Canadian Business Law

Ray Brillinger

Kathryn Filsinger

Larry Olivo

Nora Rock

Mark Walma

Camilla Wheeler

CONTRIBUTORS

Peggy Buchan

Carmen Dima

Kate Hawkins

Sheerin Kalia

William Kosar

Michelle Roy McSpurren

Philip Sworden

2007
Emond Montgomery Publications Limited
Toronto, Canada

Emond Montgomery Publications Limited
60 Shaftesbury Avenue
Toronto ON M4T 1A3
http://www.emp.ca

Printed in Canada.

We acknowledge the financial support of the Government of Canada through the Book Publishing Industry Development Program (BPIDP) for our publishing activities.

The events and characters depicted in this book are fictitious. Any similarity to actual persons, living or dead, is purely coincidental.

Acquisitions and developmental editor: Peggy Buchan
Marketing manager: Christine Davidson
Developmental editor: Kate Hawkins
Copy editor: Anita Levin
Production editor: Jim Lyons, WordsWorth Communications
Proofreader: David Handelsman, WordsWorth Communications
Text designer and typesetter: Tara Wells, WordsWorth Communications
Indexer: Paula Pike, WordsWorth Communications
Cover designer: John Vegter

Library and Archives Canada Cataloguing in Publication

Canadian business law / Kathryn Filsinger ... [et al.] ; contributors, Ray Brillinger ... [et al.].

Includes index.

ISBN 978-1-55239-101-3

1. Commercial law—Canada.   I. Filsinger, Kathryn J.

KE919.C37 2007   346.7107   C2006-906352-4
KF889.C37 2007

Contents

3 Tort Law

4 Contract Law

5 The Sale of Goods and Consumer Protection Law

6 Methods of Carrying On Business

7 Workplace Law

8 Property Law: Personal, Real, and Intellectual

9   Banking, Financing, and Debtor–Creditor Law

Publisher's Note

There are many Canadian business law texts in existence, but professors and instructors told us time and again that the *right* business law text had not yet been written. We listened carefully to requests for a student-friendly text with a risk management emphasis, for a short text with core subjects covered well, and for a clear focus on business applications. Our mettle was soon tested by the complexity of the task. This was an enormous project with many authors, contributors, reviewers, and advisers. Each brought ideas and insights to the project. The greatest challenge was to fit it all together into a cohesive text with a single voice. Through the extraordinary efforts of developmental editor Kate Hawkins, this goal has been achieved.

A simple title page cannot give all the authors and contributors their proper due. For that, a chapter-by-chapter accounting is necessary.

Chapter 1, Laws and Law Makers That Affect Business in Canada, provides an introduction to Canada's legal system. Sheerin Kalia wrote much of this chapter, with contributions from Philip Sworden.

Chapter 2, Resolving Disputes and Navigating Canada's Court System, describes the court system and process and explores the value of alternative dispute resolution to businesses. Laurence Olivo was the primary author of this chapter.

Chapter 3, Tort Law, explains the importance of tort law in numerous business contexts and shows how to protect your business against actions in negligence. The primary author of this chapter was Nora Rock, with contributions from Carmen Dima.

Chapter 4, Contract Law, provides a basic understanding of the elements of a legal contract and explores some of the pitfalls to avoid. Camilla Wheeler was the author of this chapter.

Chapter 5, The Sale of Goods and Consumer Protection Law, explains how businesses comply with consumer protection legislation such as the *Sale of Goods Act*, the *Consumer Protection Act*, and the *Competition Act*. The primary author of this chapter was Kate Hawkins, with contributions from William Kosar.

Chapter 6, Methods of Carrying On Business, explains the advantages and disadvantages of the different types of business organizations, such as sole proprietorship, partnership, and corporation. The primary author of this chapter was Mark Walma, with contributions from Peggy Buchan.

Chapter 7, Workplace Law, introduces the many laws governing the employment relationship, with particular attention to human rights and wrongful dismissal. Kathryn Filsinger and Ray Brillinger were the primary authors of this chapter.

Chapter 8, Property Law: Personal, Real, and Intellectual, describes how businesses can protect their various property interests. This chapter was written by Michelle Roy McSpurren and Peggy Buchan.

Chapter 9, Banking, Financing, and Debtor–Creditor Law, explains the legal aspects of financing a business and debt collection. Laurence Olivo was the primary author, with contributions from Nora Rock.

We would also like to thank the many other readers, reviewers, and advisers, too numerous to mention, who provided valuable feedback.

Laws and Law Makers That Affect Business in Canada

LEARNING OBJECTIVES

After reading this chapter, you should be able to:

- Describe how law affects and relates to business.

- Discuss the importance of a legal risk management scheme in reducing the chance of business losses.

- Differentiate between common law, statutes (including the constitution), and municipal bylaws as sources of Canadian law.

- Understand Canada's constitutional division of powers.

- Describe how the federal, provincial, and municipal governments regulate business activities.

- Describe how administrative law affects business people.

- Distinguish between public and private laws.

- Describe selected branches of law that affect business operations.

What Is Law?

Law consists of the body of norms, or rules, by which a society chooses to govern itself. Because laws are a reflection of a society's values, they change as the society changes. Unlike the norms or rules that govern private clubs or sporting events, laws govern all members of society, and they are enforceable by the powers of the state.

Through the law, society seeks to create a stable environment in which its members can plan their affairs with a measure of certainty and predictability. It also seeks to facilitate productive relationships and interactions among individuals, businesses, and governments. Perhaps most important, it seeks to resolve disputes peacefully. How are these objectives of society reflected in the laws that pertain to businesses?

Laws that promote certainty and predictability in business can be found, for example, in income tax requirements and in the rules that require businesses to deal

law
body of norms, or rules, by which society chooses to govern itself

honestly and in plain language with consumers. Knowing that a business is required to contribute a predictable amount every year to the public purse through income taxation allows a business owner to plan her business's affairs with reasonable certainty. Similarly, knowing that the law requires contracts involving consumers to be written in plain language leads business people to clarify their intentions, which eliminates surprises and promotes predictability in commerce.

There are many ways in which the law seeks to facilitate interactions among businesses, individuals, and governments. Human rights laws, for example, prohibit discriminatory practices in hiring and firing employees. They also require businesses to maintain workplaces that are inclusive and free of harassment. Workers who are dissatisfied with workplace interactions may formally complain to government bodies that are empowered to resolve problems.

Dispute resolution lies at the heart of business law. Regardless of the source of a dispute—be it conflict between workers and management over trade union activity, between a manufacturer and supplier over the design of a faulty product, between a government regulator and a marketing department over a questionable advertising practice—it is the role of the law to provide a method by which the matter can be resolved peacefully. The Canadian legal framework includes mediation and settlement procedures as well as adjudicating bodies, such as tribunals and courts. The law offers well-publicized guidelines so that business people can adjust their behaviour to the rules that govern us all.

In this chapter, we discuss Canadian law and its sources. In chapter 2, we examine systems of dispute resolution in Canada.

THE RULE OF LAW

rule of law
concept that every person has equal rights before the law and that the law is supreme—nobody is above the law

You may already have encountered the phrase "the **rule of law**." This phrase has several meanings. One meaning is that everyone has equal rights before the law. Any two businesses, for example, that come to court with the same legal problem should leave with the same legal resolution. Of course, in practical terms, equality before the law can be somewhat elusive. A business person who is well-educated and wealthy is far more likely to benefit from the law than someone who is poor and uneducated.

A second meaning of the rule of law is that law is supreme: nobody is above the law. All government officials, judges, and the government itself are subject to the same rules as everyone else, and this includes the same sanctions and punishments for breaking the law.

LAWYERS

It is wise for you, as a business person, to avoid becoming embroiled in legal disputes, if possible. Knowledge of the law can assist you by helping you to develop guidelines for your business's policies, procedures, and interactions. If you do become involved in a dispute, you may need to hire someone knowledgeable to give you advice about your options for dispute resolution and to predict the likelihood of success or failure if you proceed with litigation.

Qualified lawyers who are experienced in the subject matter of your dispute may be able to assist you because of their special training in identifying and resolving legal problems.

Many business law lawyers are quite capable of advising you about the various issues that will arise in your business's day-to-day operations. However, some lawyers specialize in different areas of law, such as corporate law, labour relations law, and bankruptcy law. When your legal problem is complex and specific, you may be wise to seek specialized legal advice. To find appropriate legal counsel, business people should seek referrals from trustworthy colleagues, contact their local law society office, or interview several lawyers to determine the one that can best meet their immediate and long-term needs. It is important to find a lawyer whose approach fits the organization's vision and goals.

Many businesses choose to have an ongoing relationship with a lawyer or law firm. Larger businesses may have a legal department, which employs in-house lawyers. Both in-house and outside lawyers can assist businesses by reviewing their operations to uncover and minimize legal risks, by simplifying everyday issues such as employee relations, and by examining new ventures to ensure that new legal risks are identified and addressed.

Lawyers are prohibited by their professional rules of conduct from disclosing confidential client information to third parties. Communications between clients and lawyers are also protected by **solicitor–client privilege**, a rule that prevents these communications from being used as evidence in court. This is very important to promote open communication between lawyers and their clients. Without full and accurate information, lawyers are not able to effectively advise or represent their clients.

For example, if the management of a business is concerned that it might be violating the *Environmental Protection Act*, it may wish to retain a lawyer to assess potential **liability**. It may also wish to have the lawyer draft policies and procedures to prevent violations from occurring. The protection provided by solicitor–client privilege encourages this proactive approach because management has no concern about revealing problems to its lawyers. Communications to lawyers generally cannot be used as evidence.

How Does Law Affect Business?

With the pressing concerns of promoting your business's products, attracting and keeping clients, hiring and training employees, and paying your business's bills on time, legal issues are usually the last thing on a business person's mind. Unfortunately, ignoring legal requirements and opportunities can turn even the most successful business into an unsuccessful one. Consider the following examples:

- You hire a particularly volatile employee who assaults a customer, and your business is sued.
- You fail to obtain the municipal licence you need to run your business, and city officials close you down on opening day.

Web Link

Check the Law Society of Upper Canada's (Ontario's) website at www.lsuc.on.ca for information about its lawyer referral service and the regulation of lawyers in Ontario.

Minimizing Your Risk

Find a Lawyer

- Consult colleagues or the law society to find lawyers who specialize in the matters of concern to your business.
- Interview lawyers until you find one with whom you can work.
- Add specialists if and when the need arises.

solicitor–client privilege
protection that prevents a solicitor from revealing in court communications between a lawyer and the client

liability
legal responsibility for injuries or losses suffered by another

- Your business researches, develops, and launches a new product. A competitor, who claims that your packaging is too similar to its own, brings a legal claim against you.
- A supplier is late in delivering components that are crucial for a product that you are manufacturing for a long-standing client. The supplier's late delivery results in your failure to meet your client's deadline. Your client refuses to accept late delivery and does not pay you. You believe you are entitled to compensation from the supplier.
- You are unable to meet your monthly payments on your business's various debts, so creditors petition it into bankruptcy. A trustee in bankruptcy is appointed to sell the business's assets and settle its accounts.

All of these examples involve losses for a business—lost opportunities, lost money, or lost reputation—and all of them might have been prevented. Prevention and resolution of legal problems, however, require knowledge of Canadian law. From the moment an entrepreneur begins to consider operating a business and throughout his business career, he should be turning his mind to the requirements, obstacles, and opportunities provided by law. Table 1.1 sets out some examples of the legal considerations that should accompany common business planning.

How does a business manage all of its legal considerations and risks? It is not as difficult as it first appears if the business has a plan in place. In this book, we present the legal issues that business people most commonly encounter when conducting their commercial affairs. By learning the basic principles that underlie business law, managers, owners, and employees of businesses can plan for and avert most of the well-known risks. In order to tailor strategies to suit the needs of your individual businesses, however, you should seek the advice of competent and experienced legal advisers, both at the planning stage and when particular concerns arise.

Table 1.1   Business Plans and Legal Considerations

If you ...	You must consider ...
Are choosing a name	Whether another business has the same or a similar name
Are looking for financing	Whether you can obtain a loan or want to involve partners
Have developed a new product	Whether the product could cause injury or loss to a user. If so, you might wish to redesign your product, incorporate your company to limit your exposure to liability, and purchase product liability insurance
Need to hire employees	Whether you want to hire permanent or contract staff
Need a permanent supplier of materials for your new business	Whether you want to sign an ongoing supply contract or simply order your materials on an as-needed basis
Are searching for a business location	Whether you will need a building permit to make desired changes to the premises you choose
Are marketing a new invention	Whether you should obtain a patent before informing others about your new invention

Legal Risk Management

A **legal risk management plan** allows business people to act on a proactive or reactive basis to prevent or reduce the possibility of a business loss. If you can anticipate the sorts of things that might go wrong in your workplace, you can create such a plan. For example, the next time you are in a store, mall, restaurant, theatre, airport, library, or other public facility, notice the "Caution Wet Floor" signs posted where a floor has been recently mopped. This simple measure is part of a proactive legal risk management plan. The sign is displayed to warn pedestrians to avoid a particular area or to be cautious as they walk there. A business places these signs prominently to reduce the potential for accidents and the consequent legal claims that may result.

> **legal risk management plan**
> plan that allows businesses to take action to prevent or reduce loss

If an accident does occur in a public area, a business may implement the reactive part of its risk management plan by blocking off the area to prevent further accidents, containing the problem within a specific controlled area, and preserving the accident site to gather evidence and conduct investigations. These reactive steps can assist a business if the matter results in a lawsuit because its liability for any injury or loss will depend on the evidence that a court hears regarding actions the parties took to avoid and minimize injuries and losses.

COMPONENTS OF A LEGAL RISK MANAGEMENT PLAN

To be comprehensive, a legal risk management plan should contain methodical strategies for dealing with all legal matters that a business is likely to encounter. We set out the potential components of such a plan in the sections that follow. Note that your business will need to consider each of these components in relation to every legal matter that it identifies as needing attention.

Policy Statement

A policy statement describes a business's position on a particular subject. The statement can be elaborate, for example, when describing a complete intolerance of any form of sexual harassment in the workplace. Or it can be quite simple, stating, for example, that "slip and fall" incidents are to be avoided in the workplace.

Documentation

Contracts, letters, and manuals usually include information and procedures designed to support policy statements. A contract of employment between a business and a janitor, for example, may require the janitor to follow all company policies and procedures, one of which may be erecting a "Caution Wet Floor" sign after each floor wash. Official business communications—whether to staff, customers, or suppliers—include a business's commitments to particular standards. Businesses often use procedural manuals to communicate processes and answer the questions commonly raised by various departments. These manuals can be very helpful in proactively reducing legal risk through well-planned and documented procedures directing employees on actions to take to mitigate losses and potential liability.

Training

Training and education are the most effective means of communicating company policies and procedures. Typically, businesses communicate new policies and procedures to all staff members who are affected by them, explain the importance of the new policy or procedure, train employees to meet appropriate standards, and designate a person to contact for follow-up questions. As new employees join the business, they too are educated in the business's policies and procedures.

Monitoring and Evaluating

In order to support policy goals, a business must monitor and evaluate compliance with the standards it is trying to uphold. Merely stating a policy does not turn the policy into a workplace reality. By monitoring and evaluating a policy, a business demonstrates its commitment to the standards that it sets and ensures that its employees comply. Monitoring and evaluating can help a business determine the weaknesses in its policies and procedures and allow it to make timely adjustments and corrections before problems develop.

Reviewing and Revising

It is a good idea when reviewing policies and procedures to involve various departments and consider diverse interests. When a review is properly managed, the broader the scope of opinion that a business invites in reformulating its policies, the better its policies may ultimately serve its interests.

For example, if a problem is considered from the points of view of customer service staff, auto repair staff, legal staff, and supervisory personnel, the problem may be more easily resolved than if it is considered from the point of view of a single department. Managers of the review process can measure changes suggested from various departments against the data they have gathered through monitoring and evaluation practices.

It is wise for businesses to review and revise their policies on an annual basis, as the law is always changing.

Insurance

Unfortunately, even the most careful preventive measures cannot eliminate mishaps. Accidents happen. Businesses need to acquire a sound insurance policy from a reputable insurer to limit the amount of money they may be required to pay any injured parties. By paying the insurance company a premium every month, the business protects itself against substantial financial loss.

It is important that a business's insurance agent be knowledgeable about the kinds of risks that the business undertakes in the normal course of doing business, and that these risks are reflected in its policy of insurance. Most businesses have a comprehensive insurance policy to cover potential risks. A business can, for example, insure its buildings, equipment, and inventory for protection against potential losses caused by theft and fire; it can also acquire third-party liability coverage for injuries incurred by the public while using its products. Insurance is discussed in greater detail in chapter 8.

Reactive Procedures

Many businesses set out procedures for staff to follow in the event of an accident or emergency. For example, they inform their employees of what to do in case of a fire by demonstrating the whereabouts of exits and fire extinguishers, and by educating staff about evacuation procedures and obtaining medical assistance.

Similarly, a business may have a plan that requires employees to report situations that have the potential to turn into business problems of one kind or another. Whether the potential problem involves legal matters, medical matters, public relations, or employee relations, businesses often train their employees to report significant developments immediately to designated personnel. If, for example, a staff member notices that a competitor is using the business's logo, the business may need to quickly seek a court order to stop the competitor. The business may also need to implement a communications strategy immediately to prevent consumers from confusing its product with that of its competitor. Early identification and reporting of the problem allows the business to rectify it as quickly as possible.

PUTTING THEORY INTO PRACTICE

A basic knowledge of the law's effect on a business is a crucial first step in formulating a solid risk management plan. Armed with such knowledge, you can assess each of your business's operations for potential risks. Having identified these risks, you can then devise proactive and reactive strategies for dealing with them. Table 1.2 demonstrates how you might create a risk management plan.

As table 1.2 illustrates, risk management requires a comprehensive approach to each issue that may arise for a particular business. Throughout the book, we address risk management, making suggestions about how a business can most effectively avert the risks posed by various business activities.

In order to gain knowledge of the legal environment in which your business operates, you must first identify the legal rules that apply to your operations. The assistance of legal advisers is crucial in understanding the laws that govern your commercial activities. However, your lawyer is no more than an adviser. It is you—as a business owner, manager, or employee—who is accountable for the decisions you make, based on the advice you receive from the specialists you choose to consult, including lawyers, accountants, bankers, or business entrepreneurs.

It is important for you to acquire an understanding of where Canadian law comes from, how its sources fit together, and how various types of law will affect your business. We turn now to a brief overview of the sources of Canadian law. In later chapters, we will examine individual areas of law and their role in governing the way business is conducted in Canada.

Minimizing Your Risk
Follow the Steps

Work with a lawyer to follow these steps:

- *Step 1.* Learn about the laws that govern your business.
- *Step 2.* Identify the activities that place your business at risk.
- *Step 3.* Devise proactive and reactive risk management plans to eliminate, or at least reduce, the risks you have identified.

Table 1.2   Creating a Legal Risk Management Plan

Business Area	Legal Issues	Risk Management
Operations	• Liability for injury and loss suffered on premises	• Undertake regular housekeeping, monitor conditions, and review and revise maintenance processes • Document all efforts to keep premises safe and well maintained • Purchase insurance policy and review it regularly to ensure adequate protection from losses
Finance	• Banking • Tax • Bankruptcy	• Ensure that only those with signing authority sign cheques on the business's behalf • Create a system for the yearly filing of tax returns • Create a system for the timely payment of debts
Human resources	• Responsibility for wrongful acts of employees • Protection of human rights in the workplace • Dismissal of employees	• Ensure that new employees are doing their jobs properly • Provide instruction, training, and development of behavioural standards • Institute anti-discrimination and harassment policies • Get employees' consent to, or give advance notice of, job changes • Provide notice of dismissal or pay in lieu of notice in appropriate cases
Research and development	• Patents • Product liability	• Obtain patents for new inventions • Test your new products for safety—assess and reduce risks associated with their use • Devise informative warning labels and user manuals for your products
Marketing and promotions	• Trademark and the tort of passing off • Copyright • Government regulation	• Hire an advertising company to develop a distinctive brand image and logo • Do a corporate name search • Consult a lawyer about advertising and anti-competition laws, and obey these laws
Technology	• Liability for employees' pirating of software on company computers	• Develop, distribute, and enforce computer use policy for employees - license

Sources of Law

Canadian law comes from a number of sources. It can be found in common law, which is created by judges, and in statutes, which are created by the Parliament of Canada and the provincial legislatures. It can also be found in the constitution, framework legislation that sets limits on law-making powers and on the actions of government, and in bylaws, which are created by municipal councils. Laws applicable to business come from all these sources. In the sections that follow, we examine each of these sources with particular reference to their impact on business people.

COMMON LAW

British common law became the basis for much of Canadian law when it was first transported here from England in the 1700s. It is used in all Canadian provinces and territories—except Quebec—to settle many business issues. Quebec uses a civil code, which originated in France.

The **common law** consists of rules contained in decisions made over time by various judges. The reason these rules are called "common law" is that most of them have been applied so many times that they are widely known and are considered to be well-settled law. Judges apply the same rules over and over again to create certainty and predictability in Canada's legal system. To achieve predictability, our common-law system requires courts to make decisions in accordance with precedent.

Precedent requires courts to decide similar cases in a similar way. To take a simple example, if one judge decides that a senior citizen who suffers a broken leg in an accident because of a badly designed bicycle is entitled to compensation in the amount of $150,000, another judge will award a similar amount of money to a similarly aged person who suffers a similar injury in similar circumstances. Precedent, like most principles, is more certain in theory than in practice. In reality, the common law is full of conflicting precedents on various topics, which lawyers highlight or underplay to suit their clients' interests. And the common law, as a continually evolving entity, is subject to changes, interpretations, and reversals as society changes and evolves.

How does a lawyer go about using the common law to assist a business client? Assume that Toyz Ltd. is a manufacturer of children's toys. It is being sued because a two-year-old child has choked on one of its products—a small ball—and suffered permanent brain injuries. When Toyz Ltd. hires a lawyer to defend itself, it discovers that the legal issues involved in this case are twofold:

1. Is Toyz Ltd. responsible for causing the injury?
2. If so, how much money must it pay to compensate the child for the damages he has suffered?

Toyz's lawyer must consult the common law in answering both these questions if there is no statute governing the matter. When researching the case, Toyz's lawyer will ask herself the following questions:

- Have other manufacturers been successfully sued because a child choked on a similar toy?

common law
rules contained in decisions made over time by judges

precedent
legal rule set out by the court in a decided case that can be applied to a new case

- If so, did the manufacturer of those toys affix warnings to indicate that the toy was a choking hazard for children under the age of three?
- How much money have courts awarded two-year-olds who have suffered similar injuries?

To narrow down the cases that apply to the case at hand, the lawyer will search the common law for cases with the same or similar facts. Not all facts are important in all cases, so the lawyer will use her legal skills to separate relevant facts—that is, facts that are essential to the judge's decision—from irrelevant facts. Once she has located all the cases that could be used as precedents because of their similarity, she will carefully consider the legal principles and construct a legal argument that supports Toyz's position. If there are cases that support the plaintiff, the lawyer for Toyz will do her best to explain why these cases should not be applied as precedent, arguing that the facts are different in some significant way.

Judges do not have free rein to pick and choose among precedent-bearing cases when determining the outcome of cases before them. The principle of **stare decisis** requires them to follow the decisions that judges in higher courts have made in similar cases. These cases are known as "binding" on lower courts because they must be followed. Other cases have persuasive value only. Judges may refer to persuasive cases, but they may choose whether or not to follow them. To understand which decisions are binding and which are persuasive only, it is necessary to understand Canada's court system, a topic we discuss in detail in chapter 2.

stare decisis
principle that requires
judges to follow decisions
of higher courts in similar
cases

STATUTE LAW

statute law
rules created by both the
federal Parliament and
provincial and territorial
legislatures

The second major source of law in Canada is **statute law**, or legislation. Statute law is created by a legislature: either by the federal Parliament in Ottawa or by a provincial or territorial legislature. All legislatures are the elected arms of government and are accountable to voters. Provided that a legislature acts in accordance with Canada's constitution, it can override the principles set out in common law by using clear language in a statute. Often, however, rather than override the common law, legislation embodies—or codifies—the common-law rules that have become well known and well settled. Many statutes provide principles and rules to assist in the resolution of business issues and disputes. We discuss these statutes in detail throughout this text. Table 1.3 provides you with an overview of some of the statutes with which business people need to become familiar. As table 1.3 suggests, legislatures have been very busy codifying rules.

When courts make decisions of this nature, the decisions become part of a body of law that accompanies the statute and affects the manner in which the statute is interpreted. In the rare event that one of these decisions conflicts with a statute, the statute prevails.

regulations
rules created by staff of the
Cabinet providing practical
details of how a statute is
to be implemented

Many statutes authorize the creation of **regulations**, which provide the practical details of how the statute is to be implemented. Regulations are sometimes described as being "created under statutes." They are a subordinate form of legislation, drafted by the staff of the Cabinet of the governing party. Unlike statutes, regulations are not approved and passed by the legislature.

Regulations tend to be very practical and can include lists, schedules, diagrams, forms, and charts. The information contained in regulations is just as important as

Table 1.3   A Sampling of Statutes That Affect Business

Area of Law	Name of Statute	Sample Rules
Business organizations	*Business Corporations Act*	Rules for incorporating companies that do business in Ontario
Intellectual property	*Copyright Act*	Rules protecting rights in property such as music, art, books, and theatre productions
Contracts	*Sale of Goods Act*	Rules that imply terms and conditions into commercial contracts, unless the contracting parties opt out
Employment	*Employment Standards Act, 2000*	Rules that provide minimum standards for wages, hours of work, and pregnancy leave
Bankruptcy	*Bankruptcy and Insolvency Act*	Rules determining when an act of bankruptcy has occurred
Property	*Mortgages Act*	Rules outlining the steps a creditor must take before foreclosing on a mortgage
Marketing and promotion	*Competition Act*	Rules forbidding unacceptable pricing schemes
Torts	*Occupiers' Liability Act*	Rules establishing a high duty of care owed to anyone who enters business premises with permission

that found in the primary legislation. For example, regulations made under the *Occupational Health and Safety Act* govern how hazardous materials are to be handled. If you need to consult a statute in the course of your work, you also need to consult all of the regulations made under that statute before you can have a complete understanding of your legal obligations.

CANADA'S CONSTITUTION

Canada's **constitution** is the supreme law of the land: it establishes the basic framework under which all other laws are created and the basic principles to which all other laws must conform. Until 1982, Canada's constitution was the *British North America Act*, a statute of England. It set up the framework for Canada's democracy, but only England had the power to make constitutional amendments. The *Canada Act, 1982* finally changed this and brought the power to amend the constitution home to Canada's Parliament. A truly Canadian constitution was created with the *Constitution Act, 1982*, which contains both the *Constitution Act, 1867* and the *Canadian Charter of Rights and Freedoms*.

The Division of Powers

Canada's constitution creates a **federal system of government**, which means that law-making powers are divided between the federal government and the provincial

constitution
document that establishes the basic framework under which all other laws are created and the basic principles to which all laws must conform

federal system of government
system whereby law-making powers are divided between the federal and provincial governments according to subject matter

jurisdiction
law-making authority

governments, according to subject matter. The federal government, which is located in Ottawa, has law-making authority, or **jurisdiction**, over matters of national interest; these matters affect all Canadian residents from coast to coast. This government also has law-making jurisdiction over the territories, some of which it has delegated to territorial governments. The provincial governments have jurisdiction over local matters.

Federal powers are set out in section 91 of the *Constitution Act, 1867*. They include the authority to regulate interprovincial trade and commerce and to raise money through taxation of any kind, and control over national defence, banking and printing money, the postal service, intellectual property such as patents and copyright, immigration, radio and broadcasting, and criminal law. Matters that require a national standard are generally within the jurisdiction of the federal government. For example, laws regarding customs duties and the movement of goods into and out of Canada are issues that affect Canada's status in the international community. This makes it important that the same legal standards are applied across the country.

Provincial powers are set out in section 92 of the *Constitution Act, 1867*. They include the power of direct taxation within a province, the power to create municipalities, the regulation of local trade and commerce, the regulation of property and civil rights, and, generally, all matters of a local or private nature within the province.

The federal government also has a residual power to make laws for the peace, order, and good government of Canada in respect of all matters that do not fall within provincial jurisdiction. This means that any matters that the constitution does not specifically delegate to the provinces are matters over which the federal government has jurisdiction. Table 1.4 provides a summary of federal and provincial law-making powers.

Table 1.4   Summary of Federal and Provincial Law-Making Powers

Federal Law-Making Powers (Section 91)	Provincial Law-Making Powers (Section 92)
Interprovincial and international trade	Property
Incorporation of companies operating nationally	Civil rights
National defence	Contracts
Shipping	Torts
Currency	Hospitals
Criminal law	Incorporation of companies operating in only one province
Postal service	Local trade
Residual powers	Public works
	Municipalities
	Other matters of a local or private nature

The *Civil Code of Quebec* contains rules to resolve property and contract disputes. Throughout the rest of Canada, property and contract law is contained in the common law and various statutes. The main difference between the two approaches is that Quebec's *Civil Code* provides guiding principles, whereas the common law and statutes provide more fact-specific rules for application. In all federally regulated matters—such as criminal law, taxation, constitutional law, and immigration—the citizens of Quebec are governed by the same laws that govern other Canadian citizens. From a business perspective, a company that wishes to operate in Quebec must look to the *Civil Code* for legal rules pertaining to property and contract disputes, which are the most typical kind of disputes businesses encounter.

Occasionally, one level of government passes a law that appears to intrude on the law-making power of the other. Censorship is a good example. Controlling the sale of literature and images that may be offensive to some can be viewed as either a provincial concern (trade and commerce within a province) or a federal concern (obscenity as a criminal act). Courts settle disputes such as these. If a law does not fit squarely within the control of either the provinces or the federal government, the federal government takes jurisdiction, under the principle of **paramountcy**.

Web Link

Find the *Civil Code of Quebec* on the Justice Quebec website at www.justice.gouv.qc.ca.

paramountcy
highest in power or jurisdiction

The Canadian Charter of Rights and Freedoms

Since its passage in 1982, the *Canadian Charter of Rights and Freedoms* has changed Canadian law profoundly. The Charter is part of Canada's constitution and therefore part of the supreme law of Canada. It proclaims important rights and freedoms such as equality, freedom of religion, and freedom of expression. It prohibits interference with these rights and freedoms in legislation and government actions. No government may exercise its power in a manner that infringes these rights and freedoms, unless an infringement "can be demonstrably justified in a free and democratic society."

Canadian courts are empowered to strike down any law that violates the Charter. For example, a court could strike down a law that prevents striking workers from picketing outside a business. Why? Such a law might violate workers' rights to free speech and peaceful assembly, and not be viewed as a reasonable limitation on these rights in a free and democratic society. *R v. Big M Drug Mart Ltd.* is an example of the court's striking down legislation that violated the Charter's guarantee of freedom of religion. Table 1.5 presents a sampling of other ways in which the Charter has the potential to affect business activity in Canada.

It is important to remember that the Charter grants rights and freedoms from *government* interference. It does not apply to discriminatory action taken by individuals or companies. If, for example, a business owner discriminates against members of a minority group in her hiring practices, she has not violated the Charter. Instead, she has violated human rights legislation, which we discuss in chapter 7 under the heading "Human Rights in the Workplace." The Charter applies only if a law or government action causes discrimination. Therefore, if the Ontario government passed a law that required all business owners to be Canadian citizens, this law would violate the Charter and would be struck down by the courts.

CASE IN POINT   Shopping on the Lord's Day

R v. Big M Drug Mart Ltd., [1985] 1 SCR 295; 18 DLR (4th) 321

Facts

Big M Drug Mart Ltd. was charged with violating the *Lord's Day Act*, which prohibited stores such as Big M from carrying out business on Sunday, the Christian Sabbath. In defence of the charge, Big M challenged the constitutionality of the statute on the basis that it violated the freedom of religion entrenched in the *Charter of Rights and Freedoms*. The attorney general argued that the purpose of the statute was not religious but secular—to provide a common day of rest for all.

Result

The Supreme Court of Canada held that the purpose of the statute was to impose Christian observance, not to provide a common day of rest, and struck down the *Lord's Day Act*. What may appear good and true to a majority religious group or to the state may not, for religious reasons, be imposed upon others. While Big M, as a corporation, was not capable of holding a religious belief, it was still entitled to defend the charges against it on the basis of this Charter freedom.

Business Lesson

Successful Charter challenges do not occur every day. However, it could benefit you to be aware of any constitutional issues that may arise from legislation that regulates your business. Does the law violate Charter rights? Even if the right or freedom does not apply to corporations, such as freedom of religion, your business may be able to challenge it.

Table 1.5   Charter Rights and Business Activities

Charter Right	Meaning of Right	Business Activity Affected
Equality (section 15)	Freedom from discrimination in the application and protection of the law based on specified grounds (such as age, sex, race, and religion)	Laws permitting mandatory retirement policies have been challenged
Freedom of expression (section 2(b))	Freedom to state opinions openly	Laws limiting advertising and marketing strategies have been challenged
Freedom of association (section 2(d))	Freedom to establish and belong to associations	Laws limiting the rights of workers to organize and join trade unions have been challenged
Freedom of religion (section 2(a))	Freedom to practise sincerely held beliefs of a religious or spiritual nature	Laws limiting Sunday shopping have been challenged
Mobility (section 6)	Freedom to pursue a job anywhere in Canada	Laws limiting the rights of provincially certified professionals to work in other provinces have been challenged

Reasonable Limits on Rights and Freedoms

Section 1 of the Charter provides that all rights and freedoms are subject to "reasonable limits prescribed by law." Each time a court considers whether a law violates the Charter, it must consider whether the law imposes a reasonable limit on a right or freedom. Only if the law is found to violate a right or freedom *and* cannot be justified as a reasonable limit in the particular circumstances will the courts strike the law down. In many cases, the courts will conclude that although a right or freedom has been violated, the violation is justifiable. For example, freedom of expression is not absolute. It may be limited by pornography laws, hate laws, copyright laws, advertising laws, libel and slander laws, and even noise bylaws.

Striking the Political Balance

What are the principles behind our constitutional legal system? Canada is a representative democracy in which the people vote for politicians who represent them. If the people do not like the laws passed by a legislature, they will elect different representatives at the next election. However, the democratic principle of "majority rule" may at times come into conflict with another important principle: protecting minority rights.

The *Canadian Charter of Rights and Freedoms* protects these rights by limiting the law-making powers of legislatures. As we have discussed, a court may strike down a statutory provision that was created by a legislature if the court interprets the provision to be in violation of a Charter right or freedom. In this way, the courts—through the Charter—provide a check or balance against the otherwise legitimate exercise of government power.

The *Constitution Act, 1867* also attempts to achieve balance by dividing law-making powers between the federal and provincial governments. Neither level of government holds all the power—it is shared.

MUNICIPAL BYLAWS

A third source of Canadian law rests with municipal councils. Municipal councils are the government bodies responsible for municipalities, cities, towns, and regions. Provincial governments create municipalities and pass statutes that delegate specific powers to the municipal council. The council exercises these powers by making **municipal bylaws**. These bylaws affect businesses most commonly through licensing, permits, zoning, and taxation requirements.

municipal bylaws
rules passed by municipal governments

Cities and towns are responsible for many basic services, such as fire, police, public health, traffic, public transit, garbage disposal, libraries, pools, arenas, parks, sanitation, garbage removal, snow removal, food inspection, and water use.

Land use planning is another very important municipal function that affects businesses. Bylaws determine the use of land within a municipality's boundaries. Business people need to be aware of whether areas are zoned residential, commercial, mixed residential and commercial, or industrial. If an area is zoned industrial, a business will need to know what types of industry are permitted. Municipal building codes also affect businesses, especially with respect to fire prevention.

A municipal licence or permit may be required for activities that a business wants to carry out. For example, new construction, renovation, demolition, and installation of septic systems or fences may require a building permit. Business operations for the sale of goods or services may require a sales permit, and a permit may be required before a business erects a sign.

Bylaw inspectors and enforcement officers are employed by municipalities to monitor compliance. A business that fails to comply with a relevant bylaw may be fined or shut down by the municipality. For example, a restaurant that fails to meet sanitation standards could find its operating licence suspended and its doors closed. Therefore, during the planning stages of a business and each time changes are made, it is wise to consider whether bylaws require the business to obtain any permits, licences, or approvals.

CANADIAN LAW MAKERS: AN OVERVIEW

In the sections above, we discussed three different types of law makers in Canada: federal and provincial legislatures, courts, and municipalities. Table 1.6 provides an overview of the means by which they create laws that affect Canadian business.

Administrative Law

administrative law
body of rules created by government agencies and applied to government agencies to monitor their decision-making powers

Administrative law is a branch of law that is of particular concern to business people. It incorporates the three sources of law we have summarized above: statutes, common law, and municipal bylaws. It addresses and monitors government regulation and government regulators.

Starting in the early 20th century, governments in Canada began to expand their regulation-making roles by establishing social programs and monitoring economic and various other activities. They needed to ensure that they administered these programs and activities in a way that reflected their policies and conformed to the law. For example, they needed to supervise how the programs were run, who was entitled to their benefits, and what was to be done in the event that someone failed to follow their policies.

These supervisory and administrative needs proved to be ongoing, often requiring specialized knowledge and expertise in particular areas, such as building code requirements, licensing procedures, and workplace health and safety needs. Because legislatures are not equipped to perform these supervisory and administrative functions, they delegated the power to do so to government departments and to various administrative agencies of government.

Table 1.6 Law Makers in Canada

Law Maker	Type of Law
Legislatures: federal Parliament and provincial and territorial legislatures (elected)	Statutes and regulations
Judiciary: courts (appointed)	Common law
Municipal councils (elected)	Bylaws

ADMINISTRATIVE AGENCIES

Administrative agencies are established by legislation that regulates or oversees a particular activity that is often technical or requires specialized knowledge. These agencies fall into three main categories based on function, and some agencies may carry out more than one of these functions:

1. *Advisory.* Advisory agencies provide information to governments that assist them in developing policies or running ongoing programs. The Ontario Law Reform Commission, which conducts research on legal issues and develops policy related to law reform, is an example of an advisory agency.

2. *Operational.* Operational agencies provide goods and services as directed by government legislation. The Workplace Safety and Insurance Board is an example of this kind of agency because it is directed by legislation to set up and run a system of insurance for workers injured on the job.

3. *Regulatory.* Regulatory agencies oversee and regulate the operation of a government-mandated or private activity. For example, the Liquor Control Board of Ontario licenses and oversees bars and restaurants that sell alcohol to the public. It also oversees the conduct of licensed businesses and has the power to revoke or suspend a business's licence for breach of the regulations. Some regulatory agencies settle disputes between parties that were formerly settled by the courts. The Ontario Labour Relations Board, which settles conflicts between trade unions and employers, is an example of such an agency.

Administrative agencies—whether they are called tribunals, boards, or commissions—help implement government policies and work alongside governmental departments and ministries. Table 1.7 sets out examples of administrative agencies that may be of interest to business people.

Table 1.7   Administrative Agencies That Affect Business

Administrative Agency	Function
Provincial Alcohol Commission	Grants licences to bars and restaurants, allowing them to serve alcohol to patrons
Federal Canadian Radio-television and Telecommunications Commission (CRTC)	Grants operating licences to television and radio stations across the country
Provincial Workplace Safety and Insurance Board	Grants compensation to injured workers
Federal and provincial human rights tribunals	Determines whether human rights legislation has been violated
Canadian Food Inspection Agency	Issues decisions regarding food inspection and safety
Provincial professional societies or governing bodies	Grants licences to particular professionals (for example, lawyers, accountants, architects, nurses, and pharmacists) to practise their profession
Federal Competition Tribunal	Issues decisions regarding anti-competitive and dishonest conduct in business
Municipal building departments	Conducts inspections of buildings and grant permits to alter premises

Some of the many other areas of business regulated by administrative bodies include telephone services, immigration, employment insurance, labour relations, and municipal land use and zoning. Most, if not all, administrative bodies have websites, where businesses and the public can find information about them.

SCOPE OF ADMINISTRATIVE LAW

Administrative law regulates the regulators. It consists of the body of rules that are both created by government agencies and applied to government agencies to monitor their decision-making powers. Administrative law is an extremely broad field. It includes municipal bylaws, the decisions of municipal councils, and the decisions of the many other agencies of government. Whenever a business interacts with a government agency—such as one that grants permits and licences, does inspections, or makes decisions under a regulatory system—the business is operating within the area covered by administrative law.

For example, a company may apply to a municipality for a zoning variance because it wants to expand its operations beyond those currently permitted under a bylaw. If the municipality refuses the business's application, the business's recourse is to administrative law. This body of law provides the business with answers to questions such as the following:

- Does the business have a right to a hearing before the government agency that is responsible for the rezoning decision?
- If so, what rights does the company have at the hearing?
- What rules of evidence and procedure apply?
- Does the business have a right to know the reasons for the agency's decision?
- Under what circumstances can the business get a court to hear its case?

ADMINISTRATIVE TRIBUNALS

Government agencies and departments may make administrative decisions quickly, without hearing arguments, as they do, for example, when a building inspector makes a decision on site. Administrative decisions may also be made by administrative tribunals, which consider evidence and hear arguments. An **administrative tribunal** often functions in the manner of a court, with both sides presenting arguments and providing evidence to a decision maker.

administrative tribunal government body that functions like a court and makes decisions regarding administrative matters

The decision maker in a court is a judge, who has general knowledge and experience in many areas of law. By contrast, the decision maker in an administrative tribunal is usually a specialist in a particular field. The panelists on a human rights tribunal are experts in human rights law, but may know nothing about environmental law, for example. One advantage of administrative tribunals over courts is the expertise they offer. As Canada's population increases and government regulations grow, the specialized administrative bodies can reduce government costs and respond more quickly than courts to the interests and concerns of various sectors, including businesses.

Tribunals are like courts in that they interpret and apply the law. But they also differ from courts in several significant ways. Apart from the expertise that tribunals usually bring to their subject matter, tribunals generally differ from courts in some of the ways summarized below.

- While tribunals aim for consistency when making their decisions, they are not bound by the same strict rules that require courts to follow precedents established in earlier cases.
- While they have procedural rules, many tribunals are more informal and flexible in using them than courts are.
- Tribunals may base their decisions not just on law, but also on public policy as determined by the tribunal according to the authority delegated to it under the legislation that created it.
- The rules of evidence are often much more relaxed, and evidence that would never be admitted in court is commonly admitted in a tribunal hearing.

While tribunals have more flexibility in making decisions than courts, there are some limitations on their decision-making powers. Traditionally, the legislature that establishes a tribunal imposes some controls over how the tribunal exercises its powers, as does the law generally:

- The statute that creates the tribunal determines its composition, powers, and—in some cases—its rules of procedure.
- If the legislation that creates a tribunal does not establish procedural rules, a statute such as the *Statutory Powers Procedure Act* (in Ontario) imposes rules that apply to its proceedings and require it to act fairly. Acting fairly means, at a minimum, providing reasons for a decision and an opportunity for the person or business affected to respond.
- Tribunals are government agencies. They are therefore bound by the *Canadian Charter of Rights and Freedoms* to respect the rights and freedoms set out in this constitutional document.
- Although a tribunal may develop its own procedural rules and guidelines, agency-made rules and guidelines usually require the approval of the Cabinet.

RECONSIDERATION, APPEALS, AND JUDICIAL REVIEW

If you feel that an administrative agency has dealt unfairly with your business, you have some recourse. The statutes that create tribunals often require them to take a second look at their own decisions, particularly if a party complains that a tribunal has made a factual error. Some statutes create two levels of tribunals. One level makes an initial decision about a case, and the other level acts as an appeal board to review the decision. This is the structure in place for appeals under the Ontario *Workplace Safety and Insurance Act, 1997*, for example. Other statutes create rights of appeal to courts.

Even if the statute that sets up an administrative tribunal contains no provisions about rights of reconsideration or appeal, you may still have a right to judicial review. **Judicial review** is a process in which a superior court reviews the decision of an administrative tribunal for errors of law, errors involving fairness, or errors involving a tribunal's exercise of its powers. In general, courts tend to defer to the expertise of tribunals. They rarely overturn a tribunal's decision on its merits, but may intervene if a tribunal makes a serious error of law, acts unfairly in its proceedings, or fails to follow its mandate as set out in the statute that created it.

judicial review
process whereby a court reviews the decision of an administrative tribunal

The law governing judicial review of tribunals is currently in flux. One school of thought is that the courts should intervene more often than they currently do to ensure that tribunals follow fair procedures when making decisions. The other school of thought is that tribunals need the freedom to develop policy, as well as make individual decisions, and that intervention from courts interferes with the achievement of these goals. You can expect to see further developments and changes as this area of law continues to evolve.

Public and Private Laws

public law
rules that govern the relationship among governmental agencies and between government and individuals (or corporations)

private law
rules that govern the relationship between individuals (or corporations) where there is no government involvement

tax law
rules that govern the keeping of records and payment of taxes imposed by federal, provincial, and municipal governments

Laws can be categorized as either public or private. **Public laws** govern the relationships among governmental agencies and between government and individuals. **Private laws** govern relationships among individuals and corporations in circumstances where there is no government involvement. The public laws most relevant for business are tax law, administrative law, and criminal law. The private laws of particular interest to business are contract law, tort law, property law, and the law governing business organizations. Table 1.8 provides an overview of these legal categories.

PUBLIC LAWS

Tax law is one of the branches of public law that most obviously affects business. Business people and the companies where they work pay many taxes that are authorized and imposed by the federal, provincial, and municipal governments. Examples include income tax, goods and services tax (GST), provincial sales tax (PST), and municipal property tax. Businesses must keep accurate and thorough records of all transactions and activities that have tax consequences. For example, a retail store must calculate both GST and PST on each taxable item it sells, keep records of its customers' payment of these taxes, and remit all taxes to the appropriate government departments within the time frame required by law.

Administrative law, as described earlier, cuts across many areas of substantive law as diverse as human rights and trade regulation, and focuses on the government procedures for decision-making. Wherever there is government regulation, administrative decisions must be made regarding how those regulations should be applied to individuals and businesses. This includes the granting of licences, payment of taxes, and compliance with employment standards and occupational safety laws.

Table 1.8   Public and Private Laws

Public Laws	Private Laws
Tax law	Contract law
Administrative law	Tort law
Criminal law	Business organization law
Environmental law	Property law

Administrative law is all about how decisions are made and the legal options available to individuals and businesses when decisions affect them negatively.

Criminal law sets the standards of acceptable behaviour in Canadian society. It is codified principally in the *Criminal Code,* which applies uniformly throughout the country, although the federal government has passed many other statutes that carry criminal penalties as well. While it is rare for the state to bring a criminal action against a business, it does prosecute businesses that engage in securities fraud, falsifying corporate documents, forgery, conspiracy, and bid-rigging, for example. Some experts predict that the state will increase its prosecutions of financial misrepresentation by companies and cybercrime—for example, hacking, spreading viruses, and stealing electronic data. Most violations of criminal laws can lead to severe penalties for businesses and for those who run them in the forms of both fines and prison sentences.

Environmental law is governed by all three levels of government: federal, provincial/territorial, and municipal, and can affect businesses in many ways. For example, environmental laws impose restrictions on the amount that businesses may pollute the air, water, and land; they restrict the exploitation of natural resources such as forests and fish; and they control development in cities and in rural areas.

PRIVATE LAWS

Contract law, which concerns the enforcement of private agreements, applies to an enormous amount of business activity. This area of law governs agreements between a business and its customers or clients; it also governs business-to-business agreements. Examples of contracts in the business world are endless: purchase agreements, service agreements, leases, and employment contracts are merely a few examples. The laws that govern contracts are found both in the common law and in statutes, such as the *Sale of Goods Act.* Because contracts are such a major part of doing business, we discuss contract law in detail in chapters 4 and 5.

Tort law assigns responsibility and provides compensation for injuries and damages sustained by persons or property. Like contract law, tort law is found in both common law and statutes, such as the *Occupiers' Liability Act.* Tort law imposes a duty on businesses to take care of customers, clients, and employees, and to keep them safe from injury while they are in contact with company personnel or company property. Tort law also protects the public from manufacturing or design defects that may cause injury or damage. We discuss tort law in detail in chapter 3.

Business organization law governs how businesses are structured or organized—that is, whether they are controlled by a sole owner-operator, a partnership, or a corporation. The rights and obligations of businesses and the people involved vary according to the structure under which the business is operated. Law governs matters such as incorporation, choosing the name for the business, and deciding whether to sell company shares to the public. Like other branches of private law, corporate law is contained in common law and in statutes, such as the Ontario *Business Corporations Act.* Both the federal and provincial governments have statutes that govern corporations. We discuss the law governing business organization in chapter 6.

Property law determines what a person or company owns and what it can transfer. There are three commonly distinguished categories: real, personal, and

criminal law
rules that govern the standard of acceptable behaviour in society, the breach of which results in fines and imprisonment

environmental law
rules that govern protection of the environment, restrictions on the exploitation of natural resources, and development in cities and rural areas

contract law
rules that govern the enforcement of private agreements

tort law
rules that assign responsibility and provide compensation for wrongs resulting in injuries or damages sustained by people or property

property law
collection of rules that confer rights of ownership, possession, and transferability over things

intellectual. The law of real property concerns buying, selling, and renting land, how land can be used, and the rights of those owning or occupying the land, for example, through a mortgage or lease. Personal property is property that can be moved from place to place, such as a company car, books, inventory, merchandise, and equipment. Intellectual property involves ownership of a patent, trademark, or copyright. Laws governing the various types of property are found in common law, in federal statutes such as the *Copyright Act*, and in provincial statutes such as the Ontario *Mortgages Act*. We discuss property law in chapter 8.

Chapter Summary

In this chapter, we have defined law and its purpose, illustrated the importance of legal knowledge for the operation of a successful business, provided a broad survey of Canada's legal system, and briefly described the areas of law that may affect business activities in Canada. Because almost any business activity can result in serious legal consequences, this chapter has urged you—as a business person—to identify areas of potential legal risk and devise proactive and reactive management strategies to minimize the risks of doing business.

KEY TERMS

administrative law
administrative tribunal
common law
constitution
contract law
criminal law
environmental law
federal system of government
judicial review

jurisdiction
law
liability
legal risk management plan
municipal bylaws
paramountcy
precedent
private law
property law

public law
regulations
rule of law
solicitor–client privilege
stare decisis
statute law
tax law
tort law

REFERENCES

Bankruptcy and Insolvency Act, RSC 1985, c. B-3.
Big M Drug Mart Ltd., R v., [1985] 1 SCR 295; (1985), 18 DLR (4th) 321.
Business Corporations Act, RSO 1990, c. B.16.
Civil Code of Quebec, SQ 1991, c. 64.
Competition Act, RSC 1985, c. C-34.
Constitution Act, 1867, 30 & 31 Vict., c. 3.
Constitution Act, 1982, RSC 1985, app. II, no. 44.
Copyright Act, RSC 1985, c. C-42.
Employment Standards Act, 2000, SO 2000, c. 41.
Mortgages Act, RSO 1990, c. M.40.
Occupiers' Liability Act, RSO 1990, c. O.2.
Sale of Goods Act, RSO 1990, c. S.1.
Statutory Powers Procedure Act, RSO 1990, c. S.22.
Workplace Safety and Insurance Act, 1997, SO 1997, c. 16, sched. A.

REVIEW AND DISCUSSION

True or False?

_F_   **1.** Laws promote certainty and predictability because they never change.

_T_   **2.** A company may freely disclose how it broke the law to its lawyer, because this type of communication may not be used as evidence against the company in court.

_T_   **3.** A purpose of a legal risk management plan is to reduce the risk of being sued and to reduce the amount of liability in the event of a lawsuit.

_F_   **4.** The *Canadian Charter of Rights and Freedoms* replaced human rights legislation in 1982, when Canada's constitution was brought home from England.

_T_   **5.** The courts are empowered to strike down any law that violates the Charter.

_T_   **6.** The Charter does not prohibit businesses from discriminating against racial minorities if they so choose.

_F_   **7.** Administrative tribunals have less expertise than courts.

_F_   **8.** Public laws govern actions of individuals and businesses when those actions occur in public places such as parks, roads, waterways, and the air.

Multiple Choice

1. Which definition or definitions best describe "the rule of law"?
   a.   Everyone has equal rights before the law, and nobody is above the law, including government.
   b.   The wealthy and educated are more likely to benefit from the law than the poor and uneducated, and all societies are ruled by law.
   c.   Punishment for breaking the law is imposed according to rules of conduct.
   d.   All of the above.

2. Which are components of a legal risk management plan?
   a.   operations, finance, human resources, research and development, marketing and promotions, and technology
   b.   learn the laws that govern your business, identify the activities that place your business at risk, and devise proactive and reactive plans to eliminate or reduce the risks
   c.   policy statement; documentation such as contracts, letters, and manuals that support the policy statement; training; monitoring and evaluation; review and revision of policies and procedures; insurance; and procedures in the event of an accident or emergency
   d.   common law; statutory law; municipal bylaws; and the constitution, including the Charter

3. Which statement is most accurate?
   a. Precedent is legally binding on all courts based on the principle of *stare decisis.*
   b. Precedents are often codified into statute by the legislature.
   c. Where there is a conflict between common law and statute, the statute prevails.
   d. All statutes must be supported by regulations, whereas regulations are rarely found in the common law.

4. What does the division of powers found within Canada's constitution dictate?
   a. which powers are statutory and which are derived from the common law
   b. which powers are territorial, provincial, and municipal
   c. which powers are provided to Quebec through the civil law and to the rest of Canada through the common law
   d. which powers are federal and which powers are exclusively provincial

5. Which of the following best describes the protections offered by the *Canadian Charter of Rights and Freedoms*?
   a. freedom from discrimination and harassment in the workplace and at school
   b. freedom from unreasonable government interference with respect to rights and freedoms such as equality, religion, and expression
   c. inalienable rights and freedoms, including the right to equality, the right to religion, and the freedom to express opinions
   d. the right to sue on the basis of any violations described in a, b, or c

6. Municipal bylaws affect businesses in many ways. Which list of examples most accurately reflects municipal jurisdiction?
   a. land use planning, public transit, garbage disposal, and licensing
   b. land use planning, building permits, financing, and health and safety on the job site
   c. land use planning, transit including highways and airports, and drivers' licences
   d. land use planning, banking, commerce, and health care

7. Which of these statements about administrative law is incorrect?
   a. Administrative law is about legal office administration.
   b. Administrative law is about regulation of the regulators.
   c. Administrative law comes into play whenever a business interacts with a government agency.
   d. All of the above.

8. Which of the following is *not* an example of how tribunals are different from courts?

    a. Tribunal decisions are not binding on the parties in the same way as court decisions.

    b. Tribunals usually have more informal and flexible procedures than do courts.

    c. Tribunals may consider public policy to a degree that courts usually do not.

    d. Tribunals may admit evidence that would never be admitted in a court.

Short Answer — paper, typed

1. Define law and describe its purpose.

2. Describe the steps to take in devising a legal risk management plan.   *minimizing your risk p. 7*

3. If a provincial advertising law prevented a liquor supplier from marketing its product through posters in a mall, what section of what law might the company use to challenge the law?   *Freedom of expression, Charter of Rights*

4. If your company had a dispute involving a supplier who did not deliver the goods you ordered, what area of law would apply to resolve the dispute? What area would apply if the supplier delivered defective goods that injured customers?   *Contract Law, Tort Law?*

5. A company has launched an intense promotional campaign for a new cell phone combined with an MP3 player. Just before it ran the first commercial, the Canadian Radio-television and Telecommunications Commission informed it that the advertisement is unsuitable for children and therefore cannot air until 10:00 p.m. The company believes that this limitation will severely limit its ability to market its product. What area(s) of law might apply to resolve this issue?   *Administrative Law (advisory, operational, regulatory)*

6. Which level of government—federal or provincial—has power to make laws involving airplane travel? Give reasons for your answer.   *federal*

Discussion and Debate

1. Young workers, especially summer students, are at greater risk of being injured on the job than experienced workers. Assume you are a student who has just begun working at an industrial plant. What guidance do you think your employer should provide you to prevent the possibility of your being injured?

2. As explained in this chapter, the rights and freedoms under the Charter are not absolute. For example, freedom of expression may be limited by pornography laws, hate laws, copyright laws, advertising laws, libel and slander laws, and even noise bylaws. Can the courts rationally weigh these competing values? Does it make sense for appointed judges to be making these politically sensitive decisions, or are such decisions better left to the elected legislature? What are the pros and cons of each approach? How would you personally determine the limits of free speech?

Resolving Disputes and Navigating Canada's Court System

LEARNING OBJECTIVES

After reading this chapter you should be able to:

- Describe negotiation and suggest circumstances under which various types of negotiation can assist in resolving business disputes.

- Describe various types of mediation and suggest how they can assist business people in resolving disputes.

- Describe arbitration and its role in resolving commercial disputes.

- Distinguish between the roles of mediators and arbitrators.

- Explain the litigation process in the Small Claims Court and the Superior Court.

- Describe Canada's hierarchy of courts.

- List and describe five roles of Canadian courts.

How Are Business Disputes Resolved?

As a business person in Canada, you are entitled to have any legal dispute resolved in accordance with the law in a final and binding manner. People with little experience of the law tend to think that most disputes in Canada are resolved by the courts, and certainly courts do settle many matters between opposing parties through the process of litigation.

Litigation begins when a party launches a lawsuit; it proceeds through a standard series of steps that eventually lead to a hearing before an impartial judge. When engaging in litigation, the parties to the lawsuit resolve their dispute as adversaries. Opposing lawyers usually present evidence on behalf of each party to a presiding judge. The judge determines the facts, applies the law, and eventually decides the

litigation
process of resolving disputes through a formal court process

case in favour of one party and against the other. In theory, with both parties presenting opposing points of view to the best of their abilities, the truth will emerge and justice will be done.

Litigation, however, is not the only process for resolving disputes, and courts are not the only forums. The parties themselves can gather their facts, present their points of view, and negotiate a solution to their dispute, either on their own or with the assistance of a **third party** that they have chosen, called a mediator. The parties may also select a third party to hear their evidence and arguments and then decide in favour of one side or the other. In this case, the third party is called an arbitrator. Arbitration is similar to litigation.

Negotiation, mediation, and arbitration are the three most widely used forms of **alternative dispute resolution (ADR)**. The term "alternative" refers to the fact that these forms provide an alternative to litigation. These methods are becoming increasingly popular among members of the business community.

In this chapter, we begin our consideration of dispute resolution with a discussion of the alternative methods, which in many instances can prove to be the most efficient, most flexible, and least expensive ways of settling conflicts that arise in the course of doing business. We then turn our attention to the more traditional method for resolving disputes—namely, litigation in the courts.

third party
outsider to a dispute or proceedings

alternative dispute resolution (ADR)
settlement of conflict through a process other than the court system

Alternatives to Litigation

For some time now, the people involved in the administration of justice in Canada have been concerned about the costs of and delays in taking cases to court. Experienced business people are also aware of the difficulties presented by lawsuits. In addition to the high cost of hiring lawyers, there are other problems. Issues that lie at the heart of a dispute—and that are most in need of peaceful, efficient, and lasting resolution—can often become lost in the procedural delays and complexity of litigation.

Business people have therefore sought out dispute resolution techniques that are cheaper, quicker, simpler, less formal, and less adversarial than those provided in Canada's court system. As we have mentioned, contemporary methods of dispute resolution fall within three main approaches: negotiation, mediation, and arbitration. Before discussing each of these processes, we turn now to a brief overview of some of the factors that you should keep in mind when deciding which of these techniques is right for you and your business.

FACTORS AFFECTING CHOICE OF DISPUTE RESOLUTION PROCEDURE

As an introduction, table 2.1 sets out some of the factors that will influence your choice of dispute resolution procedure. Our discussion focuses on alternative methods of dispute resolution; the litigation column in table 2.1 is provided for the purposes of comparison only.

If one party insists on litigation (and a party may do so by commencing a lawsuit), the other party is required to litigate. However, if neither insists on litigation, the parties are free to select an alternative process for resolving their dispute.

Table 2.1 A Brief Comparison of Negotiation, Mediation, Arbitration, and Litigation

	Negotiation	Mediation	Arbitration	Litigation
Participation in process	Voluntary	Voluntary, unless the parties agree otherwise beforehand	Voluntary, unless the parties agree otherwise beforehand	Involuntary
Formality	Usually informal and unstructured, although the parties can agree to structure	Degree of formality and structure depends on the mediator and the extent to which the parties accept the mediator's proposals to formalize and structure the process	Less formal than litigation, but much more formal and structured than negotiation or mediation	Highly formal, following a process prescribed by rules of practice
Party control of process	Parties control the process and may proceed with or without establishing their own rules	Mediator and parties control the process, usually with the mediator proposing rules for the process and the parties agreeing	Arbitrator controls the process	Judge controls the process
Outcome	Private agreement, enforceable as a contract	Private agreement, enforceable as a contract	Private decision by arbitrator that is usually binding, unless the parties agree beforehand to non-binding arbitration. May be subject to court review and enforceable by legal action	Public decision by judge, enforceable by the court

Formality

Is your dispute the sort that can most easily be resolved by following fixed procedural rules? Is communication in writing one of your strong points? Alternatively, would informality and flexibility assist you more? Would a frank discussion with a knowledgeable third party help you define your position? The answers to these questions may depend, in part, on your relationship with the other party to the dispute and on your relative power position.

Generally, if you and the party with whom you are in conflict are not equally powerful, and if you have a history of disputes, selecting a more formal process will tend to benefit the less powerful party. Arbitration, therefore, may be your best option if you are the weaker party. The formality and structure of arbitration, and the fact that the arbitrator resolves the dispute after hearing the evidence and arguments of the parties, will tend to protect you. If, on the other hand, the parties are in relatively equal positions of power and have no previous history of conflict, negotiation or mediation may best meet the interests of both parties. If you believe that negotiation will work best but you cannot get started, or, once started you cannot make progress, then you may want to turn to a mediator to assist you. Alternatively, if your strength lies in written rather than oral communication, then arbitration, with its requirement that the parties conclude their case with written arguments, should be the procedure you choose.

Control of the Process

How much control do you and the other party want over the resolution of your conflict? Is it vital to your relationship that you work together to resolve your conflict yourselves? Alternatively, would the intervention of a third party, such as an arbitrator or mediator, be useful in setting the ground rules and in helping both of you adhere to them?

Generally, where there is a power imbalance and a high degree of conflict, third-party control of the process may be more helpful in attaining a timely and successful resolution, so you may wish to choose arbitration or a highly structured mediation process. Where you and the other party want to control the process yourselves, negotiation and less structured mediation often will work. Remember that with mediation, it is the mediator who structures the process, usually by introducing and then obtaining support from the parties for the ground rules that she sets. Party support is essential because the more control that parties have over the process, the more likely they are to reach an agreement that satisfies their concerns.

Enforcement of Procedural Rules

Do you believe that you and the other party will follow the rules that you set for resolving your problem? If so, then negotiation may be the method for you. Would a third party be useful in ensuring that both of you adhere to the rules and in sanctioning either of you if you break the rules? If so, mediation by a forceful mediator or arbitration may be better choices.

INTERESTS AND RIGHTS

In the sections that follow, we make reference to the terms "interests" and "rights." By "interests" we mean short- and long-term business goals as well as business concerns, priorities, and aspirations. In general, interests tend to be subjective—that is, particular to individual businesses and business people. For example, where one business might place a high priority on expansion when the market for its product is hot, another might be equally concerned about limiting its operations to a level that is manageable for its existing staff. Interests are flexible: they change over time and evolve as a business evolves.

Rights, on the other hand, are entitlements. Although subject to change, they are much less flexible than interests. They are objective, rather than subjective—that is, they are identified through rational analysis or by reference to some authority. They include privileges enjoyed by individuals and businesses as a result of laws, agreements, policies, and practices. For example, the entitlement of workers to a safe workplace is a right under the *Workplace Safety and Insurance Act, 1997*. The various entitlements that business people have negotiated and incorporated into binding contracts are rights under the common law of contract. Freedom of assembly is a right under the *Canadian Charter of Rights and Freedoms*.

Dispute resolution usually focuses either on interests or on rights. Often, a rights focus tends to be simpler than an interests focus. Rights, though subject to interpretation, can usually be determined by reference to a law or to another authority. Dispute resolution that involves interests, however, broadens the field of discussion. Consideration of such matters as a business person's hopes, fears, and plans for the future of her business can require different—and often more subtle—skills than a logical analysis of rights.

In the following sections, we examine negotiation, mediation, and arbitration as vehicles for settling both interest-based and rights-based conflicts.

Negotiation

Negotiation is a process in which parties interact in an attempt to reach an agreement about their respective rights or interests. It can be extremely informal, involving a discussion over a cup of coffee. It can also be relatively formal, involving professional negotiators—often lawyers—with a written agenda, formal exchange of written proposals, and formal discussion of the respective positions of the parties. Generally, when parties speak to their own lawyers in the context of potential litigation, the content of their discussions is subject to solicitor–client privilege. This means that the lawyer may not reveal anything that has been said without the client's consent. If, however, a client makes a comment to a non-lawyer who is assisting him with negotiations, the comment is not privileged. The non-lawyer might be forced to reveal the comment made by the client in a subsequent legal proceeding. It is therefore important that you take extreme care when making comments to non-lawyers, even those you have hired to represent you.

The key feature that distinguishes negotiation from other forms of dispute resolution is that the parties control the process themselves. There is no third-party intervenor with authority to influence or settle the dispute, or to referee the discussion, or to set the rules for holding it. This means that the parties are totally responsible for what occurs and must exercise more self-control and discipline than would be the case in mediation or arbitration.

POSITIONAL NEGOTIATION

Positional negotiation is the most traditional form of negotiation. When using **positional negotiation**, you determine your position before you begin to negotiate and plan to deviate from it as little as possible. This form of negotiation is often confrontational and adversarial. As a positional negotiator, you measure your success by how little you have had to change from your original position.

Positional negotiation often occurs over the price, quantity, or delivery schedule. Assume the dispute is over price. The positional negotiator will typically take an aggressive approach—demanding either a high or low price, depending on whether she is the seller or the buyer. She will begin with an argument that supports this

positional negotiation
form of negotiation where a party takes a position with the intention of deviating as little as possible from that position

position, be very reluctant to back down or concede, and if she does, will demand disproportionately large concessions in some other area, such as delivery schedule.

INTEREST-BASED NEGOTIATION

Interest-based or **principled negotiation** involves mutual problem solving. It starts when you and the party with whom you are negotiating inquire together into the sources of your conflict. You listen to each other's concerns without judgment— that is, without dismissing these concerns as invalid or less worthy than your own. In many cases, by listening carefully to each other in this way, you can find the common ground where your interests intersect. From here, you can craft a solution in which you both win.

Interest-based negotiators do not initiate discussions with a demand and a justifying argument, but rather with an expression of their interests. For example, if the dispute is over price, the seller might explain why his price is fair and comparable to the prices of similar products. The buyer, on the other hand, might describe why she is unable to pay the price proposed by the seller. She might, for example, explain that she is experiencing a temporary cash flow problem, that the product is available elsewhere at a lower price, and that she was led to believe that there would be no price increase since last she bought the seller's product.

Principled negotiation techniques include listening for the other party's tone and underlying emotions, acknowledging the emotional content of the communication, and asking open-ended questions. Open-ended questions do not make the other party defensive because they are not designed to set traps.

Open-ended questions include the following:

- What are you trying to achieve, and why is that important to you?
- Why do you think that price is fair?

Closed questions, on the other hand, sound like this:

- Isn't it true that you intentionally decided to break the contract?
- Do you not admit that the goods you delivered were damaged?

Brainstorming is another useful technique in interest-based negotiations. Here the parties examine numerous possibilities that arise from the common ground they identify. They set out their goals and they list as many options as possible for achieving them. They then evaluate their options to determine which ones are worth examining further.

BATNA AND WATNA

BATNA and WATNA mean "best alternative to a negotiated agreement" and "worst alternative to a negotiated agreement," respectively. Both are part of interest-based negotiation, but they can be used in positional negotiation as well in order to determine an initial position. Rather than choosing a desired solution before the negotiation process begins, and rigidly locking yourself into it, as a principled negotiator you keep an open mind and begin by identifying your BATNA and your WATNA.

Here is how BATNA and WATNA might be used in the context of a negotiation over price. Assume that the price relates to a product that is sold by many vendors as well as the one with whom you are negotiating. Your BATNA or best alternative to this negotiated agreement is the best price you can obtain from another vendor for a comparable quantity of the product, delivered according to the same schedule. Once you know this alternative, you will be in a better position to negotiate with your vendor. Your WATNA is that the alternative vendor goes bankrupt or raises its price dramatically, leaving you with no product or a very expensive product. Knowing the likelihood of these "worst alternatives" will help you negotiate a fair agreement.

WHEN AND WHEN NOT TO CHOOSE NEGOTIATION

Negotiation is a useful tool in the following circumstances:

1. *You are establishing rules for resolving potential conflicts, but no actual conflict exists.* For example, assume that you are negotiating a contract with a parts supplier for your computer-servicing business. Both you and the parts supplier see the potential for an enjoyable and profitable long-term business relationship. It is wise to consider matters that could cause conflict between you while you still have a good relationship. Negotiate ground rules that will govern any future problems, such as late deliveries or late payments. This may involve the inclusion of an arbitration clause, as discussed in chapter 4 under the heading "Reading the Fine Print: Typical Terms in Business Contracts."

2. *You and the other party are both interested in advancing each other's business interests as well as your own and are willing to seek win–win solutions.* For example, your computer-servicing business might experience a temporary cash flow problem because of an overdue customer account. As a result, your business might be unable to pay its bills on time, including payment owed to the parts supplier. It is not likely in the parts supplier's interest to exercise its legal rights by repossessing parts or petitioning your business into bankruptcy. The parts supplier's interests are more likely to be served when your business is operating successfully. By negotiating with you to allow additional time to pay your bill, the parts supplier can support this shared goal.

Negotiation should be avoided in the following circumstances:

1. *The power balance is tipped unevenly, and you are the weaker party.* There are any number of reasons why one party has less bargaining power than another. For example, in a vendor–purchaser relationship, the vendor may have only a few purchasers for its goods, while the purchaser may have many vendors to choose from. This makes the vendor dependent on the purchaser and places the purchaser in a superior bargaining position. Whatever the reason for the power imbalance, the weaker party is likely to suffer in the negotiation process, particularly in a positional negotiation where the stronger party is prepared to take advantage of her power position.

2. *Your concern about maintaining a business relationship with the other party greatly exceeds the other party's concern about maintaining a business relationship with you.* Where one party is concerned with maintaining a relationship and the other is less concerned, negotiation is often not very useful. In these

cases, the party who values the business relationship is likely to make too many concessions at the negotiating table. The result is an agreement that favours one party at the expense of the other, not something that will be good for the relationship in the long run.

ENFORCING A NEGOTIATED SETTLEMENT

A negotiated settlement is a contract and may be enforced in court like any other contract. Failure to comply with the terms of the negotiated settlement is a breach of contract. We discuss these matters in chapter 4 under the headings "Consequences of a Breach of Contract," "Damages," and "Remedies Other Than Damages for Breach of Contract."

Mediation

Mediation is a dispute-resolving process in which the parties to the dispute invite a neutral third party—a mediator—to supervise or oversee their negotiations. Mediators often set rules about how the parties are to interact with each other, schedule meetings, and set the agenda for meetings. They may try to persuade the parties to move from a win–lose process toward a win–win one. Mediators may choose to bring the parties together in face-to-face negotiations or may place the parties in separate rooms and shuttle back and forth between them. It is the job of the mediator to ensure that all parties necessary in resolving a dispute are present, including experts, if required.

There is much variation in types and styles of mediation, and you should do some research before choosing a mediator. It is important that the mediator's style and approach meet your needs. We describe the major mediation models in the following sections.

FACILITATIVE MEDIATION

Facilitative mediation is appropriate when the parties to the dispute already have a strong and trusting relationship. The facilitative mediator's role is to assist the parties in communicating effectively by helping them to define and obtain the information they need to resolve their problem. This may involve facilitating brainstorming and proposing mutually beneficial exchanges. A facilitative mediator relies on the parties' mutual desire to maintain or improve their relationship while assisting them in solving whatever problem has caused the dispute. Facilitative mediation is usually interest-based, rather than rights-based.

RIGHTS-BASED MEDIATION

A typical rights-based mediator assesses which of the parties has the stronger position by determining which party's rights are most strongly supported by law. She then attempts to persuade the parties to settle on that basis. Consider a claim for wrongful dismissal by an employee who was fired without legal justification or compensation. A rights-based mediation would seek a negotiated settlement that is logically connected to the rights of the parties. Using legal rules—in this case the common-law rules related to justification and compensation—the mediator would assist the parties in looking realistically at how a court would resolve their case, for the purpose of promoting a settlement.

Rights-based mediation does not require a cooperative attitude between the parties. Because of its adversarial nature, it is best suited to situations where the parties do not have a close relationship and are not interested in fostering a long-term relationship. Interests tend to be ignored in this process.

TRANSFORMATIVE MEDIATION

Transformative mediation encourages the parties to understand the positive aspects of their relationship and to appreciate the wisdom of each other's point of view. The mediator's goal is to have the parties see themselves and each other in a different light. From the new perspective they have gained through mediation, the parties question and re-examine their own assumptions.

Transformative mediation might be used to resolve a dispute between an expanding business and the community in which it is located. For example, a transformative mediator might attempt to help the business owner understand how disruptive increased traffic and noise are for community life; he would also attempt to help community members understand the business's need to grow, and thereby generate the revenue necessary to pay rising taxes and higher salaries. Both sides might thereby be "transformed," and able to see each other in a different light. Transformation often increases the parties' respect for each other and can lead to novel solutions to entrenched problems.

WHEN AND WHEN NOT TO CHOOSE MEDIATION

Mediation can be a useful technique in the following circumstances:

1. *You and the other party are prepared to make serious efforts to resolve the issues between you.* For example, you and a supplier agree on most of the terms of a contract for the supply of material you need to make an innovative communication device. The profit potential for both of you is very great, but you are unable to agree on how to determine the price of the material, and you seem to be unable to find a way to break through the impasse.

2. *You and the other party approach your dispute with a view to exploring your mutual interests and maintaining your business relationship.* For example, you have a serious dispute about the level of service you require from a service provider for your manufacturing equipment. The service provider thinks the level is adequate for the price paid but you want a quicker response time. The quality of the service provider's work is good, and you are expanding your business by adding other factories. The situation has great potential for both parties, but you need reassurance that the service provider can handle the increased

volume. You would like to continue to use his services if possible, and he is interested in the business expansion that your plans represent for him.

3. *You and the other party want to settle a rights issue, and your mutual desire to set your own rules exceeds your desire to have a third party settle them for you.* You and your customer are entering into an agreement to cooperate on the joint production of a new product. You are having some problems working out contract details, but both realize that the cooperative venture will work best if you both participate in making the rules.

Mediation will not work in certain circumstances:

1. *You or the other party is entirely focused on power or control.* If power or control of a business relationship or a dispute is the chief concern of one or both of the parties, mediation will probably fail. Why? There will be nothing for the mediator to discuss with either of you, short of one party totally giving in.

2. *One or both parties require a public decision that resolves the dispute and sets a precedent by which future disputes are resolved.* Because mediation is a private process, it will not create a precedent for future similar disputes.

3. *The legal rights clearly favour one party and that party sees no reason to compromise.* Consider, for example, a term of a contract that unambiguously gives one party the right to terminate the agreement for any reason on giving the other party 30 days' notice. Mediation will be a fruitless exercise if that party gives the required notice and has no interest in rethinking her position.

ENFORCING A MEDIATED SETTLEMENT

When the parties have reached an agreement through a mediator, the mediator will often help them to draft a formal contract. A contract achieved through mediation is the same as any other contract: it is an exchange of promises by the parties. Like any other contract, this contract is legally binding and can be enforced by the courts if necessary.

Minimizing Your Risk

Choose Your Mediator Carefully

- Research your choice: consult other business people and your lawyer; check websites and directories.

- Check the credentials of all prospective mediators. Do they have a background where they have used mediation skills? Have they taken mediation courses from a reputable institution, such as a university or law school, that provides comprehensive training? There is no official certifier of mediators.

- If the issues are technical, consider choosing someone with background and experience with the issues. For example, someone with engineering training might be able to work more efficiently with you on a product liability dispute.

- Once you have some names, suggest them to the other parties to the mediation. If you cannot agree, consider choosing randomly from an agreed list.

Arbitration

Commercial arbitration is a more formal process than negotiation or mediation. Like mediation, arbitration requires the presence of a neutral third party to oversee and steer the process. Unlike a mediator, however, an arbitrator determines the results of the process by making a binding decision at the end of the arbitration. In this way, an arbitrator's role in an arbitration hearing resembles a judge's role in a trial.

The arbitration process, in many respects, also mirrors the court process: there is a formal procedure for presenting a case and rules of evidence to govern the material that is acceptable for presentation to the arbitrator. These rules are often more relaxed than they are in a court, and the atmosphere at an arbitration hearing is usually much less formal than in court.

Parties often use lawyers to represent them during an arbitration, especially to examine expert witnesses when presenting their cases to the arbitrator. Arbitration begins with one side presenting its case through the evidence of witnesses and relevant documents. The other party cross-examines these witnesses before presenting his own case. At the end, the arbitrator makes a decision on the basis of the evidence presented to her. The arbitrator's decision is usually binding on the parties and enforceable in the courts if the parties do not voluntarily comply. While courts can intervene through judicial review to overturn an arbitrator's decision, they do so only in very limited circumstances. (We discuss judicial review in chapter 1 under the heading "Reconsideration, Appeals, and Judicial Review.")

Most provinces have statutes that govern arbitration. These laws set minimum standards of **fundamental fairness**—the right to be heard, to hear the case against you, and to reply to the case. The statutes also provide mechanisms to enforce arbitration decisions (also called arbitration awards) in the superior courts of the provinces as if the arbitration awards were court orders.

Arbitration is generally faster and less expensive than adjudication in the courts; however, this is not always the case. For example, proceedings in Small Claims Court are relatively quick and inexpensive, parties can handle the cases themselves, and there is no arbitrator to pay. Retail sellers of expensive items such as automobiles (above the monetary jurisdiction of Small Claims Court) often include a provision in their sales contracts that requires disputes about the product to be referred to arbitration, rather than the courts. We provide a more detailed discussion of arbitration clauses in chapter 4 under the heading "Arbitration."

fundamental fairness
principle encompassing the right to be heard, the right to hear the case against you, and the right to reply to the case

WHEN AND WHEN NOT TO CHOOSE ARBITRATION

In general, arbitration can be useful in the following situations:

1. *You and the other party agree on an arbitration system before a conflict develops.* A preordained arbitration system can be particularly useful if your conflict is likely to concern technical matters that require both expert evidence and knowledgeable adjudicators for a just and speedy resolution. For example, if your conflict concerns whether machinery meets the specifications set out in the contract, an arbitrator with an engineering background could likely resolve the matter more quickly than a judge, who would need more explanatory evidence.

2. *You and the other party are concerned about each other's business interests and about maintaining a good business relationship.* While arbitration is adversarial and somewhat formal, it is less so than litigation. Particularly if you have agreed on an arbitration process before your dispute arose, arbitration may be less destructive of an ongoing relationship than a lawsuit would be. If you combine arbitration with mediation as a first step and use goodwill, you may be able to salvage the relationship.

3. *The balance of power between you and the other party is tipped against you.* Because the arbitrator controls the process and decides on the basis of rules after hearing the evidence, arbitration can prevent a more powerful party from using her power to get her way, despite the merits of the case.

Arbitration may be unhelpful in the following circumstances:

1. *The relationship is damaged beyond repair.* The more formal process of litigation might be more useful because there is less direct contact between the parties.
2. *The credibility of the parties or witnesses is an issue.* The court system may be a better place to decide the dispute since the courts have formal rules for controlling witnesses and the presentation of evidence.
3. *A party may be seeking a remedy or remedies that cannot be granted by arbitrators.* A remedy may be unavailable because of limitations in an arbitration clause or because only courts can grant the remedy being sought. For example, only courts can grant injunctions—that is, orders requiring a party to do or refrain from doing something.

ENFORCING AN ARBITRATION AWARD

Where both parties have agreed to arbitrate rather than litigate, the parties are likely to comply with the arbitrator's decisions. Where one side refuses to accept the decision, provincial arbitration legislation provides that an award may be registered in the Superior Court for enforcement as if it were an order or judgment of the Superior Court.

Minimizing Your Risk
Find the Dispute Resolution Mechanism That Is Right for You

- Reflect about the nature of your conflict, its true causes, and what you hope to achieve for your business through its resolution.
- Reflect on your relationship with the other party and assess your relative power positions.
- Decide on the degree of informality that will best serve your interests and those of the other party.
- Consider your innate dispute-resolving skills and those of the other party.
- Determine whether a third party would be likely to assist you. If so, choose a third party whom you both trust and who has the qualities necessary to address your concerns skillfully.
- Approach the process openly and with strength.
- Prepare to present your case as thoroughly and with as much convincing documentation as you can find.

Litigation

Litigation in a superior court is costly and time consuming, particularly if the case is complex and the parties are entrenched in their positions. A lawsuit can easily take up to two years or more from start to finish. The costs can run from several thousand dollars to well over $100,000, depending on the complexity of the case. In addition to paying your own legal costs, you may have to pay between one-third and two-thirds of your opponent's legal costs, if you lose. The idea behind this rule is to make you think twice before launching or defending a weak or dubious case, and to encourage you to settle your differences rather than litigate. Should you decide to litigate, however, you will need to be aware of the many steps involved.

To understand how a case proceeds to trial, consider the example of Khan World Foods Ltd. Khan is an importer and exporter of raw foods. The company has done well over the years and has recently expanded into food processing. It has purchased several pieces of food processing equipment from Food Masher Ltd. for $90,000. Unfortunately, the processing equipment keeps malfunctioning. Although Food Masher has repaired it on several occasions, it keeps breaking down. Because of the breakdowns, Khan is unable to meet delivery deadlines, and customers are beginning to look to Khan's competitors to meet their needs. Khan asks Food Masher to remove its equipment, refund the purchase price, and compensate Khan for the business it has lost. Food Masher refuses. It claims that food-processing equipment must often be adapted to the customer's needs, and that Khan should be patient. However, the patience of Farid Khan, the company's president, has run out.

THE PRE-LITIGATION PROCESS

A lawsuit begins long before a case arrives at the doorsteps of a courthouse for trial. As in the case of some alternative dispute resolution procedures, such as arbitration, a court proceeding usually requires a party to find a lawyer. We have discussed this matter in chapter 1 under the heading "Lawyers."

Consulting the Lawyer

Khan will meet with the lawyer to give her the factual details of his case and provide documents, such as invoices and emails. On the basis of this information, the lawyer will advise Khan about the pros and cons of proceeding with a lawsuit. On the basis of this advice, the lawyer will ask Khan for instructions to proceed.

All conversations between Khan on behalf of his company and the lawyer and all correspondence passing between them are privileged. The purpose of the privilege rule is to encourage clients to be completely frank with their lawyers about everything that is relevant to the case, including aspects of the case that are unfavourable to the client. When lawyers have the whole story, they are able to provide their clients with frank and effective advice.

There are some lawyer–client communications for which the client cannot claim privilege. For example, if Khan told the lawyer he was going to lie under oath when giving evidence, the lawyer would be obliged—as an officer of the court—to inform the court or, at the very least, to stop representing Khan.

Avoiding Delay

In Ontario, and other provinces and territories, there are rules of procedure that set out times within which various steps in a lawsuit must be completed. Missing one of these deadlines is not usually fatal to the lawsuit.

limitation period
time period in which a lawsuit must be commenced, after which the right to sue is lost

However, the law has also established **limitation periods**, which are time periods during which lawsuits must be brought. To establish whether a limitation period has expired, Khan and his lawyer must determine when Khan World Foods Ltd.'s right to sue Food Masher first arose. If Khan is suing in Ontario, for example, the *Limitations Act* gives Khan two years from the time it first had a reason for suing Food Masher to start its lawsuit. If Khan fails to act before the limitation period expires, it loses its right to sue Food Masher.

Limitation periods are a complex field in which lawyers are expected to be knowledgeable. If a lawyer, rather than a client, is responsible for missing a limitation period, the client can sue the lawyer for negligence. In Khan's case, this could mean that Khan would receive roughly the same compensation from the lawyer that it would have received from Food Masher if the suit against Food Masher had started within the limitation period and Khan had been successful.

Limitation periods also have some relevance for arbitrations. Some arbitration clauses provide that a proceeding must be started within a specific time period and may not be arbitrated if the specified time has elapsed.

THE LITIGATION PROCESS IN SUPERIOR COURT TRIAL DIVISION

From the commencement of proceedings, Khan's case will follow the multi-step process set out in the Ontario *Rules of Civil Procedure*. The most important of these steps are set out in the following sections.

Exchange of Pleadings

statement of claim
court document notifying a defendant of a lawsuit against him and the reasons for the proceedings

statement of defence
court document notifying the plaintiff in a lawsuit that the defendant is denying the claim, and identifying the defendant's arguments

discovery
procedure after exchange of pleadings where both parties disclose all information, including producing documents, relevant to the case

Once Khan's lawyer has reviewed the facts and researched the law, she drafts a statement of claim, which she brings to a court office. She pays a fee, and the court officially starts the process. The statement of claim is served on (delivered to) the defendant, Food Masher. Khan's **statement of claim** tells Food Masher that it is being sued and gives the reasons for the lawsuit. Food Masher then has a short period of time to file a **statement of defence**. If Food Masher fails to act in time, Khan is entitled to judgment by default, which brings an early end to the lawsuit. However, defendants usually file statements of defence. At this point, the legal position of the parties has been set out, as have the basic facts on which they rely. The exchange of the statement of claim and the statement of defence usually completes the pleadings stage of procedure.

Discovery

Once Khan and Food Masher have exchanged pleadings, they each have an outline of the facts and legal rules on which the other relies. They are now entitled to find out more details about the evidence against them through a process called discovery. **Discovery** requires that each party disclose and produce all relevant documents, except for those that they no longer have in their possession or that are privileged.

Both parties must appear at an examination for discovery to answer questions about the case posed by the opposing lawyer. There is no judge present.

Preparation for Trial

At the conclusion of the discovery process, the parties will usually attend a pre-trial conference, where a judge reviews the case, explores options for settlement with the parties, and tries to narrow the issues and facts in dispute in order to shorten the trial. Many parties settle their dispute at this stage. If they do not, they then summons witnesses, prepare their evidence, and get ready for trial.

Trial

A trial can take several days. It begins with the lawyers for each party making opening statements, which present the judge with their version of what the case is about. Because Khan is the plaintiff, Khan's lawyer examines, or questions, its witnesses first. By examining Khan's witnesses, Khan's lawyer is presenting the judge with the evidence necessary to win Khan's case. Food Masher's lawyer will then cross-examine these witnesses in an effort to discredit their evidence. When Khan has finished presenting its case, Food Masher will call and examine its witnesses, and Khan's lawyer will then cross-examine them. At the end, each lawyer will present an oral summary to the judge.

In a civil (non-criminal) case, such as Khan's, Khan—being the plaintiff—bears the **burden of proof**. This means that Khan's lawyer must convince the judge on a **balance of probabilities** that Khan's version of facts and law has more merit than Food Masher's version. If Khan is only able to establish that its version of facts and law is equally meritorious as Food Masher's, Khan loses its lawsuit.

After hearing all the evidence and all the arguments of the parties' lawyers, the judge—if sitting without a jury—gives judgment. Jury trials in civil cases are rare in Canada. If there is a jury, however, it is the jury's job to sift through the evidence to draw factual conclusions. The judge then instructs the jury on how to apply the law to their factual conclusions. After deliberating in secret, the jury renders its verdict.

burden of proof
requirement that a certain party prove a particular fact at trial

balance of probabilities
standard of proof in civil (as opposed to criminal) law indicating that one version of events is more probable than another

Post-Trial Enforcement

If Khan is successful, it will obtain a judgment that awards monetary compensation for the wrongful actions of Food Masher. The judge will also award Khan interest on this monetary compensation and some of the costs involved in bringing its lawsuit. If Food Masher refuses to pay the award voluntarily, Khan must bring further proceedings to enforce its judgment, the most common of which are set out below:

- *Judgment debtor examination.* Khan can require Food Masher to appear before a court or at a court reporter's office to answer questions about its assets, debts, and ability to pay.
- *Writ of seizure and sale.* Khan can obtain a document from the court (also called a writ of execution) and file it with the sheriff. This writ enables the sheriff to seize property belonging to Food Masher and sell it at public auction. The proceeds of the sale (minus the costs of conducting it) are then available to Khan to pay the judgment.

- *Garnishment.* If a third party, such as a customer, owes money to Food Masher, Khan can obtain a garnishment order, which requires the third party to pay the money it owes to Food Masher into court so it is available to Khan.

We discuss each of these remedies in greater detail in chapter 9 under the heading "Debt Proceedings in Superior Court."

THE LITIGATION PROCESS IN SMALL CLAIMS COURT

If Khan's claim is relatively small—under $10,000 in Ontario—Khan may choose to take his case to Small Claims Court, a division of the Superior Court. This court is designed to provide a forum where small claims can be heard quickly, efficiently, and inexpensively. Plaintiffs and defendants can conduct their cases themselves, without being represented by lawyers. Small Claims Court permits paralegal agents to represent parties in court, providing a less expensive alternative to lawyers. Because parties often represent themselves, judges tend to intervene in the process more frequently than they do in Superior Court to assist and guide parties in presenting their cases. The procedure in this court is based on that in the trial division of the Superior Court, but is much simpler in form and operation:

- Khan's lawsuit would begin when Khan files a claim and serves it on Food Masher. If Food Masher intends to defend the case, it files a defence within the time allowed. If Food Masher fails to file a defence, Khan obtains a default judgment.

Minimizing Your Risk
Litigate Only When Necessary

- Choose Small Claims Court over Superior Court if your claim qualifies.
- Consult a lawyer or paralegal or take other action to advance your claim as quickly as possible to avoid missing a limitation period.
- Seek representation from a lawyer who specializes in litigation if your case must be heard in the Superior Court.

- There is no discovery process; if there are relevant documents, Khan and Food Masher file them with the court. The case proceeds to a pre-trial conference in most cases, where the parties are encouraged to settle, and then to trial.
- Court forms are pre-printed, many requiring a party to simply follow instructions and fill in the blanks, rather than engage in legal drafting, which often requires a lawyer's skills.
- The rules about what may be used in evidence are less complicated, less formal, and less restrictive than in the Superior Court.
- Judgments are enforced in Small Claims Court in the same way that they are in the Superior Court.

Small Claims Court is a high-volume court, with many cases involving debt collections for relatively small amounts of money, such as unpaid phone, gas, or credit card bills. However, commercial parties often use this court to resolve disputes that can be quite complex legally, though large amounts of money are not involved.

Canada's Court System

We have discussed in the previous sections the trial and small claims divisions of Superior Court. These are simply two divisions of a single court that exist within a much larger judicial framework. As a business person, you will never need the extensive knowledge of the Canadian court system that a lawyer or a court administrator needs. However, because you may find yourself using Canada's court system to resolve your legal disputes, some knowledge may be useful.

Each province and territory in Canada has its own court system to try all civil and criminal cases. While the systems differ slightly from province to province, they are similar in most respects. All systems arrange courts in a hierarchy. A court's relative position in the hierarchy depends on how much authority it has to decide legal issues. Generally, the more extensive the authority, the higher the court is perceived to be. Also, the procedure in higher courts is more formal and complex.

The Hierarchy of Courts in Ontario

At the top of Ontario's four-level hierarchy are the appellate courts, which hear appeals from decisions of lower courts. The appellate courts occupy two tiers in the hierarchy: the Supreme Court of Canada is the highest court and the Ontario Court of Appeal is the second highest.

Below the appellate courts is the Superior Court of Justice. It is staffed, for the most part, by federally appointed judges and consists of several divisions, which are described below in the section entitled "The Superior Court of Justice."

Below the Superior Court of Justice is the Ontario Court of Justice, which deals with less serious criminal and civil matters.

Figure 2.1 sets out the hierarchy of courts in Ontario. In the following sections, we briefly describe the function and composition of these courts.

Figure 2.1 Hierarchy of Courts in Ontario

Supreme Court of Canada

A federally established national appeal court that hears appeals from all provincial court systems; its decisions are binding on all courts in Canada.

Ontario Court of Appeal

The highest court in the province; it hears appeals from lower provincial courts and its decisions are binding on all other courts in the province.

Superior Court of Justice

The highest trial court in the province; it includes specialized courts, such as Divisional Court and Small Claims Court; its decisions are not binding on any other courts.

Ontario Court of Justice

Includes the lower criminal courts.

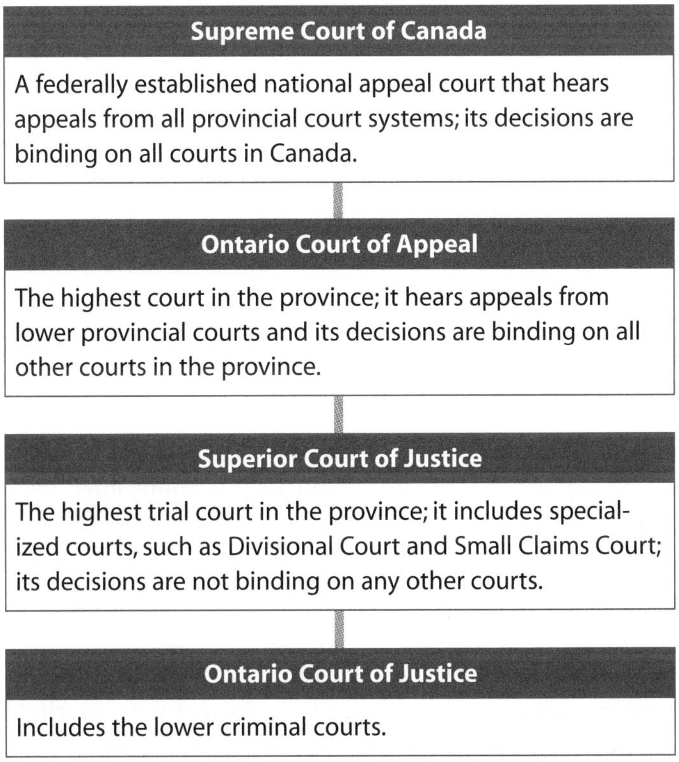

The Supreme Court of Canada

At the highest level sits the Supreme Court of Canada. This court is the most powerful court in the land and the court of last resort. It hears appeals from the provincial courts of appeal and from the highest federal courts.

The Supreme Court does not hear every appeal that is filed with it. If you want the court to hear your case, you must persuade it that your case raises issues of general public significance or reflects opposing decisions by provincial courts of appeal. Therefore, the court would not likely hear your appeal from a decision that went against you in the Ontario Court of Appeal on the interpretation of an ordinary business contract that was of no real interest to anyone but yourself and the other contracting party. It might, however, be interested in hearing your appeal if your contract had unusual implications that affected many other business contracts or if the law in the area was not yet settled.

Like most appeal courts, the Supreme Court of Canada does not hear witnesses or original evidence. The Supreme Court's job is to review the decisions of the provincial courts of appeal for errors made by judges. The court does not try or retry cases. It relies on transcripts of trials and hearings, and on arguments from lawyers in reaching its decisions. The decisions of the Supreme Court, once made, are binding on all other courts in Canada.

The Court of Appeal

Immediately below the Supreme Court of Canada is the Ontario Court of Appeal. Its job, like that of the Supreme Court of Canada, is to review the decisions of lower courts for errors, not to try or retry cases. It hears appeals from decisions about criminal and civil cases made in the Superior Court of Justice.

As a business person, you might find yourself in the Court of Appeal if you are dissatisfied with the result you obtain from the Superior Court of Justice. For example, if you think the trial court misinterpreted a contract that was being disputed, you might want to argue in the Court of Appeal that the wrong rules of contract interpretation were applied. Or if the trial court decided an issue that had been decided differently by other trial judges in other cases, you might want the court to rule on which interpretation is correct.

The Superior Court of Justice

The Superior Court of Justice consists of three divisions that are of concern to business people:

1. *Trial division.* The trial division of the Superior Court of Justice is the highest trial court in Ontario. Judges of this court are federally appointed to hear criminal and civil cases in larger cities and towns across Ontario.

   For example, you might wish to sue in this court for an unpaid account or because the other party to a contract refused to fulfill other contractual obligations.
2. *Divisional Court.* The Divisional Court hears applications for judicial review of decisions made by government agencies, such as the Ontario Human Rights Commission, the Ontario Labour Relations Board, or the Ontario

Liquor Control Board. If, for example, the Ontario Human Rights Commission finds the hiring policies of a business to be in contravention of the Ontario *Human Rights Code*, the business can appeal this decision to Divisional Court.

The Divisional Court does not substitute its own judgment for the judgment of a governmental agency whose decision is under review, and whose members often have specialized expertise in dealing with the issues before them. Rather, the Divisional Court identifies an agency's error and sends the matter back to the agency to make an appropriate decision.

3. *Small Claims Court.* The Small Claims Court has authority to hear cases where the claim is for $10,000 or less. Although any federally appointed Superior Court judge can hear such a case, these judges rarely do so. Instead, provincially appointed Small Claims Court judges and deputy judges staff this high-volume court, which has many offices across Ontario.

   The rules of procedure and the court forms in Small Claims Court are much simpler than they are in the trial division of the Superior Court of Justice. As well, there are guides available from the government to assist people who wish to represent themselves in Small Claims Court. The idea is to create a quick and inexpensive process to try small claims so that the cost of trying the case does not exceed the worth of the claim itself.

The Ontario Court of Justice

The Ontario Court of Justice is often referred to as an inferior or lower court because its power is limited by statute. (This is also true for Small Claims Court, even though it is technically part of the Superior Court system.) The court is divided into divisions that are defined by subject matter. The division most likely to affect a business person is the criminal division. As a business person, you might find yourself in the Ontario Court of Justice to testify about shoplifting in your store or a minor assault committed by an overly zealous bouncer in your bar, for example.

COURT REFORM: REDUCING COST AND DELAY

As we have noted already, the people who administer Ontario's courts are very concerned about how long it takes to try a case and how expensive the process can be. Efforts have been made to reduce cost and delay in order to make justice more easily available to everyone. Reformers have streamlined the civil trial process, established shorter time lines, created specialized courts to deal with complex cases, simplified procedures for certain types of cases, and diverted cases away from an adversarial framework where appropriate. Unfortunately, these efforts have not been very successful, and the cost of using lawyers is still prohibitive for many.

The Role of Canadian Courts

Courts have five essential roles to fulfill in Canada's judicial–political system. They resolve disputes, interpret legislation, answer constitutional questions, protect the rights and freedoms of individuals, and review the actions of government agencies.

Although these functions often overlap, we examine them individually in the following sections.

DISPUTE RESOLUTION

As we have noted, a principal role of the courts is to settle disputes between parties who have been unable to settle their differences themselves. Because the courts provide a forum for resolving conflicts peacefully, the parties have no need of resorting to remedies that involve force or fraud. The very existence of courts prevents, or at least limits, the social disorder and violence that can result when people engage in "do-it-yourself" justice.

A party who is dissatisfied with a judge's decision may appeal to a higher court, whose job it is to decide if the judge made an error. Once all rights of appeal have been exhausted, the decision is final and binds the parties. Thus, the parties' dispute is resolved.

INTERPRETATION OF LEGISLATION

In the course of deciding a dispute, a court may be called upon to determine the meaning of a statute or a regulation made under a statute. When a statute is drafted, the drafters cannot take into account every possible situation to which the statute might apply. In some cases, it is unclear how a statute is to be applied. In cases such as these, the parties will ask a court to interpret the statute to decide what it means in relation to a particular set of facts. The court's interpretation will resolve the matter for the parties to the lawsuit. It also provides guidance to others affected by the statute by allowing them to arrange their affairs so that they can predict, with reasonable certainty, the legal consequences of their actions.

CONSTITUTIONAL INTERPRETATION AND PROTECTION OF RIGHTS AND FREEDOMS

The constitution, like other legislation, must be applied to many different situations. It is the role of the courts to determine how to interpret and apply it. This can be a particularly weighty responsibility. Unlike ordinary legislation, which can always be changed and clarified if the government is dissatisfied with how the courts are interpreting and applying it, the constitution is not so easily amended. A Supreme Court of Canada ruling on the interpretation of a particular section is generally the final word on the matter.

Constitutional decisions usually involve resolutions of disputes about the powers of the federal and provincial governments and interpretations of the *Canadian Charter of Rights and Freedoms*. As we discussed in chapter 1, the creation of the Charter greatly expanded the role of Canadian courts by giving them the power to strike down laws that violate rights and freedoms, such as equality, freedom of expression, and freedom of religion. Pursuant to the Charter, the courts are responsible for safeguarding the rights and liberties of individuals against unlawful encroachments by the state. This responsibility sometimes pits courts against the state on issues that are often considered political and controversial.

REVIEW OF GOVERNMENT AGENCIES

As we observed in chapter 1 under the heading "Administrative Law," administrative boards and tribunals now resolve many disputes that arise in the course of doing business. The statutes that establish these adjudicative agencies of government often have provisions that exclude interference from courts. However, the courts have maintained their power to review the decisions of these agencies to ensure that they act fairly and do not make major legal errors in deciding cases.

Courts generally defer to the expertise of specialized government agencies and do not interfere unless the agency makes a clear and obvious error. For example, if the Ontario Labour Relations Board, after listening to both union and management representatives, comes to the conclusion that an employer has engaged in an unfair labour practice, a court will not generally interfere. The board is clearly using its expertise in considering subject matter with which it deals every day. If, however, the board comes to its conclusion without hearing from both parties or without considering a matter that is of vital importance to the issue before it, a court may order a rehearing and a new decision.

CASE IN POINT Government Policy and Interpreting Statutes

Barrie Public Utilities v. Canadian Cable Television Assn., [2003] 1 SCR 476

Facts

The Canadian Radio-television and Telecommunications Commission (CRTC) granted an order under section 43(5) of the *Telecommunications Act* permitting cable television companies to attach their cable lines to the power poles of Barrie Public Utilities.

Section 43(5) delegates such authority to the CRTC where a provider of public services is refused access to "the supporting structure of a transmission line" constructed on public property. On the basis of this wording, the CRTC decided that it had authority over the utility's poles. The CRTC relied on the telecommunications policies contained in the *Telecommunications Act* and the broadcasting policy contained in the *Broadcasting Act* to interpret the section, and concluded that "transmission line" included lines used to distribute electricity.

The case was appealed and eventually heard by the Supreme Court of Canada.

Result

The Supreme Court disagreed with the CRTC's interpretation of section 43(5) for many reasons. It held that the phrase "constructed on a highway or other public place" qualified the phrase "transmis-

sion line," and therefore the CRTC did not have jurisdiction over transmission lines on private property. Also, section 43(5) referred to "transmission lines," not "distribution lines," and because the utilities' power poles supported distribution lines, the CRTC did not have jurisdiction.

The Supreme Court also objected to the CRTC's heavy reliance on the policy objectives of the *Telecommunications Act* and the *Broadcasting Act*. While consideration of policy and legislative objectives is a legitimate approach to statutory interpretation, the CRTC wrongly used policy objectives to override the plain meaning of the statutory provisions.

Business Lesson

Government policies may be useful tools for filling in the gaps left by vague statutory provisions. However, they sometimes conflict with a strict reading of the statute. When this happens, it is the statute that prevails. If you are uncertain about the meaning of a section, or about whether to rely on a government policy, and if getting it wrong could have a significant consequence to your business, seek legal advice.

Chapter Summary

The chapter began with a discussion of the major dispute-resolving methods that business people use to avoid the risks and expense of litigation in Canadian courts. We examined negotiation, mediation, and arbitration with a view to demonstrating various techniques and illustrating particular circumstances that might prompt business people to choose one method over another. By way of comparison, we then discussed the process of litigation in Superior Court and Small Claims Court.

We then discussed the hierarchy of courts in Ontario and concluded with an analysis of the function of courts generally.

KEY TERMS

alternative dispute resolution (ADR)
balance of probabilities
burden of proof
discovery
fundamental fairness
interest-based or principled negotiation
limitation period
litigation
positional negotiation
statement of claim
statement of defence
third party

REFERENCES

Barrie Public Utilities v. Canadian Cable Television Assn., [2003] 1 SCR 476.

Canadian Charter of Rights and Freedoms, part I of the *Constitution Act, 1982*, RSC 1985, app. II, no. 44.

Constitution Act, 1867 (UK), 30 & 31 Vict., c. 3.

Limitations Act, 2002, SO 2002, c. 24.

Rules of Civil Procedure, RRO 1990, reg. 194, as amended.

Supreme Court Act, RSC 1985, c. S-26.

REVIEW AND DISCUSSION

True or False?

_F_ **1.** BATNA and WATNA are more commonly part of positional negotiation than of interest-based negotiation.

_F_ **2.** A negotiated settlement, unlike arbitration decisions, cannot be enforced.

_T_ **3.** Transformative mediation attempts to get each party to appreciate the validity of the other's point of view.

_T_ **4.** In the Superior Court, you are entitled to disclosure of the other party's documents and evidence prior to trial.

_F_ **5.** If you win a case in court, you can enforce your judgment by using garnishment to seize and sell the defendant's car.

_F_ **6.** A decision made in the trial division of the Superior Court is binding on the Court of Appeal.

Multiple Choice

1. Arbitration as a process
   a. is more formal than negotiation
   b. is more formal than litigation
   c. is controlled by the parties
   d. none of the above

2. If the parties have a history of conflict, and one is stronger than the other, the following is probably the best alternative dispute resolution process:
   a. negotiation
   b. mediation
   c. arbitration
   d. either b or c would work equally well

3. In talking about alternative dispute resolution, we often discuss rights and interests. In this context rights refer to
   a. short-term goals
   b. long-term goals
   c. business concerns, aspirations, and priorities
   d. entitlements

4. In positional negotiation you
   a. determine what outcome you want before you start and stick to it as best you can
   b. explore with the other parties what the source of the conflict is
   c. accept the other side's position as legitimate and valid
   d. ask open-ended questions
   e. none of the above

5. In the mediation process,
  a. the mediator guides discussions and imposes a settlement after hearing both sides
  b. the mediator guides discussions
  c. the mediator always keeps the parties apart during discussions
  d. the parties must not be in an adversarial position

6. You should use mediation if
  a. both parties are prepared to make serious efforts to resolve the issues
  b. both parties are prepared to explore mutual interests and wish to maintain an ongoing relationship
  c. in settling a rights issue, the parties are more interested in making their own rules than in having rules imposed on them by a third party
  d. all of the above
  e. only b and c are correct

7. You should use arbitration if
  a. the other party is stronger than you are
  b. you know the other party will comply with the arbitrator's decision
  c. you have a good working relationship and have successfully resolved interest disputes in the past
  d. all of the above
  e. none of the above

8. Solicitor–client privilege means
  a. anything your lawyer tells you cannot be repeated by you to anyone else
  b. anything you write to your lawyer cannot be revealed by either of you
  c. your lawyer has a right ahead of other creditors to payment of his bill for services
  d. third parties who provide your lawyer with information about your case cannot reveal it to anyone else
  e. your lawyer cannot reveal any information you give to him about the case without your permission

9. Small Claims Court cases differ from those in the trial division of the Superior Court in the following way:
  a. There is a limit on the amount of money you can sue for in Small Claims Court.
  b. Proceedings in the trial division of the Superior Court are faster and cheaper than in Small Claims Court.
  c. There is no discovery process in Small Claims Court.
  d. b and c.
  e. The rules of evidence are more relaxed in Small Claims Court than in the trial division of the Superior Court.

Short Answer

1. In the context of ADR, what are interests and rights, and why is the distinction between them important?

2. What is positional negotiation?

3. What is interest-based negotiation?

4. When should you choose negotiation over other dispute settlement techniques?

5. When should you choose mediation over other dispute settlement techniques?

6. When should you choose arbitration as a dispute resolution technique?

7. What are the main steps in the litigation process in the trial division of the Superior Court?

8. How does a Small Claims Court case differ from one in the trial division of the Superior Court?

9. What is the hierarchy of courts in Ontario?

10. Why do business people increasingly opt for ADR rather than civil litigation to resolve disputes?

Discussion and Debate

You are the major shareholder and CEO of Canagasso, a small Canadian scientific research and manufacturing company located near Toronto. Canagasso specializes in developing and manufacturing rare gases for use in industry, including the computer chip manufacturing industry. You have a number of customers who eagerly purchase the various gases you make as fast as you can produce them in your small factory. The profits you make have been primarily devoted to further research in the development of new gases; some of the research is quite speculative, and your researchers are encouraged to satisfy their scientific curiosity as much as they are encouraged to develop new products. Until now you have not really tried to expand the business, content to produce enough products for the current market in order to fund further research. You are not interested in finding a bigger manufacturing plant. Because of environmental controls required by most governments, changing location would be hugely expensive and time consuming. You also know all 40 of your employees by first name and are keenly aware that, at your present size, you can maintain the kind of informality and congenial relations that make Canagasso a pleasant place to work. Generally, you put a high value on good interpersonal relations among your workers. You also like to be able to finance your operations out of current earnings, and you do not seek expansion. At the same time, you would like to expand your research operations, which is your first love, almost a hobby.

Chipponad is a large market-leading computer chip manufacturer and a long-time customer of Canagasso, which supplies all of the gases used in Chipponad's computer chip manufacturing. Although large and somewhat bureaucratic, Chipponad has a reputation for being on the leading edge of product development and has long been known for the speed at which it can turn a concept or idea into a marketable product. Chipponad puts a very high value on product development and views it as the key to business success. Recently, it began to develop a new superchip. If the effort is successful, the new product is likely to dominate the worldwide market for many years and make Chipponad huge profits.

Chipponad approaches Canagasso with a proposition. It invites Canagasso to work with it in a joint venture to do the gas research and manufacturing required for the successful development of the superchip in exchange for a share of the profits.

As Canagasso's CEO in charge of negotiating the joint venture, you must do the following:

1. Identify your interests and, in that context, your BATNA and WATNA in preparation for conducting a principled negotiation process with Chipponad.
2. Do the same with respect to Chipponad's interests, BATNA, and WATNA.
3. Based on your conclusions in 1. and 2., develop a proposal that might lead to an agreement to enter the proposed joint venture.

Tort Law

LEARNING OBJECTIVES

After reading this chapter, you should be able to:

- Recognize a tort.
- Distinguish between intentional and unintentional torts.
- Describe the concept of vicarious liability.
- Describe the elements of negligence.
- Explain strict liability.

- Identify torts common in the commercial world.
- Identify defences to tort actions.
- Identify different types of damages.
- Manage business risks from a torts perspective.

What Is a Tort?

A **tort** is an action that causes injury to people or damage to property. Unlike a crime—which the law views as harming the state—a tort usually causes harm to individuals, including businesses. Examples of torts that can arise in the business world include the following:

- A grocery store fails to clean up spilled olive oil; a customer slips, falls, and breaks his leg.
- A consulting company supplies a business with inaccurate information about marketing techniques; the business acts on the information and loses several million dollars as a result.
- A nightclub owner fails to illuminate exit signs; a fire breaks out and 40 patrons die or suffer serious injury in a stampede to the door.

The state does not prosecute torts as it prosecutes crimes. In the examples above, the customer, the business, and the patrons (or their estates) must bring a lawsuit against the grocery store, the consulting firm, and the nightclub to obtain compensation for their injuries. By bringing a lawsuit, the customer, business, and patrons become **plaintiffs** in a **tort action**. By being sued, the grocery store, the consulting firm, and the nightclub become **defendants** in the tort action.

If a tort causes very serious harm, as in the fire example, it is likely that the state would launch a criminal prosecution against the person or business that was responsible for the damage. Such a prosecution, however, would be an entirely separate matter

tort
civil wrong other than breach of contract, for which damages may be sought to compensate for any harm or injury sustained

plaintiff
party who commences a lawsuit (the suing party)

tort action
lawsuit based on tort

defendant
party who is sued in a lawsuit

from any tort actions that the patrons might choose to bring. The purpose of a criminal prosecution is to *punish* lawbreakers in the name of the state and prevent further crimes. By contrast, the purpose of a tort action is to *compensate* individuals, including businesses, who have suffered injury as a result of the torts committed by others.

Many forms of harm traditionally recognized in tort law have, over time, been incorporated into various statutes as offences. For example, the *Occupiers' Liability Act* incorporates, with modifications, certain aspects of tort law that relate to visitors and business people who enter private property. Once a tort evolves into a statutory offence, the state assumes responsibility for enforcement. However, individuals may still sue in tort unless the statute specifically prohibits these lawsuits.

Predicting and minimizing potential harm to consumers and others is an ongoing responsibility of businesses that want to avoid legal liability.

The Importance of Tort Law for Business People

Torts can occur in all kinds of contexts: they are not unique to the business world. It is essential, however, for business people to be aware of the risks of tort-based litigation against their businesses:

- *Tort judgments are expensive.* Tort liability is perhaps the most significant potential source of unexpected expense for businesses. While fines under the criminal law are certainly unpleasant, they are usually predictable and well defined. Tort judgments, by contrast, are much less predictable, and large awards to plaintiffs can plunge a business into insolvency. Tort liability is a difficult risk to manage, but all businesses must consider it.
- *Tort judgments are a public relations nightmare.* Financial impact aside, a tort lawsuit can do irreparable damage to a business's reputation. Business people invest considerable resources into building trust in their products and services. Goodwill can evaporate in the face of bad press relating to a tort suit (even, sometimes, when the plaintiff's case is proven to be unfounded). Sensitive handling of tort matters—for example, knowing when to fight and when to settle—can help protect a business's valuable reputation.

It is also important for business people to understand that tort law is an essential business tool. When most business people think about tort liability, they think first about how to avoid it. However, businesses themselves are often plaintiffs in lawsuits based on tort. When harm is suffered by the actions or **omissions** of another and there is no breach of contract involved, there may be a remedy for the wronged party in tort. We consider examples such as nuisance, occupiers' liability, and passing off later in the chapter.

omission
failure to act

Vicarious Liability

vicarious liability
liability imposed on one party (often an employer) for the harmful actions or omissions of another (often an employee)

One of the most important principles in tort law—and a principle that business people must always keep in mind—is **vicarious liability**. Because of vicarious liability, businesses can be held responsible—or liable—for injuries that result from the actions of their employees. For example, if a furniture company's delivery truck driver crashes into a bus shelter while delivering furniture, the company may be held vicariously liable for the driver's conduct. The people who suffered injury at the bus shelter can sue the driver in tort, but they can also sue the employer. Vicarious liability holds an employer responsible for the torts that its employees commit while doing their jobs.

CASE IN POINT   Vicarious Liability

Teskey v. Toronto Transit Commission, 2003 CanLII 11726 (ONSC)

Facts

The Toronto Transit Commission (TTC) became concerned that there was a drug problem among TTC nightshift operators. To address it, the TTC approached an investigation agency. Through the agency, the TTC hired an investigator and trained him so that he would be able to work undercover, posing as a TTC employee.

In the course of his employment, the undercover agent reported on marijuana use and a marijuana sales transaction conducted by a TTC employee. However, the undercover agent's credibility was at issue because of his own marijuana use. A defamation claim was made by the TTC employee against the undercover agent, and, based on vicarious liability, against the TTC and the agency.

Result

The TTC was held liable for the undercover agent's actions. The court ruled that the contract between the TTC and the agent created an employer–employee relationship and that it is possible for more than one employer (the investigation agency and the TTC) to be vicariously liable for the actions of a single employee at the same time. It made no difference that the undercover agent was hired for the purpose of conducting an investigation.

Business Lesson

Remember that your business is vicariously liable for the actions of your employees. If you need temporary assistance in an area that is outside your business's usual range of expertise (for example, private investigations), hire an independent contractor, not an employee. (We discuss independent contractors in chapter 7 under the heading "Independent Contractor or Employee?")

Minimizing Your Risk
Train and Monitor Employees

- Prevent employees from committing torts through clear policies, sufficient training, and adequate monitoring.

- Carry sufficient insurance to cover the costs of employee accidents and other risks.

Joint and Several Liability

Another important concept is joint and several liability. This arises in situations where there are two or more tortfeasors, such as an employee and the business that employs him, or partners in a firm (discussed in greater detail in chapter 6, Methods of Carrying On Business), or two engineers who worked on a project. If both are held liable for the harm to the plaintiff, the *Negligence Act* provides that the plaintiff is entitled to recover the full amount of the damages from either of them.

In other words, if Joe and Maria are both liable for harm to Bob, and the court awards damages of $5,000, Bob could demand the entire amount from either Joe or Maria. This allows the plaintiff, Bob, to collect from whoever has the deepest pockets. Even if the court allocates liability between Joe and Maria such that Joe is only 10 percent responsible, he may be required to pay the entire amount. The *Negligence Act* permits him to then sue Maria for the difference.

Elements of a Tort

A tort does not exist every time a person is hurt or feels offended. A person or business that has suffered harm as a result of the actions of another must prove the elements of a tort in order to obtain compensation in tort law. The elements may vary depending on the type of tort, but they always include the following:

1. *causation*—that is, that the actions of the defendant caused the harm, and
2. *quantifiable harm*—that is, that the harm is measurable in a manner recognized by the law. (See figure 3.1.)

For example, assume that you and your friend Ravi attempt to sell antique watercolour paintings from a booth at an outdoor fair, but it rains and no one buys anything. You and Ravi quarrel and have a miserable time. You cannot bring a tort action against Ravi just because your unsuccessful business venture was his idea. Why? First, you cannot establish causation: your misery was caused by rain and a lack of interest in your wares, not by anything Ravi did. Second, even though you were uncomfortable and upset, you cannot prove quantifiable harm because the law does not, in general, provide compensation for discomfort and disappointment.

If, on the other hand, Ravi carelessly left the roof off your booth, and the paintings were ruined by the rain, you might have an action against him for the tort of negligence. At least you would be able to prove causation—that is, that Ravi's carelessness resulted in damage to the paintings. You would also be able to quantify the harm based on the appraised value of the paintings that were ruined.

Figure 3.1   Elements of a Tort

CAUSATION   +   QUANTIFIABLE HARM   ➡   TORT

To succeed in a tort action, a plaintiff must always prove causation and quantifiable harm, but there are other elements that a plaintiff must prove, depending on the nature of the tort in question. To take an obvious example, a plaintiff who claims to have suffered damages as a result of the tort of trespass must prove that the defendant did, in fact, trespass on premises lawfully occupied by the plaintiff. In the sections that follow, we discuss the elements that plaintiffs are required to prove when seeking compensation for injuries suffered as a result of various torts, both intentional and unintentional.

Categories of Torts

Torts can be categorized in a number of ways. We have grouped them in three principal categories: unintentional torts, intentional torts, and torts that can be either intentional or unintentional (see figure 3.2).

An **unintentional tort** occurs as a result of careless or negligent actions that cause unintended harm to people or businesses. Most unintentional torts fall into the large group of torts known as negligence. Product liability, occupiers' liability, and professional negligence are three subcategories of negligence. Another form of unintentional tort is known as a **strict liability tort**, which requires no proof of negligence.

An **intentional tort** occurs when a person or business deliberately harms another. Intentional torts fall into two large groups: torts involving verbal or physical aggression, and business torts.

Certain torts may be committed either intentionally or unintentionally. Trespass to land, nuisance, and invasion of privacy are all torts that can be unintentional or intentional.

unintentional tort
injury inadvertently caused to a plaintiff by a defendant

strict liability tort
unintentional tort that requires no proof of negligence

intentional tort
injury deliberately caused to a plaintiff by a defendant

Figure 3.2   Categories of Torts

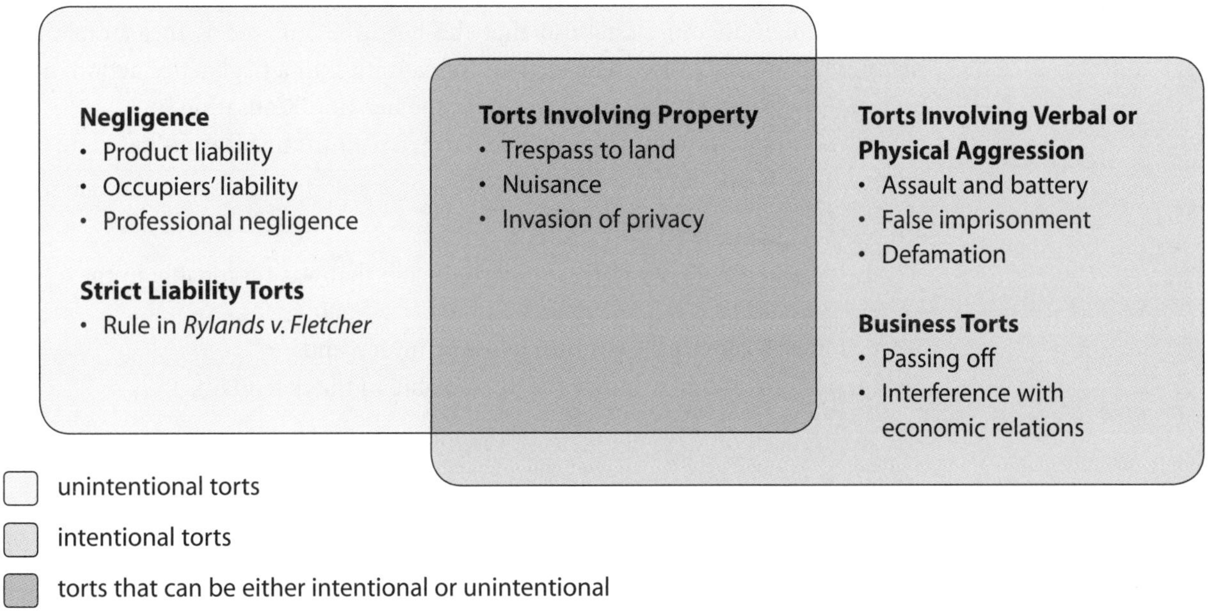

Negligence
- Product liability
- Occupiers' liability
- Professional negligence

Strict Liability Torts
- Rule in *Rylands v. Fletcher*

Torts Involving Property
- Trespass to land
- Nuisance
- Invasion of privacy

Torts Involving Verbal or Physical Aggression
- Assault and battery
- False imprisonment
- Defamation

Business Torts
- Passing off
- Interference with economic relations

☐ unintentional torts

☐ intentional torts

▨ torts that can be either intentional or unintentional

Unintentional Torts

The broadest and most significant unintentional tort that affects businesses is the tort of negligence. In order to make a successful claim in negligence, a plaintiff must establish certain elements, which we explore in the sections below.

Following our detailed discussion of negligence, we provide a brief description of strict liability.

DEFINITION AND SCOPE OF NEGLIGENCE

negligence
failure of a person to act reasonably, with the result being harm to someone else

Negligence is a tort in which a business or person commits a careless act that results in unintended harm to another. The harm is caused by either the defendant's failure to carry out a duty or the defendant's poor performance of a duty.

Negligence is an extremely broad category of tort. The torts that business people most commonly encounter fall into certain well-established subcategories of negligence. These subcategories include

- *product liability*, which occurs when a manufacturer carelessly produces defective goods that injure a member or members of the public;
- *occupiers' liability*, which occurs when a business carelessly fails to keep its premises safe for its customers and other visitors to enter; and
- *professional negligence*, which occurs when a professional, such as a lawyer, accountant, or veterinarian, acts carelessly while performing her job.

We discuss the elements of product liability, occupiers' liability, and professional negligence later in this chapter.

ELEMENTS OF NEGLIGENCE

As discussed above, to prove negligence (or any subcategory of negligence), a plaintiff must prove causation and quantifiable harm. Proof of quantifiable harm in a negligence action is the same as proof of quantifiable harm in any other tort action—the plaintiff must establish that the harm he suffered is measurable in a manner recognized in law. The element of causation in a negligence action, however, is unique. We explore it below under the heading "Causation."

In addition to proving quantifiable harm, a plaintiff in a lawsuit based on negligence must prove the following elements:

- the defendant owed him a duty of care,
- the defendant breached the standard of care that was reasonable in the circumstances,
- this breach caused the plaintiff's loss or injury, and
- the plaintiff's loss or injury was foreseeable to the defendant.

We discuss each of these elements in the following sections.

duty of care
legal duty owed by one person to another based on a relationship or on the doctrine of foreseeability

Duty of Care

A **duty of care** is a legal responsibility to avoid causing harm to others through carelessness. This duty lies at the base of all negligence claims.

In the commercial world, a duty of care arises whenever a business person or corporation becomes aware—or should reasonably become aware—that its actions or omissions could harm another. Businesses owe a duty of care to their customers, suppliers, and anyone else who could reasonably be expected to come into contact with their products or services. Businesses are responsible—they have a duty—to make sure that their products or services do not harm anyone.

Standard of Care

A **standard of care** is the degree of care that a business person or corporation must take to prevent or minimize harm to others. Every time a business sells a product, there is the possibility that harm may result from the use or misuse of the product. But how careful must a business be? For example, is a business responsible for the injuries suffered by a child who swallows the rat poison that it manufactures? Is it relevant whether the poison is labelled with warnings to keep it away from children, and is contained in a childproof bottle? What if the warning label falls off the bottle?

standard of care
degree of care that a person must take to prevent harm to others

Courts use the reasonable person test to determine the appropriate standard of care on a case-by-case basis. A **reasonable person** is defined as a normal, prudent individual who acts according to generally accepted practices and conducts her affairs in a manner generally accepted by society. The reasonable person standard also applies to corporations because, in law, a corporation is a person. That is, a corporation has the same rights and responsibilities as an individual and is held to the same standard of care—that of a reasonable corporation.

reasonable person
fictional person who, in negligence law, applies the appropriate standard of care in a given situation

If the defendant has been more careless than a reasonable person would have been in the situation, the defendant has breached the standard of care required. Appropriate standards of care vary from situation to situation. However, for consistency, courts look to previous decisions in similar cases to determine what kind of behaviour is reasonable. For example, *Jordan House Hotel Ltd.* provided the judge in *Crocker v. Sundance Northwest Resorts Ltd.* with a precedent (see the Case in Point box below). In the *Crocker* case, a ski resort business was found liable for injuries to an intoxicated customer whom resort staff allowed to compete in a snow-tube race. Even though the customer signed a waiver explaining that he entered the race at his own risk, the court held that a reasonable person would have foreseen that drunkenness increased the risk of injury; the resort's staff had a duty of care to their patron and should have stopped the man from competing.

In many business tort cases, reasonable behaviour is dictated by statute. For instance, in the rat poison example, it is no longer up to individual manufacturers to decide whether or not to securely affix a warning label to containers; a securely affixed warning label is now a statutory requirement under the *Pesticides Act*, among other statutes. However, in a complicated case—where, for example, someone has tampered with a label—courts will look to the principles established in earlier cases. They may ask, for example, whether the pesticide manufacturer performed tests on its product for tamper resistance.

In cases of professional negligence, the standard of care is generally higher than that of a reasonable person test. Professionals are typically held to the standards of their profession. For example, doctors are held to the standard of a reasonable doctor, lawyers to the standard of a reasonable lawyer, and architects to the standard of a reasonable architect. We provide more information on this topic below under the heading "Professional Negligence."

CASE IN POINT   Standard of Care: The Reasonable Bar

Jordan House Hotel Ltd. v. Menow and Honsberger, [1974] SCR 239

Facts

A patron was banned from a bar for rowdy behaviour. The bar eventually allowed him to return on the condition that he be accompanied by a responsible adult friend. One night, while his friend was away from the bar, bar staff served the patron several drinks. Although he became obviously intoxicated, the staff continued to serve him until he had to be removed for harassing other patrons. On his way home, a car struck and injured the patron.

Result

The bar was liable for the patron's injuries. Knowing the patron's reputation and that he was drunk on the night of the accident, the bar and its staff were more careless than a reasonable person would be when, instead of calling the police or arranging for a ride, they sent the patron out alone.

Business Lesson

Take appropriate preventive steps the moment you or an employee becomes aware that there is a potential for harm befalling a patron or client as a result of your actions. This may include setting clear policies and providing training for employees that addresses the specific risks inherent in your business.

Causation

To obtain compensation for a defendant's negligence, a plaintiff must prove not only that the defendant breached the standard of care owed to her, but also that the breach caused, or contributed to, the harm that she suffered.

In some cases, proving causation is straightforward. For example, consider a computer service that attempts to repair a business's computer system but does so incompetently and renders the system unworkable. Clearly, the computer service has breached the standard of care owed to the business, and clearly this breach has caused the business's loss.

In other cases, however, there may be more than one cause of harm. Consider a manufacturer who supplies defective milk cartons to a milk producer. The producer then fills the cartons with milk and sells them to a grocery store. The cartons leak, and a customer slips in a puddle of milk, breaking her wrist in the fall. On investigation, it is discovered that the leak in the carton resulted from rough handling by the shipper during transit to the store. Who caused the customer's broken wrist? Is it the store, for not cleaning up the spilled milk? Is it the shipping company, for handling the shipment too roughly? Is it the carton manufacturer, for supplying an unsuitable carton? Is it the milk producer, for shipping the milk without determining, through tests, whether the cartons were suitable for the purpose?

The answer seems to be that all the parties have jointly caused the customer's injury and are therefore jointly responsible. In a case such as this one, the court will apportion—or divide—liability among the parties. If the court determines, for example, that the grocery store was 25 percent responsible for the customer's injuries, the grocery store must pay the plaintiff 25 percent of the amount awarded to her in compensation for her injuries.

Remoteness

In order to establish the tort of negligence, a plaintiff must prove that the harm she suffered as a result of the defendant's breach of the standard of care owed to her was, in a general way, **foreseeable** by the defendant. In other words, the harm suffered by the plaintiff as a result of the defendant's breach cannot be too far removed (or "remote," as the law commonly refers to it) from the kind of harm that the defendant might anticipate.

forseeability
expectation of whether a reasonable person could predict that a certain result might follow from his actions

For example, manufacturers of television sets enclose electrical components in a protective panel. They do this not only to protect the television from breakage, but also to protect people from electrocution. They usually mark the panel with a warning discouraging unqualified people from touching the components inside. If the manufacturer fails to enclose the components or to mark the panel with a warning, electrocution is a foreseeable result. A plaintiff who suffers injury from electrocution would be able to establish that the harm was foreseeable by the manufacturer.

However, a television set can conceivably cause harm in other ways. Consider, for example, an enraged person who throws his roommate's television set out of a third-storey window. If the television set crashes through the roof of a car parked on the street below, the car owner will have trouble establishing that the damage was, from the standpoint of the television manufacturer, reasonably foreseeable. A manufacturer would almost certainly not be expected to foresee the possibility that its product could cause injury to the public by being used in this manner.

The issue of foreseeability is relevant to the kind of harm, and not usually to the degree of harm, suffered by the plaintiff. That is, as long as the defendant could have anticipated harm of the general type that actually occurred, he is usually held responsible for all the damage that results.

In the example of the leaking milk cartons, the carton manufacturer can certainly foresee that property damage could result from the leakage of milk. Even in a case where property damage is extensive and improbable—where, for example, milk leaks through a floor and damages valuable antique furniture in a basement—the carton manufacturer is likely to be held responsible for the damage. In reality, the consequences may lie beyond the normal limits of a carton manufacturer's foresight; however, it is still property damage that results from leakage, and the courts have traditionally found that it requires compensation.

NEGLIGENCE TORTS COMMON IN BUSINESS

Product liability and occupiers' liability are the two types of negligence suits that most commonly threaten businesses. Any business that designs, manufactures, or sells a product is at risk of being sued for product liability if someone alleges that the product has caused harm. Any business that invites customers or clients onto its premises is at risk of being sued for occupiers' liability if the customer or client suffers injury while on the property.

Professional negligence is a third type of unintentional tort that involves professionals such as accountants, doctors, engineers, lawyers, and veterinarians. This tort may affect businesses that deal with or employ these people. Professionals are at risk of being sued if a client or patient alleges that he suffered harm, either physical or financial, as a result of the professional's advice or services.

Product Liability

product liability
subcategory of negligence based on a defendant's liability for harm caused to others because of his defective or dangerous products

Product liability arises out of harm caused by defective or dangerous products. The harm this tort addresses may affect both people and property. For example, a defective seatbelt may result in injury to a person. A defective valve may result in water damage to a house.

The designer, manufacturer, or supplier of a product owes a duty of care to anyone who can reasonably be foreseen as a user of the product. One such user is the purchaser of the product, but there are others as well. Unlike the purchaser, these other users cannot sue for breach of contract. This is because these users lack privity of contract, a matter we discuss in chapter 4 under the heading "Identification of Parties."

Consider the example of a passenger who is injured when a seatbelt in a friend's car malfunctions during an accident. The passenger is not a party to the contract of purchase and sale between the car's owner and the dealership; nor is she a party to the contract between the car's manufacturer and the seatbelt manufacturer. She therefore cannot seek compensation for her injuries in an action for breach of contract. However, she can bring a tort action in product liability. Product liability expands the scope of plaintiffs to include all potential seatbelt users, not just those who were parties to contracts involving the sale of cars or the purchase and installation of seatbelts. Anyone who uses a seatbelt is owed a duty of care.

As in all lawsuits based on negligence, the injured passenger must still establish that the seatbelt manufacturer and/or car manufacturer breached the relevant standard of care, that the breach of this standard caused her injuries, and that her injuries were reasonably foreseeable.

Minimizing Your Risk

Reduce Lawsuits Based on Product Liability

- Test all products thoroughly to determine whether they pose any dangers.

- Document your testing.

- Eliminate potential dangers through redesign if possible.

- Apply clear and exhaustive warnings securely to products.

- Carry sufficient insurance to cover any potential liability.

Defective Products Versus Dangerous Products

A defective product is one that is designed poorly or manufactured improperly. If a product has a design problem, the defect will affect all identical products. If, however, a product has a manufacturing problem, usually only some of a manufacturer's products will be affected. In either case, the designer, manufacturer, or supplier has a duty to take reasonable steps to prevent the product from finding its way into the hands of consumers.

CASE IN POINT   The Second-Hand Helmet

Thomas v. Bell Helmets Inc., 1999 CanLII 9312 (ONCA)

Facts

A motorcyclist, who was wearing a second-hand helmet, suffered serious brain damage after colliding with a car. The motorcyclist was thrown through the air, his helmet flew off, and he landed in a ditch, hitting his head on the ground. The motorcyclist's family commenced a lawsuit on his behalf against various parties, including the other driver and the manufacturer of the helmet. All the defendants settled the case before trial with the exception of the helmet manufacturer, which disputed its liability.

Result

The helmet manufacturer was held 25 percent responsible for the motorcyclist's injuries. In 1985, the year the helmet was manufactured, Bell Helmets either knew or should have known that there was a risk of injury to a user if an ill-fitting helmet flew off on impact. This risk could have been minimized if the user had conducted a "roll off" fit test. Instructions for how to perform this test were not printed on the warning label that remained on the helmet at the time the motorcyclist purchased it. The court found that the manufacturer was liable to the motorcyclist based on the law of product liability.

Business Lesson

If you manufacture safety products, be especially vigilant in the design and content of warning labels, because it is foreseeable that products can be passed on to people who do not have other warning materials (such as user guides). Affix warning labels directly on your merchandise. Ensure that your labels exhaustively describe known risks and how to avoid them.

Certain products, such as poisons, chainsaws, and children's swimming pools, are inherently dangerous. Manufacturers of these products have a duty to warn users of the dangers and to provide clear directions about using the products safely. For this reason, warnings are now commonplace on a variety of household items. Once a manufacturer is aware that a product can cause harm, it has two choices: eliminate the potential for harm or clearly warn the user.

Minimizing Your Risk

Reduce Lawsuits Based on Defective Products

- Conduct regular and thorough quality inspections of your product at all stages of the manufacturing process.

- Document all inspections.

- Recall any products you discover to be defective if they have already reached distribution channels.

- Contact purchasers of defective products if possible.

- Carry insurance to cover any potential liability.

Occupiers' Liability

If someone is injured on your business premises, you may be required to compensate him for his injuries as a result of the tort of **occupiers' liability**. The most common example of this tort is the "slip and fall" in which a customer suffers an injury after slipping on a wet floor or icy steps.

Occupiers' liability applies to all "occupiers" of property, whether or not the occupier is an owner or tenant. An **occupier** has control of the property and is therefore responsible for keeping it safe. Occupiers owe a duty of care to anyone who enters the property that they are occupying. An occupier's standard of care—that is, how much and what type of care an occupier needs to take to protect visitors—depends to some degree on the nature of the visit.

Visitors are divided into three main groups:

1. *Invitees.* Invitees are people who come onto the property for business purposes, such as customers and suppliers.
2. *Licensees.* Licensees are people who come onto the property with permission, but not for a business purpose, such as social visitors.
3. *Trespassers.* Trespassers are people who are not invited onto the property and may in fact be on the property for an illegal purpose.

The common-law standard of care for each group of visitors differs. Traditionally, invitees were entitled to the highest standard of care—that is, to be protected from unusual dangers that the occupier knew about or should have known about; for example, unexpected obstacles such as a mop and bucket in the aisle of a darkened movie theatre. The rationale behind the high standard of care was that an occupier stands to gain economically from having invitees come onto the property.

The standard of care applicable to licensees was slightly lower than the standard that was applicable to invitees. Licensees were entitled to protection against known hazards, such as a missing balcony guardrail. The lower standard was justified on the basis that an occupier does not stand to benefit economically from the presence of licensees.

Minimizing Your Risk

Maintain the Safety of Your Business Premises

- Shovel snow and remove ice from walkways.
- Clean up spills immediately.
- Comply with building code requirements about handrails and guardrails.
- Conduct scheduled and regular inspections of your property.
- Remove and repair hazards immediately.
- Document the safety measures you take.
- Post warning notices to alert people to any special risks, such as wet floors.
- Obtain adequate insurance to cover your risks.

Trespassers were entitled to the lowest standard of care. Although trespassers are unwanted visitors, an occupier nevertheless owes them a duty of care. The standard was that they must be treated humanely, and the occupier must not wilfully disregard their safety. For example, an occupier of a commercial property who was undertaking construction could not leave a serious hazard—for example, a gaping hole in the ground—that was not cordoned off and that was accessible to a trespassing passerby.

The *Occupiers' Liability Act* has superseded the common-law standards of care for occupiers in Ontario. Under this Act, occupiers must take reasonable care to see that people (and their property, such as cars) are reasonably safe when entering business premises. This statutory standard of care is roughly similar to the standard that formerly applied only to invitees and expands its scope to include licensees as well. The Act limits an occupier's liability in the case of criminals and trespassers to dangers deliberately created to cause harm (such as a trap) or dangers created with reckless disregard (such as a gaping hole not cordoned off).

Professional Negligence

Professionals—such as lawyers, accountants, financial advisers, stockbrokers, engineers, and computer programmers—are required to meet the standard of a reasonable professional when providing their services. **Professional negligence** occurs when professionals fail to meet this standard and their shoddy service or advice harms a client.

professional negligence
tort based on a professional's failure to provide services that meet that profession's standards

Professional organizations often set standards of education, competence, and ethical conduct for their members. The law expects a person who holds herself out as a professional to have the training and qualifications that are standard in that profession and to follow approved practices when providing services.

The standard is that of a reasonable—not perfect—professional, because highly trained professionals are as human as everybody else. For example, if an architect makes an error in designing your office building and her error is one that a reasonable architect might have made, your negligence action against her will not succeed. She has not breached the standard of care of a reasonable architect. Only if her error falls outside the scope of reasonable professional competence will she be liable for professional negligence.

In some cases, the delivery of professional services gives rise to a special duty, called a **fiduciary duty**, owed by the professional to the client. A fiduciary duty is an enhanced duty of care that flows from a relationship of special trust. A lawyer who holds assets in trust for a beneficiary, for example, owes a fiduciary duty to his client. He, and all other professionals who owe a fiduciary duty to clients, must demonstrate a high standard of good faith and loyalty, as well as the competency required by his profession.

> ## Minimizing Your Risk
> ### Take Professional Care
> - If your business employs professionals, know what standards they must meet.
> - Ensure your professional employees are in good standing with their regulatory associations.
> - Keep abreast of any changes in professional standards.
> - Monitor the work of professionals through peer reviews.
> - Carry sufficient insurance to cover potential liability.

fiduciary duty
enhanced duty of care that flows from a relationship of special trust, such as a relationship between a doctor and a patient

STRICT LIABILITY TORTS AND THE RULE IN RYLANDS v. FLETCHER

While the concept of strict liability is much more commonly associated, these days, with criminal and quasi-criminal statute law, there was a historical line of tort law that incorporated the concept.

Strict liability is liability that a court imposes on defendants without the need for proof that the defendants intended to cause harm or that they were negligent. In a negligence case, the plaintiff must prove that the defendant failed to act reasonably, and that this resulted in harm to the plaintiff.

In the tort context, courts in England recognized liability for harm in the absence of intent or negligence in certain narrowly defined circumstances. Two of

Minimizing Your Risk

Exercise Due Diligence

➤ If you keep or use a potentially dangerous thing on your property, such as large quantities of water, chemicals, wild animals, or spark-generating machinery, keep or use it safely.

➤ Obey all safety guidelines, obey environmental laws, and work quickly to contain spills and attend to accidents.

➤ Because strict liability arises without negligence on your part, you may be liable even when you do everything right. Carry adequate insurance.

these circumstances were the possession of dangerous animals and blasting. In one case, the owner of a savage dog was held liable for injuries to bite victims even though he himself played no role in setting the dog loose. (In Ontario today, liability for the actions of one's dog is governed by statute.)

In other strict liability cases, contractors conducting blasting operations were held liable for blast damage on neighbouring lands even though there was no evidence that they conducted the blasting negligently.

The branch of strict liability that has found the surest foothold in modern tort law was defined in 1868 in the case of *Rylands v. Fletcher*. In that case, the defendant owned a reservoir. The reservoir burst, and water escaped through a channel of which the reservoir owner was unaware, damaging neighbouring property. The court found that the defendant was liable based on strict liability—that is, without actually being negligent.

The "rule in *Rylands v. Fletcher*" now provides that a person who has a dangerous thing on his land is liable for any damage to neighbouring lands caused by the escape of that thing, even in the absence of negligence. As you can imagine, many applications of this rule are now a part of environmental statute law, especially the discharge of contaminants into the air and water.

Intentional Torts

Unlike torts that impose strict liability or that require proof of negligent actions or omissions, intentional torts are actions by individuals or businesses that intentionally cause harm to others. Like all torts, they require proof of causation and quantifiable harm. The intentional torts that business people should be particularly aware of are described in the sections that follow.

INTENTIONAL TORTS INVOLVING VERBAL OR PHYSICAL AGGRESSION

Of course, violence and defamation are not common in a business setting. When intentional torts occur in the commercial world, they are often the result of employees losing control of their tempers or they may occur because of the nature of the business itself. Some businesses—for example, those that repossess assets that have been pledged as security—lead to stress, and conflict can arise with clients or service providers. Where dealings require sensitivity, business people should carefully screen and train their employees.

Intentional torts involving aggressive and defamatory conduct occur both within and outside the business arena. After examining them in the sections that follow, we will also explore two intentional torts that relate only to the commercial world: passing off and interference with economic relations.

Assault and Battery

The torts of assault and battery can occur in business settings. For example, a security guard may be excessively violent when detaining a suspected shoplifter or a bouncer may be overly rough in expelling patrons from a bar. Employees may also be violent toward each other, and the business that employs them may be held responsible for the resulting injuries.

While an assault is generally understood in the criminal law to be a physical attack, an **assault** in tort law is a *threat* of imminent physical harm. Assault (without contact) is unlikely to form the basis of a lawsuit because it is difficult for plaintiffs to prove that they have suffered a quantifiable harm. **Battery**, which is often claimed in conjunction with assault (as in "assault and battery"), is any intentionally harmful or socially offensive direct physical contact. When the tort of battery forms the basis of a lawsuit, it generally involves violent or sexual contact.

False Imprisonment

Retail businesses have the right to temporarily infringe on the freedom of anyone caught in the act of shoplifting. However, these detentions must be founded on reasonable grounds. If an employee or security guard detains a suspect—by means of a threat or physical restraint—without reasonable evidence that the suspect was shoplifting, a business could be sued for false imprisonment as a result of the principle of vicarious liability.

False imprisonment occurs when one person unlawfully restricts the freedom of another. The "imprisoner" need not place the victim in jail. Any unreasonable restriction on liberty is technically a tort, though it may be difficult to prove quantifiable harm from temporary detentions.

Minimizing Your Risk
Prohibit Violence and Train Employees
- Train employees to treat each other, customers, and clients with respect.
- Implement a zero-tolerance policy on workplace violence and harassment.
- If the potential for conflict is high, provide employees with advanced training in how to handle angry clients and contact appropriate authorities.
- Carry sufficient insurance to compensate victims adequately.

assault
tort in which the defendant threatens the plaintiff with physical harm

battery
tort in which the defendant engages in unwanted physical contact with the plaintiff

false imprisonment
tort in which the defendant unlawfully restricts the freedom of the plaintiff

Minimizing Your Risk
Treat Shoplifters Humanely
- Teach retail employees to use minimal force in detaining suspected shoplifters.
- Never conduct arbitrary fishing expeditions into the bags or coats of customers.
- Do not approach a customer unless you have actually observed a theft or the customer is clearly hiding something.
- Treat detainees with courtesy, and call the police immediately to minimize detention time.
- If someone objects to a physical search, do not touch him; wait for the police to arrive.
- Carry general liability insurance.

Defamation

Business people must be careful when commenting about their competitors. Negative statements about other companies, their management, or their products can result in a lawsuit.

defamation
tort based on harm to a person's or business's reputation through false statements made by the defendant

Defamation is a tort that occurs when someone makes a statement about a person or business, to at least one other person, that results in a significant loss of respect or reputation in the eyes of a reasonable or right-thinking person in the community. For example, if your car rental business advertises that your competitor does not maintain its fleet to the same standards of safety that your business does, you may be making a defamatory statement. Negative advertising—that is, advertising that focuses on the negative aspects of the competition, rather than on the positive aspects of your own product—is especially open to accusations of defamation if it lowers a competitor's reputation.

Defamation in written form is sometimes referred to as libel, and defamation in verbal form is sometimes referred to as slander. Malicious false statements made with the intention of harming a product's reputation are sometimes referred to as injurious falsehood or slander of goods.

Defences to Defamation

When confronted with an allegation of defamation, a business person can raise two defences: truth and fair comment.

◊ Truth

If your car rental business advertised that your competitor fails to maintain its fleet to the same safety standards that your business does—and you can prove that your statement is true, for example, by reference to maintenance records and safety tests—you have a complete defence. No defamation lawsuit can succeed against you.

◊ Fair Comment

The defence of fair comment is designed to encourage the expression of opinions. It is based on the notion that people can and should make up their own minds about whether a statement is true. If your statement about your competitor is an honest criticism, based on a sincere impression, rather than on facts, you may be able to succeed with a defence of fair comment. Success generally depends on two things: whether there is at least some credible evidence to back up the truth of the statement, and whether the statement was made maliciously, with intent to harm.

Therefore, if you have informally observed the state of your competitor's fleet over a number of months and judged it to be substandard, you are in a better position to raise the defence of fair comment than if your advertisement was based on no evidence at all. If your comment was motivated, at least in part, by a genuine concern for public safety, you may raise the defence of fair comment. Unsubstantiated or purely malicious comments rarely constitute fair comment.

Web Link

To learn how businesses can protect themselves from vicarious liability for employees' defamatory remarks through email and other electronic forums, visit www.cyberlibel.com/liabilit.html.

Minimizing Your Risk
Avoid Potentially Defamatory Remarks

- Review all advertising and marketing material, especially if it identifies a competitor.

- Advertise the benefits of your own product; avoid criticizing the products of competitors.

- Have a lawyer review all negative advertising.

- Train employees in media relations before they speak on behalf of your business or refer to a competitor.

- Hire public relations staff if necessary.

INTENTIONAL BUSINESS TORTS

The two most common business torts that involve intentional actions are passing off and interference with economic relations. We discuss both of these torts below.

Passing Off

Using a product name that is similar to a known brand name constitutes the tort of **passing off**. This tort is based on a misrepresentation of a product or service. For example, a watch manufacturer that calls its watches "Rollex" can expect to be sued by Rolex, the well-known watchmaker. The similarity of names could confuse customers, who might think they are buying a quality brand when, in fact, they are buying a cheap knock-off. When the Rollex watch breaks, the reputation of Rolex is diminished in the mind of the confused customer.

This kind of dishonesty in business is also addressed in consumer protection legislation (in provisions dealing with false, misleading, or deceptive representations) and in intellectual property law (in provisions dealing with trademarks). We discuss these topics in chapter 5 and chapter 8 under the headings "False, Misleading, or Deceptive Representations" and "Trademark Law," respectively.

> ### Minimizing Your Risk
> **Name Your Products Responsibly**
> - Research the marketplace before naming your products or business.
> - Register your trademarks.
> - Monitor the marketplace for product or business names that might adversely affect your business.

passing off
tort based on one party's attempt to distribute its own knock-off product or service on the pretense that it is the product or service of another party

Interference with Economic Relations

The ways in which one business may interfere with the economic relations of another are limited only by the human imagination. Some methods of interference, such as defamation, are defined as particular torts. Other methods—such as stealing confidential information, poaching key employees, hacking into computers, and inducing breaches of contract—may not be so defined. If a form of intentional damage to the economic interests of a business is not defined as a particular tort, it may be encompassed by the tort of **interference with economic relations**.

A business person must demonstrate three elements to prove that he has been the victim of interference with economic relations:

1. *intention* on the part of the defendant to injure his business,
2. *interference by illegal means* with the business's mode of earning money, and
3. *quantifiable harm.*

Because the tort of interference with economic relations requires interference *by illegal means*, it involves breaking laws or committing other torts. This could expose the defendant business to other lawsuits or criminal charges. The bad press that flows from a high-profile interference lawsuit usually outweighs any perceived advantage gained through acting in an unethical manner. It can permanently injure the reputation of both a business and its management. These are all reasons why a business should avoid conduct that puts it at risk of being sued for interference with economic relations.

Unfair competition is another way in which businesses can interfere with each other. The *Competition Act*, a federal statute, now largely governs this very complex area of law.

interference with economic relations
tort based on intentional harm, through illegal acts, to a party's means of earning money

> ### Minimizing Your Risk
> **Maintain Zero Tolerance for Illegality in Your Business**
> - Enact business policies that prohibit illegal practices.
> - Train staff to obey the law and respect the rights of competitors.

CASE IN POINT The Mutinous Barista

Cappuccino Affair Ltd. v. Haraga, 2000 ABQB 750 (CanLII)

Facts

The owner of a coffee franchise system (the franchisor) hired a director of operations, who organized an association of the franchisees and encouraged them to repudiate their franchise agreements by refusing to pay royalties to the franchisor, selling unapproved food items, refusing to accept shipments of approved coffee cups, and installing and upholstering unapproved furniture.

The franchisor fired the director of operations, but continued to suffer losses when 11 of its 13 outlets continued to breach their contracts. The franchisor applied for an **injunction** to stop the director from attempting to interfere with its contractual relations with the outlets.

Result

Because this was an application for an injunction, and not a full trial, the court needed only to find that a serious issue was raised and there was a prospect of irreparable harm. The evidence that the director had intentionally interfered with the franchisor's business relations, and that the franchisor had suffered losses as a result was sufficient. The court granted the injunction.

Business Lesson

If someone is interfering with your business, act quickly: getting an injunction to stop losses immediately is often more effective than waiting to sue on the basis of harm already done.

injunction
order of a court requiring a party to discontinue an action or prohibiting a party from taking a proposed action

Intentional or Unintentional Torts

Many torts that involve business property can be committed intentionally or unintentionally. For example, a resort owner who is mistaken about the exact extent of her property's lake frontage might build a beachside bar and seating area that encroaches onto neighbouring land; in this case, the building and use of the area would constitute unintentional trespass. By contrast, if the same resort owner plays croquet on what she knows to be the neighbour's lawn, this is intentional trespass.

COMMON BUSINESS TORTS INVOLVING PROPERTY

Three torts that involve the use of property may be of particular interest to business people: trespass to land, nuisance, and invasion of privacy. We describe these torts in the following sections.

Trespass to Land

trespass to land
tort in which the defendant, without the permission of the plaintiff, comes onto land occupied by the plaintiff

Trespass to land occurs when a person comes onto land without the express or implied permission of the occupier. Express permission is uncommon in the commercial world; implied permission is much more typical, as in the case of a retail store that invites its customers to enter its premises as frequently as possible.

Trespass usually occurs when a person refuses to leave business premises upon being asked to do so. In Ontario, the *Trespass to Property Act* now governs the tort of trespass.

Most businesses have the right to exclude whomever they want from their property. However, there are exceptions. A retail business, or other business that depends on dealings with the public, cannot unreasonably exclude potential customers or clients.

A retail business that removes or excludes a potential customer without a valid reason could face charges under a provincial or federal human rights statute. The "look" of a person is not a valid reason for removing her, particularly if the reason is based on discriminatory criteria such as race, sex, or age. For example, an electronics outlet may not remove teenagers simply because they are teenagers. However, if some of the teenagers become belligerent, disturb other customers, or destroy product displays, for example, the store has the right to remove those particular teenagers.

In detaining or removing trespassers, business owners and employees should use the minimal level of force necessary in order to avoid tort suits or criminal charges based on assault and battery or false imprisonment (both discussed above).

Businesses, such as land developers, that are not open to the public and that wish to prevent trespassing on their property must post "no trespassing" signs as described in the *Trespass to Property Act*.

> ## Minimizing Your Risk
> ### Manage Access to Your Premises
> - Post "no trespassing" signs to minimize liability in negligence and to support your enforcement of the *Trespass to Property Act*.
> - Avoid exclusion of patrons on the basis of discriminatory criteria, and train employees to respect human rights.
> - Use minimal physical contact to remove trespassers or troublemakers. If patrons resist removal, call the police.

Nuisance

Occupiers, both owners and tenants, have the right to use and enjoy their property in the usual manner. **Nuisance** is the tort of interference with that right.

For example, assume that your candy shop has been located in a quiet neighbourhood for years. Your business has attracted customers because of its location, and you have enjoyed maintaining and enhancing your premises. Sadly, a factory that has been dormant for years starts up operations, spewing foul-smelling smoke into the air and discouraging candy customers from patronizing your shop. You may have a tort action in nuisance against the factory.

Nuisances come in many different forms: sounds, smells, spills, fumes, vibrations, and other types of pollution. Often two businesses are incompatible, such as a candy shop and a factory, or a bed and breakfast and a pig farm. Municipal zoning bylaws, building codes, and environmental laws have evolved in an attempt to manage the environmental impacts of different kinds of land use; however, they have not replaced the tort of nuisance. Accidents such as broken water pipes and sewage spills can still result in nuisance lawsuits.

nuisance
tort in which the defendant interferes with the use and enjoyment of the plaintiff's property

> ## Minimizing Your Risk
> ### Be Considerate of Your Neighbours
> - Comply with all land use laws that pertain to your business.
> - Investigate technologies to control emissions, such as chemicals and exhaust fumes.
> - Choose a site suitable for your business.
> - Maintain good relations in your community.
> - Carry sufficient insurance to cover cleanup costs in the event of accidents.

Invasion of Privacy

The law requires businesses to respect the privacy of employees, customers, and clients in circumstances where these people have a reasonable expectation of privacy and where privacy of personal information is specifically protected by statute.

The tort of invasion of privacy occurs where there is an expectation of privacy, that privacy is invaded, and harm results. Clearly, the level of privacy that an employee can expect in the workplace is lower than the level of privacy that he can expect in his own home. However, a business's ability to monitor an employee's telephone and computer use and its ability to rely on video surveillance are subject to legal scrutiny. We discuss these matters in chapter 7 under the heading "Employee Surveillance and Monitoring."

Businesses must also be aware of the rights of customers and clients to guard their personal information, such as names, addresses, and consumer purchase history. Business owners who collect personal information must ensure that their operation complies with the *Personal Information Protection and Electronic Documents Act*. We discuss this legislation in chapter 5 under the heading "Consumer Privacy."

Minimizing Your Risk

Respect the Privacy of Employees and Customers

- Allow employees as much privacy as possible, being mindful of the need for business security and productivity.

- Keep up to date with changes in privacy law.

- Designate a person to deal with privacy issues.

Defending Against Tort Actions

If you or your business is confronted with a tort claim, it is usually sensible to attempt to limit your liability by defending against the lawsuit. There are three common defences to tort actions: failure to prove the tort, contributory negligence, and voluntary assumption of risk. We discuss each of these in the following sections. We also comment briefly on statutory defences, which are alternatives to defences in tort.

FAILURE TO PROVE THE TORT

burden of proof
requirement that a certain party prove a particular fact at trial

standard of proof
degree to which a party must convince a judge or jury that the allegations are true

balance of probabilities
standard of proof in civil (as opposed to criminal) law indicating that one version of events is more probable than another

As the victim of an alleged wrong, a plaintiff bears the **burden of proof**. This means that the plaintiff must present evidence showing that a particular tort occurred, that the defendant was responsible for its occurrence, and that the tort resulted in quantifiable harm to the plaintiff. Unlike in a criminal case, where the **standard of proof** is very high and the prosecutor must prove the guilt of a defendant "beyond a reasonable doubt," in a civil case a plaintiff need only prove her case on a **balance of probabilities**. This means that the plaintiff must prove that her version of events is *more likely* to be true than the version presented by the defendant.

It is the defendant's job to refute (respond to and argue against) the plaintiff's evidence in an effort to prevent the plaintiff from establishing her case. If a defendant successfully demonstrates that the plaintiff failed to show that her version of events is more likely to have occurred than his, the defendant will successfully defend his case.

For example, when refuting a negligence claim, the defendant may argue that the plaintiff has failed to prove one of the four elements of negligence. He may, for example, persuade the judge that the plaintiff has failed to prove, on a balance of probabilities, that he owes the plaintiff a duty of care. If the judge is persuaded by the defendant's arguments, the defendant wins the case. He is not required to present any evidence of his own, and he is not required to compensate the plaintiff for her losses.

Minimizing Your Risk

Challenge the Plaintiff's Case

- Consult a lawyer.
- Research the case and the nature of the plaintiff's alleged damages.
- Present credible evidence—to the court or to your lawyer—about alternative causes for the plaintiff's harm, including people other than yourself who have contributed to it.
- In appropriate cases, raise, before the court, the possibility that the plaintiff has not met the burden of proof.

CONTRIBUTORY NEGLIGENCE

Contributory negligence is a defence to all torts that involve negligence. By raising the defence of contributory negligence, the defendant claims that the plaintiff contributed to, or was partially responsible for, her own injuries. Consider, for example, a product liability case in which a plaintiff sues a lawnmower manufacturer after suffering an injury while mowing the lawn. The plaintiff claims that the lawnmower was defective and establishes the four elements of negligence on a balance of probabilities.

contributory negligence role that a plaintiff may play in negligently contributing to the cause of, or aggravation of, her own injury

The defendant manufacturer now has an opportunity to present his defence. To establish the defence of contributory negligence, he may claim, for example, that the plaintiff was partially responsible for the injuries she suffered because she tampered with the lawnmower by removing a safety guard. Like the plaintiff, the defendant must establish his defence on a balance of probabilities. If the judge finds that it is more likely than not that the plaintiff was partially responsible for the harm she suffered, the defence of contributory negligence succeeds.

When a defence of contributory negligence succeeds, a judge apportions—or distributes—liability between the plaintiff and the defendant. The judge may, for example, find that the plaintiff was 25 percent responsible for the accident by tampering with the guard, and the defendant was 75 percent responsible for the accident by selling a defective lawnmower. In deciding how the plaintiff can be fairly compensated for her injuries, the judge will apportion the plaintiff's monetary damages accordingly. If the damages she suffered can be quantified at $1,000, the defendant will be required to pay $750 and the plaintiff will be required to absorb the $250 herself (see figure 3.3). We discuss the subject of damages later in this chapter under the heading "Damages."

Minimizing Your Risk

Try to Establish Contributory Negligence

- Consider and raise the possibility that the plaintiff may have contributed to his own injuries or losses.
- Investigate the issue. Request that the plaintiff disclose all available medical or repair records to determine whether the plaintiff responded to the incident in an appropriate way.
- If you suspect contributory negligence, locate and call witnesses who can support your case.

Figure 3.3   Contributory Negligence

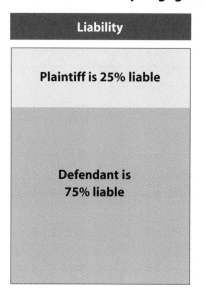
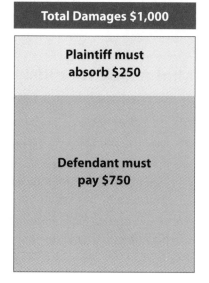

voluntary assumption of risk
defence based on proof that a plaintiff knowingly entered into a risky situation and thereby assumed responsibility for any injuries

waiver of liability
acknowledgement of risks in an activity and an agreement to assume them

VOLUNTARY ASSUMPTION OF RISK

The defence of **voluntary assumption of risk** is available to defendants who can prove, on a balance of probabilities, that a plaintiff voluntarily and knowingly put himself in a risky situation and thereby assumed responsibility for his own fate, including any injuries he suffered.

For example, a whitewater rafting company might argue voluntary assumption of risk if a customer is injured while on a rafting trip. The company might demonstrate that the plaintiff assumed the risk of injury by providing the court with a **waiver of liability**—a document signed by the customer before the rafting trip, stating that the customer was aware of the risks and had agreed to assume them.

Unlike the defence of contributory negligence, the defence of voluntary assumption of risk is a complete defence. This means that a court will not apportion the responsibility for assumption of risk between the parties. If a court determines, on a balance of probabilities, that the injured party voluntarily assumed the risk of injury, the injured party will receive no compensation. In the whitewater rafting case, the customer must bear the cost of his losses alone.

The defence of voluntary assumption of risk frequently arises in occupiers' liability cases. Consider, for example, a case in which a banker sues a construction company after suffering injury on a construction site. Although the site manager warns the banker that the premises are unsafe for untrained personnel, the banker insists on walking in a cordoned-off area and refuses to wear a hard hat. In a case such as this, a court may determine that the banker voluntarily assumed the risk of injury and is therefore responsible for her own injuries.

Minimizing Your Risk

Inform Your Customers About Risks

- If you run a business or operate a facility that poses a risk to customers, be thorough and detailed in your explanations of the risks associated with participation.

- Use signage and handouts to communicate all foreseeable risks.

- Require customers to read and sign liability waivers that have been prepared by your lawyer.

- Carry adequate insurance in case your waivers fail to hold up in court.

CASE IN POINT Not So Much Fun at the Water Park

Hutchison v. Daredevil Park Inc., 2003 CanLII 25623 (ONSC)

Facts

A customer at a water park broke his ankle while using a waterslide. The top part of the slide contained a slip-resistant tub that was designed for users to sit in before launching themselves into the steep and slippery chute. Water jets obscured the users' view of the bottom of the launching tub and the chute. An attendant at the top of the slide, who was also responsible for several other slides, did not instruct the customer on the proper use of the slide, other than to indicate when it was safe for the customer to launch himself. The customer failed to sit down in the tub before entering the chute. Although he had never used such a slide before that day, he did complete several successful runs before breaking his ankle.

There was no sign close to the entry tub directing the user to sit down in the tub. There was no luminescent line at the point of transition to the slippery surface with a warning to sit behind the line. In the 12 years of the park's operation, no one had ever suffered the same sort of accident as the customer.

Result

The court found that, while the customer voluntarily assumed some risk in using the slide, not all of the inherent risks of its use were communicated to him, and he was not fully instructed in how to use it safely. As a result, the customer was found 20 percent contributorily negligent, and the water park was liable for 80 percent of his injuries.

Business Lesson

Explain all foreseeable risks of injury to your customers, and carry adequate insurance.

STATUTORY DEFENCES

In some cases, legislative schemes, such as workplace safety insurance, compensate plaintiffs for the injuries they suffer as a result of the torts of others. Compensation offered under these programs is typically paid as an alternative to lawsuits. This means that a person who accepts statutory compensation for an injury cannot also sue a defendant in tort for the same injury. We discuss some of these compensatory legislative schemes in chapter 7 under the heading "Workplace Safety and Insurance Act, 1997."

Remedies for Torts

Once a plaintiff has proven that a defendant has committed a tort—and once the defendant has failed to raise a credible defence—the goal of the law is to provide compensation for the plaintiff. By fashioning a remedy, a court seeks, as far as practicable, to put the plaintiff back into the position in which he was before the defendant committed the tort.

Remedies take a variety of forms. We discuss some of the less common ones in chapter 4 under the headings "Specific Performance" and "Injunctions." By far, the most common tort remedy is damages, which we discuss in the following sections.

DAMAGES

damages
losses suffered as a result of the commission of a tort or the breach of a contract, or compensation awarded for these losses

Damages is the legal term for the financial compensation that a court orders a defendant to pay to a plaintiff. Damages include compensation for both pecuniary losses—that is, losses that are easily expressed in terms of money, such as medical bills—and non-pecuniary losses—that is, losses that are not easily expressed in terms of money, such as the suffering that arises as a result of the loss of a limb.

Pecuniary Damages

If a shopper breaks his leg after falling on the icy premises of a retail business, the plaintiff's **pecuniary damages** (or losses) may include the following:

pecuniary damages
damages that can be readily quantified in financial terms

- medical expenses not covered by a health insurance plan,
- wages lost from work missed while recovering,
- the cost of a babysitter for the plaintiff's children whom he cannot care for while recovering, and
- the cost of taxi trips for running errands that the plaintiff would normally run on foot.

A pecuniary damages award will require the defendant to pay for these and other pecuniary losses that the plaintiff suffered.

If a plaintiff suffers permanent or long-term injuries, a court must quantify the amount of compensation that the plaintiff will need in the future. These damages can include future wage loss and future medical expenses. They are less easily measured than losses that have already occurred. However, experts, such as actuaries, use statistics to assess the likelihood of future events and can usually assign an estimated dollar figure for future loss. Damages for future losses are pecuniary damages because they are based on the future loss of money.

Non-Pecuniary Damages

non-pecuniary damages
damages that cannot be readily quantified in financial terms

Non-pecuniary damages attempt to address losses not based on money. They are more difficult to quantify than pecuniary damages. For example, how should a court award compensation for the loss of a limb, damage to a reputation, or debilitating pain that lingers on and on? Since it is impossible to return a severed limb or erase pain and suffering, a court must determine a fair dollar figure to award instead.

Awards for non-pecuniary losses are, of necessity, somewhat arbitrary. To promote consistency in the administration of justice, courts refer to the awards that other courts have made in other cases involving similar suffering. In general, awards for non-pecuniary damages tend to be much higher in the United States than in Canada, although awards in Canada have increased significantly in the last quarter century or so.

aggravated damages
a subcategory of non-pecuniary damages awarded for intangible harm, such as harm to reputation or humiliation

Aggravated damages are a subcategory of non-pecuniary damages. They are used in cases that involve intangible harm, such as damage to reputation or humiliation.

If, for example, a competitor defames your business in a particularly high-handed way, you may claim aggravated damages.

Another subcategory of non-pecuniary damages is **punitive damages**. Courts award punitive damages when a person or a business intentionally causes harm in a vindictive and malicious way. The purpose of punitive damages is to punish the wrongdoer and discourage similar behaviour in the future. Because compensation, rather than punishment, is the primary purpose of tort law, a court will not order the payment of punitive damages unless the defendant's conduct is outrageous.

A strip search of a suspected shoplifter by an employee of a retail business would probably justify an award of punitive damages. The case of *Whiten v. Pilot Insurance Co.* provides another example of conduct sufficiently outrageous to attract punitive damages.

punitive damages
sum generally added to a damage award that is intended to compensate the plaintiff for a defendant's outrageous conduct

MITIGATION OF DAMAGES

Plaintiffs are expected to mitigate—or minimize—their damages. For example, a customer who suffers a serious cut while trying out equipment in a sporting goods store is expected to seek appropriate medical treatment to avoid infection and complications. Where a plaintiff fails to make reasonable efforts to minimize his losses, and the result is a more serious loss, such as amputation of a finger, his compensation may be limited. We discuss the topic of mitigation more fully in chapter 4 under the heading "Duty To Mitigate Damages."

CASE IN POINT Punitive Damages: A Million-Dollar Message

Whiten v. Pilot Insurance Co., [2002] 1 SCR 595; 2002 SCC 18

Facts

On a freezing night in January, the plaintiff discovered a fire in the addition attached to her house. The family fled, in pajamas, into the night. The father suffered frostbite serious enough to place him in hospital. The house burned to the ground, and the family lost three cats, some valuable antiques, and many items of sentimental value.

The family, which was suffering serious financial difficulties at the time, moved into a winterized cottage and received an initial $5,000 living expenses payment from the defendant insurance company. After a few months, the insurer stopped paying the rent on the cottage and began an aggressive campaign to challenge the family's insurance claim.

It forced the family to trial in an effort to deny the claim. The insurer alleged arson, despite the fact that none of the many investigators who examined the fire scene found any evidence that the fire was deliberately set. The family had to pay $320,000 in legal fees to recover the $345,000 in insurance money that was owed to them. By the time the case reached the Court of Appeal, the insurer had conceded that there was no basis for its arson allegations.

Result

At trial, the jury found that the insurer was required to pay the insurance claim. It also made a $1 million punitive damages award against the insurer.

The Supreme Court of Canada affirmed the jury's award of $1 million in punitive damages. The court stated that punitive damages are "imposed only if there has been high-handed, malicious, arbitrary or highly reprehensible misconduct that departs to a marked degree from ordinary standards of decent behaviour."

Business Lesson

Ensure that your conduct always meets or exceeds the ordinary standards of decent behaviour.

Chapter Summary

In this chapter, we have explored tort law and the concept of compensation that underlies it. We have focused your attention on individual torts, both intentional and unintentional, that are of interest to business people. In each instance, we have pointed out ways in which you can minimize your business risks by limiting your exposure to liability.

We have devoted particular attention to the concept of vicarious liability because it is essential that business people understand the legal responsibilities that they assume for the actions of their employees. Another area of special concern is the field of negligence law. We have therefore discussed the elements of negligence in detail, as well as the three negligence torts most commonly encountered in the business world: product liability, occupiers' liability, and professional negligence.

In addition, we have briefly explored three common defences to tort actions: failure to prove the tort, contributory negligence, and voluntary assumption of risk. This chapter concludes with a discussion of damages, the most popular form of compensation available to plaintiffs who have suffered harm as a result of the injurious actions of others.

KEY TERMS

aggravated damages
assault
balance of probabilities
battery
burden of proof
contributory negligence
damages
defamation
defendant
duty of care
false imprisonment
fiduciary duty
foreseeability
injunction

intentional tort
interference with economic
 relations
negligence
non-pecuniary damages
nuisance
occupier
occupiers' liability
omission
passing off
pecuniary damages
plaintiff
product liability
professional negligence

punitive damages
reasonable person
standard of care
standard of proof
strict liability tort
tort
tort action
trespass to land
unintentional tort
vicarious liability
voluntary assumption of risk
waiver of liability

REFERENCES

Cappuccino Affair Ltd. v. Haraga, 2000 ABQB 750 (CanLII).

Competition Act, RSC 1985, c. C-34.

Crocker v. Sundance Northwest Resorts Ltd., [1988] 1 SCR 1186.

Hutchinson v. Daredevil Park Inc., 2003 CanLII 25623 (ONSC).

Jordan House Hotel Ltd. v. Menow and Honsberger, [1974] SCR 239.

Occupiers' Liability Act, RSO 1990, c. O.2.

Personal Information Protection and Electronic Documents Act, SC 2000, c. 5.

Pesticides Act, RSO 1990, c. C.11.

Rylands v. Fletcher (1868), LR 3 HL 330.

Teskey v. Toronto Transit Commission, 2003 CanLII 11726 (ONCA).

Thomas v. Bell Helmets Inc., 1999 CanLII 9312 (ONCA).

Trespass to Property Act, RSO 1990, c. T.21.

Whiten v. Pilot Insurance Co., [2002] 1 SCR 595; 2002 SCC 18.

REVIEW AND DISCUSSION

True or False?

T **1.** The standard of proof for tort actions is on a balance of probabilities.

T **2.** Many actions that were originally torts have become offences under provincial statutes.

F **3.** To prove that a defendant has committed a tort, a plaintiff must establish that the defendant's actions were the sole cause of the harm.

T **4.** A fiduciary duty is an enhanced duty of care that flows from a relationship of special trust.

F **5.** The burden of proving a tort defence, such as voluntary assumption of risk, is on the plaintiff.

T **6.** The law assesses professional negligence according to the "reasonable professional" standard.

F **7.** An unlimited right to privacy is constitutionally recognized in Canada.

F **8.** Defamation in writing is called slander.

F **9.** The tort of assault involves violent touching.

Multiple Choice

1. Contributory negligence
   a. means that the plaintiff was partially at fault for the harm he suffered
   b. must be proven by the defendant
   c. can, if proven, limit the defendant's liability in tort
   d. all of the above

2. Remedies available for torts include
   a. prison sentences and damages
   b. specific performance and injunctions
   c. damages and injunctions
   d. restraining orders and restitution

3. Pecuniary losses recoverable in a tort action can include
   a. medical expenses
   b. the cost of lost work time
   c. the loss of future earnings because of a disabling injury
   d. all of the above

4. Negligence is established only when the plaintiff proves that the defendant could foresee
   a. that the plaintiff would purchase the defendant's goods
   b. that the plaintiff or someone like her might be harmed or incur loss as a result of the defendant's actions
   c. that the plaintiff or someone like her might be harmed or incur loss as a result of the defendant's actions, and that the full extent of the harm actually suffered by the plaintiff was also reasonably foreseeable
   d. all of the above

5. A business can attempt to limit its liability in tort by
   a. conducting safety tests on products and services and documenting test results
   b. maintaining retail and other premises in good repair and conducting regular safety patrols
   c. printing warnings on products advising of potential dangers
   d. all of the above

6. To prove defamation, a plaintiff must establish that the impugned statements
   a. are not true
   b. are not fair comment
   c. caused quantifiable harm
   d. all of the above

7. To avoid lawsuits based on the law of nuisance, business owners should
   a. buy liability insurance
   b. conduct market research before designing new products
   c. comply with all land use laws, such as zoning bylaws, building codes, and environmental laws
   d. none of the above

8. To establish that the defendant committed the tort of interference with economic relations, the plaintiff must prove that
   a. the defendant's business is a direct competitor of her own and that the defendant has gained an economic advantage over the plaintiff by illegal means
   b. the defendant intended to harm the plaintiff's business, that the defendant committed an illegal act to do so, and that the plaintiff suffered actual harm as a result
   c. the defendant intended to harm the plaintiff's business and that the harm was done with knowledge on the part of principals of the defendant's corporation
   d. the defendant committed an illegal act with the intent to harm the plaintiff's business, whether or not actual harm occurred

Short Answer

1. List five business practices that can help reduce losses from product liability lawsuits.

2. What is the difference between negligence and strict liability?

3. Why might a party decide to commence a tort action that is based on events that have also formed the basis of a criminal prosecution?

4. What kinds of factors might prompt a judge or jury to add an award of punitive damages to the regular pecuniary damage award? List at least six factors that you think might be relevant.

5. If a defendant is attempting to argue voluntary assumption of risk as a defence to a tort action, what must the defendant prove?

6. Describe an appropriate policy for a business with respect to the handling of trespassers.

7. How can a business protect itself from competitors seeking to pass off their merchandise as that of the business?

Discussion and Debate

Eco Motors Inc. is a car manufacturer that is in the final stages of production of its new fuel-efficient model, the Blast. It has just discovered that if the Blast is rear-ended at a particular angle and at a particular speed, the car will explode. Eco's accountants have calculated that the cost of changing the Blast's design outweighs the costs of the damages it will have to pay to dead and injured consumers. Eco's president raises a question: should consumers have the right to bear the risk of injury in return for a cheap car? What do you reply?

Contract Law

What Is a Contract?

A **contract** is an agreement between two or more parties that is enforceable by law. Contracts are extremely common in daily life. You may be surprised to learn that you, as a consumer, are a party to a contract every time you buy a cup of coffee, shop for groceries, rent a DVD, ride a bus, use a laundromat, or purchase any other goods or services from a commercial enterprise.

Contracts occur with equal frequency in the business world. In fact, mutually beneficial contractual transactions are the sustaining force behind most businesses. They also sustain the economy as a whole. Business contracts regulate most commercial transactions, including leasing retail or office space, purchasing or supplying inventory, storing or transporting goods, providing or receiving computer services, and insuring against losses or damages.

A contract always involves an agreement; however, not every agreement is a contract. If, for example, your aunt agrees to buy you a controlling interest in the company of your choice, you and your aunt do not have a contract. That is, if your

contract
an agreement between two or more parties that is enforceable by law

aunt subsequently decides against buying you a business interest, you have no recourse against her in law.

For an agreement to constitute a contract, it must contain four elements:

1. *An intention to create a legal relationship.* The parties to a contract must intend to enter into a relationship with one another that binds them in law. Thus, if your aunt makes a promise that is motivated, for example, by a desire to command your loyalty or annoy another family member—and she has no intention of being legally bound by it—there is no contract. For a contract to exist between you and your aunt, you both must intend to be legally bound by any promises you make to each other.

2. *Offer and acceptance.* A contract requires that one party offer to do something and that the other party accept this offer. Had Aunt Sal, through her lawyers, offered to buy you shares in a company, any hesitance on your part in accepting this offer could be evidence that no contract exists between you and Aunt Sal.

3. *Consideration.* **Consideration** is a legal concept that means each party to a contract must provide something of value to the other. Since you have promised nothing of value to Aunt Sal, her promise to buy you a corporate interest lacks consideration and therefore does not constitute a contract.

4. *Legality.* A contract must conform to the law of the land and must not violate public policy. Had Aunt Sal promised to buy you shares in exchange for your refusal to testify against her at her upcoming murder trial, your agreement would not be enforceable as a contract because it would violate public policy by interfering with the administration of justice; it would also be illegal under Canada's criminal law.

consideration
something of value
given up by each party
to a contract

We discuss these four essential elements of a contract in greater detail later in this chapter under the heading "Formation of a Contract."

In practical terms, a contract's enforceability is perhaps its principal feature. Parties are expected to live up to the obligations that they assume under the contracts that they enter into. In other words, if you enter into a business transaction—say, an agreement to purchase inventory—you are expected by the other contracting party, the courts, the business community, and society at large to honour your commitment. Failure on your part to fulfill your contractual obligations is known as a **breach of contract**, and such a breach can result in serious legal and economic consequences for you. We explore the implications of contractual breach later in this chapter under the heading "Consequences of a Breach of Contract."

breach of contract
failure to fulfill contractual
obligations

Contracts in the Business Context

There are many different types of business contracts, some of which are listed below:

- *employment contracts*—for example, contracts under which businesses engage the services of staff, on a full- or part-time basis;
- *service contracts*—for example, contracts under which businesses provide or receive services such as financial advice, research, marketing analysis, storage, transportation, cleaning, maintenance, and computer or Internet services;

- *leasing contracts*—for example, contracts under which businesses rent office space or equipment;
- *contracts for the purchase and sale of goods*—for example, contracts under which businesses purchase inventory or supplies; and
- *insurance contracts*—for example, contracts under which businesses insure themselves against loss or damage to business premises.

Much of the law that applies to contracts is common law, which has evolved over time in the courts, as we discussed in chapter 1. Sometimes, however, provincial statutes govern particular situations, such as contracts involving consumers and contracts involving the sale of goods, both of which we discuss in chapter 5. Provincial legislation also governs personal property security contracts, which we discuss in chapter 9. Contracts governing the employment of staff are subject to federal and provincial human rights legislation, which we discuss in chapter 7.

This chapter focuses on contract law as it applies to everyday business-to-business transactions. Why, in this context, is it important for businesses to live up to their contractual obligations? One reason is that a single business contract is capable of having far-reaching consequences for many enterprises over long periods of time. A successful business operator must always be looking ahead and planning for the future. If, as a general rule, businesses can depend on each other to fulfill their contractual obligations, they can run their current operations efficiently and plan for the future confidently. If, on the other hand, they are constantly gambling on whether their fellow businesses will fulfill their contractual obligations, planning becomes impossible, and economic chaos becomes likely.

Consider, for example, a retailer that enters into an agreement in June to purchase a large shipment of toys from a manufacturer for delivery in October. The retailer is planning a major toy sale during the holiday season in December. Anticipating that the manufacturer will meet its obligations to deliver the toys on time, in early September the retailer enters into a contract with a supplier of shelving. The supplier agrees to install the shelving in time to display the toys when they arrive in October. Although another supplier offers to sell children's books to the retailer at a good price, the retailer rejects the offer because he will not have room to display both the books and the toys over the holiday season. The retailer also signs a contract for a full-page advertisement in a local newspaper regarding the sale. The newspaper insists on payment in advance, so the retailer pays it when the contract is signed in mid-September. The advertisement is scheduled to appear in a mid-November edition of the newspaper. Would the retailer be wise to install shelving, pay for an advertisement, and turn down another business opportunity if he had little faith that the manufacturer would deliver the toys on time?

This type of interdependence among businesses is standard throughout most industries. The good news is that generally businesses *can* depend on one another to meet their contractual obligations, because businesses know (or should know) that if they fail to meet their contractual obligations,

- they may be sued for breach of contract, which can be very expensive, time-consuming, and stressful; and
- they may quickly obtain a bad reputation in the business community, resulting in the loss of future business opportunities.

Businesses that breach their contracts are extremely likely to lose their cases, should the breach come to the attention of a court. Because of the importance of the integrity of business transactions to the business community and the economy as a whole, courts generally rule against parties who are found to be in breach of their contractual obligations.

The Importance of Contract Law for Business People

Although most business people understand the importance of keeping their contractual promises—and do so—it is nevertheless important for all business people to know about contract law. Why?

- *Contracts can clarify your business dealings.* A contract, if carefully drafted and properly understood, can smooth business dealings by informing both you and the other party of your rights and obligations. Elimination of confusion will benefit both of you by facilitating the efficient performance of your contract.
- *Contracts can avoid unexpected and undesirable results.* An understanding of frequently used contractual terms can help you avoid surprises. Familiarity with the legal impact of these terms creates certainty about your contract's outcome. We discuss legal terms that are common in contracts later in this chapter under the heading "Reading the Fine Print: Typical Terms in Business Contracts."
- *Contracts can provide for a dispute resolution process.* You can agree beforehand on a process for resolving disputes and include this in the contract. Knowledge of contract law allows you to consider a range of dispute-resolving solutions and mechanisms before any dispute arises. This can increase your chances of maintaining a good working relationship, even in the event of a challenging development.
- *Contract law governs disputes.* Despite your best intentions, and those of the other party, contractual disputes can still arise. It is important to understand the rules that judges and arbitrators have applied in the past in order to predict the outcome that is likely in the event that your business contract dispute needs formal resolution.

Formation of a Contract

In this section, we revisit the four essential elements of a contract that we examined at the beginning of the chapter:

1. an intention to create a legal relationship,
2. offer and acceptance,
3. consideration, and
4. legality.

INTENTION TO CREATE A LEGAL RELATIONSHIP

The law presumes that the parties to a business-to-business transaction understand that the promises they make to each other carry legal consequences. That is, the law presumes that the parties to a business agreement intend that they may sue and be sued by each other if they break the promises that they have made. This **presumption** exists only in the context of the business world and the marketplace. It has no relation to family or social arrangements, such as the one involving Aunt Sal that we described at the beginning of this chapter.

presumption
a legal assumption that is made, subject to a party proving otherwise

rebuttable
capable of being refuted

Even in the commercial world, the presumption that the parties had an intention to contract is **rebuttable**, or capable of being refuted. Therefore, if you, as a business person, sue another business person for breaching a commercial agreement, a court will not require you to prove that you intended to enter into a contract; it will presume that both business parties had such an intention. However, if the other business person wishes to rebut the court's presumption by presenting evidence that you did not intend to contract—that is, did not intend your promises to be legally binding—she is entitled to do so. She is facing an uphill battle in her attempts to convince the court, though, because the presumption of the law is on your side.

> ### Minimizing Your Risk
> **Respect the Presumption To Contract**
>
> - Make only the promises that you intend to keep.
>
> - If you do not intend to be legally bound by something you say, make sure the other party understands your intention.

OFFER AND ACCEPTANCE

A contract must demonstrate a "meeting of the minds" between the parties. In other words, both parties must agree to the same thing. In a business-to-business transaction, this requirement is usually straightforward. There must be an offer by one party—for example, an offer to provide a service or product in exchange for a particular sum of money—and unconditional acceptance of that offer by the other party in the form, for example, of a signed document or a verbal agreement.

Disputes can arise when one party believes that a deal is final, while the other party believes that additional negotiations are needed, or that additional time is available to reflect on the terms of the deal before it becomes final. Disputes can also arise if one party claims that he accepted an offer—thus creating an enforceable contract—while the other party claims that the offer was no longer open for acceptance. These types of disputes are essentially about the timing or the formation of the contract, rather than about the contract's terms. Whether a court concludes that there was consensus—and thus that there was a legally binding contract—usually depends on the answer to one of the following two questions:

1. Was the offer still open when it was accepted?
2. Was acceptance of the offer properly communicated?

Was the Offer Open?

It is important for business people to know the rules about when an offer expires because offers may expire in a variety of ways. Several of the most common ways—lapse, revocation, and counteroffer—are discussed in the following sections.

Lapse

lapse
expiration of an offer

An offer may itself specify an expiry date and time. If so, once that time has passed, the offer lapses and is no longer open for acceptance. Your business may attempt to accept an offer after there has been a **lapse**, but—in law—your business's "acceptance" is nothing more than another offer. The party that originally extended the offer is free to accept your offer or to reject it. If he accepts your offer, you have a contract. If he rejects it, you have no contractual relationship.

Revocation

Whether or not an offer includes either a deadline or a promise to remain open for a particular period of time, the party who extends the offer is entitled to revoke the offer—or take it back—*at any time* before it is accepted. A business person who contemplates an offer at his leisure may be unpleasantly surprised to encounter

revocation
taking back of an offer

revocation—that is, to find that the offer is no longer open by the time he decides to accept it.

The revocation rule makes sense in view of the voluntary nature of contracts. It allows businesses to reconsider the wisdom of their offers at any time until an offer is accepted; only upon acceptance does an offer become legally binding. Because the marketplace is constantly changing, the revocation rule allows businesses to keep their positions flexible. For example, a business might put forward an offer to one party, realize that its offer is too low to obtain the goods or services that it needs to remain competitive, and revoke the offer. Or, it might put forward an offer to one party and then itself receive a highly desirable offer from another party that requires the use of the resources that it committed to the first party. In the latter case, it makes good business sense to revoke its offer to the first party and accept the offer of the second party.

option agreement
contract in which a party gives something of value to keep an offer open for a specified period of time

An exception to the revocation rule exists in the option agreement. An **option agreement** is an agreement under which a business that is contemplating an offer commits something of value—usually money—in exchange for a promise from the other party to keep the offer open for a specified length of time. An option agreement is itself a contract, in which the parties exchange mutual promises, which are of value to them both. The exchange of valuable mutual promises is a matter discussed later in this chapter under the heading "Consideration."

Business people often use option agreements when they need time to conduct market research in order to determine whether a proposal is sufficiently advantageous to them economically. They also use options when they cannot sensibly accept an offer before determining whether they can line up other related contracts. For example, a hotel chain might make an offer to a local manufacturer of organic bath products to be its exclusive supplier for a period of one year at a very attractive rate. The manufacturer might pay for an option agreement to hold the offer open long enough to determine whether or not it can meet the increased demand for its products. It might need additional equipment or staff in order to fulfill its obligations under the exclusivity offer and not want to commit before ensuring they would be available. If it is important for your business to know that an offer will remain open, either to allow you time to consider it or to negotiate related deals, you must pay for this privilege by entering into an option agreement.

Counteroffer

By accepting an offer on terms that differ from those proposed in the original offer, a business person makes a **counteroffer**. For example, if a company offers to provide cleaning services for your business premises at the rate of $35 per hour for a period of 12 months, and you respond by agreeing to the company's hourly rate for a period of 10 months only, you have made the company a counteroffer. Rather than accepting the company's offer unconditionally, you have proposed a modification to it. In law, the effect of your counteroffer is to take the company's original offer off the bargaining table. By making your counteroffer, you lose the right to accept the original offer. The cleaning company may choose to put its original offer back on the table, but you have no power to compel it to do so.

counteroffer
proposal that accepts an offer on terms differing from those in the offer

Table 4.1 provides a summary of how contracts are formed.

Table 4.1   Formation of a Contract

Scenario	Contract Formed?	Reason
A makes an offer. B accepts.	Yes	Both offer and acceptance have occurred.
A makes an offer. B rejects the offer. B later accepts the offer.	No	Offer is no longer open after B rejects it.
A makes an offer, stating deadline for acceptance. B accepts after this date.	No	Offer has lapsed. B's acceptance is a new offer.
A makes an offer. B makes a counteroffer. A rejects the counteroffer. B accepts the original offer.	No	Offer is no longer open as a result of B's counteroffer.
A makes an offer, stating the offer remains open until a certain date. A revokes the offer prior to this date. B accepts the offer after revocation but before the original deadline.	No	Offers can be revoked prior to acceptance, even if they include a promise to stay open.
A makes an offer, stating the offer remains open until a certain date. B pays money for the right to this time period. A revokes the offer prior to this date. B accepts the offer after revocation but before the date.	Yes	Option agreement operates to keep an offer open.
A makes the same offer separately to B and C. B accepts, then C accepts shortly thereafter.	Yes—two are formed.	Acceptance of offer by one party does not revoke the offer made to another party.

Was Acceptance of the Offer Properly Communicated?

Business people must also be aware of certain rules that govern the manner in which they must communicate their acceptance of an offer. Unless your contract states that you and the other party to the contract agree to implement different rules, the following are the rules that courts apply in resolving disputes about the formation and timing of contracts:

1. *A contract is formed when the party who accepts the offer communicates her acceptance to the party who makes the offer in the manner requested by the offering party.* For example, if the party who makes the offer specifies that the offer may be accepted by fax, written notice delivered by courier, or verbal notice communicated by telephone, a binding contract exists as soon as the offering party receives unconditional acceptance of her offer in one of these prescribed modes of communication.

2. *If the offer states that acceptance must be communicated in a specified form, only that form of communication can create a contract.* If, for example, an offer requires that acceptance be communicated by fax, acceptance communicated by email does not create a binding contract.

3. *Acceptance can be communicated by action alone, without requiring verbal or written confirmation.* For example, if a business places an order for delivery of office supplies and requests that the goods be delivered to its factory, the supplying company need not acknowledge receipt of the order. Its delivery of the supplies constitutes acceptance of the order and creates a binding contract at the time of delivery.

4. *Acceptance by mail occurs when the party who accepts an offer puts the acceptance in the mail.* The time when the offering party receives the acceptance is irrelevant to the formation of a contract.

5. *Electronic acceptance occurs when it enters the information system used or designated by the offering party and becomes capable of being retrieved and processed by that party.* This presumption is set out in section 22(3) of the Ontario *Electronic Commerce Act, 2000*. Whether the acceptance is communicated electronically by email or by clicking an "I accept" or "submit" button on a website, once that email message or online acceptance has reached the information system of the offering party's Internet service provider, it is deemed to have been received. This acceptance is presumed to have happened regardless of whether the intended recipient has retrieved and read the electronically transmitted information.

There are important reasons to be aware of these rules. For example, you would not want to miss out on an opportunity to enter into a beneficial business transaction simply because you failed to convey your acceptance in a timely or appropriate manner.

Minimizing Your Risk

Observe the Rules of Offer and Acceptance

- Remember that you are bound by any offer that you make and the other party accepts. If you are merely making a negotiating proposal that you do not intend to be bound by, ensure that the other party understands that your proposal is not an offer.

- When making and accepting offers, act with as much speed as wisdom allows. Do not let an offer lapse or be revoked merely because you have delayed unnecessarily.

- Remove all offers you have made from the bargaining table once you realize they are of no advantage to your business.

- Use option agreements when you need time to consider your position.

- Weigh the usefulness of making a counteroffer against the knowledge that making it will remove an original offer from the bargaining table.

- Communicate your acceptance of an offer in a manner that will bind the other party in law.

Knowledge of these rules will also help you avoid being bound twice by the same offer. This could happen unless you take care to ensure that the offer you make to one business has expired, been revoked, or been subject to a counteroffer before you make the same offer to another business. If your first offer is still open at the time you make your second offer, you might find that both offers are accepted and that you are a party to two binding contracts. In this case, unless you are able to fulfill your obligations under both contracts, you will be liable for breach. For example, assume you operate a delivery service and are upgrading your fleet of delivery trucks. You offer to sell all six trucks to a used auto wholesaler for a fixed price. Before the wholesaler gets back to you regarding the deal, one of your employees expresses interest in purchasing one of the trucks. You offer to sell it to her. If she accepts and the auto wholesaler accepts, you are contractually bound for the sale of the same vehicle twice.

CONSIDERATION

A valid contract requires consideration. Consideration is the price that the parties are each willing to pay for the contractual benefits that they expect to gain. For example, if one party agrees to supply goods and services in exchange for payment, the consideration—from the point of view of the supplier—is the goods and services; the consideration—from the point of view of the receiver of the goods—is the payment. In this situation, the parties' contract has the essential element of consideration that is required to make it valid. Any subsequent changes to the original contract also require a mutual exchange of consideration to be legally enforceable.

By contrast, a one-sided promise—such as your aunt's promise to bestow business riches—has no consideration, and therefore is not enforceable as a contract. Anyone who promises to give someone a present can always change her mind; the potential recipient will not be successful if he attempts to enforce the gift in court.

Exceptions to the Requirement of Consideration

There are a few situations in which a contract does not need consideration to be valid. If your business agrees to allow another business to pay you less than it owes you in order to satisfy a debt, no consideration is required for your promise to accept the lesser amount. This exception has been created by statute and rests on the philosophy that your business receives the benefit of avoiding the delay and costs associated with collecting the entire debt. An out-of-court settlement of a lawsuit works in much the same way. The plaintiff gives up his right to a trial in exchange for the defendant's payment of the claim.

Another exception to the consideration applies to contracts made under **seal**. A seal is essentially a special stamp or sticker added to an agreement—including a one-sided promise—to indicate the seriousness of the agreement and an intention to be legally bound by the promise. Contracts made under seal do not require consideration.

Promissory estoppel is one other exception to the consideration rule. This exception originally developed to help parties who relied on one-sided promises and

seal
symbol, stamp, etc., on a contract that indicates an intention to be legally bound; takes the place of consideration

promissory estoppel
a remedy available to a party that relies on a gratuitous promise to her detriment

suffered as a result. Consider, for example, a manufacturer that agreed to a long-term supply contract at a fixed price only to have its manufacturing costs suddenly skyrocket. It negotiates an increase in the sale price with its customer in order to remain financially viable. If the customer changes his mind and demands the return of the additional payments, the manufacturer could argue that the customer is bound by the doctrine of promissory estoppel to pay the higher price. To succeed, the manufacturer must be able to show that it relied on the customer's promise to its detriment, perhaps by showing that it incurred additional costs in order to meet its supply obligations. The manufacturer must also show that it acted with integrity throughout its dealings with the customer. It cannot, for example, have lied to the customer about its increased costs.

When you want to change the terms of a contract before you have carried out its terms, both sides must provide consideration. If they do not, the law will not enforce the change. One way to avoid problems is to agree with the other party to terminate the original contract and enter into a new one on new terms. The mutual agreement to terminate a contract provides consideration for the termination.

LEGALITY

A contract must have a legal purpose. In other words, the parties to the contract cannot agree to do something illegal. A single illegal action or promise can affect a series of business transactions by making all agreements that depend on the illegality unenforceable.

Consider a wholesale business that knowingly purchases from a supplier counterfeit goods—that is, they are copies that infringe the rights of the legitimate manufacturer and designer by violating copyright and trade legislation. The wholesaler complies with the supplier's request for payment in advance. The deadline for delivery comes and goes, and the supplier fails to deliver the goods. Since trading in counterfeit goods is illegal, the wholesaler will probably not be successful in making a claim for the return of the payment against the supplier in a Canadian court. It is likely that a court will rule that the contract is unenforceable because of its illegality.

Now assume, instead, that the wholesaler pays for the goods and receives shipment. The wholesaler then sells its newly acquired counterfeit inventory to a retailer. The goods are delivered and the retailer fails to pay for them. Once again, as a result of the illegality of the transaction, the wholesaler will have little success in collecting the money it is owed if it tries to sue the retailer.

Similarly, a business that trades in stolen property or sells illegal drugs can hardly expect to be able to enforce its business agreements through the courts.

However, some businesses dealing in legal products may find themselves faced with a similar problem. Consider the following examples:

- bans on the shipment of Canadian cattle into the United States,
- bans on pesticide use in some cities, and

- bans on the sale of toys or other children's products that fail to meet safety standards.

If a rancher near Calgary has an ongoing contract with a trucking company to transport cattle to Montana on a weekly basis, what happens when the United States announces a ban on imports? Can a pesticide manufacturer insist that a Toronto lawn care company with a contract to purchase its product in bulk proceed with its contractual obligations after the city declares a ban? Can businesses enforce similar contracts governing other products that are banned?

As you might expect, courts do not enforce contracts whose purpose has become illegal. If, for example, the pesticide manufacturer asked a court to enforce its demand that the lawn care company accept delivery of and pay for the shipment of pesticide, the court would probably declare the contract to be **void** (unenforceable). The result for the parties would be the same as if the contract had never existed. The pesticide manufacturer would bear the financial loss incurred by the loss of the market for its product. A court would neither require the lawn care company to fulfill its obligations under the original contract nor order it to compensate the manufacturer through the payment of **damages** for failing to do so. A carefully worded contract can, however, include a term that predetermines which party will bear the risk of this kind of eventuality.

> ## Minimizing Your Risk
> ### Keep Your Business Dealings Legal
>
> - Know with whom you are dealing. If your supplier is not trustworthy, you may end up paying for goods you do not receive or selling goods you do not get paid for. You could also be charged with an offence and fined for infringing copyright or violating trading laws.
>
> - Keep up with political and social developments in your industry. The sooner you know about laws or events that might adversely affect your business, the better you can prepare to minimize their effect. On the brighter side, the sooner you know about laws or events that may benefit your business, the sooner you can reap the rewards.

void
unenforceable

damages
monetary compensation
for breach of contract

The Importance of Written Contracts

The law does not require all contracts to be in writing. A mutual exchange of promises by business people over lunch, confirmed with a handshake and an intention to be bound, can constitute a binding contract, provided that the agreement is legal and represents a meeting of minds. A verbal agreement of this sort is every bit as binding as the most detailed of written contracts. In fact, many business contracts are never reduced to writing and are successfully completed without any problems.

However, for businesses, written contracts are usually preferable to verbal contracts for two reasons:

1. *Written contracts provide the parties with a record of their rights and obligations.* Documentary evidence of goods sold, services rendered, and business expenses incurred may be necessary from an accounting and tax perspective.
2. *Written contracts provide proof of the parties' agreement in the event of a dispute.* Should the parties take opposing positions regarding whether a contract exists at all, or should they disagree on the terms of the contract, a written contract provides excellent evidence of their intentions and mutual promises.

There are a number of exceptions to the general rule that contracts need not be in writing to be legally enforceable. Contracts that must be in writing include contracts related to consumer transactions (this topic is covered in chapter 5), most contracts related to the sale or leasing of land (this topic is covered in chapter 8), and

Minimizing Your Risk

Remember the Advantages of a Written Contract

- Be aware that you may be legally bound by an oral agreement.

- Avoid committing to a business agreement until the terms have been specified in a written contract. Tell your suppliers and customers that it is your company's policy not to finalize any deals without a signed contract.

- Know the person with whom you are dealing. Formalities may be less important when dealing with long-term business associates than with new business contacts about whom you have little information.

- Do not necessarily refuse to be a party to a verbal contract, but understand the risks involved. Carefully consider whether the benefits of a verbal contract outweigh the problems that might arise in the event of a dispute.

contracts that guarantee the payment of another person's debt if that person defaults on his payment obligations.

If a contractual dispute comes to court, the plaintiff (the party who launches the lawsuit) will probably argue that the defendant (the party whom the plaintiff sues) breached an existing contract. The burden will be on the plaintiff to convince the judge that her version of the case has more merit than the defendant's version. When there is little evidence beyond the testimony of the parties involved, the case will hinge on whom the judge believes.

If the parties are equally credible—that is, if the judge believes that they are both giving their honest, if perhaps mistaken, recollection of the events—and cannot decide whom to believe, the plaintiff will lose the case. Similarly, if the parties are equally incredible—that is, if the judge believes that they are both being less than truthful or perhaps exaggerating their evidence—the plaintiff will also lose. A written contract can tip the balance in the plaintiff's favour. *Macatula v. Tessier* is a case that underscores the wisdom of taking time to reduce all financial—and other—agreements to writing.

CASE IN POINT   The Advantages of Written Agreements

Macatula v. Tessier, 2003 MBCA 31

Facts

A homecare worker purchased a Lotto 6/49 ticket for her employer, a senior who was disabled with arthritis. The worker claimed that she and her employer had an agreement to share the proceeds. When the ticket holder won $11.4 million, the family of the employer, who was in possession of the winning ticket, claimed the money. The homecare worker sued the employer, claiming that the employer was in breach of their contract to share the proceeds. Although the worker had a credit card receipt to prove she had paid for the ticket, the employer insisted during the trial that she had paid her for the ticket and denied any agreement to divide the winnings.

Result

Without the evidence that a written agreement could have provided, the judge was forced to base his decision on the testimony of the parties. After hearing all the evidence, he concluded that the parties had not been "totally candid" with him. The worker's lawsuit failed because the worker did not succeed in convincing the judge that her version of events was more credible than that of her employer.

Business Lesson

Put your business agreements in writing.

WRITING A CONTRACT

The terms of a written contract constitute a record of the promises made and exchanged by the contracting parties. It is vital that the contract record these promises with as much precision as possible. Should a dispute arise, the most convenient resolution is to find a solution within the language of the contract itself.

Sometimes, however, a contract is flawed. It may fail to address significant matters, or its drafting may be vague and careless. In these cases, the terms of the contract are unlikely to provide a resolution that is acceptable to both parties in the event of a dispute. The parties may need to look to the courts as a last resort in settling their contractual differences.

RULES OF CONSTRUCTION

Over the years, the common law has developed several rules—known as the **rules of construction**—that are used in interpreting disputed contracts. Some of the most significant of these rules are set out below.

rules of construction
common-law rules used in interpreting disputed contracts

1. *Apply an objective test.* If the parties have used a vague term, such as "excellent quality," in defining, for example, the standard for oranges that one has agreed to sell to the other, a judge will apply an objective test to interpret the meaning of this term. In doing so, the judge will ask herself, "What does a reasonable person think 'excellent quality' means?" She might consult a dictionary or be guided by earlier decisions of other courts about the meaning of similar words. Surprisingly, she would probably not concern herself with what the parties themselves think "excellent quality" means. Judges act on the principle that contracts should be strictly enforced according to the ordinary meaning of the words chosen by the parties themselves.

2. *Interpret the contract against the drafter.* Under this rule of construction, a judge will prefer the interpretation offered by the party who did not draft the contract over the interpretation of the party who drafted it. The rationale for this rule may be explained by reference to the oranges example. The purchaser of the oranges, in drafting the agreement, chose to be satisfied with the term "excellent quality," and thus ran the risk that the supplier's interpretation would differ from his own. Because he failed to prevent the possibility of conflicting interpretations by failing to be more specific in his language, he must bear the burden of having the supplier's interpretation prevail over his own.

3. *Determine the parties' intentions.* Under this rule of construction, a judge will attempt to enforce a contract in accordance with the intention of the parties. However, use of this rule is often problematic when the parties take contrary positions regarding what their intention was.

THE PAROL EVIDENCE RULE

The **parol evidence rule** is another of the rules that judges use in interpreting contracts. The parol evidence rule states that if a contract is in writing and the language of the contract is clear, a court will not look beyond the contract itself to

parol evidence rule
common-law rule stating that if the language of a written contract is clear and complete, courts will not look at evidence beyond the contract to interpret it

interpret, alter, or contradict its terms. This means that a party cannot introduce evidence of statements made during negotiations unless the statements are included in the written contract. You can see the impact of the parol evidence rule in the case of *Arens v. MSA Ford Sales Ltd.*

CASE IN POINT The Parol Evidence Rule in Action

Arens v. MSA Ford Sales Ltd., 2002 BCCA 509

Facts

When negotiating the purchase of a used pickup truck, the buyer claimed that a salesman at the automobile dealership showed her an inspection report stating that the engine block was free of cracks and told her that the truck was in good running order. Eventually, she bought the truck under a written sales contract. The contract stated that the dealership made no representations and gave no warranties about the truck, that the buyer had obtained an independent inspection, and that the written contract constituted the entire agreement between the parties. The engine failed after the buyer drove the truck for 40,000 kilometres. A subsequent inspection revealed that the engine block had a hole that had been improperly repaired.

Result

The buyer's action against the dealership failed. The British Columbia Court of Appeal concluded:

> [E]vidence of the pre-contractual representations was inadmissible. Those representations are inconsistent with the terms of the written contract. The admission of that evidence would render ... terms of the written contract meaningless. ... Parol evidence cannot be admitted to vary or contradict the written agreement's express terms.

Business Lesson

Put all relevant aspects of your agreement in writing. Never rely on oral representations.

What Is in a Contract?

In theory, the content of a contract is limited by nothing but the imagination and creativity of the parties who draft it. In practice, however, contracts within particular industries tend to contain similar or identical terms because these terms have proven, over time, to be expedient for businesses. A business may choose to create individual contracts for each of its transactions, picking and choosing from an array of terms that are commonly used within its industry. We present many of these terms below under the heading "Reading the Fine Print: Typical Terms in Business Contracts." Alternatively, businesses may choose to adopt a standard contract and apply it to all transactions of a similar nature. We discuss these contracts, which are known as standard form contracts, in the following section.

STANDARD FORM CONTRACTS

A **standard form contract** is a contract that is drafted by one of the parties and imposed on the other with little or no opportunity for negotiating changes. It is often the party who provides a service or who sells a product that dictates the terms of the contract. In contrast, the party who pays for a service or purchases a product may often find himself in a "take it or leave it" situation. The use of standard form contracts is widespread, and you will often encounter the following types:

standard form contract
contract that is drafted by one of the parties and imposed on the other with little or no opportunity for negotiation

- *service agreements*—for example, contracts for office cleaning, equipment maintenance, security, and information technology;
- *commercial leases*—for example, contracts for the rental of office space or vehicles;
- *equipment rental agreements*—for example, contracts for the leasing of photocopiers and telephone systems;
- *advertising agreements*—for example, contracts for direct mail inserts, magazine display advertisements, and conference exhibition displays; and
- *insurance policies.*

Although standard form contracts tend to be one-sided and some of the standard terms may appear to be unfair, these contracts are just as enforceable between businesses as contracts that are the product of extensive negotiations. Most standard form contracts are successfully completed: the business transaction proceeds smoothly, and the terms of the contract never become contentious between the parties. Businesses should, however, exercise caution when using standard form contracts with consumers, because the law holds businesses to very strict standards in their dealings with consumers. We address this matter in chapter 5.

Businesses often find standard form contracts to be an efficient means of conducting their affairs for the following reasons:

- *Standard form contracts save time.* Rather than draft a separate agreement for every transaction, businesses are able to rely on a familiar and binding statement of their rights and obligations, and those of their clients and customers.
- *Standard form contracts reduce costs.* Businesses may be able to lower the prices they charge to their clients or customers if, for example, they can limit their liability by using a standard disclaimer clause. (We discuss these clauses in the following section under the heading "Disclaimer.")
- *Standard terms usually produce standard results in court.* The outcome of a contractual dispute may be more predictable when it is based on a standard form contract whose terms have been previously interpreted by judges. A predictable result may assist the parties in resolving their differences in a timely manner.
- *Standard terms help businesses plan for potentially adverse results.* If a business person is familiar with the meaning of a standard term, she can plan for any adverse consequences that the term could produce by, for example, buying insurance or adopting an alternative plan. If she knows that the risk created by the term is too high for her business to assume, she can refuse to enter into the contract.
- *Standard form contracts provide excellent models.* In drafting their own contracts, business people often review the standard form contracts of others and adopt the terms that are beneficial to them.

Reading the Fine Print: Typical Terms in Business Contracts

This section introduces you to a number of terms that commonly appear in business contracts. If the parties turn their minds to each of these terms, their contract should accurately reflect the bargain they have struck. Below, we discuss why you may wish to include each of these terms and how you can avoid the risks they may pose for your business.

IDENTIFICATION OF PARTIES

EXAMPLE

AGREEMENT OF PURCHASE AND SALE

BETWEEN

Premier Cement Inc., Seller

AND

#1 Contracting Co. Ltd., Buyer

Minimizing Your Risk
Identify the Parties Accurately

◀ If you are negotiating a contract on behalf of a corporation, ensure that the corporation's name—not yours—appears on the contract. If you are named personally as a party, you are liable personally.

◀ Accurately name all parties who intend to participate in the benefits and assume the obligations of the contract.

In most business transactions, identifying the parties to a contract is fairly straightforward. It is important, however, that you identify the parties correctly because only the parties to a contract may claim benefits under the contract. Conversely, only the parties to a contract can be held responsible for contractual obligations. This legal concept, which restricts the operation of a contract to those who are parties to it, is known as **privity of contract**.

In identifying the parties, ensure that you name them correctly. If the parties are individuals, use the names that appear on official documents, such as birth certificates. If they are corporations, use the names that appear on the articles of incorporation.

You may also want to include a brief description of the parties' roles in the contractual relationship, such as "Seller" and "Buyer" or "Publisher" and "Advertiser."

privity of contract
doctrine that restricts the operation of a contract to those who are parties to it

DESCRIPTION OF PRODUCT OR SERVICE

EXAMPLE

The designer will create a website using an Art Deco design, five Art Deco line drawings, and an Art Deco typeface, and featuring the colours black, jade, and salmon.

Precision in description is important. Suppose, instead of using the above phrasing, this contract for the design of a restaurant's website had stated, "The website is to have a professional appearance in keeping with the mood of the restaurant's logo."

Can you see that the website designers and the representatives of the restaurant might have different opinions about "professional appearance" and appropriate "mood"? If these differences lead to a dispute, difficult questions arise:

- Is the restaurant obliged to pay for a website it does not like?
- Do the designers have to start all over again at their own expense because the restaurant thinks that the website's appearance is not professional or in the appropriate mood?

If the parties cannot reach an amicable resolution to their dispute, they might be forced into costly and needless litigation. If, however, they had put their minds to drafting their requirements in a more specific form, these questions might never have arisen.

If the parties' dispute ends up in court, a judge will apply the rules of construction—with all their difficulty and uncertainty—in interpreting the contract for the parties. (We have discussed these rules earlier in this chapter under the heading "Rules of Construction.") The judge is unlikely to allow the parties to produce any evidence beyond that set out in the contract itself in keeping with the parol evidence rule (also discussed above).

> **Minimizing Your Risk**
> **Describe Products or Services Precisely**
> - Be as precise as possible when describing the products or services covered by your agreement.

QUANTITY

EXAMPLE

The seller agrees to sell and the buyer agrees to buy 100 cases of Ontario's Best Organic Pea Soup, provided that each case contains 24 28-ounce jars of Ontario's Best Organic Pea Soup.

It is important to specify the quantity of goods or materials that an agreement covers. If, for example, the parties agree to buy and sell a product that comes in cases, ensure that the contract specifies the number of cans, jars, or other containers within each case. Consider, for example, the difference to the parties between a case containing 24 28-ounce jars and a case containing 12 12-ounce jars.

> **Minimizing Your Risk**
> **Specify Quantity Accurately**
> - Be as accurate as possible when specifying quantity.
> - If your industry has commonly understood measurements, such as "barrel," use them.

QUALITY

EXAMPLE

The seller agrees to deliver only inspected and graded beef products that fall into the Canada AA or higher grades.

If a contract covers the purchase and sale of various cuts of beef to be served at a fundraising gala at your hotel, you may want to specify that the meat has been inspected and graded in accordance with federal or provincial standards. If the contract includes no description of the quality of meat required to satisfy the supplier's obligations, you cannot assume that you will be supplied with the grade of beef that you are expecting.

As with any other contractual term, specificity regarding quality will not necessarily guarantee that a supplier will deliver satisfactory goods. However, such a term will give the buyer recourse against the supplier for breach of contract in the event that the goods are substandard. (We cover various modes of recourse later on in the chapter under the headings "Damages" and "Remedies Other Than Damages for Breach of Contract.")

> **Minimizing Your Risk**
> **Express Your Agreement About Quality**
> - Where possible, refer to relevant quality control standards, or samples of comparable quality to eliminate surprises and misunderstandings when a product or service is delivered.

Another type of contractual term allows for the delivery of substandard goods. If, for example, the parties agree that the buyer will purchase goods "as is"—that is, with existing bumps, dents, and other flaws—they must specify this to be the case in their contract.

PRICING

EXAMPLE 1

Contract price: $_____*
* Note: Price is subject to change on 30 days' notice in writing to the purchaser.

EXAMPLE 2

"Product price" means the weekly average price published by the Market Analysis Division of Agriculture and Agri-Food Canada in its *Weekly Price Summary*, online at www.agr.gc.ca/mad-dam/.

EXAMPLE 3

In the event of an increase in the price of labour and/or materials necessary for the completion of this project, the supplier reserves the right to increase the project price by up to 10 percent over the original price on reasonable notice to the purchaser.

If possible, always incorporate some flexibility into the contract's pricing clause, particularly if your business arrangement extends over a period of time. Is there a chance that your costs will increase over the duration of the contract? Is there a chance that you will need additional resources to complete the project if you are running behind schedule? The original contract price may account for these contingencies, but a flexible pricing clause, such as one of the three examples above, may provide greater protection.

A flexible pricing clause must be reasonable from both parties' point of view. If the pricing clause creates too much uncertainty, the vulnerable party should reconsider the wisdom of signing the contract. *MJM Custom Fabrications Inc. v. Big Drum Inc.* illustrates the pitfalls of failing to be specific about the pricing of contractual changes and extras.

Minimizing Your Risk
Allow for Flexibility When Pricing a Product or Service

- Consider tying the price of any product that you distribute or manufacture to a market price, particularly in long-term contracts.

- Negotiate a fixed price if you are the buyer of a product that is prone to fluctuations in price.

- Build in a price cushion to compensate for unexpected costs, or consider a pricing clause that allows for adjustments if you are providing a service.

- Reopen negotiations immediately if pricing problems arise while the contract is in force; do not wait until the contract has been completed before speaking up.

CASE IN POINT Keeping Track of Prices

MJM Custom Fabrications Inc. v. Big Drum Inc., 2005 CanLII 34584 (ONSC)

Facts

A purchaser contracted with a manufacturer to pay $21,000 for the creation of a chocolate system. Because the initial sketches—on which the price was based—were incomplete, the parties implemented a number of design changes during the manufacturing stage at the request of the purchaser. The purchaser knew that there would be additional expenses associated with the changes; however, when the manufacturer delivered its final invoice in the amount of $41,363, the purchaser refused to pay the full amount. The manufacturer sued for the balance of $14,597.

Result

The Ontario Superior Court of Justice concluded that the extra work and materials were worth approximately two-thirds of the amount charged, resulting in a judgment in favour of the manufacturer of $6,500. The judge stated, "the only reasonable method of analysis is to start with the fixed price contract, as it was never [revoked], and calculate the value of the extras." He also made the following comments that identify the real costs associated with this dispute:

> Having listened to the evidence, I fail to understand how reasonably intelligent business people would allow their dispute over a small amount of money to proceed to trial. From an economic perspective, it made no sense both in terms of actual expense as well as the time away from their respective businesses. Further, a business relationship of many years has now been destroyed by this dispute.

Business Lesson

Use a flexible pricing clause to predetermine the basis for calculating increases to the initial price, or agree on the price of any changes to the original contract before any extra work is performed.

PAYMENT

EXAMPLE 1

Unless otherwise agreed, payment terms are cash on order.

EXAMPLE 2

A downpayment of 15 percent of the contract price is due on signing. Balance in full is due within 30 days after completion of the services.

EXAMPLE 3

Terms of payment: Payment in full on delivery of the goods by cash, certified cheque, money order, or credit card only.

EXAMPLE 4

Upon acceptance of the terms of this development agreement, the customer will receive an invoice requiring a minimum deposit of 50 percent of the contract price to commence work. A second invoice for 25 percent will be sent 30 days later. A third and final invoice for the remaining 25 percent will be sent upon completion of the services. Payment is due immediately upon receipt. If payment is not received within 30 days of each invoice date, a late fee of $35 will be added to the outstanding amount. Any amounts outstanding 60 days past the invoice date will incur simple interest charges of 10 percent per annum to the date payment is received in full.

EXAMPLE 5

Payment options: The club offers members a pre-authorized payment plan to pay annual fees. The plan consists of 11 equal monthly payments withdrawn from the member's bank account on the first business day of the months of February to December inclusive. A $75 administrative fee applies to this option and will be withdrawn at the time of the first payment.

Does a contract require payment

- before delivery of a product or service,
- at the time of delivery of a product or service, or
- after delivery of a product or service?

Minimizing Your Risk

Tailor Payment Clauses To Meet Your Needs

- ◄ Consider partial payments over the duration of long-term contracts.

- ◄ Obtain financing if necessary when payment is required on acceptance or before delivery.

If payment matters to your business (and presumably it does), make sure to include a clause regarding payment terms in your contract.

If your business is providing a service over time, can you wait to be paid until the conclusion of the project, or do you need a source of interim revenue to pay for ongoing expenses? Have you any concerns that the other party will pay and/or pay on time? If you answered yes to either of these questions, you would be wise to include a schedule of partial payments.

A schedule of partial payments makes good business sense. If the other party refuses or neglects to make a scheduled payment, you will have recourse against her for breach of contract. You will also have advance warning of potential problems, and you may be able to minimize your losses by pulling out of the project.

DEADLINE

EXAMPLE 1

CONTRACT DEADLINE
A 50 percent deposit for each exhibitor space you request must accompany your signed contract by January 15; payment in full is due by February 15.

EXAMPLE 2

All advertising materials must reach the publisher at least 24 hours before the weekday edition and 72 hours before the Saturday edition of the publication in which the advertisement is to appear. Advertisements cancelled because of a delay or missed deadline will be charged to the client.

EXAMPLE 3

Date work is to begin: _____
Date work is to be completed: _____

It is particularly important to include a deadline clause that covers delivery or other matters related to a contract's duration when

- a deadline is crucial to a project's effectiveness or
- several contracts are dependent on each other.

For example, on a construction project, if a cement company is late in pouring the foundation of a building, the later phases of construction may need to be postponed. If the contract between the general contractor and the cement company states a date for completion of the foundation, the cement company should bear the burden of any additional costs associated with the rescheduling of later stages of the project.

> **Minimizing Your Risk**
>
> **Remember the Importance of Timing**
>
> ➤ Record all deadlines on your calendar or in your appointment book to avoid missing business obligations or opportunities.
>
> ➤ Include enough flexibility in deadline terms to account for unexpected events that may result in delays.
>
> ➤ Remember the risks and costs associated with late completion and be prepared to accept them.

LIQUIDATED DAMAGES

EXAMPLE 1

If the customer is in breach of this service agreement, the present value of the charges applicable for the unexpired portion of the contract period will become immediately due and payable.

EXAMPLE 2

Notwithstanding any other provision in this contract, the designer's liability for damages arising out of its performance or failure under this agreement shall not exceed the contract fee.

liquidated damages clause
clause in a contract that provides for the payment of money if a certain event—usually a specified breach of contract— occurs; also known as an "acceleration clause"

A **liquidated damages clause** (also known as an acceleration clause) provides for the payment of money if a certain event happens; this event is usually a specified breach of contract. For example, if a business breaches a contract with a lender by failing to meet a loan payment, a liquidated damages clause may make all outstanding loan payments due and payable immediately. Alternatively, a contract that specifies a deadline for delivery of a product or service may also contain a clause that states a sum that will become owing if a party fails to meet the deadline. A liquidated damages clause that is tailored to the duration of a breach may state an amount that becomes owing for each hour or day that a payment or delivery is late.

The effect of a liquidated damages clause is to quantify, in advance of a problem, the compensation that one party will pay to the other in the event that a problem arises. In general, it is wise for parties—while their relationship is still cordial—to anticipate whatever problems might occur in the performance of the contract and to plan for compensating the party who will suffer loss as a result of such a problem.

Provided that liquidated damages clauses address the matter of compensation, the courts are generally willing to enforce them. However, if a clause that purports to be a liquidated damages clause is merely a penalty clause in disguise, the courts are reluctant to use their powers of enforcement. The court analyzed this matter in the case of *32262 B.C. Ltd. v. See-Rite Optical Ltd.*

> **Minimizing Your Risk**
>
> **Negotiate a Liquidated Damages Clause and Use It Sensibly**
>
> ➤ Negotiate a liquidated damages clause that fairly estimates the amount of compensation necessary in the event of a breach of contract.
>
> ➤ If there is a breach of contract, use the liquidated damages clause as a starting point for negotiating a fair resolution of your dispute with the other party.
>
> ➤ If there is a breach of contract, also use the liquidated damages clause to determine whether a lawsuit or other formal dispute-resolving procedure is financially worthwhile for your business.

CASE IN POINT Liquidated Damages as Compensation, Not Penalty

32262 B.C. Ltd. v. See-Rite Optical Ltd., [1998] 9 WWR 442 (Alta. CA)

Facts

The defendant rented a business sign from the plaintiff under a standard form contract that included a liquidated damages clause. When the defendant stopped making monthly rental payments, the plaintiff sued for damages. The liquidated damages clause gave the plaintiff the right to receive an amount equal to the total of all monthly payments owing for the outstanding term of the contract. With 70 months' rental remaining before the contract expired, this was a significant amount.

The primary issue in the case was whether the liquidated damages clause was so oppressive as to amount to a penalty clause, or whether it was a genuine pre-estimate of damages for breach of contract for which the plaintiff was entitled to compensation.

Result

The Alberta Court of Appeal ruled in favour of the plaintiff, concluding that the amount due under the liquidated damages clause "was closely related to the amount to which [the plaintiff] would have been entitled according to principles of general contract law." The defendant was ordered to pay damages amounting to the outstanding 70 months' sign rental, plus interest and legal fees.

Business Lesson

Ensure that a liquidated damages clause addresses compensation, and is not a penalty clause in disguise.

ARBITRATION

EXAMPLE 1

Any dispute in connection with this agreement must be settled by arbitration in accordance with the provisions of the Ontario *Arbitration Act, 1991*.

EXAMPLE 2

10.1. In the event of any dispute between the parties arising from the meaning or effect of any clause or matter contained in this agreement, or arising from the rights and liabilities of the parties, the parties will try to settle the matter on an amicable basis.

10.2. If the parties cannot resolve the matter on an amicable basis, they will refer the dispute to an independent third-party mediator.

10.3. If the parties cannot reach a settlement in accordance with the procedures outlined in clause 10.1 or 10.2 above, they will refer the dispute to arbitration to be settled in accordance with the Ontario *Arbitration Act, 1991* by one arbitrator.

10.4 The arbitration will be held in London, Ontario.

An arbitration clause specifies that the parties agree to resolve all disputes that arise under their contract through arbitration, rather than through litigation (a lawsuit). In Ontario, the arbitration process is generally governed by the *Arbitration Act, 1991*.

We have already described some of the advantages of arbitration over litigation in chapter 2. These can include confidentiality, relative flexibility, speed of process, and industry-specific expertise of the arbitrator.

If the parties include an arbitration clause in a contract, they give up the option of bringing a lawsuit. Should a party to such a contract attempt to launch a lawsuit despite the arbitration clause, the other party can ask a court to stay the lawsuit—that is, to put it on hold permanently.

The second example shows an arbitration–mediation clause. It is clearly more detailed than the first and reflects the seriousness of the parties' goal to minimize the costs associated with a contractual dispute. In this example, the parties have enlarged the arbitration clause to include an agreement to resolve their differences amicably or with the assistance of mandatory mediation.

As we have observed in chapter 2, mediation is another way for business people to settle their disputes out of court. A neutral third party, the mediator, helps the parties look for a solution that resolves their dispute, ideally leading to a win–win result. Unlike judges, a mediator does not have the power to reach a decision and impose it on the parties. The mediator focuses on understanding each party's interests and helping the parties communicate their positions in an effort to reach a mutual agreement.

Mediation is a relatively informal process and is completely confidential. It is particularly helpful in maintaining ongoing business relationships when a dispute arises. In Ontario, mediation is now a mandatory component of most civil cases that proceed through the regular court process.

> **Minimizing Your Risk**
> **Sue Only If You Have To**
> - Use an arbitration or a mediation–arbitration clause to increase the likelihood of an early resolution of a dispute and to avoid the high cost of litigation.

AUTOMATIC RENEWAL

EXAMPLE

When this agreement expires, or when any extension of this agreement expires, the parties agree to renew the agreement for a further term of 12 months, and automatically to renew the agreement thereafter for a further identical term. If, however, at least 30 days before the expiry of this agreement, or any extension of this agreement, either party gives the other party written notice of his intention to terminate the agreement at the end of the then-current term, the agreement is so terminated.

Many contracts for the provision of a service or the rental of equipment or space extend over a period of time. Examples include contracts for renting photocopiers, hosting websites, advertising products in bus shelters, and providing janitorial services. These contracts may contain an automatic renewal clause, which states that the contract is to be automatically renewed for a specified period time, usually one month or one year.

> **Minimizing Your Risk**
> **Comply with Notice Requirements**
> - If you do not intend to renew a contract that contains an automatic renewal clause, take care to give notice within the time and in the manner that the contract specifies.

These contracts may include terms that require one party to give the other party notice of an intention to terminate the agreement. If they do contain such a term, it is necessary to comply with the notice requirements in order to avoid automatic renewal of the contract.

CANCELLATION

EXAMPLE 1

If you terminate your Service prior to the end of the term (if applicable) you agree to pay us $20 times the number of months remaining in the term, to a maximum of $200.

Rogers may allow for the cancellation of your Service without penalty with the following conditions:

- device is returned in complete and original condition to the store where it was purchased (if customer-owned hardware, this condition does not apply) and
- cancellation is requested within 30 days from date of activation and
- your account has incurred less than 30 minutes of airtime usage or 150 Kilobytes of data usage.

You will be billed for any local airtime, data, roaming and long distance charges incurred up to the point of deactivation. (Rogers/AT&T Wireless Agreement, Form # 375ONT-51-03 — 07/02)

EXAMPLE 2

The Purchaser must give written notice of cancellation to the Supplier at the address indicated at the end of this agreement. The Purchaser will be refunded a percentage of the full invoiced amount based on the following schedule:

Number of days remaining until the event:	Amount refunded:
180 or more	Full amount less $100 administrative fee
90 to 179 days	75% of full invoiced amount
14 to 89 days	50% of full invoiced amount
7 to 13 days	25% of full invoiced amount
Less than 7 days	No refund

A cancellation clause specifies the rights and obligations of the parties in the event that one of them decides to terminate the agreement. Parties often choose to include cancellation clauses in contracts involving services or products to be delivered after the contract is signed or to be delivered over a period of time. Types of contracts that usually include cancellation clauses include:

- contracts for exhibition space at upcoming trade shows,
- contracts for advertising in future editions of magazines, and
- multi-year contracts for cellular telephone services.

Long-term contracts, or contracts for future services, often come with cost savings for purchasers. However, these contracts may include cancellation penalties, such as those contained in the two examples above. A wise business person should always weigh the benefit of saving money on product or service costs against the risk of losing money on cancellation fees. In some instances, a business person may choose to keep his options flexible by refusing to sign a contract until he is ready to receive or provide services or goods. He might prefer to pay a higher price for month-to-month service than to run the financial risk of cancelling a long-term contract. His choice should be dictated by a clear-headed appraisal of his business's circumstances and prospects.

Cancellation clauses can work to your advantage as well. They can provide a release from a long-term contract at a known and agreeable price. Depending on the situation, it may be beneficial for you to pay the costs of early cancellation in order to take advantage of a better opportunity or to limit even greater losses that would be associated with completing the contract.

> **Minimizing Your Risk**
> **Be Mindful of Cancellation Penalties**
>
> ◄ Weigh the risks of cancellation penalties against the prospect of savings on long-term contracts and contracts covering future events.
>
> ◄ Weigh the cost of completing a contract against the benefits that you could gain through early cancellation, despite having to pay a cancellation fee.

CONDITION PRECEDENT

EXAMPLE

This agreement is subject to a first mortgage being made available to the purchaser on or before _____, in the amount of $ _____ at an interest rate not to exceed ___ percent per annum with a ___ year amortization period, ___ year term, and repayment of approximately $_____ per month, including principal and interest (plus 1/12 of the annual taxes, if required by the mortgagee). This clause is for the sole benefit of the purchaser.

This agreement is subject to the purchaser's obtaining municipal approval on or before _____ of a minor zoning bylaw variance to permit construction of a building (not to exceed 40,000 square feet) zoned for industrial use on the subject property.

In a **condition precedent** clause, a contract specifies that something must happen before a party is required to fulfill her contractual obligations.

Conditions precedent are commonly found in agreements to buy and sell real estate. A condition precedent may, for example, make completion of the contract conditional on the purchaser's obtaining financing or permission to rezone a property within a certain time period.

During the waiting period specified in a condition precedent clause, the contract exists as an enforceable agreement, and the parties have certain obligations under it. The purchaser is obliged in law to make a genuine effort to fulfill the condition, and the vendor is obliged to wait and see whether the purchaser succeeds in complying with the condition. In the real estate example, the purchaser must try to obtain the necessary financing and rezoning, and the vendor must wait and see whether the purchaser succeeds in obtaining financing and approval for rezoning; the vendor cannot sell the property to someone else during the waiting period.

If the purchaser's efforts are ultimately unsuccessful, the condition precedent is not fulfilled. Therefore, the sale falls through because the purchaser's obligation to buy ceases to exist.

condition precedent
a clause in a contract specifying that something must happen before a party is required to perform his obligations under the contract

When might a business person want to include a condition precedent in a contract? She may want to do so if she does not want to bind her business to a contractual obligation without knowing that something essential to a contract is available or has occurred. For example, a manufacturer may need to know that it can obtain an adequate supply of a necessary ingredient at a fair price in order to commit to a manufacturing project. A computer business may need to know that it has access to the expert personnel essential to performing computer services before undertaking a large job. Both the manufacturer and the computer service would be wise to use a condition precedent to relieve themselves of all obligations under the contract should the essential ingredient or the personnel prove to be unavailable.

CONDITION SUBSEQUENT

EXAMPLE

This contract will automatically terminate in the event that the purchaser orders less than the quota for four consecutive weeks.

A **condition subsequent** terminates a contract when a specified event or circumstance occurs. Until such an occurrence, the parties must perform their obligations under the contract. If the specified event or circumstance never occurs, the contract remains enforceable, and the parties are responsible for living up to all obligations they have assumed under it.

A business person may choose to include a condition subsequent in a contract if he is certain in advance that he no longer wishes to be contractually bound to a business arrangement if a particular circumstance arises. For example, a business owner may choose to terminate a contract with a sales representative or a distributor if the sales representative or distributor fails to meet sales or distribution targets.

The condition subsequent clause also has several other useful functions. It clarifies the sales or distribution standards that are required for the contract to remain operative. It also provides a means of terminating the contract in the event that one party's performance falls below a specified standard without the need for resorting to allegations about contractual breach.

> **Minimizing Your Risk**
>
> **Use Conditions Precedent or Subsequent To Terminate Disadvantageous Contracts**
>
> ◀ Before contracting, determine preliminary elements that are essential for your business to carry out its obligations under the contract.
>
> ◀ Use conditions precedent to confirm that these elements are in place if the contract is to be binding.
>
> ◀ Before contracting, determine the circumstances that would jeopardize an agreement. Use conditions subsequent to have your contract terminate if these circumstances present themselves.

condition subsequent
occurrence of an event or circumstance that results in the termination of contractual obligations

DEPOSIT

EXAMPLE

This agreement will terminate if the unpaid balance is not paid on or before the purchase completion date, and the deposit paid by the purchaser will be forfeited to the vendor.

A contract may require a deposit of a fixed amount or a percentage of the total contract price. Deposit clauses are commonly found in contracts involving tenders for bids on government projects, as illustrated in the case of *Dhillon v. City of Coquitlam*, or contracts for the sale of property. It is important to read deposit clauses carefully because they may specify that a deposit will be forfeited if the purchaser fails to complete the transaction.

Minimizing Your Risk

Protect Your Deposit

- If missing a deadline may result in your forfeiting a deposit, make sure you have a good reminder system in place.

- If meeting a deadline depends on the performance of work by others, follow up to ensure that all obligations are being fulfilled to avoid having your deposit forfeited.

CASE IN POINT Forfeiture of Deposit

Dhillon v. City of Coquitlam, 2004 BCSC 924

Facts

The City of Coquitlam advertised its intention to offer 22 undeveloped lots for sale through a bid process. A newspaper advertisement invited interested parties to obtain and submit bid packages. The bid packages specified the minimum bid price and required bidders to include a deposit of 10 percent of the total bid amount. The package contained an information sheet that stated, "Deposits will be defaulted if the successful bidders do not complete their obligations by October 14, 2003." It also included a copy of the agreement of purchase and sale that the successful bidders were required to sign. The plaintiffs were the successful bidders. They signed and submitted the agreement of purchase and sale, along with a 10 percent deposit of $23,559. The contract contained the following provision:

> [U]nless the Unpaid Balance is paid on or before the Completion Date, the Vendor [the City of Coquitlam] may, at the Vendor's option, terminate this Agreement and in that case, the amount paid by the Purchaser will be absolutely forfeited to the Vendor.

The plaintiffs intended to sell the property immediately to another purchaser after closing the deal with the City of Coquitlam. Apparently, a dispute arose with this subsequent agreement that prevented the plaintiffs' lawyer from receiving the funds necessary to complete the contract with the City of Coquitlam on time. Since the city did not receive the funds before the October 14, 2003 deadline, it refused to refund the deposit, and the plaintiffs sued to get the money back.

Result

The British Columbia Supreme Court decided in the city's favour. Because the clause calling for forfeit of the deposit was reasonable and did not constitute a penalty, the clause was enforceable.

Business Lesson

When your contractual obligations depend on the actions of a third party, know whom you are dealing with, and remember that this party's inaction may put your deposit at risk.

DISCLAIMER

EXAMPLE

10.1 The responsibility of the warehouse, unless otherwise stated, is the reasonable care and diligence required by law.

10.2 The warehouse's liability with respect to any one package deposited with it is limited to $40 unless the depositor has declared in writing a valuation in excess of $40 and paid the additional charge specified to cover the warehouse's liability.

The above clause is a simplified version of the one contained in the case of *London Drugs Ltd. v. Kuehne & Nagel International Ltd.* In that case, the Supreme Court of Canada held that the clause was effective to limit the liability of the warehouse and its employees after a transformer was damaged while being moved. Although the actual damage suffered by the owner of the transformer was $33,955, liability for the warehouse and its employees was limited to $40 as a result of the disclaimer clause.

As we have stated, a party who fails to fulfill her obligations under a contract can expect to be held liable for breaching the contract. Liability for breach obliges the breaching party to compensate the party who has fulfilled his contractual obligations. There are a number of ways in which compensation may be provided. The most common is the payment of a sum of money, known as damages. When the parties include a **disclaimer clause** (also known as a limitation of liability clause) in their agreement, they can limit the amount or the type of damages that they might otherwise be required to pay.

disclaimer clause
clause in a contract that limits the amount or type of damages that the parties might otherwise be required to pay; also known as a "limitation of liability clause"

Disclaimer clauses are common in business contracts, and they can have a very limiting effect on what a non-breaching party can expect to recover by way of compensation. The extent of the limitation of liability depends on the wording of the clause. A sensible business person must consider any disclaimer clauses with care and assess the risk of their potential application. Questions that might prove helpful in this regard are the following:

- How well do you know the party who is protecting himself from potential liability?
- How likely is this party to breach the contract?
- If he breaches the contract, what are the likely consequences?
- Is the risk of suffering these consequences acceptable to you?
- Can you protect your business against these consequences in another way?

Minimizing Your Risk
Understand the Impact of a Disclaimer Clause

- Include a disclaimer clause in your contracts to reasonably limit the potential liability of your business.

- Weigh the risks of signing a contract with a disclaimer clause. How serious an impact might it have on your business? Are there ways for you to protect yourself, such as by purchasing adequate insurance?

Sometimes the clause itself will dictate the wise course of action. For instance, in the warehousing example at the beginning of this section, a business that stores a package whose value exceeds $40 would be wise to pay the additional fee required to increase the warehouse's liability.

The purchase of insurance, either by means of the payment of an additional fee, as in the warehouse example, or under a separate contract of insurance, may be all you need to resolve the riskier aspects of disclaimer clauses. The case of *Dryburgh v. Oak Bay Marina (1992) Ltd.* illustrates the dangers of failing to protect against disclaimer clauses.

CASE IN POINT   Disclaimer Clause? Think Insurance!

Dryburgh v. Oak Bay Marina (1992) Ltd., 2001 FCT 671

Facts

The plaintiff's yacht was damaged when a dock broke loose at a marina and drifted aground. The plaintiff alleged that the dock broke loose because it was poorly designed, constructed, maintained, and/or supervised. The following is an excerpt from the disclaimer clause contained in the parties' moorage contract:

> All vessels, boathouse and ancillary equipment of the Owner stored or moored on the Company's premises shall be solely at the Owner's risk, and the Company shall not be responsible under any circumstances for any loss or damage caused thereto whether caused by the negligence of the Company, its servants or agents, or the acts of third parties, or otherwise.

The plaintiff sued the marina and one of its employees, claiming damages for negligence and breach of contract.

Result

The Federal Court Trial Division held that the clause was effective to protect both the marina and its employee from any liability for damage to the plaintiff's yacht. The judge commented, "Anyone reading the clause would certainly, if acting reasonably, take out proper insurance to cover the losses which the clause purports to exclude."

Business Lesson

Consider your insurance needs before signing a contract that contains a disclaimer clause.

ENTIRE AGREEMENT

EXAMPLE

This contract constitutes the entire agreement between the parties. There are no representations or warranties—express or implied, statutory or otherwise—and no collateral agreements other than those expressly referred to in this contract.

An entire agreement clause reinforces the parol evidence rule (see page 95). If a dispute regarding the meaning of a contract comes to trial, a party may not introduce evidence of statements made during negotiations unless these statements are included in the written agreement. The Ontario Court of Appeal, in the case of *KPMG Inc. v. Canadian Imperial Bank of Commerce*, summarized this concept as follows:

> The cardinal interpretive rule of contracts ... is that the court should give effect to the intention of the parties

Minimizing Your Risk
Write Your Entire Contract Clearly

- Ensure that your contract states your entire agreement because you may not be able to rely on any statements, whether oral or written, that are not recorded in it.

- Write your contract clearly to prevent a court from rewriting it for you.

as expressed in their written agreement. Where that intention is plainly expressed in the language of the agreement, the court should not stray beyond the four corners of the agreement.

It is worth noting that the prohibition against considering evidence external to a contract refers only to contracts whose terms are clearly expressed. If a contract contains an unclear or ambiguous term, a judge may consider external evidence for the purpose of clarifying the ambiguity.

EXCLUSION

EXAMPLE 1

The service provider shall not be required to provide any services relating to problems arising out of (1) the customer's use of the software in a manner for which it was not designed; (2) operation of the software in a hardware environment not recommended by the service provider; (3) operation of the computer on which the software is installed in environmental conditions outside those recommended by the computer manufacturer; or (4) the customer's negligence, misuse, or modification of the software.

EXAMPLE 2

This service contract DOES NOT COVER repairs or replacements resulting from defects, damage, or deterioration that arise from normal use, wear and tear, exposure, misuse, alteration, negligence, or accidents, and any damage from overheating.

exclusion clause
clause in a contract that excuses parties from their contractual obligations in specified circumstances

An **exclusion clause** excuses a party from her contractual obligations under certain circumstances. They are frequently seen in insurance contracts, although they appear in other contracts as well, such as service and extended warranty contracts. They differ from disclaimer clauses (although disclaimer clauses are sometimes referred to as exclusionary clauses) by directly affecting the scope of the coverage or services that are the subject of the agreement.

It is a good risk management policy for businesses to purchase insurance and, depending on the circumstances, extended service agreements or warranties to cover various potential losses. However, it is important to be wary of the exclusion clauses that these types of contracts often contain. For example, an insurance contract covering damage to property generally excludes liability for loss or damage resulting from the intentional or criminal acts of the party insured under the contract. Similarly, insurance contracts generally exclude liability for conduct resulting in injury to another party where the insured's intentional or criminal conduct has caused an injury.

endorsement
additional terms added on to a standard form or existing contract

You should also be alert to the **endorsements** that insurers often add to insurance contracts either to limit or to expand their coverage. For example, an insurance contract covering a jewellery store may include an endorsement that requires the insured business to install surveillance equipment and security devices in order for the insurance to be effective.

The interpretation of insurance contracts has been the subject of many court decisions and is a topic that is beyond the scope of this book. However, from a business perspective, it is worth knowing that courts generally interpret exclusion clauses strictly against the insurers who drafted them, in accordance with the rule 2.

set out earlier in this chapter under the heading "Rules of Construction." Courts also tend to interpret coverage provisions broadly, which means that they give effect to the coverage clauses whenever possible.

Minimizing Your Risk

Carefully Examine Exclusion Clauses

◄ Read the contract carefully. Only a thorough reading will reveal restrictions on the insurance or services that may be vital for your business.

◄ If you are the service provider, review whether the restrictions are sufficiently broad. Would your business benefit from excluding even more from the scope of your agreement?

◄ Ask yourself: how badly does your business need the contract? How many exclusions is it prepared to accept? How many restrictions will the other party accept?

FORCE MAJEURE

EXAMPLE

The supplier shall not be liable for any losses or damages resulting from acts of God, war, terrorist acts, labour unrest, currency devaluations, government-imposed restrictions on the sale or distribution of the product, or any other delays or failure in performance resulting from causes beyond the supplier's reasonable control.

A *force majeure* is a significant and unanticipated event—such as a war or a natural disaster—that is beyond the control of the parties and prevents them from carrying out the terms of the contract; the effect of a *force majeure* is to terminate the contract. By inserting a *force majeure* clause in a contract, the parties can exempt themselves from liability for damage caused by events that lie beyond their control.

Like disclaimer clauses, *force majeure* clauses allocate the risk of loss in certain circumstances. They specify that one or both of the parties will not bear the risk of specified losses. As long as the parties are aware of the existence of a *force majeure* clause and its potential impact, they can make wise business choices, such as purchasing insurance or adopting contingency plans. For example, if you are concerned that extreme weather might interfere with the performance of your contractual obligations in a particular place, put a deposit on an alternative location to serve as a backup.

If a contract lacks a clause that allocates the risk of loss in the case of a *force majeure* or other unforeseen event that makes the performance of the contract impossible, the legal concept known as **frustration** may apply. Frustration occurs when performance of a contract according to its original terms becomes impossible or radically different from what the parties intended. It will not apply simply because performance of a party's obligations becomes onerous or expensive.

Under the common law, application of the doctrine of frustration meant that the loss would "lie where it falls." For example, consider a contract under which a

force majeure
significant and unanticipated event—such as a natural disaster—that is beyond the control of the parties and makes fulfillment of contractual obligations impossible

frustration
a legal doctrine that allocates the risk of loss in the event that a contract becomes impossible to perform and the contract is silent regarding the issue

processing company agrees to buy tomatoes and has prepaid the farmer for the crop. If the crop is severely damaged by a severe and unforeseen hailstorm, under the common law the processing company would bear the loss. Although the farmer was unable to deliver the crop, he would have been entitled to keep the money that the processing company paid him. The *Frustrated Contracts Act* has changed this outcome. If it is established that a contract has been legally frustrated, a party who paid for a benefit that it did not receive will be entitled to recover the amount it paid.

GOVERNING LAW

EXAMPLE

The parties agree to construe and enforce this agreement in accordance with the applicable laws of Prince Edward Island and of Canada. The parties also agree to treat this agreement in all respects as a Prince Edward Island contract.

If the parties carry on business in different jurisdictions, it is necessary to designate the law that is to prevail in the event of a dispute. While the law is relatively uniform throughout the Canadian provinces and territories, it is not identical. Also, Canadian law may differ from the law of China, Brazil, or the United States, for example, in ways that profoundly affect a contract. Different countries may have different rules about interpreting contracts as well as different procedures for bringing disputes before courts or arbitrators. By including a governing law clause (also known as a choice-of-law clause), the parties can choose the law that they want to govern their dealings. They can thereby eliminate the uncertainty of unexpected (and perhaps unwelcome) legal results.

INDEMNITY

EXAMPLE 1

The client unconditionally guarantees that any elements of text, graphics, photos, designs, trademarks, or other artwork furnished to the website designer for inclusion in the project are owned by the client, or that the client has permission from the rightful owner to use each of these elements. The client also agrees to protect, indemnify, and defend the website designer and its subcontractors from any liability, including any claim or lawsuit (and related legal fees and court costs)—threatened or actual—arising from the use of the elements furnished by the client. (Adapted from NetSites LLC, "Web Site Design Contract," www.net-sites.com/contract.htm.)

EXAMPLE 2

The renter shall indemnify and protect the venue from all claims, damages, suits, and actions whatsoever, including any claims for any personal injury (including death resulting therefrom) or any loss of or damages to property that arise out of or in connection with the entry onto and use of the venue's facilities on the dates specified in this agreement. If the venue is made a party to any litigation commenced by or against the renter, the renter shall promptly indemnify and hold harmless the venue and shall pay to the venue all costs and expenses incurred or paid by the venue in connection with such litigation. (Adapted from *Potvin v. Canadian Museum of Nature*.)

To indemnify means to protect another party from loss or legal responsibility, or to compensate that party for losses or expenses. An **indemnity clause** in a contract requires one of the parties to pay for any losses or expenses that the other party may incur as a result of claims related to the contract. Inevitably, the party required to do the indemnifying is the party whose actions or omissions lie at the root of the claim.

indemnity clause
clause in a contract that requires one of the parties to pay for any losses or expenses that the other party may incur as a result of claims related to the contract

For example, consider the position of the website designer in the example at the beginning of this section. She frequently uses many types of text and artwork in creating websites for her clients. She lacks the time and knowledge to research the various claims made by her clients, or to check the legitimacy of every photograph, logo, or piece of artwork her clients submit to her for inclusion in their websites.

What if it turns out that a piece of artwork contains something that infringes the copyright of another artist? Or what if the language in a piece of submitted text is defamatory of a competing business or product? The designer could be named as a defendant in a lawsuit alleging tort liability and/or copyright infringement. To protect herself from the costs associated with defending such a claim, the website designer can include an indemnity clause in her contract with the advertiser. This clause requires the client—who is in the best position to know whether the material is legitimate—to pay for any expenses or losses incurred by the designer as a result of carrying out her contractual obligations.

The following list provides several examples of situations in which indemnity clauses can effectively shift responsibility for risks associated with various business transactions in accordance with the parties' agreement:

- In a contract for the provision of maintenance services in an office building, the maintenance company may agree to indemnify the building occupants against any claims for personal injuries that arise from allegations that the building was improperly maintained.
- In a construction contract, an electrical subcontractor may agree to indemnify the general contractor against any claims for loss or damage that arise from allegations that the electrical work was faulty.
- In a software licensing agreement, the purchaser of the licence may agree to indemnify the software company for any claims that may arise against it from the purchaser's improper use of the software.

It is important to note that an indemnity clause cannot be so broadly worded that it protects a party against its own wrongdoing or negligence. This type of clause will be narrowly interpreted to disallow a party's immunity from responsibility for its own negligence. For example, in *Potvin*, the court ruled that the indemnity clause (see example 2 above) did not apply when a person suffered injury after falling on the

> ## Minimizing Your Risk
> ### Keep Indemnification Obligations in Mind
>
> - Ensure that you have obtained all necessary permissions when providing copy or graphics for an advertisement, website, or brochure.
>
> - Check to see that your commercial liability insurance covers claims for indemnity.

exterior stairs of a rented premises. It found that the injury suffered by the person attending the event hosted by the renter was unrelated to the event itself. The court therefore held that there was insufficient connection between the renter and the injury to invoke the venue's indemnification clause.

VENUE

EXAMPLE 1

The parties agree to submit to the courts of Ontario.

EXAMPLE 2

The parties agree to submit to arbitration in Ontario.

venue
place where a contractual
dispute will be litigated

A **venue** clause states the place where the parties agree to settle any contractual disputes. It is related to, but differs from, a governing law clause, whose purpose is to state the law that governs the parties' contractual relationship. Under a venue clause, the parties could, for example, agree to settle their differences in Prince Edward Island. Under a governing law clause, they could agree to apply Ontario law there.

It is wise to include a venue clause in a contract because it can be very expensive and time-consuming to travel to a distant place—even within Canada—for the purpose of litigating a dispute. When dealing with disputes in countries other than Canada, a party may be faced with the additional challenges of hiring a foreign lawyer, communicating in a foreign language, and navigating a foreign legal system.

If you succeed in negotiating a venue clause that allows you to resolve your disputes in Canada, you have gained a major contractual advantage. If you fail in your attempt to negotiate such a clause, you may decide that the business risks of submitting to the dispute resolution procedures of another country outweigh the business advantages of entering into the contract.

A venue clause will not necessarily prevent a party to a contractual dispute from starting a lawsuit in a place other than the one specified in the contract. However, if your business is sued in a foreign country, and your contract contains a venue clause stating that Ontario is the appropriate place to resolve any disputes, you have some recourse. You, or lawyers acting on your behalf in the foreign jurisdiction, can argue that the foreign lawsuit should be stayed or dismissed for lack of jurisdiction. Your chances of success probably depend on the foreign jurisdiction. Canadian courts will enforce these clauses and stay lawsuits brought in Canada when the venue clause provides for resolution in another place.

Minimizing Your Risk

Designate the Place Where You Will Resolve Contractual Disputes

- Include a venue clause to ensure that disputes will be resolved in a location convenient for your business.
- Before entering into a contract with a foreign venue clause, assess whether the potential risks and costs of foreign procedures are acceptable to your business.

Whatever happens, do not ignore a lawsuit brought against your business in a foreign place. Even if you believe the lawsuit was brought in the wrong place and any judgment against your business should be ineffective, it is perilous to ignore the proceedings. As long as there is a real and substantial connection between the foreign jurisdiction and the subject matter of the lawsuit—and assuming the lawsuit followed procedures that are consistent with Canada's concept of due process and fundamental fairness—it is likely that the foreign judgment can be enforced in Canada.

MISSING TERMS

Contract disputes commonly occur when the parties fail to include essential terms in their agreement. Missing terms are problematic for a number of reasons, several of which we have discussed earlier in this chapter under the headings "Rules of Construction" and "The Parol Evidence Rule."

If the parties fail to express their contractual intentions within the written terms of their agreement, the courts are willing—under certain limited circumstances—to imply terms. An **implied term** is one that a court inserts—or implies— into a contract when it believes that the term is necessary to give effect to the parties' intentions. Several examples of situations in which courts may imply contractual terms are provided below:

- *Custom within an industry.* If, for example, it is customary within the construction industry that interest is payable on accounts that are overdue for 30 days, a court may imply a term allowing an unpaid seller to collect interest from a buyer who refuses to pay within this time.
- *Obligations of good faith.* If, for example, a contracting party has undertaken to obtain financing to complete a contractual obligation, a court may imply a term requiring that the party use good faith or his best efforts in obtaining this financing. Implying such a term prevents the party from using inadequate efforts to avoid his obligations under the contract.
- *Business effectiveness.* If, for example, the actions of one party undermine the business effectiveness of another party, a court may imply an obligation to refrain from such actions. In *Nickel Developments Ltd. v. Canada Safeway Ltd.*, a case involving a commercial lease, the Manitoba Court of Appeal implied a term that the parties intended the premises to be occupied. In this case, a supermarket was a tenant of a shopping mall under a 20-year lease. Thirteen years into the lease, the supermarket closed because it was operating a more profitable store close by. It continued to pay the rent, allowing the store to remain vacant. This action had a negative impact on attracting customers to the shopping mall. The mall owner successfully sued for breach of contract. The court implied an obligation of continuous operation on the part of the tenant in order to give business efficacy to a commercial shopping centre operation.
- *Obvious omission.* If, for example, the price is missing from a contract for the sale of goods or services, a court or tribunal will imply a reasonable price.

Before a court will imply a term in a contract, the party who seeks to have the term included must satisfy the court that

- the term reflects the intention of the parties, and
- the term is reasonable, clear, and does not contradict an **express term** in the contract.

Whether or not a court chooses to imply a term is completely dependent on the circumstances of a case and the evidence presented by the parties. Because litigation is unpredictable, it is extremely unwise for business people to rely on courts to imply missing terms. Business people should take care that their contracts are complete and comprehensive from the outset.

implied term
term that will be inserted by law into a contract when necessary to give effect to the parties' intentions

express term
term specified in writing

Missing terms can be imported into contracts by legislation. For example, Ontario's *Sale of Goods Act*, which we examine in detail in chapter 5, applies to contracts involving the sale of physical goods. As a result of this Act, all such contracts in Ontario contain the following implied terms, unless the parties agree otherwise:

- the seller has a right to sell the goods;
- the goods are not subject to any encumbrances, such as liens;
- the goods correspond accurately to a description or sample; and
- the goods are of merchantable quality or reasonably fit for a purpose specified by the purchaser.

In order for these terms not to apply, the parties must include a term in their contract that prohibits the application of the Act.

Consequences of a Breach of Contract

You should now understand the importance of contract terms and fulfilling your obligations under the contract. You should also appreciate how you can use specific contract terms to plan for and resolve potential conflicts arising out of the agreement. Unfortunately, unanticipated events can still take your business by surprise and interfere with a contractual transaction. This can result in a breach of the contract and the need to assess the possible consequences.

WHAT CONSTITUTES A BREACH OF CONTRACT?

Although most contracts are successfully completed according to their terms, there will always be occasions when parties fail to live up to their contractual obligations. The following are examples of situations that may constitute a breach of contract:

- A product or service fails to meet the quality or description specified in the contract.
- A product or service is not delivered.
- A product is delivered after the delivery date specified in the contract.
- A project remains incomplete after the deadline specified in the contract.
- No payment is made.

A breach of contract may be intentional or unintentional. Consider a contract that turns out to be highly unprofitable for one of the parties. Although the party may have intended to complete the contract when she signed it, she eventually realizes that it is less expensive for her business to breach the contract than to continue fulfilling her contractual obligations at a much higher cost than she originally anticipated. Perhaps a business owner signs a contract to deliver a product, or to provide a service, and shortly thereafter receives a more lucrative offer for his product or service from another business. He may decide that cancelling the first contract in order to enter into the second is financially irresistible.

An unintentional breach may occur when fulfillment of one contract depends on the successful completion of another. Consider a construction project in which many contracts are interdependent. A delay at any stage may create a ripple effect throughout the remaining stages and result in a breach of completion deadlines. A caterer may have contracted to supply lobster for a charity gala, relying on a standing order from its regular supplier. If there is an unexpected shortage of lobster, the caterer may be in breach of his contract if he substitutes prawns or scallops. External forces such as governmental bans on fishing for endangered species, natural disasters, political unrest, or labour disputes may also affect the performance of contractual obligations, perhaps making them impossible.

To determine whether a circumstance constitutes a breach of contract—and to predict the consequences of that breach—the parties must look first to the terms of their agreement. For example, a sensible caterer will include contractual language that allows for some flexibility in the proposed menu. Terms such as "subject to availability" or "an equivalent substitution at the caterer's discretion" may be useful in this regard. If a catering contract contains this type of language, the substitution of prawns or scallops for lobster is unlikely to be regarded as a breach of contract.

A business owner who is in the habit of cancelling less lucrative contracts in favour of more lucrative ones may also be in the habit of including cancellation clauses in his contracts. In this case, the terms of the cancellation clause will dictate the consequences of early cancellation. As long as the actions of the business owner fall within the terms of the cancellation clause, the business will probably have a good defence in an action against it for breach of contract. (We discussed cancellation clauses in detail earlier in this chapter.)

Similarly, if the contract contains a liquidated damages clause, an exclusion clause, or a disclaimer clause, the consequences of one party's breaching the contract—and the remedies available to the non-breaching party—may be clear. These clauses, which we discussed earlier in this chapter, will usually tell the non-breaching party whether starting a lawsuit for breach of contract is a sensible business option.

BREACH OF CONDITION OR BREACH OF WARRANTY?

Does a breach of contract by one party absolve the other party of his obligations under a contract? In other words, does a breach allow the non-breaching party to treat the contract as though it were at an end? The answer depends on the nature of the breach.

If the breach is a serious one that involves an important term—or **condition**—of the contract, the non-breaching party is free of all further obligations under the contract. Breach of a condition allows the non-breaching party to treat the contract as if it were at an end. It also gives the non-breaching party a right to claim compensation for any losses, or damages, that flow from the breach.

However, if the breach is less serious and involves a relatively minor contractual term—or **warranty**—the non-breaching party must fulfill its remaining obligations under the contract. The non-breaching party does, however, have the right to claim damages as compensation for losses it has suffered as a result of the breach.

In practical terms, distinguishing between a condition and a warranty is important for one reason only: it allows the parties to know whether they must continue to live up to their contractual obligations after a breach has occurred. Breach of a

condition
important term of a contract whose breach frees the non-breaching party from all further obligations under the contract

warranty
minor term of a contract whose breach requires the non-breaching party to continue to fulfill her remaining obligations under the contract

condition ends a contract. Breach of a warranty does not end a contract. As long as a contract is in existence, the parties are obliged to honour their contractual obligations. However, once a contract ceases to exist, the parties' contractual obligations cease to exist as well.

It is sometimes difficult to distinguish between a condition and a warranty. Terms that are conditions in some contracts may be warranties in others because their relative importance may vary from contract to contract. Consider, for example, a contractual term that states the parties' agreement about the timing of delivery of a toy shipment. If the timing is crucial to meet a holiday market, the delivery term is probably a condition. This means that the buyer is probably safe in rejecting a late shipment and claiming damages from the supplier. If, however, the delivery is intended for mid-season restocking and the toy market is relatively calm, the term may be a warranty. In this case, the buyer should accept and pay for delivery in accordance with the terms of the contract before making a damages claim against the supplier.

It is extremely wise for parties to specify whether the terms in their contract are conditions or warranties. For example, a delivery term in the toy store situation might read, "It is a condition of this contract that the Goods be delivered on or before October 31." If the parties do not specify whether a term is a condition or a warranty, the non-breaching party cannot be certain of how to react to the other party's breach. She will not know whether she can safely consider the contract to be at an end or whether she is still obliged to fulfill her contractual obligations and accept delivery.

VICARIOUS LIABILITY FOR BREACH BY EMPLOYEES

In the context of tort law, we observed that businesses can be held responsible—or liable—for injuries that result from the actions of their employees. The principle of vicarious liability also operates in contract law together with the principle of **vicarious performance**. Generally speaking, a business's contractual obligations are fulfilled by people whom the business employs or retains. For example:

vicarious performance carrying out of contractual obligations by employees of a business

- Packages are delivered by delivery staff, even though the parties to the delivery contract are the customer and the delivery company.
- Advertising slogans or product logos are designed by creative staff, even though the parties to the advertising contract are the customer and the advertising agency.
- Products are manufactured by factory workers, even though the parties to the contract of purchase and sale are the purchaser and the manufacturing company.

These situations demonstrate the concept of vicarious performance of the contract. In each of these examples, if a business's employee fails to perform the work in accordance with the terms of the contract—for example, fails to deliver a package on time, design an acceptable logo, or produce a flawless product—it is the business that is sued. The business is therefore vicariously liable for the employee's breach of the contract.

> ## Minimizing Your Risk
> **Avoid, Plan for, and Respond Sensibly to Breaches of Contract**
> - Avoid gaining a reputation for habitually breaching your contracts.
> - Use cancellation, liquidated damages, exclusion, or disclaimer clauses in your contracts to predetermine the financial cost of a breach.
> - In the event of a breach, check the wording of the contract to determine whether the breach is of a condition or a warranty.
> - Be prepared to fulfill your obligations in the event of a breach of warranty by the other party.
> - Monitor the work of employees to ensure that they do not jeopardize your contractual obligations.

Damages

As we have seen, there is much that contracting parties can do to anticipate the possibility of a breach and to address it within the terms of their contract. What happens, however, if a contract is silent about breach and its consequences? The general rule is that any breach, no matter how large or small, entitles the non-breaching party to compensation.

In the commercial world, compensation usually takes the form of monetary damages. The subject of damages eventually evolves into an examination of how much money the breaching party is required to pay to the non-breaching party in order to compensate him for the breach. If a damages claim ends up in court, a judge applies the test set out in the case of *Hadley v. Baxendale* to determine the **quantum**, or amount, of the damages:

quantum
amount

> The non-breaching party should be compensated to the extent of the loss of benefits that were within the reasonable contemplation of the parties when the contract was made.

In other words, the damages should be sufficient to put the non-breaching party in the position he would have been in had the contract not been breached, but only to the extent that the damages were foreseeable. For example, if a store enters into a contract for the design of a website and the design company breaches the contract by failing to meet the design specifications, the store may be entitled to the costs it incurs in hiring another company to complete the website according to the original agreement.

However, it is unlikely that the store would be successful in claiming compensation for loss of profits due to the delay, because it would likely be difficult to prove that this risk was foreseeable when the contract was made.

DUTY TO MITIGATE DAMAGES

duty to mitigate
obligation to take all reasonable steps to lessen losses suffered

The non-breaching party has an obligation to keep her losses to a minimum. This obligation is known as the **duty to mitigate**. Because of the duty to mitigate, a breaching party is not required to pay for losses that the non-breaching party could have avoided with reasonable efforts. Consider the following examples.

Assume that a scientific research conference includes an exhibition area, where interested businesses can, for a fee, set up booths to demonstrate their products or services. Because there is limited exhibition space, exhibitors must reserve a booth and pay a 50 percent deposit at the time of booking. One week before the conference, an exhibitor notifies the conference organizers that it is pulling out of the exhibition. It refuses to pay the balance of the booth rental fee. There is no cancellation clause in its contract with the organizers.

The exhibitor is probably in breach of the contract because when it reserved the booth, it entered into a binding agreement to exhibit at the conference and pay the outstanding balance of the booth rental fee. As a consequence, the conference organizers may be entitled not only to keep the 50 percent deposit but also to make a claim for the outstanding balance. This would put the conference organizers in the position they expected to be in had the exhibitor not breached the contract.

In order to mitigate their losses, however, the conference organizers are under a duty to make reasonable efforts to find a replacement exhibitor. If they are able to rent out the space to a different business, they may have no losses and therefore no claim for damages in compensation. The good fortune of the breaching party in avoiding payment of 50 percent of the fee may seem unfair. However, from a business perspective, the conference organizers are also in a much better position than they would have been had they gone to court to attempt to recoup their losses.

Why go to the trouble of making a claim against another party if there is a more practical solution available? *Carr v. Killam* is a recent New Brunswick case that illustrates the need for exercising good judgment in mitigating losses after suffering a contractual breach.

REMOTE DAMAGES

As we discussed in chapter 3 in the context of tort law, compensation is not available for losses that are considered too remote from a harm-producing activity. In contract law, compensation is similarly unavailable when the losses suffered by the non-breaching party are too remote—or distant—from the actions of the breaching party. Generally, courts do not compensate for losses that the breaching party could not reasonably have foreseen. For example, if an air conditioning system is improperly installed in a shopping mall, the contractor may be liable for any related structural damage, the cost of reinstalling the system correctly, and loss of profit by any businesses that were forced to close during the time of the installation and repair. All of these consequences are reasonably foreseeable.

However, imagine that the air conditioning system was improperly installed in a newly built shopping centre and pushed the construction schedule off target by several months. The shopping mall owner could claim the cost of the reinstallation and perhaps finaning costs associated with the delay in construction. It could probably also claim the reasonably anticipated lease payments that it was unable to collect as a result of the delay. But what if there was a significant downturn in the economy during those few months? It is unlikely that the shopping mall owner could also claim the difference between the future lease payments that it could have

CASE IN POINT Mitigation of Damages

Carr v. Killam, 2005 NBQB 260

Facts

The purchaser bought a small building located in Westfield, New Brunswick for $2,000. He intended to move the building to property he owned in Seeley's Cove. The contract for the sale of the building required that it be removed from the Westfield site by a specified date. The purchaser contracted with a mover to move the building for $8,000, and he paid a deposit of $3,000. As the deadline for moving the building approached, the mover demanded a further deposit of $1,000. The contract was silent with respect to the deposit amount, and the purchaser refused to pay the additional $1,000. After the deadline for moving the building came and went, the purchaser sued the mover for breach of contract, claiming the following damages:

- $3,000 downpayment,
- $2,000 paid for the building,
- $4,000 for the value of the unmoved building,
- $4,025 for road improvements to his Seeley's Cove property to move the building to an appropriate location on the lot,
- $880 paid to workers who prepared his property at Seeley's Cove,
- $780 for his own time,
- $100 to remove an electrical mast that would have impeded the moving of the building from its original location,
- $260 for miscellaneous expenses (including gas and a tree trimmer), and
- $50,000 for the estimated increased value that would have resulted from the addition of the building to his Seeley's Cove property.

Result

The New Brunswick Court of Queen's Bench rejected almost all of the damages claimed by the purchaser because the purchaser knew that if he paid the additional $1,000 deposit, the mover would likely have fulfilled his contractual obligation to move the building. By refusing to pay the $1,000, the purchaser effectively accepted the mover's breach of the contract. The reasonable course of action was for the purchaser to mitigate his losses by retaining another contractor to move the building. All claims—except for the return of the $3,000 deposit—flowed directly from the purchaser's failure to mitigate, rather than from the mover's breach of the contract.

Business Lesson

Following a contractual breach, mitigate your losses immediately.

collected from tenants in a vital economy, had the leases been entered into at the time of the original construction deadline, and the lease payments that it can collect in a now-stagnant economy. The air conditioning contractor could be successful in arguing that it could not reasonably have foreseen these consequences of its breach of contract.

Courts frequently find damage claims for lost profits to be too remote to merit compensation. It is very difficult for non-breaching parties to prove that they would have earned a profit but for the breach. So many factors other than contractual breach—such as market conditions or personnel shifts—can affect a business's profits and losses. Business owners are wise to remember that a breach of contract will not result in a windfall for the non-breaching party.

PUNITIVE DAMAGES

Courts and arbitrators award punitive damages to punish a party who has breached a contract, rather than to compensate a party who has complied with it. To award punitive damages, a court must be satisfied that the conduct of the breaching party is sufficiently reprehensible to warrant monetary punishment. An insurance company's conduct met this standard in *Whiten v. Pilot Insurance Co.*, a Case in Point in chapter 3. The jury in *Whiten* evidently believed that the insurance company knew from the outset that its arson claim was contrived and unsustainable and, further, that it was denying the claim to force the plaintiff to settle for less than she was entitled to.

ALTERNATIVE METHODS FOR PERFORMANCE

Sometimes a contract specifies that it can be fulfilled in one of several ways—that is, the contract provides for alternative methods for performance. How are damages to be measured if a party breaches such a contract? In *Hamilton v. Open Window Bakery Ltd.*, the Supreme Court of Canada recently ruled that the correct test for measuring damages is to apply the method that is least profitable to the plaintiff, and least burdensome to the defendant.

Minimizing Your Risk
Prepare To Justify Your Damages

- Keep all records and documents that pertain to losses flowing from contractual breaches.

- Take immediate steps to mitigate your losses.

- Do not expect compensation for damages that are too remote from a breach.

- Ensure that your conduct toward the other party is honest, reasonable, and businesslike.

CASE IN POINT Damages Under Contracts with Alternative Performance Methods

Hamilton v. Open Window Bakery Ltd., 2004 SCC 9

Facts

An agent contracted with a bakery to be its exclusive sales and marketing representative in Japan for a term of 36 months. The contract allowed the bakery to terminate the contract either

1. "without notice … if the Agent acts in a manner which is detrimental to the reputation and well being" of the bakery, or
2. "with notice to the Agent effective after the commencement of the 19th month of the term herein, on three (3) months' notice."

Approximately 16 months into the contract, the bakery sent a letter to the agent terminating the agreement immediately on the basis of allegations that she had deliberately falsified ingredient lists and disclosed confidential information to a competitor. Subsequently, it also sent her another letter in accordance with its right to terminate by giving notice as specified under the second item above.

At trial, the judge found no evidence that the agent had acted dishonestly or fraudulently. The bakery had therefore breached the contract by terminating the contract without giving the appropriate notice. The trial judge awarded the agent damages in an amount reflecting the payments she would have received under the remainder of the 36-month contract, less an allowance of 25 percent to reflect the fact that the bakery could have validly terminated the contract on three months' notice.

Result

The Supreme Court of Canada reduced the damages that the bakery was required to pay. The bakery was liable only for the amount that the agent would have received if the bakery had given notice immediately after the 19th month to terminate the contract at the end of the 22nd month.

The court did not apply the general rule that a non-breaching party is entitled to be restored to the position she would have been in if the contract had been carried out according to its terms. Rather, because the contract allowed for alternative methods of performance, the court applied the rule that the non-breaching party is entitled to be restored only to the position she would have been in had the least beneficial contractual alternative been performed.

Business Lesson

Keep termination provisions as flexible as possible, particularly in long-term contracts. What seems like a great business relationship at the beginning may sour over time.

Remedies Other Than Damages for Breach of Contract

Damages cannot always compensate a party for a breach of contract. In the following sections, we briefly discuss two remedies other than damages: specific performance and injunctions.

SPECIFIC PERFORMANCE

specific performance
requirement by a court that a party complete her obligations under a contract

A court order for **specific performance** of a contract requires that the parties perform a contract in accordance with its terms. For example, consider a contract to sell land that is unique, such as the only commercial property on a popular waterfront. If the seller signs an agreement of purchase and sale, but subsequently changes her mind and refuses to complete the transaction, a court may order her to specifically perform the contract—that is, to sell the buyer the property that she agreed to sell him. If the court orders specific performance of the contract, the seller must complete the transaction and transfer title to the property to the buyer. She may not substitute another property, nor may she pay damages instead of fulfilling her contractual obligations.

INJUNCTIONS

injunction
court order that requires a party to stop doing something specific

An **injunction** is a court order that requires a party not to do something specific. For example, an injunction could order a business to stop using a business name or slogan that is similar to that of a trademark registered to another business.

Injunctions can be useful in the context of breach of employment contracts. Consider an employment contract that contains a clause that prohibits an employee from working for his employer's competitor, or establishing a competitive business, within six months of leaving his job. If the employee breaches this clause by, for example, establishing his own competitive business within five months of leaving his job, the former employer may obtain an injunction requiring the former employee to shut down his business in order to comply with the terms of the contract.

interim injunction
temporary injunction, pending a final hearing; see "injunction"

Depending on the nature of the business, speed in shutting down the competition may be crucial. In most jurisdictions, a court procedure is available to apply for an interlocutory or **interim injunction** (see, for example, rule 40 of the Ontario *Rules of Civil Procedure*). The party seeking the injunction would otherwise have to wait for its case to wind its way to a conclusion through the regular court process. If the following three-part test is met, a court may grant an injunction that can take effect immediately:

1. Is there a serious issue to be tried?
2. Will the party applying for the injunction suffer irreparable harm if the interim injunction is not granted?
3. Which party will suffer the greater harm from granting or refusing an injunction prior to trial?

Minimizing Your Risk

Seek the Remedy That Is Right for You

- Seek damages if monetary compensation is adequate for the losses you have suffered.

- Consider a claim for specific performance if your loss cannot be compensated by money but, rather, by the completion of the original terms of the contract.

- Seek an injunction to stop behaviour that is injurious to your business.

Allegations of violation of a non-solicitation or non-competition clause in an employment contract can lead to the granting of an interim injunction.

Unenforceable Agreements

The great majority of contractual obligations are enforceable. However, in a few limited circumstances, a court or arbitrator (where the parties use private arbitration to resolve the dispute) may relieve a party of the contractual obligations that he has agreed to assume. From a business perspective, it is important to know the factors and conduct that may jeopardize a business transaction. If you can anticipate problems, you can avoid creating them or stumbling into them.

Unenforceable agreements stem from situations in which one party feels that she has been taken advantage of, has been misled, or has otherwise made a bad deal. A party who wants to be relieved of contractual obligations may claim that an agreement is unenforceable in one of two contexts:

1. *Defensively.* A party may raise her objection to the enforceability of an agreement if she is sued for breach of that agreement.
2. *Assertively.* A party may raise her objection to the enforceability of an agreement by asking a court or arbitrator to declare that an agreement is unenforceable, whether or not the agreement has been breached.

If a party is able to make a convincing claim—or to raise a convincing defence—based on any of the circumstances outlined in the following sections, a court or arbitrator may relieve the party of her contractual obligations.

MISREPRESENTATION OF MATERIAL FACT

Did one of the parties make a false statement that persuaded the other party to enter into the deal, and was this statement important to the agreement as a whole? The statement in issue is one made outside of the actual terms of the contract. As a general rule, to render an agreement unenforceable, the **misrepresentation**—or false statement—must be a statement of fact, not opinion, that the deceived party relied on in entering into the agreement.

misrepresentation
false statement of fact

rescind
treat as if the contract were never made

The deceived party need not prove that the other party made the misrepresentation intentionally. However, whether the misrepresentation was made innocently, negligently, or fraudulently may affect the remedies available. For example, if a party misrepresents a material fact because he honestly (but mistakenly) believes it to be true, the party who relied on the statement and entered into a contract because of it is only entitled to **rescind** the contract. This means that a judge will attempt to put the parties back to their original positions. However, this may not always be possible, in which case the party who was deceived by the innocent misrepresentation will bear the loss. However, if the misrepresentation is negligent (for example, where the party who made the misrepresentation

> ## Minimizing Your Risk
> ### Don't Make Factual Representations That Cannot Be Supported
>
> - Be careful what is said both outside and within the express terms of the contract. If a party relies on your untrue or unchecked factual representations, he may be able to rescind the contract or collect damages.
>
> - If a particular fact about a service or product is important to your decision to enter into a contract, get it in writing as an express term of the contract.

failed to do the necessary research to back up the claim) or fraudulent (in other words, intentionally deceptive), the party who relied on the statement and entered into the contract may be entitled to monetary damages as well as an order or rescission.

MISTAKE

Is one of the parties taking advantage of a serious mistake in the contract? Because courts and arbitrators take the enforcement of contracts very seriously, it is difficult for a party to successfully argue that a contract should not be enforced because of a mistake. Parties are expected to read and understand the terms of any agreements they sign. Therefore, a simple oversight or mathematical error is unlikely to render a contract void or unenforceable. However, the doctrine of mistake may apply where the mistake is found to be a fundamental mistake, as in the following case. In *Dyson et al. v. Moser*, Marjorie Moser purchased in interest in a trailer park from George Dyson. The purchase was financed in part by means of a promissory note in the amount of $86,000, which included the following provision:

> … together with interest thereon at the rate of Ten (10%) per cent per annum calculated annually from the 8th day of March, 1978 which shall be payable in regular monthly instalments of Four Hundred Dollars ($400.00) from and including the 8th day of April, 1978 and to continue on the 8th day of each and every month thereafter until the full sum of $86,000 and interest accrued thereon has been fully paid and satisfied.

Mrs. Moser made regular payments on the promissory note from April 1978 until the death of Mr. Dyson in May 2000. She made a further payment of $1,600 on September 5, 2000, following which she met with the executors of Mr. Dyson's estate, his two sons, to discuss settling the amount outstanding on the promissory note. Based on calculations made by Mrs. Moser's accountant and the late George Dyson, it was believed that the outstanding amount was in excess of $20,000. At a meeting on September 7, 2000, Mrs. Moser and George Dyson's son, Norman Dyson, signed the following handwritten document:

> The final total payment agreement on the note between late G.F. Dyson & Marjorie Moser is $24,000 (twenty-four thousand) provided payment is made within 14 days.

> Payment subject to release document prepared by lawyer & signed by both parties.

Mrs. Moser made two further payments of $400 each on October 3, 2000 and November 3, 2000. In late November 2000 she received advice from a different accountant that she had actually overpaid the amount due on the promissory note and refused to make any further payments. Norman and his brother Ross, as representatives of the estate of their father, George Dyson, sued Mrs. Moser, seeking to enforce the September 7, 2000 agreement and claiming judgment of the outstanding $23,200. The key issue was whether a mistake had been made in the calculation of interest on the original promissory note. When the parties signed the September 7, 2000 agreement, both had received and relied on calculations based on interest compounded monthly, rather than annually. The trial judge concluded that interest was to be compounded annually, resulting in an overpayment by Mrs. Moser in the amount of $921.01. The trial judge refused to enforce the September 7, 2000 agreement, applying the doctrine of mistake as follows:

> I am satisfied that, in this case, despite the desire to uphold an apparent contract, there has been a mistake, shared by both parties, relating to the facts as they existed at the time the purported agreement was made which rendered the subject matter of the purported contract essentially and radically different from the subject which the parties believed to exist. If there was, in fact, no indebtedness under a proper construction of the promissory note, rather than a substantial indebtedness as believed by both parties, the subject matter of the proposed contract does become "essentially and radically different" from what was understood to be the case by the parties.

Minimizing Your Risk
Avoid Mistakes

➤ Know what you are signing (including the fine print), proofread the document, and double-check all details.

DURESS, UNDUE INFLUENCE, AND THE UNCONSCIONABLE AGREEMENT

Was one of the parties pressured into making the deal? A party may claim that he was forced to enter into an agreement under **duress**—that is, under threat of physical or serious economic harm. However, in the business-to-business context, financial pressure is more likely to arise than physical threat. This is called economic duress.

duress
pressure to enter into a contract by way of threat of physical or economic harm

Consider a vacation resort that was undergoing renovations on a tight schedule in order to receive booked guests during the busy summer season. What if, midway through the job, the contractor demanded a change to the contract—more money or she would not complete the work? Because of the tight schedule and the threat of not being ready in time for customers, the resort might pay the money. Arguably, this extortionate behaviour by the contractor would amount to economic duress.

A party who claims duress must prove that the pressure exerted exceeded ordinary commercial pressure. A court or arbitrator will not void an agreement unless it is convinced that the threatened party did not freely consent to the terms of the agreement. Economic duress is difficult to prove. It will only be successful if the party claiming that it was under duress can persuade the court that it had no realistic alternative but to submit to the pressure.

Undue influence is similar to duress. A party may claim to be the victim of undue influence if the pressure exerted by the other party deprived him of the ability to exercise his free will when he entered into the agreement.

undue influence
pressure exerted on a weaker party that deprives that party of his ability to exercise his judgment or free will

There is a presumption of undue influence where there is a special relationship between the parties that is unbalanced in terms of power—such as that of lawyer and client or doctor and patient. Undue influence may arise in other relationships, such as employer and employee or husband and wife, but there is no presumption—the weaker party must prove it.

Consider a wrongful dismissal situation, where an employer fires an employee without a good reason and without providing sufficient notice. The employer might pressure the employee to sign a termination agreement, releasing the employer of all liability (and effectively preventing the employee from suing for wrongful dismissal). The employer might offer a small payment in return for signing the agreement, but threaten that the offer expires in an hour. A distraught

Minimizing Your Risk
Don't Be Pressured into a Risky Deal

- If you are unsure about a business opportunity, get a second opinion from a trusted source.

- Seek independent legal advice, and make sure the other party has an opportunity to do likewise.

- If it is your position that you were pressured into an agreement against your will, assert this position at the first opportunity.

- Do not exert undue pressure on a business partner or employee—it may give them an excuse to get out of the deal.

employee, worried about paying his bills and unaware of his entitlement to a much larger sum, might accept this offer. These facts would support an allegation of undue influence.

To avoid allegations of undue influence, businesses can encourage employees to obtain **independent legal advice** before they sign any contract, including an employment agreement, confidentiality agreement, or termination agreement. Be sure to provide sufficient time for employees to consult with their own lawyer before entering into the transaction.

An **unconscionable agreement** is one in which the terms are so unreasonably one-sided that the court will not enforce the agreement. The test for this is strict—a gross inequality of bargaining power or a gross inadequacy of benefit to the weaker party.

CASE IN POINT Unconscionability and Economic Duress

Upper Valley Dodge Chrysler Ltd. v. Cronier (Estate), 2004 CanLII 34431 (ONSC)

Facts
William Morgan, a successful entrepreneur, lent $160,000 to the unsophisticated Cronier family for their small wood-cutting business. The Croniers had substantial debts already. Morgan took a chattel mortgage on equipment worth about $270,000 but also insisted on taking a mortgage on the Cronier family home. The interest rate charged was 14 percent and the Croniers did not receive independent legal advice. They made payments on the debt sporadically. Years later, after the death of Mr. Cronier, Morgan demanded full payment of the loan, which, with accumulated interest, had grown to over $500,000. Issues raised included unconscionability and economic duress.

Result
The court held that the terms of the loan were not unfair. The rate of interest was reasonable in 1988 when the loan was made. Morgan's insistence on taking a mortgage on the family home was not unreasonable; nor was it economic duress, because the Croniers had other creditors, and the equipment could easily have been sold without Morgan's knowledge. The issue of unconscionability must be based upon the nature and terms of the agreement entered into at the time that the agreement was contracted. The Croniers had an opportunity to obtain independent legal advice but chose not to do so. The Croniers did not take any steps to avoid the contract and only claimed economic duress years later when Morgan demanded payment.

Business Lesson
Unconscionability and economic duress are very hard to prove. If you intend to make allegations like these, it is important to do so as soon as possible. Acquiescence to the contract over a period of time will undermine your argument that you were forced into it.

MINORS

Was one of the parties a **minor**—that is, under the age of majority (18 years in Ontario)—when the agreement was entered into? This issue is less likely to arise in a business-to-business context than in a business-to-consumer context. However, all business people should be aware that minors have the option of being excused from most contractual obligations.

If you are dealing with a young entrepreneur, you may wish to confirm her age before signing a contract with her. If she is under the age of majority, be aware of and assess the risk that she may not be required to fulfill her contractual obligations. And do not expect to hold her parents accountable unless they are also parties to the contract or have signed a **guarantee**. A guarantee is an independent contract in which the guarantors (for example, the parents of a minor) agree to assume liability for the financial obligations of another person (for example, their child). If that person (the child) defaults on her obligations under a separate contract, the guarantors (parents) will be obligated to pay the amount owing based on the guarantee.

CAPACITY

Was one of the parties suffering from a mental condition, or was he so impaired by drugs or alcohol that he did not know what he was doing when he entered into an agreement? Persons under the influence of drugs or alcohol, or suffering from a mental condition, may be able to argue that they lacked the capacity—or legal capability—to contract.

Being a minor, as we have seen, is a form of legal incapacity because minors do not have the same obligations as adults when entering into contracts. To escape contractual responsibility, a minor need only prove that he was incapacitated because of his age at the time he entered into an agreement. Proof of incapacity is not so simple for those who attempt to avoid contractual responsibility on the basis of mental impairment or intoxication by drugs or alcohol.

A person suffering from impairment as a result of mental condition, drugs, or alcohol must prove both that she was incapacitated when she entered into the agreement and that the other party was aware of her condition. Impairment claims are essentially claims that one party has taken advantage of the other as a result of a temporary or permanent mental condition.

independent legal advice
legal advice regarding a contract obtained from a different lawyer than the lawyer who drafted the contract

unconscionable agreement
agreement so inequitably one-sided that it is unenforceable

minor
person under the age of majority

guarantee
contract whereby a party assumes responsibility for another party's financial obligations if that other party defaults on payment

Minimizing Your Risk
Consider Capacity Before Signing a Contract
- If in doubt about someone's capacity to contract, ask for proof of age.
- Insist on a guarantee before contracting with a minor.
- Avoid finalizing business transactions at social or other events where alcohol is consumed.

What Can You Do About a Breach of Contract?

If a party breaches a contract to which you are a party, you have several courses of action available to you. You can

- ignore the breach,
- negotiate a compromise that is agreeable to both you and the other party,
- seek alternative dispute resolution services, or
- litigate your differences in court.

We discuss each of these options briefly below.

IGNORE THE BREACH

A breach of contract may have a very minor effect on your business. For example, if a caterer is forced to substitute a menu that is of equal value—but not identical—to the contracted menu, you may be wiser to ignore the breach than to expend time and energy in seeking a remedy. If the breaching party is a business with which you have an ongoing relationship, ignoring a breach may work to the advantage of both of you in the long run. By forgiving a breach on one occasion, your business may be forgiven on another.

NEGOTIATE A COMPROMISE

A breach of contract may cause frustration, perhaps even anger. But as a business person, you must try not to let your emotions interfere with your sound judgment. The most cost-effective and sensible solution to a breach of contract may be to negotiate a resolution with the other party. If possible, work with the other party to understand the reason for the breach and the problems caused by it. Negotiating a reasonable compensation payment may enhance your future relationship with the other party and save everyone money in the long run. Negotiation also allows you to explore creative solutions to the problem and to prevent future breaches.

release
document that absolves the breaching party of liability for any contract-related claims that the non-breaching party might make in the future

Once you have resolved your dispute by way of negotiation, the breaching party should ask the non-breaching party to sign a release. A **release** absolves the breaching party of liability for any contract-related claims that the non-breaching party might make in the future. Alternatively, you can draw up a new contract that revokes the original one and sets out the terms of your new agreement. The purpose of the release or the new contract is to bind you both to your compromise agreement and prevent either of you from altering your newly negotiated position.

USE ALTERNATIVE DISPUTE RESOLUTION (ADR)

The expense and uncertainty of litigation has led to the establishment of the various alternative dispute resolution services that we describe in detail in chapter 2. If negotiations with the other party fail to resolve your dispute, you should consider engaging the services of an independent third party to help settle your differences. Two popular forms of ADR are mediation and arbitration. Mediation, the less formal of the two processes, can assist you by pointing out the strengths and weaknesses of both parties' positions. Mediators are skilled in suggesting mutually beneficial compromises. If you succeed in resolving your dispute through mediation, you will want to ensure that a release is signed for the reasons pointed out above. Arbitration, as we have already discussed, produces a binding result that is enforceable through the courts.

USE LITIGATION

Litigation in the courts has become a prohibitively expensive and time-consuming process. It is, however, an option to consider as a last resort.

Chapter Summary

In this chapter, we began our discussion with an examination of the characteristics and elements of a contract, noting the prevalence of contracts in the business world. Although most contracts need not be in writing, we described the many advantages of written contracts; the most notable is certainty. We also examined various rules by which courts interpret contracts that are imperfectly drafted.

The bulk of the chapter was devoted to an examination of clauses that are commonly found in business contracts, such as disclaimer clauses, indemnity clauses, clauses respecting quality of goods and timing of delivery, venue clauses, and governing law clauses, to name but a few. In each instance, we advised you to take specific steps to minimize your contractual risks by using these clauses wisely and to your advantage.

We then discussed breach of contract and remedies for breach, including damages, specific performance, and injunctions. Next, we discussed unenforceable agreements. We concluded the chapter with a discussion of the courses of action you can take in the event of a breach of contract.

KEY TERMS

breach of contract	frustration	quantum
condition	guarantee	rebuttable
condition precedent	implied term	release
condition subsequent	indemnity clause	rescind
consideration	independent legal advice	revocation
contract	injunction	rules of construction
counteroffer	interim injunction	seal
damages	lapse	specific performance
disclaimer clause	liquidated damages clause	standard form contract
duress	minor	unconscionable agreement
duty to mitigate	misrepresentation	undue influence
economic duress	option agreement	venue
endorsement	parol evidence rule	vicarious performance
exclusion clause	presumption	void
express term	privity of contract	warranty
force majeure	promissory estoppel	

REFERENCES

32262 B.C. Ltd. v. See-Rite Optical Ltd., [1998] 9 WWR 442 (Alta. CA).

Arbitration Act, 1991, SO 1991, c. 17.

Arens v. MSA Ford Sales Ltd., 2002 BCCA 509.

Carr v. Killam, 2005 NBQB 260.

Dhillon v. City of Coquitlam, 2004 BCSC 924.

Dryburgh v. Oak Bay Marina (1992) Ltd., 2001 FCT 671.

Dyson et al. v. Moser, 2003 BCSC 1720.

Electronic Commerce Act, 2000, SO 2000, c. 17.

Hamilton v. Open Window Bakery Ltd., 2004 SCC 9.

Hadley v. Baxendale (1854), 9 Ex. 341, 156 ER 145.

KPMG Inc. v. Canadian Imperial Bank of Commerce, 1998 CanLII 1908 (ONCA).

London Drugs Ltd. v. Kuehne & Nagel International Ltd., [1992] 3 SCR 299.

Macatula v. Tessier, 2003 MBCA 31.

MJM Custom Fabrications Inc. v. Big Drum Inc., 205 CanLII 34584 (ONSC).

Nickel Developments Ltd. v. Canada Safeway Ltd., 2001 MBCA 79; (2001), 199 DLR (4th) 629.

Potvin v. Canadian Museum of Nature, 2001 CanLII 6709 (ONSC).

Sale of Goods Act, RSO 1990, c. S.1, as amended.

Upper Valley Dodge Chrysler Ltd. v. Cronier (Estate), 2004 CanLII 34431 (ONSC).

Whiten v. Pilot Insurance Co., [2002] 1 SCR 595.

REVIEW AND DISCUSSION

True or False?

___T___ 1. Family members who enter into business agreements with one another may have difficulty proving they intended the agreement to be legally binding.

___F___ 2. If an offer specifies that it must be accepted by fax before a certain deadline, your acceptance by email message before the deadline will result in a legally binding contract.

___F___ 3. Your business is running into financial difficulties and you persuade one of your customers to pay more for your marketing research services than the original contract specified. If your customer changes his mind and refuses to pay the additional amount, you would likely be successful if you sued him for breach of contract.

___F___ 4. When you pay cash for toothpaste at the local corner store and do not receive a receipt from the vendor, the transaction is not a legally binding contract.

___F___ 5. Your business purchases a new computer. A week later you see the same model at a different store at a significantly lower price and realize you paid too much. If you attempt to return the computer to the store where you bought it, the store must refund your money.

_____ **6.** Contract law presumes that business people understand that their promises to one another will be enforced by courts and tribunals.

_____ **7.** It is possible for a business to prove that it did not intend a promise to be legally binding.

_____ **8.** If you shake hands on the essential terms of a business transaction, it will not be legally binding until a contract is written up and signed by the parties.

_____ **9.** A business should always refuse to deal with businesses that do not put their agreements in writing.

_____ **10.** If an essential term of a contract is not precise, resulting in a contractual dispute that ends up in court, the plaintiff's subjective interpretation of the term will prevail.

_____ **11.** Standard form contracts are one-sided and will not be enforced by the courts.

Multiple Choice

The questions below are based on the following facts:

Toronto Organic Foods Wholesale Distributors Ltd. (TOFWD) distributes organic fruits and vegetables and other organic products to several stores in Toronto. On September 1, TOFWD entered into a one-year contract with "Organics for You" (Organics), an upscale specialty food shop. The contract was negotiated by TOFWD's president, Anton, and Ying Li, Organics' sales manager. Under the terms of the contract, TOFWD is to supply a minimum weekly quantity of products to Organics. TOFWD is to deliver 2 cases each of 7 varieties of organic fruits and vegetables, 2 cases each of 2 types of packaged organic pasta, and 2 cases of pasta sauce, for a total of 20 cases of goods (the "quota"), to Organics on the first day of every week. Organics owes TOFWD $500 for each weekly shipment, payable within 14 days of delivery. If Organics wants to add more cases, or to order fewer cases than the regularly scheduled quota, it must provide TOFWD with notice of the change at least two business days before the scheduled delivery date.

1. Who are the proper parties to the contract?
   a. Anton and Ying Li
   b. Anton and Organics for You
   c. TOFWD and Ying Li
   d. TOFWD and Organics for You
   e. the presidents of the two companies

2. In order for the contract to be legally enforceable,
   a. it must be in writing
   b. it must be made under seal
   c. it must be complete
   d. one of the parties must take legal proceedings against the other
   e. all of the above

3. The contract between TOFWD and Organics is legally enforceable because the terms agreed upon in the contract include

    a.   agreement by one party to do or not do something
    b.   agreement by both parties to do or not do something
    c.   agreement by one party to pay money to the other
    d.   agreement by both parties to pay money to each other
    e.   none of the above

4. If the contract is TOFWD's standard form contract, and Organics for You later wishes to get out of it, a court or tribunal will generally

    a.   rule in favour of Organics and allow it to get out of the contract
    b.   enforce the contract
    c.   review the relevant federal legislation to see if the contract is enforceable
    d.   change the terms of the contract to make them fair
    e.   none of the above

5. Below are a number of additional terms or clauses contained in the contract between TOFWD and Organics. Select which of the following categories best describes each term or clause:

A—condition precedent
B—entire agreement clause
C—disclaimer or limitation of liability clause
D—liquidated damages clause
E—none of the above

    a.   "This contract will automatically terminate in the event that Organics orders less than the quota for four consecutive weeks."
    b.   "If TOFWD fails to deliver the weekly supply of products to Organics on or before the first day of each week, TOFWD shall pay Organics $100 for each day that the delivery is late."
    c.   "TOFWD shall not be liable to Organics in respect of any losses, damages, costs, or claims resulting from circumstances that are not within the control of TOFWD."
    d.   "This is the entire agreement between the parties, covering everything agreed or understood in connection with the subject matter of this transaction. No oral promises, conditions, warranties, representations, understandings, or interpretations were relied on by either party in order to execute this contract."
     e.   "Except as otherwise provided in this contract, TOFWD's liability shall include all damages proximately caused by the breach of any condition or warranty in this contract, or negligent conduct on the part of TOFWD, but such liability shall in no event include any indirect, incidental, or consequential damages, including any loss of profit."
    f.   "Weekly shipment price = $500*
         * Price is set on a sliding scale and will be automatically adjusted to reflect fluctuations exceeding 10 percent in costs associated with delivering the product."

The next three questions are based on the following additional facts:

TOFWD employs Sam on a part-time basis to assist with deliveries. On October 3, Sam accompanies the company president, Anton, for the weekly delivery of 20 cases of organic foods to Organics. Sam and Anton arrive at Organics at approximately 4:30 p.m. The products are unloaded into a storeroom at the back of the store. Sam inadvertently stacks the cases too high and they tip over, knocking over a nearby 10-gallon drum of organic cooking oil that spills onto the floor of the storeroom and seeps into the rest of the store, creating a slippery mess. Organics is forced to close down for the remainder of the day while the spill is cleaned up. The cost of the cleanup and replacement of products damaged by the oil is $1,200. In addition, Organics estimates that it lost $1,500 in profits because it was closed during its busiest time of the day.

6. If Organics sues TOFWD and Sam for breach of contract as a result of this incident, which of the following statements is true?
   a. TOFWD will not be liable for Sam's mistake.
   b. TOFWD's liability for Sam's mistake will be limited to $500.
   c. TOFWD's liability for Sam's mistake will be limited to $1,200.
   d. Sam will not be liable for his mistake.
   e. None of the above.

7. If Organics wishes to obtain compensation from TOFWD and Sam for breach of contract as a result of this incident, which of the following statements best describes the most cost-efficient route for Organics to pursue?
   a. Organics should negotiate a settlement directly with TOFWD.
   b. Organics should proceed by way of arbitration.
   c. Organics should proceed by way of mediation.
   d. Organics should proceed by way of Small Claims Court.
   e. Any of the above.

8. Organics' decision to sue TOFWD for breach of the contract may be affected by
   a. the amount of money in dispute
   b. the impact of suing on the reputation of Organics
   c. the possibility of getting the stock from a different supplier
   d. the price of the stock from another supplier
   e. all of the above

Short Answer

1. Your business is running into financial difficulties and you persuade one of your customers to pay more for your marketing research services than the original contract specified. If your customer changes her mind and refuses to pay the additional amount, what can you do?

2. Why is it important to uphold the integrity of contractual agreements?

3. Why is it important for business people to know about contract law?

4. You work for a company that manufactures a specialty line of commercial shelving suitable for retail displays. Your manufacturing costs have been rising steadily, and you have been negotiating with a new supplier for a key

component of the shelving units. The supplier's latest offer is to supply the component for a reasonable, fixed price if your company commits to a minimum monthly purchase for a period of 12 months.

   a. What are the risks associated with taking time to consider the offer before accepting it?

   b. What can your business do to ensure that the offer remains open while you take time to consider whether to accept the offer?

   c. What happens if your company responds by agreeing to a six-month commitment?

   d. If the supplier specifies a deadline for acceptance, can she cancel the offer ahead of time? *Yes, but before acceptance*

   e. If the supplier specifies a deadline for acceptance, can you accept the offer after the deadline expires? *No, but can present counteroffer*

   f. If the supplier has made the same offer to both your company and one of your competitors, at the same time, what risks does she run? *undersupply making cx unhappy*

5. Your business enters into a contract for the delivery of a shipment of toys from Asia. When they are delivered, you discover that they are counterfeit goods.

   a. If the goods have been paid for, what can you do to get your money back? *crt can't enforce contract (it's illegal) → just try to negotiate*

   b. If you have attempted to deliver the goods to local toy stores, and they refuse to accept delivery and pay for the goods, will a court make them pay or award damages to your business? *no (it's illegal)*

6. What are some examples of situations where a court will imply a missing term into a contract? *interest on ovrdue debts (?)*

7. What might constitute a breach of contract? *p.118*

8. Explain the remedies available if a breach of contract involves a condition versus a warranty. *p.119*

9. What is the obligation of a non-breaching party to mitigate its damages? *p.121*

10. What courses of action are available to a business when the other party to a contract breaches it? *p.132*

Discussion and Debate

George is an entrepreneur who works in the sex trade. Like his colleagues, he works hard to earn a living. Since he does not ply his trade in a brothel or with minors and since he does not violate other relevant laws, George's actual labour is legal in Canada. As a society, however, we tend not to enforce the business contracts that George and his colleagues make with their clients. If one of George's clients refuses to pay him for his services, should George—like other business people—be able to take the client to court? Give reasons for your answer.

The Sale of Goods and Consumer Protection Law

LEARNING OBJECTIVES

After reading this chapter, you should be able to:

- Explain the effect of the *Sale of Goods Act* on conditions and warranties, passage of title, and remedies for breach of contracts.

- Comment on the effects of e-commerce on recent legal developments.

- Understand consumers' rights under the *Consumer Protection Act, 2002* to truthful and timely information about products and services.

- Describe unfair practices under the *Consumer Protection Act, 2002* and comment on the penalties imposed on businesses that engage in them.

- Identify anti-competitive trade practices and misleading marketing techniques that are prohibited by the federal *Competition Act*.

- Describe the roles played by the *Food and Drugs Act* and the *Consumer Packaging and Labelling Act* in protecting the safety of consumers.

- Explain the effect of the *Personal Information Protection and Electronic Documents Act* on a business's responsibility to treat consumers' personal information confidentially.

What Are Sale of Goods and Consumer Protection Laws?

Sale of goods law governs the buying and selling of tangible objects and products; it is chiefly statutory and in Ontario is contained in the *Sale of Goods Act*. Consumer protection law is much broader in scope than sale of goods law. It applies to services as well as to goods, and it also affects areas such as consumer safety, information, and privacy. Consumer protection law is also statutory for the most part. It, however, is contained in various statutes and regulations passed by the provinces and territories, as well as the federal government.

Codified—or statutory—laws regarding the sale of goods are significantly older than the more specialized statutes that protect consumers today. Both consumer protection and sale of goods laws, however, can be viewed as compassionate updates of the Latin maxim *caveat emptor*. **Caveat emptor**, which roughly translates to "buyer beware" or "let the buyer take care of himself," is an expression of the philosophy that dominated the early common law of the marketplace. Under this law, which was based on the law of contract, buyers and sellers were expected to conduct whatever investigations were appropriate and to include whatever contractual terms were necessary to protect their interests. Oversights naturally led to inequities, and courts, reluctant to allow inequity to prevail, began to chip away at the strict doctrine of *caveat emptor*.

In Ontario, the *Sale of Goods Act* is the principal statute that governs commercial sales transactions. It is based on 19th-century British legislation that codifies the early mellowing of the common law respecting the rights of buyers and sellers. It is applicable to business-to-business sales, as well as to transactions that involve consumers. The Act by no means provides the comprehensive protection provided to consumers under the *Consumer Protection Act, 2002*. This recent statute, unlike the *Sale of Goods Act*, applies to services as well as products, and does not apply to business-to-business transactions. It operates principally by empowering consumers: adding to the rights they already have under the *Sale of Goods Act* and allowing them to seek remedies directly from businesses that have offended or cheated them. The *Consumer Protection Act, 2002* also empowers the state to exact heavy penalties against businesses that fail to respect consumers' rights.

The federal government has enacted a great deal of legislation to protect the rights and safety of consumers. The *Competition Act* restricts, monitors, and penalizes anti-competitive business tactics and dishonest marketing. Rather than empowering consumers directly, the Act protects their interests primarily by means of state intervention: either through the operations of the federal Competition Bureau and Competition Tribunal, or through prosecution in the criminal courts.

In addition to protecting the interests of consumers in the business arena, the federal government monitors consumer safety with the *Food and Drugs Act* and the *Consumer Packaging and Labelling Act*. The most recent federal contribution in the field of consumers' rights is the *Personal Information Protection and Electronic Documents Act*. This statute protects personal and sensitive information about consumers by requiring businesses to comply with rules and procedures regarding the collection, use, and disclosure of this material.

With the relatively recent advent of e-commerce—that is, business conducted over the Internet—federal and provincial governments have been passing legislation to address the new risks and challenges. Ontario, for example, has added the *Electronic Commerce Act, 2000* to the list of statutes that business people must be aware of in order to confidently buy and sell goods over the Internet. As a business person, it is necessary for you to become familiar with these laws in order to deal with the many situations that arise when buying and selling products and services and in dealing with consumers. Consider the following examples, each of which is resolvable by reference to one or several of the statutes that we have mentioned in the preceding paragraphs.

- You sell fish, which you buy from a wholesaler, to the public at a stand in a market. You offer friendly service, have low prices, and advertise widely, so you have many customers. Lately, you have had trouble getting non-farmed

---

caveat emptor
Latin maxim that translates roughly to "buyer beware"

trout. You suspect that your competitors, through the wholesaler, may be trying to squeeze you out of business because you pose a competitive threat. Where do you turn for help?

- You want to run a business through a website on the Internet selling cookbooks to consumers. You have heard that you must take particular care in providing your customers with information about your products as well as your business. Where do you look for guidance?

- The company you work for is about to market a revolutionary anti-balding cream. Your cousin, an actor and minor celebrity, has agreed to help with the advertising campaign. Although your cousin has never tried the cream, he is willing to go on television and tell the public how effective it is. What should your marketing department do?

The Importance of Sale of Goods and Consumer Protection Law for Business People

The purchase and sale of goods and services is the essence of modern commerce. It is impossible to imagine a business that will not be involved in these activities many times during its existence. Because consumerism is so essential to the contemporary economy, the law in this area will continue to evolve, and it is important for business people to keep pace with it. Knowledge of this area of law will be of particular assistance to you in the following ways:

- *Sale of goods law can assist commercial parties in negotiating deals and resolving disputes.* Contractual terms that the *Sale of Goods Act* implies into contracts concerning the quality of goods and the passage of ownership responsibilities provide a background against which parties can negotiate commercial sales. These statutory terms are imposed by law, only in contracts involving consumers. Businesses entering contracts with other businesses can choose to waive these terms; however, the terms can provide a default solution for parties who are otherwise unable to reach an agreement.

- *Laws governing competition in the marketplace leave room for innovation and initiative by new businesses.* Competition laws, which protect consumers by eliminating business practices that are designed to restrict trade, also protect young businesses by allowing them to compete for their share of a market that is free of monopoly. By knowing the laws that govern fair competition, you can bring businesses that compete unfairly to the attention of the appropriate authorities, and thus create room for your own growing enterprise.

- *By conforming to laws that protect consumers, you contribute to the health of your business.* Laws that enforce fair and open dealings, require services to match promises, and protect vulnerable people from exploitation are codifications of good business practice and attract a loyal customer base.

- *By conforming to laws that protect consumer health and safety, you promote your business's reputation as a good citizen.* Clean water and safe food, safe drugs and other chemical products properly labelled—all contribute to your positive reputation.

The Sale of Goods Act

The Ontario *Sale of Goods Act* is one of many pieces of legislation that codifies the common law that governed the sale of goods in late 19th-century Britain. Similar statutes have been adopted throughout much of the common-law world, including Canada, Pakistan, Hong Kong, New Zealand, and Australia. This law has even found its way into the US *Uniform Commercial Code*. The Ontario *Sale of Goods Act* applies not only to sales involving consumers but also to business-to-business sales transactions. In fact, the most common application of the Act is in the business arena.

It is important to remember that a contract for the sale of goods remains a contract, and therefore all of the ordinary rules of contract law apply, except where they are modified by the *Sale of Goods Act*. The Act defines a "contract of sale of goods" as "a contract whereby the seller transfers or agrees to transfer the property in the goods to the buyer for a money consideration, called the price." The goods either may exist in the present, such as merchandise on a store shelf, or may be expected to exist in the future, such as merchandise that is currently being manufactured for future sale.

APPLICATION OF THE ACT

The *Sale of Goods Act* applies only to tangible personal property—that is, goods that you can actually touch, such as automobiles, MP3 players, or heads of lettuce. The Act does not apply to goods that represent monetary worth—such as stocks, bonds, or currency—unless they are collected for their aesthetic or historical, rather than their financial, value. Further, the Act applies only to goods, and not to the services that may be delivered along with them.

If a buyer purchases something that is a mixture of goods and services, the *Sale of Goods Act* applies only if the contract is primarily for goods. For example, it would not apply to the receipt of a permanent wave service at a hairdressing business, because the consumer's contract with the hairdresser is for the purchase of work and materials, not merely for the sale of the chemicals that the hairdresser uses in the process, and the services and goods cannot be separated for practical purposes. The contract is therefore not covered by the Act. A further limitation is that the Act applies only to contracts in which goods are exchanged for money. It does not apply when goods are traded for other goods or services, as they are in a barter transaction.

The Act applies automatically to *all* sales of goods involving consumers. It also applies to sales between businesses unless the parties to the contract specifically exclude the Act. Any contract that attempts to exclude the operation of the Act must do so clearly, as demonstrated in *Gregorio v. Intrans-Corp.*

CONDITIONS AND WARRANTIES

The conditions and warranties that the *Sale of Goods Act* implies into contracts significantly soften the harsh doctrine of *caveat emptor*. These conditions and warranties are contractual terms specifically designed to keep commercial dealings fair

CASE IN POINT   When Contracting Out of the Sale of Goods Act, Make Your Intentions Clear

Gregorio v. Intrans-Corp., 1994 CanLII 2241 (ONCA)

Facts

The purchaser bought a truck from a dealer for $100,000. From the time he bought it until he sold it seven years later, the truck had serious problems with excessive vibration and misalignment of the frame. The problems forced the purchaser to repeatedly spend money on repairs and to lose trucking income when the truck was in the shop.

The trial judge found that the truck's performance fell short of the purchaser's reasonable expectations and imposed liability on the dealer under the *Sale of Goods Act*.

The dealer argued that it was not responsible for economic loss (lost trucking income), because there was a clause in the written warranty, signed by the purchaser, waiving responsibility for this type of loss. However, the dealer did not bring this clause to the purchaser's attention until after the contract was made.

Result

The Ontario Court of Appeal upheld the trial judge's decision. The dealer could not rely on the waiver clause. The court agreed with earlier case law that stated that a seller cannot rely on a waiver clause unless the seller makes reasonable efforts to bring the clause to the attention of the buyer before or at the time of the making of the contract. The dealer did nothing to bring the clause to the purchaser's attention until four days after he picked up the truck and five days after he signed the contract. The dealer was liable for the purchaser's economic loss.

Business Lesson

If you are a seller who wants to contract out of the *Sale of Goods Act*, do so explicitly and clearly, bringing all waivers to the buyer's attention before the contract is signed and performed.

and honest. In general, a condition is a major contractual term; a warranty is a minor contractual term, although some warranties are extremely significant. The distinction between implied conditions and implied warranties is the same as the distinction between express conditions and express warranties (those written into the contract by the parties)—the breach of a condition brings the contract to an end, and the breach of a warranty does not. A seller's breach of an implied condition in a contract for the sale of goods allows the buyer to reject the goods and ignore all further contractual obligations. (We discuss conditions and warranties in detail in chapter 4 under the heading "Breach of Condition or Breach of Warranty?")

Implied Conditions

The major conditions implied into contracts by the *Sale of Goods Act* are the following:

- The seller has the right to sell the goods.
- Any goods sold by description will match the description by which they are sold.
- The goods are fit for the purpose for which the buyer purchases them if the seller is aware of the buyer's purpose.
- Any goods sold by description are of merchantable quality.
- Any goods sold by sample will match the sample by which they are sold.

We examine each of these conditions below.

Right To Sell

Section 13(a) of the Act sets out the implied condition that the seller has the right to sell the goods. The goods must be owned by the seller or will be owned by the seller at a future time, when the seller will be able to transfer ownership in the goods to the buyer. Should the goods turn out to be stolen, the seller has no right to sell them and would therefore be in breach of this implied condition.

Sale by Description

Section 14 of the *Sale of Goods Act* requires goods sold by description to match the description by which they are sold. For example, a buyer who orders goods from a catalogue is entitled to receive the same goods that he ordered, not others of similar quality. This implied condition is also applicable where a buyer specifically picks out an item. For example, if a buyer comes to the pet store where you work, views a tank full of fish, and declares he wants "that one," he is entitled to receive the specific fish he agreed to purchase.

Fitness for Purpose

Section 15 requires that if a buyer makes her purpose in buying certain goods known to the seller—either expressly or by implication—and shows that she is relying on the seller's skill or judgment, the goods must be reasonably fit for the buyer's purpose. It is unnecessary for a buyer to inform a seller of her purpose if she intends to use the goods for their ordinary purpose. For example, if a customer asks a retailer to recommend a good umbrella, she is relying on the retailer's knowledge to acquire a reliable device to shield her from the rain. If the retailer sells her a parasol, which is good for shading her from the sun but collapses in the rain, the retailer has breached the implied condition of fitness for purpose.

merchantable quality
quality sufficiently high to allow goods to be placed for sale as they are, without the need for repairs or other intervention

Merchantable Quality

Section 15 of the Act also requires goods sold by description to be of **merchantable quality**—that is, of reasonable quality, taking into account their price. For example, if a customer relies on a grocer's sign that says "farm-fresh milk," pays a premium price, and later discovers that the milk is sour, the grocer has breached the implied condition of merchantable quality.

Merchantability covers goods, packaging, and labelling. Assume, for example, that the goods consist of dolls packed in cardboard boxes with clear plastic display windows. If, when the shipment arrives, the dolls are undamaged but the plastic windows have been pierced or ripped during shipping, the goods are not of merchantable quality. However, the seller is not liable to the buyer for reasonably discoverable defects if the buyer actually inspects the goods before sale and accepts them. If, for example, a buyer examines and purchases a shipment of lumber that, at a quick glance, clearly has noticeable knots in the wood on many boards, the buyer cannot later reject the load based on these defects.

Sale by Sample

Section 16(2) of the Act requires goods sold by sample to match the sample. For example, a buyer may come to a seller's studio and order a jacket "just like the one on display." To comply with the requirements of the *Sale of Goods Act*, the jacket delivered to the buyer must match the sample that the seller showed him. A buyer must be allowed a reasonable opportunity to compare any delivered goods with the sample that prompted the sale. Again, the seller bears no liability for reasonably discoverable defects, such as seams that are carelessly finished, if the buyer accepts the goods after inspecting them.

Implied Warranties

There are only two implied warranties under the *Sale of Goods Act*: that the buyer will enjoy quiet possession of the goods and that the goods are free of encumbrances.

Quiet Possession of Goods

Section 13(b) of the Act states that the buyer is entitled to "have and enjoy quiet possession of the goods." This means that a buyer is entitled to use the goods she has bought without interference from third parties who might claim an interest in them. This provision has rarely been the subject of an action for damages.

Goods Free of Encumbrances

Section 13(c) of the Act creates the implied warranty that the goods are sold free of "any charge or encumbrance in favour of any third party, not declared or known to the buyer before or at the time when the contract is made." If, for example, a buyer purchases a tractor from a seller who fails to inform her that the tractor is subject to a lien, the seller is in breach of the implied warranty that the tractor is free of encumbrances.

> **Minimizing Your Risk**
>
> **Comply with or Exclude Implied Conditions and Warranties Where Business-to-Business Sale**
>
> - Determine whether there are any implied conditions or warranties that you wish to exclude from your sales transaction.
> - Negotiate their exclusion accordingly.
> - Meet all implied conditions and warranties unless you specifically exclude them from your contract in the clearest possible terms.

TRANSFERRING THE RIGHTS AND RESPONSIBILITIES OF OWNERSHIP

In addition to implying conditions and warranties into contracts for the purchase and sale of goods, the *Sale of Goods Act* also provides rules regarding the passage of the rights and responsibilities of ownership of these goods. Anyone who has **title** to property—such as cars, desks, and computers—has ownership rights in that property. Ownership rights allow a business to sell, lease, give, possess, or dispose of its property in any manner authorized by law. A contract of sale is an agreement to transfer these ownership rights.

The physical transfer of property does not necessarily transfer ownership. For example, a consumer may purchase a car from a dealership, paying for it in full and thereby gaining title to it under a contract of sale. However, the customer may choose to leave the car with the dealership until the dealer outfits it with, for example, the spotted velour upholstery that the customer requires.

Why is it important to pinpoint the moment when title to goods passes from a seller to a buyer? Transfer of title determines transfer of risk and responsibility for loss. Thus, if the risk of loss in a sale of lumber has passed to a buyer, the buyer bears responsibility for the loss that occurs when the warehouse in which the lumber is stored burns down. If risk has not yet passed to the buyer, the seller bears the responsibility for the loss. If the goods are insured, transfer of title—and therefore of risk—determines whether the buyer's or the seller's insurance will pay for the goods.

Section 19 of the *Sale of Goods Act* codifies five rules that determine when title to goods—and therefore rights and responsibilities of ownership—pass from seller to buyer. Commercial buyers and sellers may choose to stipulate other terms for passage of title. However, if no contrary intention appears to exist in the contract, the following five rules apply.

Rule 1: Transfer of Specific Goods in Deliverable State

When there is an unconditional sale of specific goods in a deliverable state, title passes to the buyer when the contract is made. It is irrelevant whether the time of payment or the time of delivery is postponed. **Specific goods** are goods that are identified and agreed upon at the time the contract is made. A **deliverable state** is a state in which the goods are ready to go. Nothing further needs to be done; for example, there is no need for finishing, weighing, or packaging.

Therefore, if a consumer inspects and agrees to buy your entire stock of spotted velour upholstery, and you immediately move the upholstery to the loading docks for shipping, title passes to the consumer as soon as the contract is concluded. It is irrelevant that the consumer is not contractually obliged to pay for the upholstery immediately or that you are required to deliver it at a later time.

Rule 2: Goods Must Be Put in Deliverable State

When a contract for the sale of specific goods requires the seller to do something to the goods to put them in a deliverable state, title does not pass until that thing is done and the buyer receives notice that it has been done.

This rule covers situations in which the seller is contractually obliged to alter goods in order to make them deliverable—such as paint them, add options to them, or package them. Therefore, if a consumer agrees to buy a cabinet once it is varnished, title passes as soon as the cabinet is varnished and the consumer has been notified that the cabinet is varnished.

Rule 3: Seller Must Do Something To Ascertain Price

When a contract for the sale of specific goods in a deliverable state requires a seller to weigh, measure, test, or perform another act to ascertain the price of the goods, title does not pass until the act is performed and the buyer has notice that it has been performed.

This rule covers situations in which goods are already in a deliverable state, and a contract of sale requires a seller to perform an act that quantifies or qualifies the goods. For example, if a business person agrees to buy all the whole wheat flour in a warehouse after the seller weighs it to determine the price and tests it for purity, title to the flour passes only after the seller has weighed and tested it and the business person has been notified that these acts have been completed.

Rule 4: Goods on Approval

Furniture and rugs are among the commodities often sold on approval. When a seller delivers goods to a buyer on approval, property passes to the buyer

- when the buyer signifies approval or acceptance, or otherwise adopts the transaction (for example, the buyer tells the seller she is keeping the carpet);
- when the time fixed for return of the goods passes and the buyer keeps the goods, without giving notice of rejection (for example, the sales contract calls for an approval term of 30 days, and this time passes without comment from the buyer); or
- when a reasonable time for the return of the goods passes, the contract contains no fixed time for returning the goods, and the buyer keeps the goods, without giving notice of rejection (for example, the sales contract contains no specified term for approval, but a reasonable 30-day term lapses without comment from the buyer).

If a buyer purchases a carpet for her office, for example, and takes it with her "on approval," title passes to the buyer in any of the following circumstances:

- she tells the seller she is keeping the carpet;
- the sales contract calls for an approval term of, say, 30 days, and this time passes without comment from the buyer; or
- the sales contract contains no specified term for approval, but a reasonable 30-day term lapses without comment from the buyer.

Rule 5: Unascertained Goods

In a contract that calls for the sale of unascertained or future goods by description, title to the goods passes to the buyer once the goods are unconditionally acquired

unascertained goods
goods that are not yet separated from the stock of the seller and set aside for a particular buyer

future goods
goods that have not yet come into being at the time a contract is made, such as an agricultural crop, or goods that have not yet been manufactured

in a deliverable state—either by the seller with the acceptance of the buyer, or by the buyer with the acceptance of the seller. Acceptance may be expressed or implied and may be given either before or after the goods are acquired.

Unlike the other rules, which cover agreements to buy and sell specific goods, rule 5 deals with agreements to buy and sell unascertained goods or future goods—that is, goods to be delivered at a future date. **Unascertained goods** are goods that are not yet set aside and identifiable as the subject of the contract at the time the contract is made. For example, a warehouse may be full of sugar in 50-kilogram sacks. The sugar is unascertained until the seller sets aside the sugar for delivery to the buyer by, for example, putting it in a separate part of the warehouse for later delivery to the buyer. **Future goods** are goods that are not yet made by a factory or a craftsperson, such as custom-made shoes or clothing.

REMEDIES AVAILABLE TO THE BUYER

If a seller breaches a condition of a contract of sale—regardless of whether the condition is implied by statute or expressed in the contract—the buyer may be entitled to repudiate the contract, as we explained above under the heading "Remedies for Breach of Implied Conditions and Warranties." The buyer has the right to refuse payment for the goods, or if he has already paid the seller, he can recover his money from the seller. If a seller breaches a warranty, either one that is expressed in the contract or one that is implied by statute, the buyer's only remedy is damages.

If the seller fails to deliver the goods, the buyer can buy the goods elsewhere—if this is possible—and sue the seller for the difference between the contract price and the price that the buyer actually had to pay. For example, if Ahmed agreed to purchase 10,000 back-scratchers at $1.00 each from D'Arcy, and D'Arcy failed to deliver them, Ahmed may purchase comparable back-scratchers from Nancy. If Nancy charges $1.20 each, Ahmed may sue D'Arcy for $2,000.00 (additional $0.20 per back-scratcher × 10,000 back-scratchers purchased).

A small variance in the quantity of goods delivered will not likely amount to a breach of a contract of sale, unless the contract specifically states otherwise. However, if the seller delivers a quantity that is materially less than the buyer agreed to purchase, the buyer may reject the whole shipment, or she may complete the transaction at the contract rate (see s. 29(1)). For example, if a buyer agrees to purchase 10,000 pairs of shoes for a total purchase price of $33,595.00, but the seller only delivers 9,876 pairs of shoes, the buyer has an option: she may either reject the entire delivery, or she may purchase the number of shoes delivered at the contract rate ($33,595.00 ÷ 10,000 = $3.3595 per pair) for a total of $33,178.42 (9,876 pairs × $3.3595 per pair). Section 29(2) of the *Sale of Goods Act* also deals with the situation in which a seller delivers a greater quantity to the buyer than she ordered. In this case the buyer has three options: reject the entire delivery, accept what she contracted to buy (10,000 pairs of shoes in our example) and reject the excess, or accept the entire order. If she chooses to accept the entire order, she will pay for the shoes at the contract rate.

Although section 50 of the Act allows for the remedy of specific performance, courts are reluctant to use it. If specific performance is ordered, a seller is required to deliver and a buyer is required to pay for goods in accordance with the terms of the contract of sale. (We discuss this remedy in chapter 4 under the heading "Specific Performance.") This remedy is usually reserved for goods that are antiques, works of art, or other unique objects whose loss cannot be compensated for by damages.

REMEDIES AVAILABLE TO THE SELLER

Because sales are contract-based transactions, the parties to a sale have at their disposal the usual common-law contract remedies of damages, repudiation, and specific performance in the event of a breach of contract. The *Sale of Goods Act* also creates further protections for buyers and sellers. For sellers, these take the form of special remedies, including an action for the sale price, a **seller's lien**, and stoppage in transit.

seller's lien
security interest under the *Sale of Goods Act* that allows a seller to keep and resell goods to discharge an insolvent buyer's debt

While these remedies were very important at one time, they are rarely used now. Modern banking practices—which allow a seller to require assurances of a buyer's solvency before dealing with the buyer—and modern rules with respect to security interests in goods have made reliance on these remedies nearly obsolete in today's commercial world. We discuss modern banking and security interests at length in chapter 9.

LIMITS ON THE PROTECTION OFFERED BY THE SALE OF GOODS ACT

The *Sale of Goods Act*, as we have noted, is applicable only to the sale of tangible goods, not to the sale of land, the sale of services, or to any barter transaction. Because its purpose is to protect contracting parties only, the Act offers retail customers no protection from breach of warranties by the manufacturers of goods.

Over the years, legislatures have recognized the need to provide more comprehensive protections for consumers than the *Sale of Goods Act* affords. Although the Act arguably provides adequate protection for commercial buyers and sellers, who are relatively sophisticated in their knowledge of the pitfalls of commerce, consumers are thought to require additional safeguards. Therefore, both provincial legislatures and the Parliament of Canada have responded with statutes designed, in various ways, to protect the interests of the consuming public. We explore these statutes following a brief discussion of e-commerce.

E-Commerce

The ability to transact business over the Internet—that is, to participate in e-commerce (electronic commerce)—is a tremendous and relatively recent development. E-commerce brings together buyers and sellers from all over the world and provides unprecedented opportunities for the exchange of goods, services, and ideas.

Traditional contract law applies to Internet transactions. However, the Internet also introduces numerous new issues and risks. Some of these risks are being addressed with legislation, such as the federal *Personal Information Protection and Electronic Documents Act* (PIPEDA, which we return to later in this chapter), the Ontario *Consumer Protection Act, 2002*, and the Ontario *Electronic Commerce Act, 2000* (ECA). However, the law governing e-commerce is currently in a state of flux as businesses, consumers, citizens, and governments negotiate the rules of this new game.

As a business person, if you are engaged in e-commerce, you may find that some of the following matters are of concern to you:

- the authenticity of electronic documents and signatures, and whether these signatures are binding;
- the place to resolve a dispute when the parties to a contract are from different regions;
- the laws that apply when contracting parties from different countries, with different laws, are involved;
- the time that the contract is created; and
- the people who have access to your personal information and credit card number.

Authenticity of Documents and Electronic Signatures

As we noted in chapter 4, there is no legal necessity that a contract be in writing to be enforceable; however, a written agreement certainly makes the existence of a contract and its specifics much easier to prove. How can you achieve contractual certainty on the Internet, where documents may be readily altered, and where it is easy to assume a false identity?

PIPEDA, a federal Act, and provincial electronic commerce statutes, such as Ontario's ECA, address this concern by recognizing electronic documents and "signature equivalents" that are protected by password or encryption. Any contract that can be entered into in writing and on paper can be entered into electronically. Electronic documents and signatures are the equivalent of written contracts signed by hand.

Place for Dispute Resolution

The international capabilities of e-commerce can create problems where the contracting parties are located in different countries or jurisdictions. Imagine, for example, a dispute arising between an Internet service provider located in the United States, a vendor in Canada, and a purchaser in Spain. If there is a contractual dispute, where will it be resolved? Each of the parties may have legitimate reasons for arguing that the dispute should be resolved on its own soil.

Lawsuits are always expensive. Lawsuits in foreign countries are even more so. As the Canadian vendor, it would be foolhardy to ignore a lawsuit launched against you in either the United States or Spain because international treaties may provide that a foreign judgment is enforceable by Canadian courts. This means your Canadian assets could be seized.

Some Internet contracts have tried to create predictability about the place where disputes will be resolved by specifying the place for resolution in the contract. If your business uses the Internet to sell goods to international customers, you would be wise to draft a term in your standard contract that provides that any contractual disagreements are to be heard in Ontario. Rather than engaging in expensive and lengthy litigation, you might also draft a clause that requires disputes to be submitted to binding arbitration, as described in chapter 2. We have provided examples of both sorts of clauses in chapter 4 under the heading "Venue."

Applicable Law for Dispute Resolution

While basic common law contract principles, such as offer and acceptance, are similar in most parts of the world, the details of contract law are not. Statutes governing consumer protection, fraud, sales tax, and illegal commercial activity (such as gambling) override the common law and vary widely among countries. Businesses that buy and sell over the Internet risk running afoul of the laws and regulations of other jurisdictions. It is nearly impossible to ensure absolute compliance with the laws of every jurisdiction; however, businesses that are extensively engaged in e-commerce should seek legal advice to minimize their risks.

Buyers and sellers may include a clause in their contracts that specifies the law that will govern their disputes. This is known as a governing law clause, and we have provided an example of such a clause in chapter 4 under the heading "Governing Law." If your business uses e-commerce to sell goods to international customers, your standard contract could provide that any contractual disagreements are to be resolved according to the laws of Ontario. Courts generally respect the choices that the parties have expressed in their contracts, unless there are public policy concerns such as tax avoidance or criminality.

Timing of Formation of Contract

Most business contracts are created when one party makes an offer and the other party communicates her acceptance of this offer. With e-commerce, this process can occur very quickly, and it is sometimes difficult to determine when an offer is made or accepted. The timing of an offer and the acceptance of it can be of critical importance in some circumstances. For example, consider an offer that expires after 24 hours. When does the 24 hours start running: when the e-mail is sent, when the e-mail is received, or when the e-mail is opened and read? If acceptance is not communicated within the correct 24-hour time period, a contract does not exist.

Statutes such as Ontario's ECA have adopted the rule that unless the parties specify otherwise, an offer exists as soon as the party making the offer hits the "send" button, and acceptance occurs when the acceptance message is received, whether or not the message is opened and read. The Ontario ECA provides that the offer and the acceptance may be made by means of electronic communication, such as sending an e-mail or clicking an icon.

Minimizing Your Risk

Take E-commerce Precautions

- Know that you may legally obligate yourself to a contract simply by clicking an icon.

- Create a standard form e-commerce contract providing that Ontario law governs contractual disputes, and that Ontario courts or an Ontario arbitrator has authority to resolve contractual disputes.

- Remember that an e-mail message or other electronic communication may constitute an offer or acceptance.

- Be aware that an electronic communication is deemed received at the time it is sent, regardless of whether the recipient has read your message.

- Implement strategies to protect the privacy rights conferred by PIPEDA if your business collects, uses, or discloses personal information in the course of its commercial activities.

Web Link

The following is a list of e-commerce legislation in Canada, which can be found at http://canada.justice.gc.ca:

- Canada: *Personal Information Protection and Electronic Documents Act*, SC 2000, c. 5

- Saskatchewan: *Electronic Information and Documents Act*, SS 2000, c. E-7.22

- Manitoba: *Electronic Commerce and Information Act*, CCSM, c. E55

- Ontario: *Electronic Commerce Act, 2000*, SO 2000, c. 17 (in force October 16, 2000)

- Nova Scotia: *Electronic Commerce Act*, SNS 2000, c. 26

- Yukon: *Electronic Commerce Act*, SY 2000, c. 10

- British Columbia: *Electronic Transactions Act*, SBC 2001, c. 10

- Quebec: *An Act to establish a legal framework for information technology*, SQ 2001, c. 32

Protection of Privacy

There are a number of security measures that may be taken to preserve the confidentiality of credit card numbers and personal identifying information exchanged over the Internet. Federal and provincial legislation concerning e-commerce sets out standards for protection of the privacy of information exchanged electronically. Most commercial websites post privacy policies, have secure transaction logos, and use encryption to prevent credit card information from being intercepted.

Since January 1, 2004, PIPEDA has applied to all businesses in Canada that collect, use, or disclose personal information in the course of commercial activities. It explicitly extends protection to information that businesses have built up over time before the passage of the Act. Several provinces have enacted legislation that is similar to PIPEDA, and others are expected to do likewise. We discuss PIPEDA in detail later in this chapter under the heading "The Personal Information Protection and Electronic Documents Act."

The Consumer Protection Act, 2002

consumer
purchaser who buys or otherwise obtains goods for her own use, not for business purposes

Amendments to the *Consumer Protection Act, 2002* came into force in Ontario in the summer of 2005. This statute is comprehensive and designed to give consumers rights over and above those provided in the *Sale of Goods Act* and the common law of contract. It operates by adding to the existing rights of consumers, not by substituting new rights for the ones that already exist. The Act defines a **consumer** to mean an "individual acting for personal, family or household purposes and does

Http://www.e-laws.gov.on.ca/html/statutes/english/elaws_statutes_02c30_e.htm

not include a person who is acting for business purposes." Therefore, if your business conducts its affairs only with other commercial enterprises, and does not concern itself with consumers, the Act does not apply to you. The Act governs consumer transactions of all kinds (including barter transactions), other than those specifically excluded, such as transactions involving professional services (for example, the services of accountants and engineers) and transactions involving the purchase, sale, or lease of most real property.

CLARITY

The *Consumer Protection Act, 2002* stresses the principle that clarity is essential in all your dealings with consumers. When required by the Act to disclose or deliver information to consumers, you must present this information in a form that is "clear, comprehensible and prominent." To emphasize its concern for clarity, the Act codifies the common-law rule that any ambiguous contractual information or provisions drafted by a business are to be "interpreted to the benefit of the consumer." (We discuss this common-law concept in detail in chapter 4 under the heading "Rules of Construction.")

CONSUMER RIGHTS AND WARRANTIES

Part II of the *Consumer Protection Act, 2002* sets out certain rights of consumers and certain warranties that operate in their favour. The Act makes it illegal for businesses to contract out of the implied conditions and warranties under the *Sale of Goods Act* when dealing with consumers. It also extends protection from goods to services by requiring businesses to warrant that all services supplied to consumers are of a "reasonably acceptable quality."

The Act requires businesses to honour all estimates they make to consumers for goods or services within a 10 percent margin of error. A consumer may require any business that exceeds the estimate by more than 10 percent to provide goods or services at the estimated price.

The Act also makes negative-option marketing—that is, demanding payment for unsolicited goods or services—illegal. For example, a cable company may not unilaterally decide to add new channels and charge customers for them. Rather, each customer must be asked if he would like to purchase access to the new channels.

The courts are also using damages awards to punish businesses for cavalier attitudes about the protection of consumers. Recently, the Supreme Court of Canada restored a punitive damages award made by the trial judge in *Prebushewski v. Dodge City Auto (1984) Ltd.*

UNFAIR PRACTICES

Part III of the Act describes three types of unfair practices:

1. making false, misleading, or deceptive representations;
2. making unconscionable representations, and
3. pressuring consumers into renegotiating the terms of a transaction by holding on to their goods.

CASE IN POINT   Sell Only Safe Products and Correct All Product Deficiencies Quickly

Prebushewski v. Dodge City Auto (1984) Ltd., 2005 SCC 28 (CanLII)

Facts

The consumer bought a brand new Dodge Ram half-ton truck from a dealership. She and her husband drove the truck without incident for 16 months until, one day, the husband's employer noticed a fire outside the office. The husband ran outside to discover the truck in flames. It was completely destroyed.

Both the dealer and the manufacturer denied liability, referring the consumer and her husband to their insurer. After some investigation, it was determined that the fire was caused by a defect in the daytime running light system. A representative of the manufacturer eventually testified that the manufacturer had known of this defect for several years without issuing a recall.

The trial court found a breach of a statutory warranty under the Saskatchewan *Consumer Protection Act*. In addition to ordering regular damages of about $40,000, the trial judge ordered exemplary (punitive) damages of $25,000 against the manufacturer and dealer. The manufacturer and dealer appealed to the Court of Appeal and were successful in having the exemplary damage award struck out. The consumer appealed to the Supreme Court of Canada.

Result

The Supreme Court of Canada restored the order of exemplary damages, finding that the consumer protection legislation had increased the accessibility of exemplary damages (under the common law, it is very difficult to win damages of this kind). (The Ontario *Consumer Protection Act, 2002* also permits awards of exemplary damages under section 18(11).)

Business Lesson

If you sell consumer products and are aware of any serious defects, you may find yourself liable for punitive damages—on top of regular damages—if you do not act quickly to resolve problems with the products. Denying responsibility for known problems makes matters worse.

False, Misleading, or Deceptive Representations

Section 14 of the Act prohibits businesses from making a variety of dishonest representations to consumers, among which are the following:

- that the goods or services have sponsorship, approval, performance characteristics, accessories, uses, ingredients, benefits, or qualities they do not have;
- that the goods or services are of a particular standard, quality, grade, style, or model, if they are not;
- that the goods are new, or unused, if they are not (this excludes the reasonable use of goods to test or prepare them for delivery);

- that the goods or services are available for a reason that does not exist;
- that the goods or services are available or can be delivered or performed when the person making the representation knows or ought to know they are not available or cannot be delivered or performed;
- that a service, part, replacement, or repair is needed or advisable, if it is not;
- that a specific price advantage exists, if it does not;
- that uses exaggeration, innuendo, or ambiguity about a material fact, or that fails to state a material fact if the use or failure deceives or tends to deceive;
- that misrepresents the purpose of any charge or proposed charge; and
- that misrepresents or exaggerates the benefits that are likely to flow to a consumer if the consumer helps a person obtain new or potential customers.

The list is comprehensive and clearly intended to promote honest dealings by prohibiting any form of dishonest communication by business people with consumers.

Unconscionable Representations

Section 15 of the Act provides a list of certain practices that a court or tribunal may take into account in determining whether a representation made to a consumer is unconscionable. The Act does not specifically define the term "unconscionable," but the representations that it sets out as examples of unconscionable conduct are clearly those that shock the moral sense of the average person. Under section 15, if the person who makes a representation—or that person's employer or principal—knows or ought to know that any of the following situations is true, the representation is unconscionable:

- that the consumer is not reasonably able to protect his or her interests because of disability, ignorance, illiteracy, or inability to understand the language of an agreement;
- that the price grossly exceeds the price at which similar goods or services are readily available;
- that the consumer is unable to receive a substantial benefit from the subject matter of the representation;
- that there is no reasonable probability that the consumer will be able to pay for the goods or services in full;
- that the consumer transaction is excessively one-sided in favour of someone other than the consumer;
- that the terms of the consumer transaction are so adverse to the consumer as to be inequitable;
- that a statement of opinion is misleading and the consumer is likely to rely on it to his or her detriment; or
- that the consumer is being subjected to undue pressure to enter into a consumer transaction.

This is not an exhaustive list. Other circumstances of an equally serious nature, or arising from a similarly inequitable balance of power between the parties to the transaction, can render a representation unconscionable. *De Maeseneer v. Degamo* is a case in which the conduct of a business person clearly falls afoul of many of the prohibitions in section 15.

CASE IN POINT An Unconscionable Transaction

De Maeseneer v. Degamo, 2002 BCPC 303 (CanLII)

Facts

A person ran a money-lending business whose clientele was primarily women from the Philippines who were employed in British Columbia as domestic workers.

When a client fell behind on loan payments, the lender sued her and her co-signers for the outstanding money. The client filed a counterclaim (a defendant's claim against a plaintiff), alleging that the lender was charging a criminal or unconscionable rate of interest.

The lender charged a high rate of interest (24 percent annually to start) that increased if the borrower defaulted. In addition, he charged fees for missed payments, delayed payments, and NSF cheques. He extended loans to borrowers who had defaulted or paid late in the past, and the client was one of these customers. The lender also extended new loans instead of consolidating loans to existing customers, so that a customer who was in default would find herself paying multiple sets of late payment/missed payment/NSF fees. The court found that the effect of these business practices was that the client was actually paying an interest rate of 63 percent on her first loan and a rate of 56 percent on her second loan.

Result

The court found that the 63 percent rate of interest on the first loan was above the criminal rate of interest (60 percent). After considering, among other sources of law, the British Columbia *Consumer Protection Act*, the court found that the 56 percent interest rate on the second loan was an unconscionable rate of interest, particularly since the client was unsophisticated and had only a basic grasp of English.

The court required that the client repay the principal on her loans. It did not require her to pay fees or interest at the contract rate; instead, it set a reasonable interest rate.

Business Lesson

Resist all unconscionable representations, and train your staff to do the same. The Ontario *Consumer Protection Act, 2002* would apply even more strictly to these facts than did the British Columbia Act. Under the Ontario legislation, a court would likely have had evidence to find that the loan contract amounted to unconscionable representations falling within the description of at least six of the eight examples from section 15 listed above. Loan transactions of this nature, if challenged in an Ontario court, could be held to be unenforceable.

Renegotiation of Terms

Section 16 of the Act sets out another form of unfair practice in relation to consumers. Businesses are prohibited from using their custody or control of a consumer's goods to pressure the consumer into renegotiating the terms of a consumer transaction. For example, imagine a situation in which a business runs a computer repair shop and has temporary custody of a customer's malfunctioning computer. A manager cannot negotiate a price for doing the necessary repairs that is higher than the price that the business has specified in its contract by threatening to hold on to the computer for a longer period of time than the customer has agreed to.

Enforcement by Consumers

Section 18 of the *Consumer Protection Act, 2002* gives consumers who have been the victim of an unfair practice the right to rescind a contract—that is, treat the contract as if it were at an end—within one year from when the contract was entered into. A consumer must notify the business of her intention to rescind. If the business fails to respond, the consumer can commence legal proceedings 30 days later. The consumer also has the right to seek any remedies that are available to her in law, including compensatory damages and punitive damages. If the sum involved is $10,000 or less, the process is inexpensive and the consumer does not need a lawyer.

Staff members at the Ministry of Government Services are available to assist consumers. They may ask consumers to file a formal complaint, which might lead to an investigation into the incident and prosecution of the business or business person involved.

Web Link

Check the Ministry of Government Services website at www.gov.on.ca/MGS/en/ConsProt/050451.html for up-to-date information about the services that the Ontario government offers consumers.

Penalties

The government is serious about prosecuting business people who engage in unfair practices. An individual convicted of committing an unfair practice faces a maximum fine of $50,000 or a maximum prison term of two years less a day or both; a corporation that commits an unfair practice faces a maximum fine of $250,000.

Web Link

Check the Canadian Marketing Association's guide to the *Consumer Protection Act, 2002* at www.the-cma.org/regulatory/consumerprotection.cfm for additional information about key aspects of this legislation.

Minimizing Your Risk

Be Frank with Consumers

- Ensure that you and your staff communicate clearly and truthfully with consumers when discussing your products and services.

- Resist the urge to make exaggerated or ambiguous claims.

- Take particular care when consumers have language difficulties, mental disabilities, or other impediments that make them vulnerable.

- Establish a fair price and stick to it.

- Establish a competent customer relations program to deal with complaints and to act as an early warning system for the need to re-educate staff.

RIGHTS AND OBLIGATIONS FOR
SPECIFIC TRANSACTIONS

Part IV of the *Consumer Protection Act, 2002* sets out rights and obligations regarding specific consumer agreements, including the following:

- *Internet agreements.* These are agreements entered into by means of text-based Internet communications, such as on websites where consumers place online orders.
- *Remote agreements.* These agreements, which are usually made by telephone, fax, or mail, are defined as agreements in which consumers and business people "are not present together."
- *Future performance agreements.* These are agreements between a consumer and a business (other than Internet or remote agreements) in which delivery, performance, or payment in full is not made at the time the agreement is made.
- *Direct agreements.* These are agreements (other than Internet agreements, remote agreements, or future performance agreements) negotiated or made with consumers at any place other than a supplier's place of business or a market, trade fair, or exhibition; direct agreements are frequently entered into at a consumer's home with door-to-door sellers.
- *Personal development service agreements.* These are agreements that require payment in advance for such services as fitness or martial arts instruction.

Consumers who enter into any of these agreements have rights concerning disclosure of information and cancellation. In certain instances, it also provides a **cooling-off period**—that is, a period during which consumers can cancel their contracts without providing businesses with any justification for doing so. Table 5.1 provides a summary of these statutory rights and obligations.

cooling-off period
period set by statute during which a consumer who has made a contract can change his mind and repudiate it

---

Minimizing Your Risk
Be Ready To Prove That Consumers Consent to Transactions

- Give consumers the opportunity to decline agreements and correct errors before finalizing deals.

- Obtain signatures to indicate consumers' acceptance.

- When selling over the Internet, provide an order confirmation page before consumers finalize the agreement.

- When selling by telephone, confirm that an order has been placed and that the customer wants to proceed.

- When selling in a store, give the consumers a copy of the agreement to review before signing.

Table 5.1 Rights and Obligations Under Specific Consumer Agreements

Type of Agreement	Examples	Minimum Amount	Disclosure, Information Delivery, and Other Requirements	Cooling-Off Period	Cancellation Rights
Internet	• Consumer places online order	• Consumer's total potential payment obligation exceeds $50	• Before consumer enters into agreement, business must disclose specific information set out in the regulation, such as description of goods, price, and statement of cancellation rights, in a form that consumer can retain and print • Consumer must have opportunity to accept or decline agreement and to correct errors before entering into agreement • Business must deliver copy of agreement to consumer after it is entered into	• None	• Consumer may cancel within seven days of receiving a copy of the agreement if disclosure requirements are not met or if she is not given an opportunity to decline the agreement or to correct errors • Consumer may cancel within 30 days of entering into the agreement if the agreement is not delivered in prescribed form
Remote	• Consumer responds to telemarketing call • Consumer purchases goods from mail-order catalogue	Consumer's total potential payment obligation exceeds $50	• Before consumer enters into agreement, business must disclose, orally or in writing, specific information set out in regulation, such as description of goods, price, and statement of cancellation rights; disclosure is adequate if it refers consumer to pre-existing publication that sets out required information • Consumer must have opportunity to accept or decline agreement and to correct errors before entering into agreement • Business must deliver copy of agreement to consumer after it is entered into in a form that consumer can retain	• None	• Consumer may cancel within seven days of receiving a copy of the agreement if disclosure requirements are not met or if she is not given an opportunity to decline the agreement or to correct errors • Consumer may cancel within one year of entering into the agreement if the agreement is not delivered in prescribed form

(Table 5.1 is continued on the next page)

Table 5.1   Continued

Future performance	• Consumer buys goods at store, provides downpayment, and agrees to pay balance of purchase price on delivery of goods	• Consumer's total potential payment obligation exceeds $50	• Agreement must be in writing • Agreement must disclose specific information set out in the regulation, such as description of goods, price, and statement of cancellation rights • Consumer must have opportunity to accept or decline agreement and to correct errors before entering into agreement • Business must deliver copy of agreement to consumer after it is entered into in a form that consumer can retain	• None	• Consumer may cancel within one year of entering into the agreement if the agreement is not delivered in prescribed form • Consumer may cancel any time before delivery if delivery is not made within 30 days after the delivery date specified in contract, an amended delivery date specified in writing by the consumer, or the date that the agreement was entered into if no delivery date is specified
Direct	• Consumer signs agreement presented by door-to-door salesperson	• Consumer's total potential payment obligation exceeds $50	• Agreement must be in writing • Agreement must disclose specific information set out in the regulation, such as description of goods, price, and statement of cancellation rights • Agreement must be delivered to consumer in a form that consumer can retain	• Consumer can cancel for any reason within 10 days after receiving written copy of agreement	Consumer may cancel within one year after entering into the agreement if she does not receive a copy of the agreement
Personal development service	• Consumer pays in advance for fitness club, martial arts instruction, or business's assistance with dieting	• Consumer's total potential payment obligation exceeds $50	• Agreement must be in writing • Agreement must disclose specific information set out in regulation, such as description of services, price, and statement of cancellation rights • Agreement must be delivered to consumer in a form that consumer can retain • Agreement can extend no longer than one year after services are made available to consumer • Consumer must have option of paying for services monthly	• Consumer may cancel, without giving any reason, within 10 days after receiving a copy of the agreement or when services become available (whichever is later)	• Consumer may cancel within one year after date of entering into agreement if agreement is not delivered in prescribed form

MOTOR VEHICLE AND OTHER REPAIRS

Part VI of the *Consumer Protection Act, 2002* contains provisions to ensure that businesses treat consumers fairly when repairing automobiles or other goods. It also requires businesses to post signs in the workplace to advise consumers of their rights under the Act. If your business does this sort of work, you will need a thorough knowledge of the Act's requirements. The most important of these requirements are described in the paragraphs below.

Businesses must provide consumers with estimates before performing any repairs unless three conditions are met:

- the repairer offers to give the consumer an estimate and the consumer declines the offer;
- the consumer authorizes the maximum amount that he will pay the repairer; and
- the repairer charges no more than this amount.

The estimate must be in writing and contain specifics about the repairer, the vehicle to be repaired, and the parts and services required, and it must provide an itemized list of costs.

Businesses may not charge fees for estimates unless the consumer agrees to the fee in advance. Consumers must authorize repairs, usually in writing. Businesses must take care to supply consumers with accurate estimates since they cannot charge consumers more than 10 percent above their estimate.

In addition to the warranties under the *Sale of Goods Act* and the general warranty under the *Consumer Protection Act, 2002* that services are to be of "reasonably acceptable quality," part VI also contains a specific warranty about vehicle repairs. Repairers are required to warrant parts and labour for a minimum of 90 days or 5,000 kilometres, whichever comes first. In the event that problems arise from the parts or labour, a consumer is usually entitled to recover the cost of work or repairs and reasonable towing charges.

> **Minimizing Your Risk**
> **Be Fair When Doing Repairs**
> - Post required signs to advise consumers of their rights.
> - Provide consumers with accurate written estimates.
> - Obtain required consents before proceeding with repairs.

CREDIT GRANTING AND CREDIT REPORTING

In Ontario, the *Consumer Reporting Act* and the *Collection Agencies Act* operate in conjunction with the *Consumer Protection Act, 2002* to protect consumers against unscrupulous lenders and collection practices. The willingness of a lender—whether a bank, credit card company, or a seller—to extend credit to a consumer depends on the consumer's history of successful repayment. Credit-reporting agencies collect this information and sell it to lenders and others for a fee. In most provinces, a consumer must give her consent before businesses and other potential creditors can obtain this information. In Ontario, the *Consumer Reporting Act* governs the collection and dissemination of information about consumers' creditworthiness. If a lender—including a business—denies credit to a consumer, it must give the consumer the name and address of the credit-reporting agency so that she may contact it to verify the credit information provided. A consumer is entitled to examine her file free of cost, and an agency is required to correct any information that proves to be inaccurate.

Collection Agencies

From time to time, businesses may employ agencies to assist them in collecting outstanding debts from consumers, usually in return for a percentage of the amount collected. In Ontario, collection agencies are governed by the *Collection Agencies Act*. If your business is involved in debt collection, you must become thoroughly knowledgeable about this Act and its general regulation. The legislation prohibits businesses from trying to collect a debt without attempting to inform consumers, in writing, that they have been hired to do so. It also prohibits them from making harassing telephone calls or personal visits, as well as from giving false information that could be harmful to a consumer or his family. The general regulation also limits the times during which these agencies may attempt to collect debts—for example, collection attempts are prohibited on Sundays and statutory holidays, and must be made between 7 a.m. and 9 p.m. on other days.

> **Minimizing Your Risk**
>
> **Comply with Consumer Credit Laws**
>
> ◀ Obtain consumers' consent before approaching credit-reporting agencies.
>
> ◀ Collect debts in a civilized and lawful manner.

The Competition Act

Canadian lawmakers clearly consider competition to be a hallmark of a fair and free marketplace. In 1889, Canada became the first country in the world to introduce legislation governing marketplace competition. Since then, the federal government has added to the list of practices it prohibits.

Today, the *Competition Act* is the principal federal statute in the consumer protection field. Because the Act is federal, it applies throughout Canada. It operates not by empowering consumers directly, but by restricting, monitoring, and penalizing anti-competitive and dishonest conduct in business. It applies to both goods and services. By restricting practices that discourage competition, the Act is intended to stimulate competitive conduct and to eliminate misleading advertising and abusive marketing schemes. The *Competition Act* operates chiefly by empowering the state to take action against those who violate its provisions, either by using the criminal law system or the services of the Competition Bureau and the Competition Tribunal. It also allows, in limited circumstances, for civil lawsuits by businesses and others who have been victimized by anti-competitive behaviour.

The commissioner of competition oversees the operation of the Competition Bureau and is responsible for the investigation of complaints about violations of the Act, including complaints made by private individuals. In addition, the commissioner is responsible for overseeing the enforcement of other legislation, including the *Consumer Packaging and Labelling Act*, which we discuss later in this chapter.

The Competition Tribunal is the principal enforcement body under the *Competition Act*. This tribunal is unique, composed of judges of the Federal Court and people who receive some training in law but are not lawyers or judges by profession. Appeals from the tribunal's decisions go to the Federal Court of Canada. Failure to comply with an order of the tribunal constitutes criminal contempt of court, with its attendant penalties.

The tribunal deals chiefly with **reviewable practices**—that is, offences under that Act that are resolved by voluntary agreement or by order of the tribunal. Examples of these offences include tied selling, exclusive dealing, market restriction,

> **Web Link**
>
> Check the Competition Bureau's website at www.competitionbureau .gc.ca/ for tools and services to assist your business in complying with the *Competition Act*.

reviewable practices commercial practices that seem to offend the *Competition Act* and that therefore may be subject to review by the tribunal and refusal to supply, all of which we discuss in detail below. The tribunal has the power to investigate, review, and make orders to restore competition. It also has other powers, including the power to order the removal of customs duties imposed on foreign goods to stimulate competition.

The commissioner has the power to refer offences under the Act that constitute criminal conduct to the attorney general for prosecution. Criminal conduct includes offences such as conspiracy and bid-rigging, which we discuss below.

In addition to reviewable practices and criminal conduct, there is another small category of mixed offences under the *Competition Act*. (This category includes the offence of misleading advertising.) When dealing with these offences, the commissioner has the power to decide whether to forward them for prosecution in the criminal courts or to treat them as reviewable practices. The commissioner's decision is based on whether a business has acted intentionally or recklessly in committing an offence. If, for example, a business has systematically and deliberately engaged in a course of misleading advertising over time, prosecution in the criminal courts is likely.

Figure 5.1 sets out the means by which an offence under the *Competition Act* comes to the attention of the commissioner, the Competition Tribunal, or the courts.

Figure 5.1   Investigations and Prosecutions Under the Competition Act

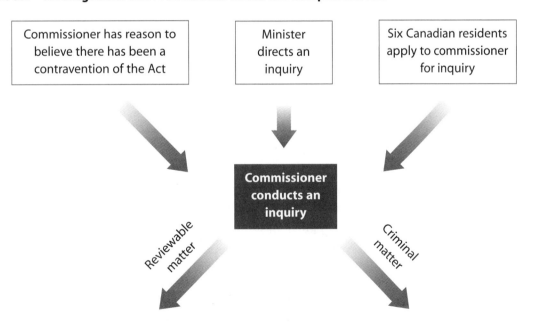

RESTRICTIVE TRADE PRACTICES

restrictive trade practices
practices, some of which
are defined by the
Competition Act, that tend
to limit freedom of trade
and competition in the
marketplace

Restrictive trade practices prohibited under the *Competition Act* can be divided into three categories:

1. practices related to the nature of a business,
2. practices that arise from dealings between a business and its competitors, and
3. practices that arise from dealings between a business and its customers.

Practices Related to the Nature of a Business: Dominant Businesses and Mergers

Businesses that become dominant in the marketplace can commit offences under the *Competition Act* either by eliminating competition or by merging with competitors. It is not an offence to become dominant, nor is it an offence to merge with another business. However, these activities can become offences under the Act when they are likely to reduce or eliminate competition. There is no precise method of determining when this likelihood arises. However, if a combined enterprise is potentially able to control half the market, the commission will probably be interested in investigating.

Abuse of Dominant Position

Abuse of dominant position is a reviewable offence under the *Competition Act*. Section 78 of the Act lists several ways in which a business can abuse a dominant position, among which are the following:

- *cutting profit margins*—for example, a supplier sells goods in the consumer marketplace at a lower price than the one it charges retailers and
- *using loss leaders*—for example, a business temporarily sells goods at a cut-rate price to eliminate a competitor that cannot afford to lower its prices, even temporarily.

Mergers

Section 91 of the Act defines "merger" as the direct or indirect acquisition or establishment "of control over or significant interest in the whole or a part of a business of a competitor, supplier, customer or other person." If a business's merger is likely to lessen competition substantially, the business has committed a reviewable offence, and the Competition Tribunal is empowered to dissolve the merger or take any other action necessary to restore competition in the marketplace.

Because of their significance as vehicles for airing diverse points of view, the news media are businesses in which healthy competition is extremely important. Although *Canada (Director of Investigation and Research) v. Southam Inc.* is a case that merely concerned an advertising supplement, it has wider implications.

Practices Related to Dealings with Competitors

Conspiracy and bid-rigging are both criminal offences under the *Competition Act* that are designed to lessen competition among businesses.

CASE IN POINT   Media Monopoly

Canada (Director of Investigation and Research) v. Southam Inc., 1991 CanLII 1702 (CT)

Facts

The defendant corporation, a media giant, purchased two British Columbia newspapers: the *North Shore News* and the *Real Estate Weekly*. The *North Shore News*, a profitable and widely read newspaper, contained a weekly real estate supplement. Before the defendant corporation purchased the papers, this supplement and the *Real Estate Weekly* were the only two real estate advertising papers distributed on the North Shore.

The Competition Tribunal's director of investigation and research brought an application asking the tribunal to order that the corporation sell one or the other of the two papers, alleging that the defendant's ownership of both papers eliminated competition in the real estate market in the area. The defendant proposed, as an alternative remedy, that the *North Shore News* begin to carry, as an insert, an independent real estate supplement referred to as "HOMES."

Result

The tribunal found that the corporation's ownership of both the *Real Estate Weekly* and the *North Shore News* eliminated competition in the real estate advertising sales market in the region. It was unconvinced that an independent HOMES supplement would be as attractive to advertisers or as financially viable as the existing *North Shore News* supplement (which at the time of the merger was slightly outperforming the *Real Estate Weekly*). The tribunal also believed that it lacked the power to make the order the defendant requested.

The tribunal ordered the corporation to sell either the *North Shore News* or the *Real Estate Weekly* to restore competition in the marketplace.

Business Lesson

The media giant in this case put forward a creative anti-competitive remedy as an alternative to a sale of its assets, and the tribunal gave this remedy very serious consideration before rejecting it. When you are involved in a difficult case, it can never hurt to ask that the court "think outside the box" when crafting a remedy.

Conspiracy

Section 45 of the Act defines **conspiracy** broadly as an agreement between two or more parties to unduly

- limit facilities for transporting, producing, manufacturing, supplying, storing, or dealing in any product;
- prevent or limit the manufacture or production of a product or to enhance its price unreasonably;
- prevent or lessen competition in the production, manufacture, purchase, barter, sale, storage, rental, transportation, or supply of a product; or
- otherwise restrain or injure competition.

conspiracy
act of planning or working together or both, on the part of two or more parties, to jointly commit an illegal activity

In a conspiracy to fix prices, for example, the Crown must prove beyond a reasonable doubt not only that the conspiring businesses agreed to fix the prices but also that they knew that their agreement would lessen competition. Conspiracies are difficult to prove, and penalties are high: as much as $10 million in fines and five years' imprisonment.

Bid-Rigging

bid-rigging
illegal trade practice in which bidders conspire to influence a contract price by having certain bidders place artificially high bids to favour another party to the scheme

Bid-rigging is a specialized form of conspiracy that occurs when two or more competitors secretly agree about the prices they will bid on a public tender in an effort to control the bidding process to suit their collective needs. For example, three companies—Sneak Co., Sly Co., and Connive Co.—may decide that they will take turns in submitting the lowest bid on a public works project that invites three separate tenders. When it is Sly Co.'s turn to win the bid, Sneak Co. and Connive Co. will deliberately bid high, and Sly Co. will bid low. The companies will rearrange the high and low bids on the next tender. By acting in this way, Sneak Co., Sly Co., and Connive Co. have effectively conspired to fix the prices of the public works project by subverting the bidding process.

Bid-rigging is an offence prohibited under section 47 of the Act. Business people convicted of bid-rigging face fines "in the discretion of the court" and terms of up to five years' imprisonment.

Practices Related to Dealings with Customers

Under the *Competition Act*, certain practices related to dealings with customers are reviewable offences. Others are criminal offences because they are generally viewed as being more serious in nature. Below, we set out examples of both types of offences.

Reviewable Offences

The *Competition Act* prohibits a number of practices that restrict the supply of goods, usually from one business to another. Refusal to deal is a reviewable offence under section 75 of the Act. Exclusive dealing, tied selling, and market restriction are all reviewable offences under section 77.

refusal to deal
inappropriate refusal, by a commercial party for its own advantage, to enter into commerce with another party, despite the second party's willingness to meet the commercial party's business terms

Refusal to deal occurs when a supplier refuses to sell goods to a customer on the same terms as other customers, and this creates "an adverse effect on competition in a market." For example, if Diesel Ballet refuses to supply tutus to General Ballet Emporium on the same terms as it sells them to Tip Toe Ballet Supplies—even though General is able to meet these terms and Diesel has stock available to fill General's order—Diesel is engaging in the reviewable offence of refusal to deal. It is giving an advantage to one customer at the expense of another.

exclusive dealing
practice whereby a commercial party requires another commercial party to deal exclusively with it in order to secure a business advantage

Exclusive dealing occurs when a supplier requires its customer to limit its dealings with other suppliers or not buy from them at all. Thus, if Diesel Ballet refuses to supply tutus to General Ballet Emporium simply because General also carries tutus manufactured by Diesel's arch-rival, Acme Stage Threads, Diesel is engaging in the reviewable offence of exclusive dealing. It is punishing a customer for not favouring it over other suppliers.

Tied selling occurs when a supplier ties the supply of one product to the purchase of another product. For example, if Diesel Ballet refuses to supply General Ballet Emporium with the Knock'em Dead Tutu, a highly profitable model, unless General also agrees to purchase the Dainty Dud Tutu, a marginally profitable item that Diesel plans to discontinue, Diesel is engaging in the reviewable offence of tied selling. It is coercing a customer to buy an unwanted product by threatening to refuse to sell the wanted product.

Market restriction occurs when a supplier imposes restrictions on its customers concerning the persons to whom they may resell a product. For example, if Diesel Ballet refuses to allow General Ballet Emporium to sell its wares to ballet students, insisting instead that only professional dancers can buy its tutus, Diesel is engaging in the reviewable offence of market restriction.

Criminal Offences

Section 50 of the *Competition Act* creates the criminal offences of price discrimination, predatory pricing, and price maintenance.

Price discrimination is a practice whereby a supplier systematically offers different pricing terms and conditions to competing customers on sales of equal volume. The prohibition against price discrimination is designed to encourage competition in the marketplace by preventing large or powerful buyers from obtaining lower prices than small or less powerful buyers from suppliers. Essentially, the Act requires that all buyers be treated equally when the terms of sale are the same.

For example, if General Ballet Emporium buys 25,000 tutus from Diesel Ballet at $100 per tutu for delivery in 30 days, with payment to be made within 45 days, Tip Toe Ballet Supplies is entitled to buy tutus from Diesel at the same price as General if the conditions of sale are comparable. If Diesel refuses to sell tutus to Tip Toe for the same price, it is engaging in the criminal offence of price discrimination.

Similarly, if General insists on a rate that is preferential to Tip Toe's, General is also engaging in price discrimination. In other words, the *Competition Act* considers both the supplier and the buyer to be equally at fault.

If, however, Tip Toe wants a 60-day payment term or a shipment of only 15,000 tutus, it cannot insist that Diesel supply tutus to it at the same price that Diesel supplied them to General, because the conditions of sale are different.

Predatory pricing occurs when sellers set their prices unreasonably low with the intention of reducing or eliminating their competition, on either a regional or a broader basis. It is not, of course, an offence to lower prices. On the contrary, the impetus of the Act is to encourage competition. Suspicions, however, would certainly be aroused at the Competition Bureau if, for

tied selling
practice whereby a seller requires a buyer to buy one product or service in order to gain commercial access to, or a better price on, another product or service

market restriction
a practice whereby a seller forces a buyer to restrict eligible resale customers for the seller's goods

price discrimination
practice whereby a supplier systematically offers different pricing terms and conditions to competing customers on sales of equal volume

Minimizing Your Risk
Protect Your Business Against Anti-Competitive Business Practices

- If you suspect anti-competitive business practices, compare the information that you have with the practices described above. If the circumstances match, you may have grounds for making a complaint.

- Contact the Competition Bureau of Canada (www.competitionbureau.gc.ca) to make your complaint. The bureau prefers to receive complaints by means of its online inquiry/complaint form but will also accept complaints by phone, fax, or mail.

- Provide succinct and relevant information about yourself, the company to which the complaint relates, and the conduct that you are complaining about. This may involve descriptions of the relevant products and services, pricing particulars, and other details.

- Wait for the bureau to review your information and decide whether a formal inquiry into the matter is warranted.

predatory pricing
practice whereby a
seller sets her prices
unreasonably low (usually
eliminating any profit
margin or selling at a loss)
to drive competitors out of
the market

price maintenance
practice whereby a seller
attempts to control the
resale price of goods by
preventing a retailer from
discounting the price

example, General Ballet Emporium raised its prices immediately after it drove Tip Toe Ballet Supplies out of business because of its tutu-pricing activities.

Price maintenance is a practice that attempts to define the prices at which goods are sold or resold. A manufacturer's suggested retail price is just that: a suggested price. Any attempt by a manufacturer to control the final selling price is prohibited, especially if the manufacturer threatens or uses sanctions against a retailer.

A seller does, however, have a right to refuse goods to a retailer that uses its products as loss leaders (popularly known as "door crasher specials"). For example, assume that General Ballet Emporium is in the habit of selling foot repair cream at the special price of $5 per tube to the first 50 customers through its doors every Saturday morning, in the hope that some customers will linger and buy a pair of ballet shoes as well. General's actual cost is $10 per tube. Diesel Ballet, which manufactures foot repair cream, is entitled to refuse to supply General with its product to use in this way.

Canada v. UCAR Inc. is a case that elevates the stakes considerably beyond those involved in the foot cream wars. It provides you with a glimpse of conspiracy and price maintenance within the international world of commerce.

PROMOTING AND ADVERTISING PRODUCTS

The *Competition Act* protects consumers by prohibiting misleading or false advertising and a number of other questionable promotional activities that are set out below.

Misleading Advertising

Misleading advertising is one of the offences under the *Competition Act* that the commissioner of competition has the power to treat as a reviewable matter or send for prosecution in the criminal courts. Section 52 of the Act defines false or misleading advertising broadly, so as to catch not only those businesses that deliberately lie when promoting their products, but also those businesses that intentionally or otherwise stretch the truth to create erroneously grand impressions about their products in the minds of consumers. To fall outside the boundaries of legal advertising, a false representation must be "material"—that is, it must apply to the statements that lure a customer to a place of business or influence a customer's decision to buy a particular product.

Sales and Bargain Prices

Generally, it is a reviewable offence under the *Competition Act* for a seller to state that a price is less than the ordinary price when it is not. The Act thereby seeks to ensure that the terms "on sale," "reduced," "clearance," and "bargain" are truthful reflections of reality. The ordinary price is the price at which goods are usually sold in a given market at specified volumes in a given time period.

Performance Claims and Testimonials

Statements about the performance of a product or a service may fall within the *Competition Act*'s general provisions concerning misleading advertising. It is also

Web Link

Advertising Standards Canada is the Canadian advertising industry's self-regulatory body. Check its website at www.adstandards.com for an advertising copy review service and other useful information.

CASE IN POINT An International Conspiracy To Fix Electrode Prices

Canada v. UCAR Inc., 1999 CanLII 7636 (FC)

Facts

UCAR Inc. and SGL Canada Inc. were sellers of graphite electrodes and controlled over 90 percent of the Canadian market. The most important worldwide manufacturer of these electrodes was UCAR International.

UCAR Inc. (the Canadian seller) and SGL formed a conspiracy, together with other graphite electrode sellers in Canada and with the participation of UCAR International, to maintain graphite electrode prices. The conspiracy involved cooperation among the sellers to share information about sales volume, to allocate sales volume among themselves, to refuse to discount the price of graphite electrodes, and to maintain high prices for the electrodes within the Canadian marketplace and beyond. The conspiracy was organized by top executives and was maintained for over five years by means of regular meetings and code names.

In 1997, the conspiracy had caused turmoil and firings at UCAR International. Shortly thereafter, UCAR Inc. approached the Competition Tribunal with disclosures about the conspiracy and ultimately pled guilty as a company. (Some executives pled guilty individually also.)

Result

The Federal Court of Canada found that UCAR Inc.'s actions did indeed constitute conspiracy to maintain prices, that the conspiracy was masterminded by UCAR International's president, chief executive officer, and chief operations officer, and that the conspiracy adversely affected Canada's steel and aluminum industries. Having made sales of $214 million during the conspiracy period, UCAR Inc. volunteered to make restitution to its Canadian customers in the amount of $19 million. By the time of sentencing, it had already paid out $4 million of that offer.

Taking into account the mitigating effect of UCAR Inc.'s confession, guilty plea, and restitution commitment, the court sentenced the company to a fine of $11 million. Individual officers were also fined.

Business Lesson

Setting prices for your goods in cooperation with your competitors may result in very substantial fines. Pleading guilty and making a fair offer of restitution can have a favourable influence on the penalties imposed by a court.

reviewable conduct under section 74.01 of the Act to make a representation about a quality of a product that is not based on an "adequate and proper test." Thus, Diesel Ballet cannot state that its foot cream "enhances toe strength" and "stops bleeding fast" when it has no tests to authenticate its claims.

Testimonials are acceptable, provided that they are accurately stated and reasonably current, and provided that those who endorse products have actually used or evaluated them.

Minimizing Your Risk

Compete Fairly in the Marketplace

- Ensure that all staff members responsible for advertising are knowledgeable about your products' assets and limitations.
- Use pricing policies that treat all customers equally.
- Allow retailers to set their own prices.
- Ensure that your distribution channels and any agreements with competitors allow for free and open competition in the marketplace.
- Encourage managers to create a corporate culture that rewards compliance with the *Competition Act*.
- Ensure that all employees whose job might tempt them to engage in anti-competitive behaviour are aware of the penalties for failing to comply with the law.

Consumer Safety

All Canadian provinces, as well as the federal government, have enacted legislation to protect the health and safety of consumers. In the sections that follow, we briefly examine two such pieces of federal legislation: the *Food and Drugs Act* and the *Hazardous Products Act*.

THE FOOD AND DRUGS ACT

The need for strict and protective food and drug laws has been apparent to governments and the public for years. The thalidomide tragedy of the late 1950s and the early 1960s galvanized public attention after thousands of human birth defects resulted from pregnant women ingesting a drug that was touted for its ability to cure morning sickness. Over the years, the subsequent discovery of carcinogenic and other harmful properties of many food additives, artificial sweeteners, and growth hormones have increased the public's concerns about its health and safety. Today, people require their governments to monitor the safe marketing of the food and drugs that are available for their consumption.

The *Food and Drugs Act* is one of Canada's oldest statutes. It prohibits

- the manufacture or sale of any article of food containing poisonous or harmful substances, or food that has been prepared, preserved, packaged, or stored in unsanitary conditions;
- the importation or shipment between provinces of any food that does not meet prescribed standards;
- false or misleading labelling or advertising;
- the sale of drugs that do not meet advertised standards or the standards imposed by law; and
- misleading drug claims.

People also monitor their governments. In the recent past, for example, concerns have been raised that Canada lags far behind European countries in protecting its population from carcinogens in goods sold on grocery shelves. Wendy Mesley, a highly respected Canadian broadcaster and journalist, has made the following comment in this regard: "Stuff that's sold on our shelves here is reformatted with carcinogens taken out of them, or at least, much reduced, to be sold over there [Europe]. Because of health concerns, there are bans on products in Europe that we eat everyday." (*Globe and Mail*, March 4, 2006, p. R3.)

Provisions Regarding Food

Health Canada and the Canadian Food Inspection Agency (CFIA) are the federal government bodies that are responsible for food-labelling policies in Canada under the *Food and Drugs Act*. Health Canada is responsible for policies that affect health and safety, such as nutritional content, allergens, and special dietary needs. The CFIA is responsible for enforcing the standards set by Health Canada through the delivery of all federal inspection services, by monitoring the humane handling of food animals, and by enforcing laws against fraudulent food labelling and other illegal practices related to food.

Food safety intervention, while scientifically complex, is straightforward in its goal of preventing, removing, or suppressing the growth of micro-organisms. Growers of food are held responsible for the hygiene of the people who work for them. Rules for the stewardship of land and water are designed to reduce microbial hazards. Harvesting equipment must be cleaned and maintained in accordance with government standards.

If you work in a business that involves processing or manufacturing, you can expect regular visits from employees of the CFIA to oversee

- the quality of your wash water, which must meet Canadian drinking water guidelines;
- your controls against cross-contamination;
- an appropriate anti-microbial treatment program;
- maintenance of hygiene standards for workers and equipment; and
- maintenance of temperature control.

If your business involves the retailing of food, you must refrigerate displays of packaged fresh foods. Inspectors from the CFIA's retail food program oversee grocery store compliance with food safety standards. Officers also investigate consumer and trade complaints about food products. Responsibility for retail food safety is shared with provincial health units. In Ontario, municipal public health units are responsible for health and safety concerns in local grocery stores and restaurants, and assess these businesses for compliance with regulations. Non-complying businesses can be charged under the *Food Premises Regulation* made under the *Health Protection and Promotion Act*.

Proposed amendments to the *Food and Drugs Act* will require that a "nutrition facts table" be added to the labels of foods, with certain exemptions, such as raw meat and fish, fresh vegetables, and food destined for sale in restaurants. The information may be presented either in separate English and French versions, or a combined bilingual format. The labelling requirement came into effect for large manufacturers on December 12, 2005 and will come into effect for small manufacturers on December 12, 2007.

Bottled water is monitored under the *Food and Drugs Act* and its regulations. Health Canada establishes health and safety standards for bottled water and develops labelling policies related to health and nutrition. The CFIA develops standards related to packaging, labelling, and advertising; it also handles all inspection and enforcement duties.

Provisions Regarding Drugs

The *Food and Drugs Act* also regulates drugs sold in Canada. The definition of "drug" is very broad; it includes any substance or mixture of substances manufactured or advertised regarding "diagnosis, treatment, mitigation or prevention of disease, disorder, an abnormal physical state, or its symptoms, in human beings or animals" and "restoring, correcting or modifying organic functions in human beings or animals."

To market a new drug in Canada, you must make a "new drug submission" to the minister of health. Your submission must contain details about the drug's potency, purity, stability, and safety; test reports; the purpose of the drug; conditions recommended for its use; and evidence of its clinical effectiveness.

Health Claims

There is a huge market today for healthy foods. Business people may be tempted to make exaggerated claims about their products in order to increase sales. There are, however, legal, as well as ethical, constraints on this practice. Under the *Food and Drugs Act*, there are three principal barriers to making diet-related health claims about foods.

1. A manufacturer who makes a claim about a particular nutrient within a food risks having the food fall within the Act's definition of "drug." Should this happen, it will be necessary to make a new drug submission in order to comply with the Act.
2. It is a violation of the Act to advertise a food (or drug) as a treatment, preventative, or cure for specified diseases, including depression, arthritis, impotence, and nausea associated with pregnancy.
3. The Act severely restricts the extent to which claims may be made for the "action or effect" of core nutrients. The government regulates these claims closely. They are allowed only if appropriate proof of their accuracy (in the form of clinical trials) is available and has been accepted by Health Canada. For example, peppermint tea is a widely respected remedy for indigestion, but its precise effects have not been documented under controls considered adequate by the government. Therefore, while it is probably acceptable to advertise a peppermint tea as "the overindulger's best friend," more specific claims—for example, a claim that the tea "provides complete relief in under 30 minutes"—would violate the regulations.

Web Link

Check Health Canada's website at www.hc-sc .gc.ca for up-to-date information about consumer product safety.

Penalties

Failure to comply with the requirements of the *Food and Drugs Act* can result in fines and imprisonment. The penalties are particularly harsh if the offence relates to food, in which case the maximum fine is $250,000 and the maximum jail term is three years.

HAZARDOUS PRODUCTS ACT

The *Hazardous Products Act* provides at least 23 categories of "restricted" products that must be labelled in a specific manner or meet certain standards to be legally sold in Canada. The Act lists certain requirements for potentially dangerous products—such as toxic, flammable, or highly reactive substances—as well as products that are particularly hazardous. If these products are sold to the public, they must contain hazard symbols, be accompanied by product information sheets, and display appropriate labelling.

Toxic, flammable, and highly reactive substances must have labels explaining, through symbols and bilingual warning statements, the nature of the hazard and precautionary measures to take when using the product. As well, products sold for use in industrial or commercial establishments must contain label information about potential workplace hazards.

Minimizing Your Risk
Respect Public Health and Safety

- Institute policies in your manufacturing or retail food business to ensure compliance with all hygiene, health, and labelling requirements under the *Food and Drugs Act* and the *Hazardous Products Act*.

- Keep abreast of changes in the law by consulting a lawyer who specializes in your business's field or by contacting Health Canada.

- Enlist the assistance of managers and other staff in maintaining healthy and safe manufacturing and retailing policies.

- Facilitate and expedite government inspections.

Consumer Information

The federal government has responded to the public's need for information on both the *Food and Drugs Act* and the *Consumer Packaging and Labelling Act*, among other laws. In the sections that follow, we provide a brief overview of the range of protection offered by these statutes, the mechanisms for their enforcement, and the penalties for their breach.

CONSUMER PACKAGING AND LABELLING ACT

Canadian law requires that prepackaged consumer products be labelled accurately and meaningfully to help consumers make informed purchasing decisions. The federal *Consumer Packaging and Labelling Act* regulates the information that must be provided to consumers on labels that are affixed to prepackaged products, other than products that qualify as a "device" or "drug" within the meaning of the *Food and Drugs Act*. The *Consumer Packaging and Labelling Act* defines "prepackaged product" broadly to include "any product that is packaged in a container in such a manner that it is ordinarily sold to or used or purchased by a consumer without being re-packaged."

The *Consumer Packaging and Labelling Act* requires the following information to appear on product labels:

- the common or generic name of the product;
- a declaration of the product's net quantity; and
- the identity and address of the person by or for whom the product was manufactured, sold, or imported—that is, dealer identification.

If the product is imported, one of the following dealer identification formats must be used:

- the name and address of a Canadian dealer accompanied by the words "imported by" or "imported for,"
- the country of origin adjacent to the name and address of the Canadian dealer, or
- the name and address of a dealer located outside Canada.

The regulations also dictate the placement of labels, generally requiring that they appear on a "principal display panel" or prominent surface of the product. Of course, all mandatory information, other than the dealer identification, must appear in both English and French.

The Act prescribes standard container sizes for a number of consumer products, such as toothpaste, shampoo, biscuits, cookies, powdered laundry detergents, soaps, wine, aerosol deodorants, shaving cream, aerosol hairspray, refined sugar syrup, and peanut butter.

Exemptions

There are a few general exemptions. Prepackaged products produced or manufactured for commercial or industrial use that will not be resold to consumers as prepackaged products are exempt from the Act's requirements. Prepackaged products produced or manufactured only for export or for sale to a duty free store are similarly exempt. Consumer textile articles subject to regulation under the *Textile Labelling Act* and certain artists' materials are exempt, as are replacement parts for vehicles, appliances, and other durable consumer goods unless they are to be displayed for sale to consumers.

Enforcement and Penalties

The provisions of the *Consumer Packaging and Labelling Act* are enforced by inspectors, who can be appointed under the *Department of Industry Act*, the *Food and Drugs Act*, or the *Canadian Food Inspection Agency Act*. These inspectors have powers to enter the premises of those who deal in prepackaged products to inspect the packages and labels for evidence of compliance. If an inspector finds a non-compliant label, she can seize the mislabelled product and detain it until the dealer or manufacturer brings the packaging into compliance with the law. If the dealer does not do so, the product can be forfeited to the government (usually for destruction) after all appeals of the seizure have been exhausted. For serious cases of mislabelling or refusal to comply with labelling regulations, the Act imposes fines. Interfering with an inspector or blocking a search, seizure, or forfeiture constitutes an offence.

FOOD AND DRUGS ACT

The *Food and Drugs Act* contains a broad prohibition against advertising "any prepackaged product that has applied to it a label containing any false or misleading representation that relates to or may be regarded as relating to that product." False or misleading representation includes representations concerning

- net quantity,
- specific contents,
- quality,
- performance,
- function,
- origin, and
- method of manufacture or production.

Penalties and Enforcement

Goods found to be in contravention of the Act may be seized by an inspector appointed under the Act. Penalties include fines of up to $10,000 for contraventions of the Act, except when they relate to food, where the maximum penalty is a $250,000 fine and a prison term of three years.

Consumer Privacy

Historically, the common law has not recognized the right to privacy as a distinct right enjoyed by consumers in Canada. In the past, the privacy of consumers has been protected by the practical difficulties of locating and compiling voluminous records. However, in the contemporary electronic age, where personal information can be compiled and transferred in seconds, privacy concerns have deepened. The federal government, followed by several provincial governments, has responded by passing legislation that safeguards the privacy of personal information.

Web Link

Check the Office of the Privacy Commissioner of Canada's website at www.privcom.gc.ca for helpful information about PIPEDA.

THE PERSONAL INFORMATION PROTECTION AND ELECTRONIC DOCUMENTS ACT

The *Personal Information Protection and Electronic Documents Act* (PIPEDA) is a federal statute that affects both a business's relationship with its employees and a business's relationships with its customers and clients. We discuss the aspects of the Act that relate to employees in chapter 7. Here, we consider how PIPEDA governs a business's right to collect, use, and disclose personal information about its customers and clients.

What Is Personal Information?

The term **personal information** is broadly defined in PIPEDA. It includes any information about "an identifiable individual," whether recorded or not. Protection does not extend to the type of information that appears on a business card: a customer's name, title, business address, and business telephone number. Some of the kinds of personal information that are protected under PIPEDA include a person's

personal information
under the *Personal Information Protection and Electronic Documents Act* (PIPEDA), any information about "an identifiable individual," whether recorded or not

- age, address, and identification numbers;
- residential telephone numbers and personal email address;
- sex, religion, ethnicity, and marital status;
- photograph, opinions, and income;

- relevant dates, such as a birth date; and
- credit records, loan records, and purchasing and spending habits.

Regardless of the form in which a business collects personal information—on paper, electronically, in a recording, or on a fax machine—businesses should strictly adhere to the 10 PIPEDA principles that are listed in the following section.

Fair Information Principles

fair information principles
10 principles, set out in the *Personal Information Protection and Electronic Documents Act* (PIPEDA), that guide the collection, use, protection, and disclosure of personal information

PIPEDA sets out 10 **fair information principles** that underlie the collection, use, protection, and disclosure of personal information about a business's clients and customers.

1. *Be accountable.* If your business collects personal information, appoint one person to ensure that your business is complying with PIPEDA. This person should be responsible for analyzing how your business handles personal information about clients and customers. What personal information does your business collect and why? Where does your business keep this information and how does it secure the information? Who has access to the information? To whom does your business disclose it? When does your business discard it and how?

   Your PIPEDA expert must then develop and implement policies and procedures to protect personal information. She should ensure that all front-line staff receives thorough training in responding appropriately to inquiries. If your business transfers personal information to another business for processing, your business should ensure that the information receives a comparable level of protection while in the hands of the other business.

2. *Identify the purpose of collection.* Your business must let your customers and clients know why it is collecting their personal information. Any forms or documents used to collect personal information must include
   a. an explanation of why you need the information and how you will use it—for example, to open an account, verify creditworthiness, provide benefits, or process a magazine subscription; and
   b. a list of those to whom the information will be disclosed.

3. *Get consent.* The individual to whom the personal information relates must consent before you collect it. There are exceptions to this principle, but they are limited in scope, applying, for example, when the information is already publicly available. The form of consent depends on the sensitivity of the personal information. Collection or use of medical, financial, or other sensitive data requires express consent. If a business had been using or disclosing information before PIPEDA came into effect, it must go back to the individual involved and obtain her consent. Your business should not make consent a condition for supplying a product or service, unless the information is necessary to meet a legitimate purpose that is specifically identified.

4. *Limit collection.* Your business can collect only information that is necessary for its stated purposes. For example, in the course of conducting a credit check, a business cannot collect information related to an individual's religious affiliation.

5. *Limit use, disclosure, and retention.* Generally, your business cannot use the information collected for any purpose other than the one stated. You must not disclose the information to third parties unless they obtain a new consent that authorizes the new disclosure. For example, information regarding dependants gathered for life insurance purposes cannot be transferred to a medical insurer for the purpose of obtaining medical coverage without obtaining fresh consent. There are a few exceptions to the rule against disclosure without consent, such as where the information is disclosed to a lawyer who is representing your business, or for the purpose of collecting a debt owed to your business by the individual. Personal information should be disposed of when it is no longer needed.

6. *Be accurate.* Use or disclosure of out-of-date or incomplete information can harm an individual. Your business should ensure that all information it discloses is accurate and current.

7. *Provide safeguards.* Your business should protect personal information against loss, theft, or unauthorized access. For example, written information should be kept in locked drawers with keys accessible only to those who need access. The most sensitive information should receive a higher level of protection through such devices as security clearances, passwords, and encrypted computerized data.

8. *Be open.* Your business should make privacy policies and procedures readily available to customers, clients, employees, and suppliers. Front-line supervisors should be familiar with them.

9. *Give individuals access.* Your business must generally provide individuals with details about the personal information being held about them and the means to gain access to it, upon request.

10. *Provide recourse.* Your business should establish a procedure to deal with complaints about its compliance with PIPEDA. It should investigate all complaints, notify the individual of the outcome of the investigation, correct any inaccuracies and instances of non-compliance, and record all decisions.

Application of PIPEDA

PIPEDA applies to both federally and provincially regulated businesses that collect, use, or disclose personal information in the course of *commercial* activities, such as creating, selling, bartering, or leasing customer lists, unless the province in which the business is situated has passed comparable legislation. In that case, the provincial law applies. Ontario has not yet passed comparable legislation.

Redress for Customers and Clients

A customer or client may make a complaint about the handling of his personal information to the Office of the Privacy Commissioner of Canada. The privacy commissioner has broad powers to investigate complaints, and may apply to the Federal Court for an order requiring an offending business to change its practices, or requiring it to pay damages to the individual. Additional penalties for non-compliance include maximum fines of $100,000.

Minimizing Your Risk
Comply with PIPEDA

➤ Ensure that your business complies with PIPEDA's 10 fair information principles.

➤ If in doubt as to your legal obligations under PIPEDA, consult a lawyer or the Office of the Privacy Commissioner of Canada.

Chapter Summary

In this chapter, we enlarged the examination of contract law that we began in chapter 4 by focusing on the statutes that govern business-to-business and business-to-consumer contracts in Ontario—namely, the *Sale of Goods Act* and the *Consumer Protection Act, 2002*. We also provided a brief discussion of the new contractual challenges posed by the widespread use of e-commerce. We examined the function of the federal Competition Bureau and Competition Tribunal in administering and enforcing the *Competition Act*, legislation designed to address the economic and social problems posed by anti-competitive conduct and dishonest business practices. We also discussed reviewable practices and criminal conduct under this Act. Throughout the chapter, we considered the protection of consumers in its broadest sense, reviewing the statutory means by which the law protects the integrity, economic viability, safety, and privacy rights of consumers.

KEY TERMS

bid-rigging
caveat emptor
consignment
conspiracy
consumer
cooling-off period
deliverable state
exclusive dealing

fair information principles
future goods
market restriction
merchantable quality
personal information
predatory pricing
price discrimination
price maintenance

refusal to deal
restrictive trade practices
reviewable practices
seller's lien
specific goods
tied selling
title
unascertained goods

REFERENCES

Canada (Director of Investigation and Research) v. Southam Inc., 1991 CanLII 1702 (CT).
Canadian Food Inspection Agency Act, SC 1997, c. C-6.
Collection Agencies Act, RSO 1990, c. C.14.
Competition Act, RSC 1985, c. C-34.
Consumer Packaging and Labelling Act, RSC 1985, c. C-38.
Consumer Protection Act, 2002, SO 2002, c. 30, sched. A.
De Maeseneer v. Degamo, 2002 BCPC 303 (CanLII).
Electronic Commerce Act, 2000, SO 2000, c. 17.
Food and Drugs Act, RSC 1985, c. F-27.
General Regulation to the Collection Agencies Act, RRO 1990, reg. 74.
General Regulation to the Consumer Protection Act, 2002, O. reg. 17/05.
Gregorio v. Intrans-Corp., 1994 CanLII 2241 (ONCA).
Health Protection and Promotion Act, RSO 1990, c. H.7.
Hazardous Products Act, RSC 1985, c. H-3.
Motor Vehicle Safety Act, SC 1993, c. 16.
Personal Information Protection and Electronic Documents Act, SC 2000, c. 5.
Prebushewski v. Dodge City Auto (1984) Ltd., 2005 SCC 28 (CanLII).
Sale of Goods Act, RSO 1990, c. S.1.
Textile Labelling Act, RSC 1985, c. T-10.
United States Uniform Commercial Code.

REVIEW AND DISCUSSION

True or False?

_F_   1. Leases are governed by the *Sale of Goods Act.*

_T_   2. Fitness for intended purpose is an implied condition under the *Sale of Goods Act.*

_T_   3. Specific performance is a remedy available in special circumstances only.

_F_   4. Unpaid sellers have no statutory remedies.

_T_   5. The *Consumer Protection Act, 2002* requires that ambiguous contract terms be construed in favour of the consumer.

_F_   6. The *Consumer Protection Act, 2002* creates a 10-day cooling-off period for all consumer transactions.

_F_   7. The *Consumer Protection Act, 2002* requires that the final bill for service for which an estimate was given is equal to or less than the estimate.

_F_   8. A supplier has the right to tell a retailer how much to charge for its products.

_T_   9. The *Competition Act* applies to both goods and services.

_T_   10. It is an offence under the *Competition Act* for a company to merge with another and become dominant in the marketplace.

_T_   11. The *Personal Information Protection and Electronic Documents Act* applies to a company's collection and maintenance of personal information for its own marketing purposes.

Multiple Choice

1. In which of the following areas does the *Sale of Goods Act* not imply terms?
    a.   merchantable quality
    b.   right to sell goods
    c.   fair price for goods
    d.   fitness for purpose

2. To which of the following does the *Sale of Goods Act* apply?
    a.   the sale of a car
    b.   the rental of an apartment
    c.   the sale of a house
    d.   the rental of a motel

3. Ashley purchased a used farm tractor for $9,500. She later discovered that the previous owner's bank had a lien on the tractor. Under the *Sale of Goods Act*, this is most likely a breach of _____, which would allow her the remedy of _____.
    a.   warranty/rescission
    b.   condition/rescission
    c.   warranty/damages
    d.   condition/damages

4. The *Consumer Protection Act, 2002* would *not* cover
   a. a professional manicure
   b. the two-month rental of a summer cottage
   c. the purchase of a car
   d. the delivery of high-speed cable Internet service to a home business

5. An unconscionable representation
   a. is a criminal act
   b. gives a buyer the automatic right to exemplary damages
   c. can be evidence that a transaction is unfair and supports a buyer's right to a remedy
   d. is irrelevant because of the *caveat emptor* rule

6. The main objective of the *Competition Act* and other laws regulating marketing practices include
   a. ensuring a supply that is adequate to meet the demands of consumers
   b. ensuring that inventories held by retailers do not become excessive
   c. protecting consumers from unfair selling practices
   d. encouraging development of innovative new products

7. Lang runs a chain of health food supermarkets that offer a number of products that other major grocery retailers have not stocked in the past. Lang has enjoyed a loyal and steadily growing clientele. Recently, however, he has noticed that the major grocery retailers are offering several of his products, such as rice snacks, organic herbs, and oils at prices so low that he cannot possibly match them without losing money. Lang suspects that the major supermarkets are selling these items below cost, or at unreasonably low levels, in order to drive him out of business. If prosecuted under the *Competition Act*, the supermarket chains are most likely to be found guilty of
   a. the criminal offence of predatory pricing
   b. the reviewable offence of discriminatory pricing
   c. the reviewable offence of price maintenance
   d. the criminal offence of price maintenance

8. Marie is the CEO of Minox Ltée, a small machine shop that does business with several large auto manufacturers. Several years ago, the CEO of a competitor asked Marie whether Minox would like to "go in with us." Maria did not understand the CEO's meaning at the time and said she was not interested. The more she thought about the incident, however, the more she realized that her competitor might have been proposing a conspiracy. Recently, she has begun to notice that the prices of her competitors' products are always the same as hers and wonders if she should report this to the Competition Bureau. Which of the following courses of action is her best solution?
   a. Marie should report the incident.
   b. Marie should not report the incident because she could be charged with conspiracy.
   c. Marie should not make a report, because conspiracy requires at least three conspiring parties, and Marie is unsure how many companies are involved.
   d. Marie should not report, because, as a private citizen, she has no standing to bring a complaint before the Competition Tribunal.

Short Answer

1. When does title to goods pass from seller to buyer?

2. If Mario trades his wristwatch for an umbrella at a flea market, can he rely on the *Sale of Goods Act* to ensure that the umbrella will be of merchantable quality?

3. What is a cooling-off period, and how does it differ from the one-year statutory limitation period for repudiation of unfair consumer contracts?

4. Explain what requirements an Internet seller must meet, at the time of a sales transaction and shortly afterward, to comply with the *Consumer Protection Act, 2002.*

5. Why does the law extend special protections to consumers, as opposed to business parties?

6. A national women's fashion retailer, Shirley Opaque, had placed price tags on garments indicating a "regular" and "sale" price, when in fact the garments were not sold in any significant quantity or for any reasonable period of time at the "regular" price. Assess this marketing technique in relation to the *Competition Act.*

7. How and by whom is food safety enforced under the *Food and Drugs Act*?

8. How is PIPEDA enforced?

Discussion and Debate

1. There is an organic market in a major North American city where the farmers share a vision about sustainable agriculture and responsible methods of cultivation. These farmers, who are well acquainted with the needs of their urban clientele, meet regularly to discuss who will grow what crops and in what quantity. They also set prices that fairly compensate them for their skills, their labour, the materials they use, and the risks they take in doing the job they do; they each agree to sell their goods at these prices. Having replaced competition with cooperation as their governing marketing principle, the farmers believe that they work for one another. Consider the example of this market when discussing the following questions:
   a. Are there any limits on the desirability of competition in commerce? If so, what are they? If not, why is this so?
   b. What would be the consequences for commerce and society in general if more businesses shared their talents, resources, and customers on a cooperative basis? When discussing this question, make reference to a particular industry to explain your point of view.

2. Many businesses claim that they "put the consumer first" or "always listen to their customers' concerns." In ever-increasing numbers, however, businesses are installing elaborate telephone systems to avoid allowing their customers to speak to a human representative. Should a business that engages in this practice be subject to prosecution or penalties under the *Competition Act* or the *Consumer Protection Act, 2002*? Give reasons for your answer.

6 Methods of Carrying On Business

LEARNING OBJECTIVES

After reading this chapter, you should be able to:

- List the various structures that business people choose for carrying on business.

- Explain the legal characteristics of and describe the benefits and disadvantages of carrying on business as a sole proprietorship.

- Distinguish between a general partnership, a limited partnership, and a limited liability partnership.

- Discuss the advantages and limitations of each type of partnership.

- Describe the contents of a partnership agreement.

- Explain the legal characteristics of a corporation and the advantages and disadvantages of adopting a corporate structure.

- Distinguish between private and public corporations.

- Describe the roles of directors, shareholders, officers, managers, and other employees of corporations.

- Describe agency and discuss its application to business.

- Distinguish joint ventures from business organizations.

- Discuss the implications of running a franchise.

What Are Methods of Carrying On Business?

Canadian law offers a variety of ways in which a person or a group of persons can carry on business. The most common of these methods of carrying on business are the sole proprietorship, the partnership, and the corporation. Each of these methods—or **business structures**—involves a legal regime that governs all aspects of a business's existence: its creation, the manner in which it conducts its internal affairs,

business structure
method of carrying on business that dictates all aspects of a business's creation and operation

its relationship to other businesses, the way in which it pays its taxes, and the extent to which it is legally responsible for its own liabilities, to name a few.

All businesses involve some legal structure. For example, even if your Uncle Izzy opens his doors to neighbours who pay him to read their fortunes, Uncle Izzy is working within a business structure: he is a sole proprietor. By virtue of reading fortunes for money, Uncle Izzy becomes subject to the established body of law related to sole proprietorships. For example, he is personally liable to pay tax on the income that his fortune-telling business produces; he may be liable for injuries that his customers suffer while they are on his premises; and, if he decides to adopt a business name other than his own—such as Izzy's Fabulous Fortunes—he is required to register the name.

Other examples of situations that involve business structures, or methods of carrying on business, include the following:

- After graduating from university, a young veterinarian decides to join the veterinary practice of her spouse. The couple will have to consider the various partnership options that are available to them as methods of carrying on business.
- A costume-designing business is about to collapse because it has just lost a large contract with a major drama festival. The business's owner needs to obtain sales representation but does not have the funds necessary to hire permanent staff. He should consider agency as a method of preserving his business.
- A family company grows so substantially that it decides to launch itself internationally, but it needs capital to cover the costs of expansion. The company should consider the advantages of offering its shares to the general public.

Every method of carrying on business has its advantages and disadvantages regarding, for example, flexibility, cost, complexity, and protection for its owners. In this chapter, we discuss these matters in relation to the most common methods of carrying on business:

- sole proprietorships;
- partnerships, including general, limited, and limited liability partnerships;
- corporations, both private and public;
- agencies;
- joint ventures; and
- franchises.

In addition, we explore the procedures required by law to set up these business structures and maintain their operations smoothly.

The various methods of carrying on business offer a business person interesting opportunities for defining significant business relationships: not only the legal relationship between the people who own and run the businesses, but also the legal relationship between their businesses and the people who run, finance, and work for them. A partner in a general partnership, for example, enjoys different rights and obligations in relation to his partner than a director of a private corporation enjoys in relation to other directors and shareholders of the corporation. An owner of a sole proprietorship, such as Uncle Izzy, has a very different legal relationship with Izzy's Fabulous Fortunes than, for example, a franchisee of a fast food outlet has with the multinational conglomerate that sold him his franchise. In the sections

Web Link

More information on business registration in Ontario can be found on the About website at http://sbinfocanada .about.com/od/ bizregistration.

that follow, we examine the various roles that business people play within the business structures they adopt to carry on business.

The Importance of Choosing a Business Structure

There are many reasons why you, as a business person, should understand the legal alternatives available for structuring your business. Choosing the most suitable business structure will have a major impact on the smooth operation of your enterprise.

- *Business structures clarify your legal relationships with colleagues and co-workers.* Whether you choose to work alone and engage people to help you on an as-needed basis, to work with a group of trusted colleagues who share the financial burden of your business's ups and downs, or to establish a multinational business empire, the type of business structure you adopt dictates the legal roles of all the participants in your enterprise. If you are a director of a private corporation, for example, your rights and responsibilities in relation to the business's officers, managers, and shareholders are defined in detail in statutes and the common law.
- *Choosing the appropriate business structure can strike the right balance between your need for simplicity and your need to limit your potential liability.* Your choice allows you to assume, share, or relinquish personal responsibility for your business's liabilities. As a sole proprietor, for example, you assume unlimited liability for your business. On the other hand, as a shareholder in a corporation, your personal assets are generally safe from your business's creditors.
- *Choosing the appropriate business structure can help you plan for the future.* Your choice can assist you in planning and implementing future expansions or other modifications of your business. For example, you could incorporate a private company in anticipation of becoming a public company some day.
- *Your choice of business structure will affect the amount of professional assistance that is required.* The different legal requirements of business structures will determine whether, and how often, you need to engage the professional assistance of lawyers or accountants, for example.

> ## Web Link
> **Visit Canada Business at www.cbsc.org for information about different business structures and government requirements for registration.**

Sole Proprietorships

The **sole proprietorship** is the most basic method of carrying on business. As its name suggests, a single (sole) person owns and operates the business (as its proprietor). There is no legal separation between the person and the business. The owner is the business, and the business is the owner.

There are thousands of these kinds of businesses across Canada because they are easy to set up, easy to run, and do not involve a great deal of interaction with the government. Your local variety store, the car repair shop up the street, and your favourite neighbourhood restaurant may all be examples of sole proprietorships.

sole proprietorship method of carrying on business whereby one person owns and operates the business, with no legal separation between the owner and the business

CREATION

A sole proprietorship is created as soon as someone opens a business that interacts with the public. For example, if you open a candy store, you become a sole proprietor. If the sign you post on the store merely gives your name and adds a title such as "Confectioner," you are able to carry on business with minimal legal requirements.

However, if you wish to use a name for your business other than your own name, you must register that name under the *Business Names Act* in Ontario (or similar legislation in other provinces). If, for example, you decide to call your store "Candyland Treats," you must register your business's name with the government. This registration requirement exists to ensure that members of the public who interact with your business will know who to take legal action against if problems arise. If, for example, someone slips on a wet floor in Candyland Treats, he can search the government database for your name, as the owner/proprietor, and then file a lawsuit against you.

Registering the name of a sole proprietorship involves filling out the appropriate form (likely available online), paying the required fee (usually less than $100), and submitting both to the appropriate provincial government office. The form includes the name and address of the sole proprietor and the name and address of the business. Failure to register a business name in Ontario may result in a fine of up to $2,000.

It is worth noting that registration of your business name may not protect you against others using it. If you want to prevent a competing business from using your name, consider registering it as a trademark under the *Trade-marks Act*. We discuss this matter in greater detail in chapter 8.

LEGAL CHARACTERISTICS

A sole proprietorship has no legal existence apart from its owner. It therefore cannot, on its own, sue another individual or business, nor can it be sued on its own. The owner is the legal entity that must sue on behalf of the business and that will be sued for the misdeeds of the business.

A sole proprietorship cannot enter into contracts; rather, its owner enters into contracts on its behalf and is responsible for fulfilling any contractual obligations related to the business. It does not file its own income tax return; instead, its owner claims income derived from the business and deducts business expenses on her personal tax return.

CONDUCTING BUSINESS

In most cases, sole proprietorships are small businesses with few or no employees. They usually operate from a single location (possibly home-based) and offer a limited number of products or services. Many Internet-based businesses are sole proprietorships.

A sole proprietor runs her business on her own or with the help of friends or family members whom she may or may not formally pay. She might, however, employ two or three people to help her as salespeople or stock people. If her business has expanded to that level, she would likely also employ a bookkeeper to maintain her financial records, to ensure that her taxes are paid and collected, to handle her payroll obligations, and to pay her suppliers.

ADVANTAGES AND DISADVANTAGES

Cost and Complexity

Simplicity is the key advantage of carrying on business as a sole proprietorship. Other than registering your business name with the provincial government (and obtaining business and other licences that may be required by the municipality for your particular type of operation), you have no other requirements to fulfill. You can decide to open a business and be up and running almost immediately as a sole proprietor.

You can make important decisions about your business easily, without changing documentation, obtaining approvals, or consulting others. Therefore, if your candy store does not work out and you decide to sell electronic equipment instead, you can do so almost immediately—without having to convince partners, corporate directors, or shareholders that it is a good idea, and without having to revise partnership agreements, articles of incorporation, or other documents.

Tax Implications

The Canada Revenue Agency treats a sole proprietorship as a source of income (or business loss) for its owner. Any profit (income minus legitimate expenses) earned by the business is added to any other income of the owner. Also, losses incurred by the business can be set off against the owner's income from other sources in order to reduce tax.

As a sole proprietor, you submit your business income and expense information with your personal income tax return. You are required to file a schedule of the income and expenses of your business, and add the net income of the business to your income from all other sources. In other words, the tax department simply treats income from your sole proprietorship as another source of your personal income, along with income from employment, rental property, or investments.

Like other forms of business, a sole proprietorship allows you, as owner, to employ people, including members of your family. This can work as an income-splitting arrangement, giving you an opportunity to save tax by diverting income from your pocket to that of a family member who pays tax at a lower rate than you do. In this manner, your business income stays in your family and may be subject to lower tax rates.

Liability

The main disadvantage of choosing to operate a business as a sole proprietorship is the legal liability of the owner. Because the owner and the business are one in the eyes of the law, the owner is legally liable for any injury (whether physical or financial) that the business may cause to others. This means that the owner is personally subject to **unlimited liability**.

unlimited liability
full responsibility for any debt incurred or loss caused by a business

Minimizing Your Risk

Equip Your Sole Proprietorship for Doing Business

- If you wish to use a business name other than your own name, register it to avoid fines.

- Obtain all licences required by your municipality for operating your type of business.

- Collect and pay all applicable taxes.

- Carry sufficient insurance to cover claims against your business, remembering that a claim against your business is a claim against you.

- Hire a bookkeeper if the complexity of your business (or your personal lack of record-keeping skills) warrants it.

As a result, if someone comes into Candyland Treats, slips on the wet floor, falls, and breaks his leg, he may sue you directly for damages. Because your sole proprietorship is unable to enter into contracts, you, as owner, become responsible for all contractual obligations of your business, and you become personally liable for any breaches of contract. If Candyland Treats fails to pay its suppliers, you are personally liable for paying the full amount owing. A creditor can force you to sell your personal assets (such as your house and your investments) to meet the obligations of your business. And, if Candyland Treats goes into bankruptcy, it takes you with it.

Considerations Concerning Expansion

Only one person can own a sole proprietorship. If the business expands significantly—or if it requires an infusion of money to continue to operate or to expand—the owner may wish to bring other individuals in as co-owners. In order to do this, it is necessary to convert the business to a structure other than a sole proprietorship: either a partnership or a corporation.

Introduction to Partnerships

partnership or firm
method of carrying on business whereby two or more persons operate a business, with no legal separation between the owners and the business

A **partnership**, also called a **firm**, is an unincorporated business that is owned by two or more persons. These people—the partners—can be individuals, corporations, or other unincorporated businesses (sole proprietorships or partnerships). Often, the partners join together in order to conduct a business in a manner that is efficient and effective for all of them. Groups of professionals who join together to offer their services to the public, such as lawyers, accountants, and dentists, often use partnerships as a means of carrying on business.

Partners have the right to organize their affairs and to determine their rights and obligations within the partnership by way of a partnership agreement. However, a partnership agreement is not mandatory for most partnerships. A **partnership agreement** is a document signed by all partners that sets out the basic terms of how the business will operate. Some agreements are very simple; others are extremely complex. Many partnership agreements include terms setting out how individual partners may choose (or be required) to leave the partnership, what happens if the partnership ceases to operate, and other important end-of-relationship issues. We discuss these agreements in greater detail later in this chapter under the heading "Partnership Agreements."

partnership agreement
contract signed by all partners that sets out how the partnership will operate and how it will end

Partnerships, like sole proprietorships, are not legally independent from the people who compose them. Partners may be liable for the conduct of other partners. The extent of this liability depends on the nature of the partnership and the terms of whatever partnership agreements the partners have entered into.

In Ontario, partnerships are governed primarily by the *Partnerships Act* and the *Limited Partnerships Act*, which lay out the general requirements of this form of business. Generally, a partnership exists where the partners agree to do the following:

- pool their capital for a common purpose—that is, running the business;
- plan to share in the profit or loss of the business;
- make decisions and manage the business together;
- exercise authority to bind the partnership to contracts with third parties; and
- share liability.

The three types of partnerships in Canada, which differ depending on how liability and other responsibilities are shared between the partners, are

1. the general partnership,
2. the limited partnership, and
3. the limited liability partnership.

This chapter explores each type of partnership separately. Table 6.1 later in the chapter summarizes and compares various aspects of these three types of partnerships.

General Partnership

The general partnership is the most common form of partnership in Canada. However, limited liability partnerships—recognized in Ontario for the first time in 1998—have become increasingly popular.

CREATION

A **general partnership** is created when two or more individuals come together to run an unincorporated business. If no agreement is registered with the appropriate government office specifying that the partnership is a limited partnership or a limited liability partnership, the law assumes that the parties have created a general partnership.

general partnership
partnership that is not registered with the government as a limited or limited liability partnership

Unless the partners sign a partnership agreement that sets out other terms, all partners in a general partnership share responsibility for the business, operate the business together, and share the profits and liability equally.

The name of a general partnership is often simply the combined names of the individual partners, for example, Chiu, Li, and Jackson. However, more inventive names, such as Holistic Dental Heaven or Mr. Leather's Loungewear, can be used as well. As with sole proprietorships, the name of a partnership must be registered under the *Business Names Act* if it operates under a business name that is different from the names of the partners.

LEGAL CHARACTERISTICS

A general partnership, like any other kind of partnership, is not an independent legal entity. It cannot, therefore, enter into legally binding contracts or protect its owners (the partners) from legal liabilities for injuries (either physical or financial) caused by the firm.

As a result, the individual partners in a general partnership are **jointly and severally liable** for the actions of the firm. This means that they divide liability equally and are also each entirely liable for the firm's actions. Therefore, if a restaurant

joint and several liability
financial responsibility requiring all parties to contribute equally but also making each party responsible for the entire amount owed

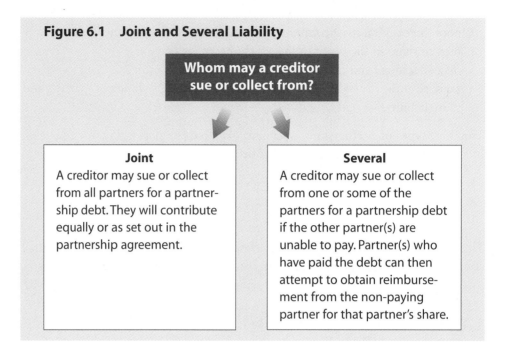

Figure 6.1   Joint and Several Liability

Whom may a creditor sue or collect from?

Joint
A creditor may sue or collect from all partners for a partnership debt. They will contribute equally or as set out in the partnership agreement.

Several
A creditor may sue or collect from one or some of the partners for a partnership debt if the other partner(s) are unable to pay. Partner(s) who have paid the debt can then attempt to obtain reimbursement from the non-paying partner for that partner's share.

partnership served tainted fish, a patron fell ill, and a court ordered the firm to make a compensatory payment to the patron, each partner is responsible for contributing an equal share of the payment. If, however, one partner is unable to pay his share, the others must make up the difference because each is individually responsible for paying the entire amount. In seeking a compensatory payment, a patron would sue the firm collectively and each partner individually.

If you decide to run your business as a general partnership, you may be liable for the conduct of each of your partners. The law views you as representing—or as acting as an agent for—both the firm and each of your partners individually. (We discuss the concept of agency later in this chapter.) As a result, if one of your partners makes a serious error that harms a client, you and every other partner in your firm could be legally responsible for compensating the client for all losses that result from the error.

As in the case of a sole proprietorship, each partner may be liable to the full extent of her personal assets for all debts and other obligations of the partnership. This means that you could lose your home, your investments, and all your savings if any of the partners in your firm makes a costly error. It is this factor that contributed most to the creation of the limited liability partnership, which we discuss below.

CONDUCTING BUSINESS

In a general partnership, all partners are equal (subject, of course, to the terms of any partnership agreement). Each partner has equal power and equal responsibility. The partners generally reach decisions through informal or formal discussion and agreement. Business income is usually used first to pay the expenses of the partnership. It is then allocated to any long-term planning projects the partnership may have, and the rest is then divided among the partners. Unless a partnership agreement provides otherwise, profits of the business are divided equally.

Depending on the size of the partnership—and some partnerships can become huge enterprises—decisions about the day-to-day operations of the firm may be made by all the partners or by a small group of partners specifically chosen to make these decisions.

In a two-person firm, for example, the partners would typically discuss day-to-day, and even major, decisions affecting the firm over their morning tea or over lunch. In a firm with 400 partners, however, a representative group of, say, five partners would make day-to-day decisions, and similar committees would make more specialized decisions—for example, decisions about the firm's computer resources, the hiring and firing of support staff, and the allocation of profits.

ADVANTAGES AND DISADVANTAGES

Cost and Complexity

The general partnership has the advantage of simplicity when smaller groups of people choose to work together. A general partnership is inexpensive, easy to set up, and easy to run. As long as it remains small, its operations can be flexible.

Tax Implications

Like the sole proprietorship, business profits of the partnership become part of the personal income of its owners—the partners—for the purpose of income tax. The firm keeps accounts of its income and expenses in order to calculate its annual profit (or loss). The profit (or loss) is then apportioned to each partner either equally or otherwise in accordance with the terms of the partnership agreement. Each partner then includes her share of the firm's profits as business income in her personal tax return.

Liability

Not surprisingly, the biggest disadvantage of the general partnership is general liability. Each partner is personally liable for the debts and obligations of the firm. If the firm cannot pay its employees or its bills, the individual partners must do so. If a person slips and falls in the firm's reception area, the individual partners may be liable for his injuries. Each partner's liability is limitless, which means that each partner will have to honour the firm's obligations until all her assets are depleted.

This liability exists even if the firm is sued as a result of a single partner's error. In this regard, every partner acts as a sort of insurer for the mistakes of the others.

Limitless liability may be less of a concern in a two-person firm, where the partners trust and are able to monitor each other, than in a larger firm. Of course, the larger the firm, the more partners there are to share the cost of mistakes.

Considerations Concerning the Pooling of Resources

Partners have the advantage of working together to run their business. They can help each other reduce expenses and attract and keep customers. Also, each partner has the comfort of knowing that his partners are there to support him when he is obliged to deal with—and pay for—problems.

Whereas four separate accountants working on their own would each incur the cost of hiring an assistant, renting an office, and buying a computer system, the same four accountants could form a partnership and reduce some of these costs. The rental of one large space with four rooms and a reception area will likely be cheaper than the rental of four smaller offices. The partners could share the cost of a photocopier and other office equipment and may be able to hire fewer staff together than they might need if they were all working separately. These "economies of scale" increase as the firm grows larger. With these financial savings, the firm may also be able to offer its clients lower prices for its services while still maintaining an adequate profit margin.

In addition, four accountants working in partnership might be able to pursue and attract large clients whose needs are beyond the capacity of one accountant working alone. The accountants might have different strengths—both personal and professional—that they could pool to provide better service to their clients.

Limited Partnership

limited partnership
partnership composed of a minimum of one general partner and one limited partner who provides money or property to the firm and shares in the profits but who does not participate in the business affairs of the firm and whose liability is limited to exclude any personal assets

A **limited partnership** has one or more general partners and one or more limited partners. The limited partners provide the firm with money and other property (but not services), in exchange for a share in any profits. The main purpose of a limited partnership is to provide a method for the partnership to raise capital.

As their name suggests, limited partners are limited in their level of participation in the firm. Their names generally cannot be included in the name of the firm, they cannot take part in the management of the firm, but their liability for the firm's obligations is also limited. If the firm accumulates debts or is sued, the only thing a limited partner can lose is her investment in the firm and any profits to which she might be or might become entitled. Her personal assets are not at risk.

The general partners, meanwhile, have the same rights, responsibilities, and liabilities as the partners in a general partnership. They operate the firm, take profits from the firm, and are liable for the debts and obligations of the firm. Their liability is, once again, limitless.

CREATION

Unlike a general partnership, which can form without any government involvement, a limited partnership is formed when a partnership declaration is filed under a provincial limited partnership statute—in Ontario, the *Limited Partnerships Act*. The declaration must include basic information such as the names and contact information of all general and limited partners.

LEGAL CHARACTERISTICS

Like all partnerships, a limited partnership is not a separate legal entity. It is not separate from the partners. The general partners operate and sign on its behalf: they are personally liable for its debts and obligations in an unlimited fashion. The limited partners' liability is limited to their investment in the firm and their share of the firm's profits.

The law views all general partners as agents of the firm with the legal authority to bind the firm and all its general partners to an agreement with third parties such as suppliers and customers. Provided that a partner is acting in the normal course of the partnership's business, third parties can generally rely on their reasonable belief that a general partner has this authority.

Limited partners may also be agents in circumstances described in the partnership agreement. However, if a limited partner takes on a managerial role with respect to the partnership's business, he risks losing his "limited" status and opens himself up to the liability of a general partner.

CONDUCTING BUSINESS

A limited partnership usually conducts its business in the same manner as a general partnership of similar size and focus. As mentioned above, the limited partners may not take part in the management of the firm without risking the loss of their protected status.

A limited partner may require the return of his investment in the firm under certain circumstances. These circumstances are set out in the governing statute or in the partnership agreement. If the firm is unwilling or unable to return the limited partner's investment as required, the limited partner could force the firm to dissolve and distribute its assets.

ADVANTAGES AND DISADVANTAGES

Cost and Complexity

The limited partnership is a more complex business structure than the general partnership, and it requires more documentation. For example, the *Limited Partnerships Act* in Ontario requires that a current record of the limited partners be kept on the premises and be made available for inspection by the public. This record includes names and contact information of all limited partners and the amount of money or value of property contributed to the partnership by each limited partner.

A carefully drafted partnership agreement—though a significant business expense when drafted by a lawyer—is particularly important in outlining the obligations and rights of both types of partners. All partners must be careful to follow the rules applicable to their roles in the firm—that is, general partners must adhere to the rules relating to general partners, and limited partners must adhere to the rules relating to limited partners. A limited partner who steps over the boundaries of his role, as described in the partnership agreement or *Limited Partnerships Act*, runs the risk of losing the protection of his limited partner status and gaining the liabilities of a general partner.

Tax Implications

The tax implications for a limited partnership are basically the same as for a general partnership. Each partner's share of the profits is combined with that partner's other income in calculating taxes.

Liability

As discussed above, the general partners have unlimited liability for the debts and obligations of the partnership. The liability of the limited partner is usually limited to his investment in the firm.

Minimizing Your Risk

Consider Taking On a Silent Partner If You Need to Raise Capital

- Before raising capital on riskier terms, weigh the advantages of taking on a limited partner to finance your business operations.

- If you are a limited partner, be careful not to jeopardize your status by assuming management responsibilities.

- File a limited partnership declaration that includes all the information required by the *Limited Partnerships Act*.

- Maintain records and make them available for inspection as required by the *Limited Partnerships Act*.

- Clarify the rights and obligations of all partners in a limited partnership agreement.

- Define the circumstances under which a limited partner expects the return of his investment in the partnership agreement.

Considerations Concerning Financing

A limited partnership has many of the advantages of a general partnership. It has the additional advantage of allowing people to become involved in the business without assuming the risks or responsibilities of a full general partner. This increases the firm's ability to attract investors, or "silent partners," as an inexpensive and low-risk method of obtaining capital.

For example, an entrepreneurial college student who starts a lawn-mowing business may need capital to buy a good-quality lawnmower and other equipment, to lease a truck, and to place advertisements in local newspapers. She could borrow the money, but she would then be personally liable for the debt (as a sole proprietor). If the business failed, she would still have to pay back the money, plus interest, even if the sale of the business assets, such as the lawnmower, did not cover the debt.

Alternatively, the student could find someone willing to join the business as a limited partner, to provide the needed capital in return for a portion of any profits. If the business failed and there were no profits, the limited partner would be entitled to the return of his investment only to the extent that the assets of the business covered it.

limited liability partnership (LLP) partnership composed of partners in certain professions, such as lawyers and accountants, who have the same liabilities as those in a general partnership except that partners are not liable for the professional negligence of other partners or employees supervised by other partners

Limited Liability Partnership

The **limited liability partnership (LLP)** is the newest type of partnership in Canada, available only to certain professionals (such as lawyers and chartered accountants) whose governing bodies allow their members to use the limited liability option. It is designed to offer the flexibility and simplicity of a general partnership while avoiding the disadvantage of unlimited liability for all partners. In essence, it is a midway point between a general partnership and a corporation in terms of liability.

CREATION

A limited liability partnership is created in Ontario when two or more people enter into a written partnership agreement that designates the partnership as a limited liability partnership and states that the *Partnerships Act* governs the agreement. Limited liability partnerships must also register their names under the *Business Names Act* before they may legally conduct business.

LEGAL CHARACTERISTICS

The limited liability partnership's legal characteristics are similar to those of a general partnership with one crucial difference: in a limited liability partnership, a partner is *not* liable for the professional negligence of the other partners. Therefore, if a lawyer provides negligent advice to a client resulting in financial harm to the client, the other lawyers in the firm will not be liable. This limitation on liability is not only in respect of negligent acts or omissions of other partners in the firm, but also of any person who is under the control and supervision of other partners of the firm, such as an associate lawyer or law clerk.

A partner in a limited liability partnership is liable only for the following:

- the general debts and obligations of the firm that do not arise from negligent acts or omissions and
- the debts and obligations that arise from the partner's own negligent acts or omissions, or the negligent acts or omissions of any person (employee, agent, or representative) who is under that partner's direct control and supervision.

CONDUCTING BUSINESS

Limited liability partnerships conduct their business in the same manner that general partnerships of similar size and focus conduct their business. The firm must, however, include the words "limited liability partnership" or the initials "LLP" in its name.

ADVANTAGES AND DISADVANTAGES

Cost and Complexity

The limited liability partnership offers greater flexibility and simplicity than the corporation, which we discuss at length below. Because professionals such as lawyers and accountants are not legally permitted to form corporations for the purpose of practising their profession, the limited liability partnership offers them at least some of the protection from personal liability that the corporation offers.

Tax Implications

The tax implications for a limited liability partnership are substantially the same as for a general partnership and a limited partnership.

Liability

As mentioned above, each partner in a limited liability partnership is liable for the general debts and obligations of the firm and for her own professional negligence. However, each partner is protected from liability for the negligence of the other partners in the firm. For some professionals—such as lawyers—whose governing bodies do not allow their members to incorporate their practices, the limited liability partnership is the best partnership option available from the standpoint of protection from personal liability. The increasing popularity of this form of partnership for law and accounting firms provides eloquent testimony to the attractiveness of this protection.

Table 6.1   Comparison of the Three Types of Partnerships

	General Partnership	Limited Partnership	Limited Liability Partnership
Typical example	Two friends go into business together; they share capital costs, debts, work, profit, and liability.	A sole proprietor needs capital and finds investors who become limited partners; they provide capital, share debts, and are entitled to profit, but they do not work in the business and have limited liability. The sole proprietor becomes a general partner.	A group of accountants form a partnership; they share capital costs, debts, work, and profit, and they are not liable for each other's professional negligence.
Liability	All partners are jointly and severally liable for each other's debts and negligence, including professional negligence. Liability is unlimited.	There must be at least one general partner who is fully liable for the debts of the firm and any negligence of the other partners. Liability of general partners is limitless. Limited liability partners are liable for the debts of the firm and any negligence of the other partners only to the extent provided in the partnership agreement (usually to the extent of their capital investment).	Some or all partners may be limited liability partners, who are liable only for the general debts of the firm and not for the professional negligence of the other partners.
Decision making and profit taking	Partners often make decisions and share profit equally. A partnership agreement may provide that some partners have more decision-making power and are entitled to more profit (usually because of a larger initial investment) than others.	Limited partners have no decision-making powers. If they become involved in business decisions, they risk losing their limited liability status. Limited partners are entitled to profit according to the terms of the partnership agreement.	Limited liability partners may have decision-making powers and are entitled to profit according to the terms of the partnership agreement.

Partnership Agreements

A partnership agreement is the contract on which a partnership is founded. It is enforceable through the courts by any of the parties who sign it. With the exception of limited liability partnerships, which require a partnership agreement, other partnerships may operate without an agreement, in which case the terms of the *Partnerships Act* and *Limited Partnerships Act* govern the operation and dissolution of the partnership. However, it is generally unwise to rely on the Act: it is not comprehensive, and the partners are in a better position than the government to tailor their agreement to their circumstances and the needs of their business.

A partnership agreement allows the members of a partnership—at the beginning of their business relationship, when goodwill is strong among them—to come to an agreement on all issues that are relevant to their business. This includes both the day-to-day management and more potentially contentious issues that may cause problems for the business in the future.

The business's lawyer usually drafts the partnership agreement. In many cases, individual partners obtain independent legal advice before signing the agreement. Once signed, the agreement governs how the business will operate, how disputes will be resolved, and, if necessary, how the partnership will come to an end. The following is a list of some of the matters that a comprehensive partnership agreement usually covers:

- *financial matters*, such as bank accounts, signing authority for cheques and other documents, accountants and auditors, and borrowing privileges and limits;
- *compensation matters*, such as division of profits, allocation of vacation time, and provisions governing illnesses;
- *business matters*, including scope and limits on the firm's areas of business;
- *management matters*, such as responsibility for hiring and managing employees, ordering office supplies, paying bills, and arranging for the office to be cleaned;
- *membership*, such as adding new partners and removing existing ones; and
- *dissolution of the partnership*, with or without the consent of all partners.

Agreements can be amended from time to time as the needs of the partnership change. An amendment process that is satisfactory to the partners can be included in the agreement itself.

Corporations

The creation of a **corporation** involves the birth of a distinct legal entity, one that has almost all the rights and obligations of an individual and one that enjoys an existence independent of its creators. If the people who created the corporation die, the corporation continues to exist.

The subject of corporations is incredibly complex. There are numerous voluminous statutes and regulations governing corporations, both at the provincial and federal level. Entire books have been written on very small areas of corporate law, and it is not possible to present more than a brief overview of the subject here.

corporation
method of carrying on business by means of a legal entity that is distinct from its creators and enjoys almost all the rights and obligations of an individual

A corporation, familiarly called a company, can be created to run any type of business, large or small. Corporations can themselves create other corporations. They can buy or sell other businesses, enter into contracts, own property, and exert influence. They are very useful in many ways, but the complexity of their creation and operation can make them too expensive and too difficult to be useful for extremely small businesses.

We will explore the differences between private corporations and public corporations later in this chapter. These terms are no longer included in most Canadian statutes, but they are popularly used to indicate whether the company's shares are available for sale to the public. The shares of **private corporations** are held by a small group of people who usually know each other, such as family members or business associates. **Public corporations** sell their shares to the public at large and are subject to a much greater degree of government regulation as a result.

private corporation
corporation whose shares are held by one person or a small group of people and are not offered to the public

public corporation
corporation whose shares are offered for sale to the public

THE PLAYERS

A corporation is distinct from the people who create it, the people who own it, the people who work for it, and the people who manage and run it. We discuss the roles played by people throughout the existence of a corporation in the sections that follow. A diagram of these players appears in figure 6.2.

Incorporators

incorporator
individual or other corporation that causes a corporation to come into existence by filing the required documentation

The creators of a corporation are called its incorporators. An **incorporator**—who may be an individual or another corporation—completes and files the required documents, assembles the initial capital (money), and causes a corporation to come into existence and begin operations. The incorporators are likely to be the initial officers and directors of the corporation, and they are also likely to be its shareholders. The incorporators may remain a part of the corporate structure throughout the life of the corporation, or they may part ways with the corporation at some point during its existence. The corporation, in such a case, continues without them. Incorporators are not legally liable for the debts and obligations of the corporation unless they are also directors of the corporation and, even then, in only very rare circumstances.

Figure 6.2   Corporate Players

Shareholders (elect directors)

Directors (hire officers)

Officers/Senior Management (hire other employees)

Employees

Shareholders

A **shareholder** is an owner of a corporation. The vehicle of ownership is a share: by owning shares in a corporation, a shareholder owns an interest in the assets of the corporation, and may have a voice in how the corporation operates. The rights of share ownership differ according to the type of shares that the shareholder owns and the terms of any shareholders' agreement that may exist.

The rights of a shareholder may include the following:

- the right to vote in the election of the directors of the corporation,
- the right to share in the profits of the corporation in the form of dividends,
- the right to sell some or all of his shares to others,

- the right to share in the assets of the corporation if it is wound up,
- the right to be protected from oppressive acts of the directors or other share-holders, and
- the right to review the corporation's accounts.

Shareholders are generally not liable for the debts and obligations of the corporation.

Directors

A **director** of a corporation is responsible for making major decisions regarding the affairs of the corporation. The directors are the minds of the corporation. Because of this special relationship between corporations and their directors, directors owe a duty—called a **fiduciary duty**—to act in good faith and with reasonable care and competence in the corporation's best interests. This duty requires directors to put the corporation's interests before their own personal financial interests.

Directors are elected by shareholders and must report to shareholders at regular shareholders' meetings. Directors are generally protected against liability for the debts and obligations of the corporation, with a few exceptions, which we discuss below under the heading "Directors' and Officers' Liability."

Officers

An **officer** of a corporation is responsible for the day-to-day operation of a corporation under the supervision of the directors. Officers are members of senior management and may have titles such as chief executive officer, president, chief financial officer, or chief operations officer. Like directors, officers owe a duty to act with reasonable care and competence, and are generally protected against liability for the debts and obligations of the corporation, with a few exceptions.

CREATION

In order to create a corporation, the incorporators must submit an application to the appropriate government office. In Canada, the application must include draft **articles of incorporation**. Included in the articles are the name of the corporation, the location of the head office, the names and addresses of the incorporators, the names and addresses of the corporation's first directors, the number and types of shares that are to be sold, a statement of any restrictions placed on the rights associated with each type of share, a statement of the corporation's business purpose, and the signatures of the incorporators.

The directors named in the articles of incorporation are responsible for setting up and running the corporation on a day-to-day basis. Setting up involves actions such as creating the minute book, adopting the corporate seal, creating and issuing appropriate share certificates, holding inaugural directors' and shareholders' meetings, and appointing auditors for the corporation's financial records.

Statutes such as the *Canada Business Corporations Act* and the Ontario *Business Corporations Act* require corporations to keep corporate records, including a corporate **minute book** that keeps track of all the corporation's important papers, such as the articles of incorporation and amendments, the names and contact information for directors and shareholders, details of share transactions (when shares are issued, bought, or sold), minutes of directors' and shareholders' meetings, copies of any resolutions passed at these meetings, bylaws and amendments, and copies of any unanimous shareholders' agreements. The minute book must be kept up to date and available for review by directors, shareholders, and other interested parties.

corporate seal
imprint made on corporate contracts and other documents that communicates the intention to bind the corporation

The **corporate seal** is a mechanism that was historically used by corporations to communicate their intention to be bound by a written contract. The use of the seal made it clear that it was the corporation, rather than the individuals acting on its behalf, that was binding itself to the terms of the contract. Physically, the seal is a device that is used to create an imprint on paper documents, which is usually kept with the minute book in the offices of the corporation or its legal adviser. The use of a corporate seal is no longer required by many corporate statutes such as the *Canada Business Corporations Act* and the Ontario *Business Corporations Act*, but some corporations choose to use it anyway.

share certificate
document that represents the ownership of shares of a corporation

A **share certificate** is a document that represents the ownership of shares in the corporation. It is signed by the officers or directors of the corporation and is given to shareholders to represent their rights within the corporation. The Ontario *Business Corporations Act* (and other business corporations legislation) severely restricts the advertisement and sale of shares in a private corporation.

The Ontario *Business Corporations Act* (and other similar legislation) also requires the directors to hold directors' and shareholders' meetings within a specified time after the date of registration of the corporation and at regular intervals thereafter. At the shareholders' first meeting, the shareholders elect the corporation's board of directors. The first elected board may include all, some, or none of the incorporators. The board then begins to run the business with a view to earning a profit for the shareholders.

If you decided to incorporate your business, Candyland Treats, you would be required to follow all of the steps outlined above. You would likely consult both a lawyer and an accountant during the process of incorporation. You would pay for their services as well as the cost of the name search, the registration fee (about $500), and the costs of setting up the corporation. You would also need to hire and pay an auditor to review the books as required by the corporation's shareholders.

You could decide to issue shares only to yourself at the outset in order to maintain control of your corporation. You could also name yourself as the corporation's sole director. By keeping things this simple, you could basically run the business as if you were a sole proprietor, with the exception that you would have to maintain the corporate minute book and pay corporate taxes.

A corporate structure also gives you the flexibility to involve others, such as friends and family members, in your business. They can provide start-up funds by buying shares in the corporation, thus providing it with capital and allowing them the opportunity to share in the future profits of the corporation. They can also act as officers or directors of the corporation, bringing their skills to its operation while, perhaps, being paid by the corporation for their efforts.

Federal or Provincial Incorporation

You can choose to file articles of incorporation with a province or with the federal government. Provincial incorporation is generally simpler and cheaper than federal incorporation but gives the corporation full legal rights only in the province of incorporation. Federal incorporation, on the other hand, gives the corporation full legal rights across Canada. This includes the right to use the corporation's name and to stop other businesses from using it.

Federal corporations are governed by the *Canada Business Corporations Act*, and provincial corporations are governed by provincial statutes, such as the *Business Corporations Act* in Ontario. The provisions of these corporate statutes are similar, but there is some variation.

Naming the Corporation

The articles of incorporation must be accompanied by proof that the incorporators have searched the appropriate government databases to ensure that the name they propose to give the corporation is not currently being used by any other corporation in the province or across Canada. This is known as a NUANS (newly updated automated name search) report. If you propose a name that is too similar to the name of an existing corporation and likely to cause confusion, the government will not accept your articles of incorporation.

Instead of naming your corporation, you may accept a number issued to your corporation by the government. In this case, your corporation becomes known as a "numbered company." If, subsequent to incorporation, your numbered company decides to adopt a name, you must then obtain the NUANS report and register the name.

Once a corporation is registered with a particular name, it has the right to protect that name from being used by any other business operating where the corporation was incorporated or where the corporation has registered its name. You could, therefore, incorporate your Candyland Treats business in New Brunswick, register the name in Manitoba and Alberta, and then stop any other business from using that name in all three of those provinces. Alternatively, you could incorporate your business federally, giving you the right to do business and to protect the business name in all Canadian provinces and territories.

The corporation must include a form of the words "corporation," "incorporated," or "limited" (or their French equivalents) in its name. These words can appear in full or abbreviated form. Your business might therefore be known as Candyland Treats Ltd.

Figure 6.3 sets out the steps involved in the creation of any corporation.

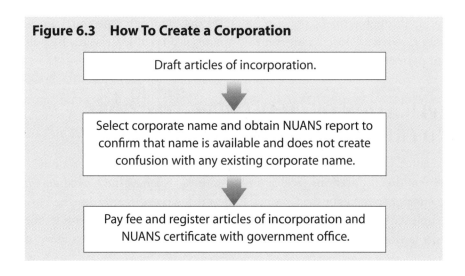

Figure 6.3 How To Create a Corporation

Draft articles of incorporation.

Select corporate name and obtain NUANS report to confirm that name is available and does not create confusion with any existing corporate name.

Pay fee and register articles of incorporation and NUANS certificate with government office.

LEGAL CHARACTERISTICS AND LIABILITY ISSUES

A corporation is a distinct legal entity that has almost all the rights and obligations of an individual. A corporation can enter into and be bound by contracts; it can own property; it can sue and be sued in its own right. A corporation exists independent of its shareholders, directors, and employees.

Because a corporation is an independent legal entity, it is responsible for its own debts and obligations. Except in certain very limited circumstances, a corporate structure protects shareholders, employees, officers, and directors from personal liability of any kind for the debts and obligations of the corporation. Whereas a sole proprietor or a partner faces unlimited liability for the debts and obligations of her business, the shareholder, employee, officer, and director are generally protected.

This is a huge advantage. If the corporation is forced into bankruptcy for any reason (as a result, for example, of poor earnings, insurmountable debt, or losses from lawsuits), generally no asset of its shareholders, directors, or employees can be used to pay the debts of the corporation. The corporation goes down on its own.

This principle of corporate law dates back to 1897 and the landmark case of *Salomon v. A. Salomon & Co. Ltd.*, where a court established that a corporation is a legal entity separate from its shareholders.

From a risk management perspective, Salomon was wise to incorporate. Had his business remained a sole proprietorship, he would have been personally liable for the debts of his shoe business. He would not have been able to collect on his personal loan to the business.

However, creating a corporation is not a simple and foolproof method of protecting yourself from the debts and liabilities of your business. In the case of a small start-up business, loans from financial institutions, such as banks and trust companies, are usually needed as a source of capital. In order to approve a loan, a bank or trust company generally requires collateral. If the corporation has no assets, this means that the business people involved in the corporation must provide the financial institution with personal guarantees.

For example, you, as sole proprietor of Candyland Treats, may decide to operate through a corporation, Candyland Treats Ltd. You anticipate that one of the benefits will be protection against liability and debts. However, in order to receive the bank loan of $50,000 that you need to expand your business into fundraising sales of candy through schools, the bank requires that you sign a personal guarantee. Should Candyland Treats Ltd. run into financial difficulties, the bank could demand payment of the loan from you personally.

APPLICATION OF CHARTER PROTECTIONS AND CRIMINAL LAW TO CORPORATIONS

What other implications flow from the special legal status of corporations? What treatment do corporations receive under statutes—such as the *Canadian Charter of Rights and Freedoms* or the *Criminal Code*—that were primarily designed to apply to people? Generally, whether the special legal status of corporations entitles them to the protections of the Charter depends on the type of right or freedom under

CASE IN POINT Corporations Are Separate Entities

Salomon v. A. Salomon & Co. Ltd., [1897] AC 22 (HL)

Facts

Aron Salomon was the sole proprietor of a successful shoe manufacturing business. For the purpose of eventual transfer of the business to his children, he decided to create a corporation called A. Salomon & Co. Ltd. to operate his business. He issued nearly all of the shares to himself, with only a very few to his wife and children, giving him complete control of all business decisions.

Aron Salomon intended to sell the shoe manufacturing business to A. Salomon & Co. Ltd., but the newly created company had no money. Therefore, he personally loaned the money to the company and took a mortgage on the company's assets. He was now a secured creditor of A. Salomon & Co. Ltd.

Labour troubles eventually led to the business becoming insolvent, and there was a dispute among the company's creditors. As a secured creditor, Aron Salomon claimed that he was entitled to repayment of his loan before the other creditors, such as suppliers, who were unsecured. This would have left nothing for the other creditors. These creditors claimed that Aron Salomon should be held personally liable for the company's debts, to the extent that the company assets were not sufficient to cover them.

Result

The (British) House of Lords held that A. Salomon & Co. Ltd. was a legal entity separate from Aron Salomon. Therefore, Aron Salomon was not personally liable for the debts owed by the company. He was also entitled to payment of his loan ahead of the unsecured creditors from the sale of the company's assets.

Business Lesson

When seeking to limit your personal liability, a corporation may be your best choice of business structure.

---

consideration. For example, freedom of expression has been interpreted as extending to corporations in the case of *Irwin Toy Ltd. v. Quebec (Attorney General),* but the right to equality and the freedom of religion have been restricted to human beings.

Does criminal law apply to corporations? A corporation cannot be sent to jail for criminal acts, but governments are more and more willing to create criminal offences (such as environmental offences) for which corporations can be found guilty and punished through substantial fines. In some cases, the directors of a corporation may be jailed for serious criminal offences perpetrated by the corporation.

DIRECTORS' AND OFFICERS' LIABILITY

Every director and officer of a corporation must use reasonable care, diligence, and skill in the course of carrying out his duties. This fiduciary duty of care, originating in the common law, is codified in corporate statutes such as the *Canada Business*

CASE IN POINT Charter Protections Are Limited for Corporations

Irwin Toy Ltd. v. Quebec (Attorney General), [1989] 1 SCR 927

Facts

Certain sections of Quebec's *Consumer Protection Act* imposed restrictions on advertising to children. The Act included various penalties, such as fines and terms of imprisonment, for those found guilty of committing an offence. Naturally, corporations cannot be imprisoned, so the legislation also deemed corporate directors to be liable and subject to imprisonment, in appropriate cases.

A corporation was charged under the *Consumer Protection Act* for violations of the restricted advertising provisions. (Its individual directors were not charged, however.) The corporation challenged the validity of the legislation on numerous grounds, including that it offended two Charter-guaranteed rights: (1) freedom of expression and (2) the right to life, liberty, and security of the person. It argued that the right to freedom of expression included the right of a business to advertise to children as well as adults. It also argued that the Act contained vague and uncertain provisions, and, since one of the penalties for breach of the Act was imprisonment, this gave rise to a potential deprivation of liberty.

Result

The Supreme Court of Canada agreed that freedom of expression applied to a business's right to advertise. However, it held that the limits on this freedom were justifiable because children can suffer harm as a result of advertising directed at them. With respect to the right to life, liberty, and security of the person, the court decided that the provision protects the "security of the *person*," not the "security of *property*." It does not extend to artificial persons, such as corporations.

Business Lesson

Do not rely on the Charter to protect the rights and freedoms of corporations as if they were individuals. Even when a court is willing to protect a corporate right or freedom—such as the freedom of expression—it may find that limiting the right or freedom is justifiable to protect a larger public interest, such as the well-being of children.

Corporations Act and the Ontario *Business Corporations Act*. Corporate officers and directors are held both to an objective and to a subjective standard, as follows:

- *Objective standard.* Did the officer's or director's conduct match that of a reasonable officer or director?
- *Subjective standard.* Was the officer's or director's conduct reasonable, given her actual knowledge and skill in the circumstances?

Generally, it is not enough for a director or officer to say that she tried her best. However, if a unanimous shareholders' agreement transfers a director's power to the shareholders, a director is relieved from liability. Also, a director who relies in good faith on incorrect financial statements prepared by an officer or auditor is not usually held liable for a breach of her duty.

Directors and officers also have obligations, and are subject to liability, under legislation intended to protect the public, such as environmental protection statutes and workplace statutes that protect employees. This liability can be substantial—as high as hundreds of thousands of dollars in fines—and can even result in prison terms.

Most of these offences are strict liability offences, meaning that the Crown need not prove intent or even negligence. Once the facts of the charge are proven by the Crown—for example, if it was proven that toxic chemicals were released into a river by a corporation—the onus is then on the accused director or officer to prove that he personally did everything reasonable in the circumstances to prevent the offence from occurring. This defence of **due diligence** can be supported by evidence of corporate policies and procedures in place to prevent these events.

due diligence
defence that claims a person did everything reasonable to prevent an offence from occurring

In the case of the *Employment Standards Act, 2000*, offences are absolute liability offences, meaning there is no defence.

Table 6.2 illustrates the statutory obligations of directors and officers under three Ontario statutes.

Table 6.2   Statutory Obligations of Directors and Officers

	Occupational Health and Safety Act	*Employment Standards Act, 2000*	*Environmental Protection Act*
Duty	Every director and officer of a corporation must take all reasonable care to ensure that the corporation complies with the Act, regulations, or court orders made under the Act.	The directors of an employer corporation are jointly and severally liable for wages if the corporation is insolvent and certain conditions have been met.	Every director or officer of a corporation has a duty to take all reasonable care to prevent the corporation from polluting contrary to the Act, or otherwise violating the Act, regulations, or court orders made under the Act.
Liability	The penalty on conviction is a fine of up to $25,000 and/or imprisonment for up to one year.	The directors of an employer corporation are jointly and severally liable to the employees for all debts not exceeding six months' wages.	Depending on the offence, the penalty on conviction may be a fine of up to $50,000 per day that the offence occurs (for first conviction) and up to $100,000 per day (for each subsequent conviction) and/or imprisonment for up to one year. Penalties for other offences include fines of up to $4 million on first conviction (increasing for subsequent convictions) and/or imprisonment for up to five years.
Defence	The onus is on the accused to prove due diligence—that every precaution reasonable in the circumstances was taken. This is a strict liability offence.	There is no defence. This is an absolute liability offence.	The onus is on the accused to prove due diligence—that she carried out the duty in connection with that contravention. This is a strict liability offence.

CASE IN POINT Officers and Directors Can Be Liable for Corporate Pollution

R v. Bata Industries Ltd. (1995), 25 OR (3d) 321 (CA)

Facts

A chemical waste barrel storage site at a corporation's shoe manufacturing facility had been neglected to the point that more than 200 containers, in various sizes and stages of decay, sat rusting and exposed to the elements. One of the directors, who was also president, visited the facility only twice a year, and another director visited about once a month. At some point, however, both directors had personal knowledge of the problem but failed to take effective steps to remedy the situation.

When the corporation was convicted of causing or allowing the discharge of liquid industrial waste, the two directors were also found personally liable for failing to take "all reasonable care" under the *Ontario Water Resources Act* and the *Environmental Protection Act*. The directors were fined $12,000 each. The judge prohibited the corporation from reimbursing the directors for the amounts they were required to pay in fines. The directors appealed their sentences.

Result

The court confirmed the personal liability of the directors, although it reduced their fines to $6,000 each. Environmental legislation obliges corporate officers and directors to establish a pollution prevention system. This includes being aware of industry standards, supervising the program established for the company, and reviewing environmental compliance reports submitted by other corporate officers. Although directors are entitled to place reasonable reliance on those to whom various tasks are delegated, ultimately they remain responsible to ensure that the company complies in full with its environmental responsibilities. The standard of care expected of them varies according to their degree of personal contact with the plant, and according to their knowledge of the environmental problems on site.

Business Lesson

Directors are ultimately responsible for ensuring a company's compliance with environmental laws. They cannot insulate themselves from liability by delegating compliance tasks to others.

SALE OF A CORPORATION

Because ownership of a corporation is represented by the ownership of shares, a corporation is never really sold. Its assets can be sold and some or all of its shares can be sold, but the corporation itself remains intact. For example, Breadspreads Ltd. may sell one of its factories, or even one of its product lines, such as applesauce, to another business. However, the corporation called Breadspreads Ltd. continues to exist, even though the factory and the applesauce line are no longer its assets.

A shareholder of Breadspreads Ltd. might disagree with management's decision to sell the factory and the applesauce line, and choose to sell her shares. If the company is a public company, with shares traded on a stock exchange such as the Toronto Stock Exchange or the New York Stock Exchange, she will simply sell the shares through the exchange to a willing buyer. The buyer will become a shareholder.

It is extremely rare for one person to own all of the shares in a large public corporation. A single person may, however, acquire a controlling interest in the corporation (by buying, for example, more than 50 percent of the shares from their previous owners). A controlling interest allows the person to control who is elected to the board of directors and, through the board, how the corporation is operated. However, having a controlling interest in a corporation does not mean the shareholder "owns" the corporation: he simply owns the majority of the company's shares.

In a smaller, private business, if the directors/shareholders wish to sell their business, they can find an interested purchaser who will then purchase either all the assets of the corporation or all the shares of the corporation.

WINDING UP

The voluntary dissolution and windup of a corporation is generally governed by the same statute that creates the corporation (such as the *Canada Business Corporations Act* or the Ontario *Business Corporations Act*). However, if a corporation begins bankruptcy proceedings, the provisions of the federal *Bankruptcy and Insolvency Act* dictate how the corporation's affairs must be terminated. (We discuss bankruptcy and insolvency in chapter 9.) A corporation is required by statute to maintain its corporate records for a fixed period after dissolution. Any legal proceedings by or against the corporation that were begun before the corporation's dissolution are allowed to continue as though the corporation still exists.

CONDUCTING BUSINESS

Officers, managers, supervisors, and other employees of a corporation carry out a corporation's day-to-day business. If you are the sole shareholder and director of Candyland Treats Ltd., for example, you make all the business decisions and may, in fact, do all the corporation's work. You may wear all the hats: shareholder, director, officer, and employee.

If there are other shareholders or if other people help you with the company's day-to-day business, the process is more complicated. You cannot make decisions about running the business of Candyland Treats Ltd. unilaterally. Large companies with many employees have very complex corporate structures because there are so many people involved in the corporation's day-to-day affairs.

TAXATION IMPLICATIONS

Corporations have a more complex tax structure than non-corporate vehicles for carrying on business. The corporation generates income of its own, pays its own expenses, assumes its own liabilities, and ends up with its own profit or loss in each fiscal year. The government taxes a corporation on its own income in much the same way that it taxes an individual. A corporation is required to prepare and file its own tax returns each year and to pay taxes on its profit.

The corporation may also be required to pay business taxes to the local municipality and to collect and pay GST on the goods and services that it uses and provides. These other taxes are expenses of the corporation for the purpose of calculating its federal income tax.

Shareholders must include dividends (representing a share of the profits) as income in their personal income tax returns. Thus, in essence, the government taxes the profits of corporations twice: once as corporate income and then again as personal income of the shareholders. A dividend tax credit available to shareholders partially offsets this double taxation.

PROFITS

Once all tax is paid, the corporation can use the remainder of its profit as its board of directors sees fit: to expand, replace existing equipment and buildings, pay bonuses for directors and officers, provide raises or bonuses for its employees, save for future plans, or pay dividends to its shareholders. The law requires the board of directors to act fairly and intelligently in deciding what to do with any profits the corporation earns.

For example, growth companies (companies whose revenue is growing quickly) usually reinvest heavily in expansion, and may not pay dividends. Shareholders may be satisfied with this situation if the company's growth is reflected in rising share prices. Mature companies that do not enjoy substantial revenue and profit growth are more likely to pay their profits directly to shareholders by way of dividends. Ultimately, the shareholders who elect the directors will have a voice in how the profits are used.

SHAREHOLDERS' AGREEMENTS

shareholders' agreement
contract that governs the relationship between shareholders or between shareholders and a corporation, or governs how the corporation conducts its business

A **shareholders' agreement** is an enforceable contract designed to govern how two or more shareholders conduct their relationship with the corporation or how the corporation itself conducts its business. Some shareholders' agreements are signed by all shareholders—or, in the case of a more complex corporation where not all shares are voting shares—by all shareholders who are entitled to vote on the affairs of the corporation; these are known as "unanimous shareholders' agreements."

Unanimous shareholders' agreements can be comprehensive—they cover most or all matters concerning how the corporation is run—or they may be limited to one or a few issues related to the relationship among the shareholders or between the shareholders and the corporation.

Agreements that involve only some of the shareholders with voting shares are known as "non-unanimous shareholders' agreements." A non-unanimous shareholders' agreement is, by definition, limited in its scope. In it, certain shareholders might agree to vote on specific corporate issues in specific ways. For example, imagine a corporation in which six individuals own voting shares. One individual owns 40 percent of the voting shares and the other five shareholders each own 12 percent of the voting shares. The 40 percent shareholder will be able to control, for example, who is elected to the board of directors as long as she gets any one of the other five to vote with her or if she is able to split the votes of the other five members in some other way. The five smaller shareholders may not like this state of affairs and may decide, as a group, to enter into a shareholders' agreement in which they agree to vote together in the election of the board. As a result, the five smaller shareholders can effectively control the vote and elect a board that pleases them.

Unanimous shareholders' agreements can also be limited in scope. These agreements often involve issues around the ownership of shares rather than the operation of the corporation. For example, all shareholders in a corporation can agree to ensure that shares in the corporation are not transferred to third parties without the consent of the other shareholders. A unanimous shareholders' agreement can, for example, require each shareholder to take legal steps to ensure that the shares are protected from division of property in the event of a marriage breakdown, are not included in the estate of a deceased shareholder, and cannot be pledged as security for a debt. (The latter requirement would help to avoid the possibility of a lender becoming the owner of the shares in the event that a shareholder defaulted on the debt.)

A comprehensive unanimous shareholders' agreement has a different use. In it, the shareholders of a corporation can set out in detail how they wish the corporation to be managed and operated. This agreement, which is usually included with the articles of incorporation, effectively limits the ability of the directors of the corporation to run the business. If a unanimous shareholders' agreement exists, the directors cannot make decisions that run contrary to the terms of the agreement. The comprehensive unanimous shareholders' agreement can be used to help the close-knit shareholders of a private corporation ensure that no outsider becomes an owner of shares in the corporation, or to ensure that the corporation will operate in a fashion that is acceptable to all shareholders, rather than leaving decisions to individual votes at different meetings.

The comprehensive unanimous shareholders' agreement is similar in its scope to the partnership agreement discussed above. It would include clauses that address such issues as

- the creation, issuance, and transfer of shares by the corporation or the shareholders;
- the business of the corporation;
- the day-to-day operation of the corporation;
- payment of dividends to shareholders;
- compensation for directors;
- the scheduling and running of shareholders' meetings; and
- financial matters, such as banking, accountants and auditors, reports to shareholders, and borrowing limits.

A unanimous shareholders' agreement allows a private corporation to enjoy the flexibility that a partnership offers, while still taking advantage of the benefits of incorporation.

Minimizing Your Risk

Understand the Limits of Corporate Protection

- Remember that a corporation does not always enjoy the same protections as an individual under the Charter.
- Be aware that the directors are personally responsible for a corporation's compliance with environmental and other laws that protect the public.
- Be aware that personal guarantees for loans will erode the liability protection offered by incorporation.
- Remember that directors are answerable for their actions to their corporation's owners: its shareholders.

Private Versus Public Corporations

As we have noted earlier, a private corporation's shares are not offered for sale to the general public. For this reason, it is sometimes referred to as a "closely held corporation" or a "non-offering corporation." It differs from a public corporation (also known as an "offering corporation"), which does issue shares for public sale.

The law imposes fewer requirements on private corporations than on public ones. A private corporation is simpler to create and to operate than a public corporation, but its ability to raise capital for operations and growth is more limited. At any point in its existence, a private corporation can "go public" if it follows the steps set out in the applicable legislation.

CREATION

Private and public corporations are created in much the same way; there are, however, some differences. The single most significant difference is that before shares in a public corporation are offered for sale to the public, the incorporators (in the case of a new public corporation) or the corporation (in the case of a private corporation going public) must prepare and distribute a document called a prospectus.

prospectus
document containing detailed financial information about a corporation that is required before sale of shares to the public

A **prospectus** is a very complex, highly regulated document. Its purpose is to ensure that any member of the public who is contemplating spending his money to purchase shares in the corporation has sufficient reliable information about the corporation, its financial health, and its future prospects to make the decision wisely. Governments require that potential investors have access to reliable information before investing.

The prospectus is too complex a document to describe in detail here. Corporate statutes obligate corporations to prepare and circulate a prospectus to potential investors before offering any of their shares to the public. A corporation or the individuals who create and distribute its prospectus are legally responsible for the accuracy of the information contained in the prospectus. If it contains false or misleading information, whoever circulated the prospectus may be sued by anyone who suffered a loss as a result of relying on it.

ADVANTAGES AND DISADVANTAGES

Raising Capital

The major advantage of a public corporation over a private corporation is that a public corporation has the ability to raise capital by selling shares to the public. As any corporation grows, it may require an influx of money to take advantage of a new business opportunity or to add to its production capacity. The group that owns a private corporation may not have enough money to meet the corporation's needs. By going public, a corporation can attract investment by all kinds of people.

The public corporation is the method of carrying on business best suited to larger enterprises that require a great deal of capital to operate. By providing the corporation access to the pockets of the investing public, the public corporation allows a business to grow.

Share Ownership and Control

The disadvantage of a public corporation, clearly, is loss of control: the more voting shares owned by different members of the public, the less control any one shareholder or group of shareholders has. It is often more difficult to convince members of the public to invest in a corporation that is controlled by a small, fixed group than it is to attract them to a corporation in which they will have a say in operations.

Ownership of a public corporation is potentially much more volatile. Because any member of the public can buy shares in the corporation, there is the possibility that any person can—at any time—become the controlling shareholder. In some cases, a takeover of ownership of a public corporation is "hostile"—that is, the person buying shares in an effort to gain control is doing so contrary to the wishes of the directors, officers, and (perhaps) some of the corporation's existing shareholders.

Cost and Complexity

Setting up and running any corporation is significantly more costly and complex than setting up and running either a sole proprietorship or a partnership. However, a public corporation is by far the most expensive and complex. The potential involvement of members of the public as shareholders creates a whole new set of requirements with regard to financial record keeping, auditing, and reporting, which contribute to the cost of running this type of corporation.

Tax Implications

Sometimes a private corporation is created for the operation of a family business, with minimizing tax as a primary goal. For example, the corporation's share structure can be used to divert income to the lowest earners in the family business, thereby taking advantage of the low earner's low marginal income tax rate. The structuring of income flow is an extremely complex subject, well beyond the scope of this chapter.

Liability and Accountability

The protection against liability that incorporation offers to business owners generally applies to both private and public companies. However, because a public corporation, by definition, involves members of the public in the ownership of the business, the activities and decisions of its directors and officers may be more closely scrutinized by shareholders and securities commissions (the government bodies that regulate the sale of shares of public companies). The law demands greater care with regard to reports of meetings, and audit and budgeting requirements.

A director of a public corporation is much more likely to be called to task for her decisions than is a director of a private corporation, in which she is likely a major shareholder or the relative of a major shareholder. Unanimous shareholders' agreements, discussed earlier, are one method for shareholders to restrict the discretion of the corporation's directors. Statutory remedies that can be used to level the inequality between minority and controlling shareholders are also available under many corporate statutes. Corporate statutes also give shareholders strong protections against inappropriate conduct by the directors or other shareholders of a public corporation.

Minority shareholders who have suffered unfair treatment at the hands of majority shareholders can apply to the court to force the corporation to buy their shares at fair market value or a judicially set fair price. In some jurisdictions, including Ontario, the court has broad discretion to make orders where a shareholder can demonstrate "oppression"—direct and individual harm. These orders may include, but are not restricted to, the following:

- an order restraining the conduct complained of,
- an order appointing a receiver or receiver-manager,
- an order to regulate a corporation's affairs by amending the articles or bylaws or creating or amending a unanimous shareholders' agreement,
- an order replacing directors,
- an order compensating an aggrieved person, or
- an order winding up the corporation.

Parties other than minority shareholders, such as creditors of the corporation, may also use the oppression remedy in certain circumstances.

CASE IN POINT Oppression Remedy

Downtown Eatery (1993) Ltd. v. Ontario (2001), 54 OR (3d) 161 (CA)

Facts
Grad and Grosman owned and operated two nightclubs in Toronto. Alouche worked as a manager of one of the clubs, and received his paycheque from Best Beaver, a related company controlled by Grad and Grosman. When Alouche was fired, he sued Best Beaver for wrongful dismissal. In the midst of the lawsuit there was a major reorganization of the Grad-Grosman companies, and Best Beaver ceased to do business. Alouche was awarded $59,906.76 in damages, but was unable to collect the money from the defunct Best Beaver. Alouche sued Grad and Grosman personally, on the basis of the oppression remedy.

Result
Harm caused to the complainant by oppressive conduct need not be intentional for the oppression remedy to apply. Although the winding up of Best Beaver was not designed to deprive Alouche of the damages awarded to him, that was in fact the result. Grad and Grosman, as the only shareholders of Best Beaver, benefited from this restructuring. As a result, the court ordered them to pay Alouche the amount of the judgment against Best Beaver.

Business Lesson
Parties other than minority shareholders, such as creditors, may also use the oppression remedy in certain circumstances. The protection against liability enjoyed by the shareholders of a corporation is not absolute.

Considerations Concerning Control and Growth

The corporation is a complex, highly regulated method of carrying on business. It has many advantages but, when numerous people are involved as directors and shareholders, it can become very difficult to control and manage. Changes to the corporation's structure, mandate, business process, or operations cannot be made quickly and easily. Meetings must be held, approvals obtained, and votes taken. In many cases, significant changes must be discussed and voted on at shareholders' and directors' meetings, and must be recorded in the corporate minute book. This can adversely affect the business's ability to respond rapidly to changes in a competitive climate.

On the other hand, the corporate form can accommodate the growth of a small business into a massive enterprise. Even with the simplest of articles and the most conservative of share structures, a corporation can become immense and immensely powerful. It can create other corporations under its own control (subsidiaries), it can amalgamate with other existing corporations, and it can enter into a partnership with other corporations or people.

Corporations of any size require the services of legal, accounting, and other advisers to meet their obligations under the law, to compete effectively in business, and, if necessary, to terminate operations.

Table 6.3 provides a comparison of some aspects of private and public corporations. Figure 6.4 is a graphic presentation of the cost, complexity, and liability exposure factors of various business structures, including private and public corporations.

> **Minimizing Your Risk**
> **Understand the Complexities of Going Public**
> - Consult an experienced lawyer before undertaking the responsibilities of steering a corporation through the process of going public.
> - Ensure that your company's prospectus is professionally drafted to comply with statutory requirements.
> - Expect and prepare for ongoing monitoring by government regulators.

Table 6.3 Comparison of Private and Public Corporations

	Private Corporation	Public Corporation
Typical example	A sole proprietorship or small partnership wants the liability protection of a corporation; the owner(s) want to maintain control and do not need to raise a large amount of capital.	A successful business needs a large amount of capital to grow; its owners are willing to forgo a degree of control, in order to raise money, by selling shares to the public.
Raising capital	More difficult to raise capital.	Can continuously raise capital by issuing more shares, provided there are interested buyers.
Regulation	Less regulation because its shares are not sold to the public.	More regulation—particularly regarding public financial disclosure—because its shares are sold to the public.
Cost and complexity	Less complex and expensive because there is less regulation.	More complex and expensive because of onerous regulation, especially regarding public financial disclosure.
Share ownership and control	Control is retained by one shareholder or a small group of shareholders.	Because more shares are issued, sold, and traded, control is less concentrated and more susceptible to change.

Figure 6.4   Cost, Complexity, and Liability Exposure in Business Structures

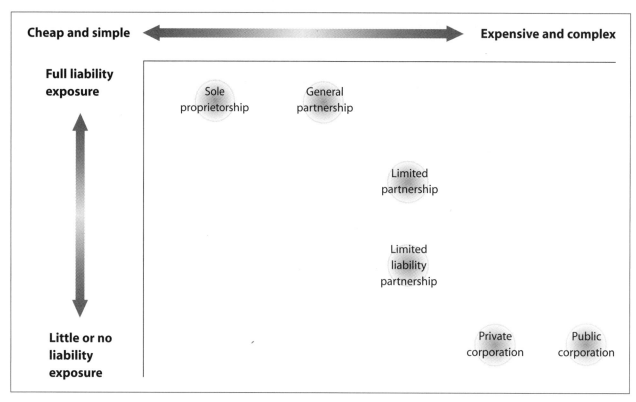

Agency

An **agent** is a person with the authority (or apparent authority) to represent another person, persons, or corporation (called the **principal**). The agent acts on the principal's behalf in an interaction with a third party and affects the legal position or interests of the principal. An agent can, for example, bind a principal to a contract with a third party. Figure 6.5 demonstrates this situation.

You may have heard the terms "signing agent" or "signing authority." These terms apply to an agent who has the authority to sign contracts or cheques on behalf of a principal. These documents are signed "per" the principal.

In the business world, an agency relationship commonly arises in contractual situations. For example, an employee can act as an agent for his employer when negotiating a contract with a customer. In this case, the employer, as a principal, may be obliged to fill the customer's order at the price negotiated by the employee. Binding contracts may also be signed by partners as agents of partnerships and by incorporators as agents of soon-to-be-incorporated businesses.

Agency can also be used as a form of business organization. For example, you—as the sole proprietor of Candyland Treats—may choose to hire a sales agent to sell candy to local schools for fundraising. This sales agent is not your employee, but rather an independent contractor as described in chapter 7 under the heading "Independent Contractor or Employee?" According to agency law, if the sales agent signs a candy sales contract with a school, the school can enforce this contract against you, the principal.

Figure 6.5   Contractual Relationship Between Principal, Agent, and Third Party

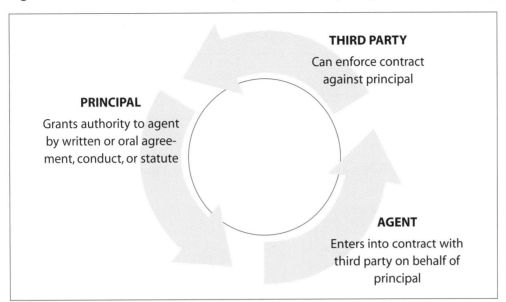

We return to each of these situations that involve agency—soon-to-be-incorporated businesses, employment relationships, partnerships, and agency as a method of carrying on business—in greater detail later in the chapter. We now turn to an exploration of the characteristics of all agency relationships and the authority—both real and apparent—of agents.

CHARACTERISTICS OF AGENCY

The basic characteristics of an agent–principal relationship are as follows:

- The agent has the authority (either real or apparent) to represent and bind the principal to a contract with a third party.
- The agent has a duty to represent the principal fairly and to act in the best interests of the principal while representing him.
- Any third party with whom the agent deals has the right to rely on the agent's authority and to hold the principal legally responsible for its dealings with the agent.

APPARENT AUTHORITY

The existence of an agency relationship is usually clear, and agents usually act within the scope of the authority granted by their principals. However, sometimes an agent may act outside of the scope of her authority. For example, if you—as the owner of Candyland Treats—tell a sales agent that she is not authorized to offer discounts to your customers, what happens if she negotiates a contract that involves a discount? Can that school enforce the contract against Candyland Treats?

The answer may be yes. If Candyland Treats allows the school to assume that the person who signs the contract has the authority to act as its agent, Candyland Treats may be bound by the person's apparent authority. The case of *Steinman v. Snarey* demonstrates this point.

CASE IN POINT   An Agent Can Bind His Principal

Steinman v. Snarey, [1987] OJ no. 2400 (Dist. Ct.); aff'd. [1988] OJ no. 2917 (HCJ)

Facts

The plaintiff customer gave a well-respected life insurance agent $16,000 to deposit in a five-year investment. However, the agent, who worked for a life insurance company, did not invest the money; instead, he fraudulently took it for himself, along with investment money from other customers. By the time his fraud came to light, the money was gone. The plaintiff customer sued the insurance company for whom the agent worked, claiming he was entitled to return of the money that the agent had misappropriated. The company responded by claiming that the customer had dealt with the agent in a *private* capacity, not in the capacity of the company's agent, and therefore it was not responsible for his losses.

Result

The company was found liable to the customer for the funds that the agent had misappropriated. The agent had persuaded the customer that he was purchasing a legitimate investment that was offered by the company. He also led the customer to believe that he was acting on behalf of his principal, the company, in offering the investment. The investment was the kind that the company normally offered to the public. As a result, the agent's misrepresentation and his acceptance of the customer's money were well within the scope of the agent's authority. The company was therefore bound by the agent's conduct and liable to the customer for the agent's wrongdoing.

Business Lesson

Remember that if an agent of your business is acting within the scope of his authority, your business may be bound by even fraudulent conduct on the agent's part.

AGENCY AND SOON-TO-BE-INCORPORATED BUSINESSES

pre-incorporation contract
contract entered into between a third party and the incorporators of a soon-to-be-incorporated business

ratify
acknowledge corporate liability for a contract entered into on behalf of a business before incorporation

Before a corporation comes into legal existence, its incorporators often wish to set the business in motion. They may, for example, want to sign leases on buildings, sign contracts to purchase equipment and materials, and even enter into sales contracts with customers of the future corporation. Because the corporation does not yet exist, it does not itself have the legal standing to do these things.

However, the incorporators can sign **pre-incorporation contracts**, advising the other parties that they are doing so as agents for the soon-to-be-created corporation. The corporation can then **ratify**—or adopt—the contracts after incorporation has taken place. Once the newly formed corporation has officially ratified the contract—or, in the language of agency law, once the corporation has acknowledged its incorporators' authority to act as its pre-incorporation agent—the corporation becomes legally liable for the contracts as principal in the agency relationship.

It must be noted, however, that the incorporator who signed the contract will be personally liable for the contract if the corporation does not come into existence or if it refuses to adopt the contract after its incorporation.

AGENCY AND THE EMPLOYMENT RELATIONSHIP

Employees who are carrying out the business of their employer and acting within the scope of their authority (or apparent authority) are agents of the employer. The agency relationship usually involves executives, such as officers of a corporation, who make major decisions that affect the business. It is reasonable for third parties who deal with these executives to rely on the representations that they make on behalf of the business.

If there are any restrictions on the authority of executives, such as procedures they must follow before striking a deal with a third party, it is the business's responsibility to communicate these limitations to the third party. Otherwise, it will be bound to the contract because the executive had apparent authority. In the context of corporate management, this concept is sometimes called the "indoor management rule," and it has been codified in corporate statutes.

Employees other than executives may also act as agents for their employer. For example, cashiers in clothing stores enter into simple contracts with customers every day on behalf of their employers. These employees can also bind their employer, even when they act beyond the scope of their actual authority. For example, even if it is against store policy, a cashier may act within the scope of her apparent authority in making an agreement with a customer that the customer can return a sweater and repurchase it the next week during a scheduled sale. In this case, the store is probably legally required to fulfill this commitment to the customer.

AGENCY AND PARTNERSHIP

All partners are agents of their partnership. This common-law rule has been codified in the *Partnerships Act*, and it means that any contract made by a partner in the course of the partnership business generally binds the other partners. It is therefore important that partners follow the rules of the partnership and not act beyond the scope of their authority as defined in their partnership agreement.

AGENCY AS A METHOD OF CARRYING ON BUSINESS

A person, including an individual or a business, may choose to become an agent as a method of earning money. In fact, he can create a business whose sole role is acting as an agent for another business. Your cousin, for example, could become a sales agent of Candyland Treats and derive his only business income from this undertaking.

An agent may also have a number of clients. For example, real estate or talent agents usually have many clients—or principals—whom they represent. This form of agency is most common in the representation of athletes, musicians, writers, and performers: a knowledgeable person sets up business as an agent and recruits clients from one or more professions. Sports agents, for example, often limit themselves to representing athletes in one or two particular sports, but may represent dozens of athletes within those sports. The agent earns commission on the contracts she negotiates between her clients and the sports teams for which they play, and may also negotiate sponsorship deals.

agency agreement
contract between principal and agent that describes the agent's rights and authority

The principal in an agency relationship may also have several agents. For example, Candyland Treats may have different agents representing it in different parts of the province or the country. Each agent would enter into an **agency agreement** that would set out the sales territory (the geographic area in which the sales agent is to operate), the commission rate, the time period covered by the agreement, the scope of the agent's authority (the agent may, for example, be allowed to approach public schools but not colleges and universities), and how the agency relationship is to be governed.

The advantage for Candyland Treats is that it can assemble a devoted and enthusiastic sales force without assuming all the legal obligations of hiring full-time employees. The advantage for the agents is that they have flexibility in setting their own schedules and in choosing how to approach clients; they can also control their incomes, earning as much as they need or want in a particular year.

An agency relationship can also be implied from the circumstances or from past behaviour. If, for example, your cousin has been selling your candy to local schools for a year on a commission basis, but with no formal agency agreement, an agency relationship exists between you and your cousin.

Minimizing Your Risk

Take Care in Creating and Defining Agency Relationships

- Provide written clarification of all agency relationships to ensure that agents act only within the scope of their defined authority.

- Advise third parties with whom your business contracts of any limitations on the authority of your agents.

- Avoid personal liability by ensuring that soon-to-be-incorporated businesses ratify all pre-incorporation contracts.

- Use a partnership agreement to define and clarify the roles of all members of a partnership.

- Consider agency as a cost-efficient means of obtaining staff on an as-needed basis.

Joint Ventures

joint venture
temporary relationship created for the purpose of completing one or a series of business projects

A **joint venture** is not a form of carrying on business; rather, it is a temporary relationship between two or more people or businesses that come together for the purpose of completing one or a series of specific projects. The members of a joint venture can be individuals, sole proprietorships, partnerships, or corporations. A joint venture need not be registered with the government or undergo any other official process, and it rarely has a name.

If you wanted Candyland Treats to join forces with the children's bookstore and the children's clothing store in your neighbourhood to hold a one-day street party, you could undertake this project as a joint venture. Candyland Treats would have no legal relationship with the other stores, apart from the relationship created for this one-day event. Your relationship could be defined and governed by a written agreement between Candyland Treats and the other stores. It would cover all matters related to the event, such as who does what, who pays for what, and who is entitled to what portion of the income; it would also address matters such as insurance, security, permits, crowd control, and food supply.

The joint venture, as an approach to a particular project or series of projects, has its advantages. It is fairly simple and quick to put together, and it has a natural end. It allows businesses to work together for a brief period to their mutual advantage, then to go their separate ways at the end of the project with no impact on their individual operations or legal status.

There are, however, some disadvantages. If a joint venture agreement is not carefully and properly prepared, problems can arise among the members regarding how to share profits (or losses) and how to deal with liabilities. There is also the possibility that members of the venture may not put their full efforts into the project. You might find, for example, that you are too busy operating Candyland Treats to put much effort into the street party; the joint venture would suffer as a result, and the other two businesses could end up losing money, losing clients, or even facing lawsuits as a result of your inattentiveness.

Minimizing Your Risk
Create Written Agreements Before Entering Joint Ventures

- Determine the legal requirements of your joint venture, such as permits and security, and satisfy them.

- Obtain adequate insurance coverage to protect you from liability.

- Draft and sign a written agreement that defines the responsibilities of participants in the venture.

- Devise a formula or other method for sharing profits and losses and include it in your written agreement.

Franchises

A **franchise** is a right to operate a business using the name, products, business methods, and advertising of another business. Franchises exist all over Canada, particularly in the fast food and convenience store industries. Sometimes it is difficult to tell whether a particular business is simply a member of a chain of stores all owned by the same corporation or a franchise of a larger corporation.

In a typical franchise situation, a large and established corporation enters into agreements with smaller business enterprises (sole proprietorships, partnerships, or other corporations). For a fee (or a percentage of the profit), the large corporation (the franchisor) allows the small enterprise (the franchisee) to operate in a particular location and sell the products of the franchisor.

The franchise agreement between the two businesses is often extremely detailed. It governs almost every aspect of the business relationship and usually favours the franchisor. In essence, the prospective franchisee knows that the franchisor is successful and well known; the franchisee is therefore willing to have the franchisor control her business in order to profit from the success of the franchisor.

A franchise agreement usually includes the requirement that

- the franchisee sell only products supplied by the franchisor, in the form in which they are supplied, to the standards set by the franchisor;
- the franchisee set up and decorate the business premises exactly as required by the franchisor so that the outlet resembles all other franchises;
- the franchisee pay both an initial franchise fee and a periodic royalty to the franchisor, often a percentage of the profit of the franchise;
- the franchisee provide audited financial statements to the franchisor on a regular basis;

franchise
right to operate a business using the name, products, business methods, and advertising of another business

- the franchisee contribute a certain amount of money to the franchisor's advertising fund, which the franchisor then uses to advertise the franchise across its territory (national, provincial, or local);
- the franchisee offer specials and discounts only as directed by the franchisor;
- the franchisee limit her business to a given territory (when, for example, delivering fast foods);
- the franchisee maintain the business premises, the service offered to the public, and the products offered for sale to the standards of the franchisor;
- the franchisee establish and maintain sufficient liability insurance on the business and protect the franchisor from any legal liabilities that may arise; and
- the franchisee participate in any group scheme or organization that the franchisor might set up (for example, the central call centre of a pizza business).

The agreement also usually includes an acknowledgement that the franchisor may, at any time, revoke the franchise agreement if the franchisee fails to live up to any of her obligations under the agreement.

Many Canadian jurisdictions have taken an active approach to regulating franchises in recent years. More regulations are appearing, requiring franchisors to provide reliable information to prospective franchisees about the business, its products, the terms of the franchise agreement, and the franchisor's financial situation. The increased disclosure requirements make it easier for a prospective franchisee to make an informed and intelligent decision about entering into a franchise agreement with a particular franchisor.

There are many advantages to the franchise method of carrying on business for both parties. The franchisee enjoys some of the advantages of running her own business while knowing that she is offering a popular product and that she is supported by strong advertising and the guidance of experts from the franchisor. A franchisee who is inexperienced in running a business may benefit greatly from the guidance of an experienced franchisor. If, at a later time, the franchisee chooses to run her own business, she can take the lessons she has learned from the experience of operating the franchise and apply them at her new business.

The sale of franchises allows the franchisor to expand quickly into new territories while not taking the full risk and cost of the new ventures upon itself. The franchisor, by choosing its franchisees wisely, obtains the services of strong local managers with a powerful interest in making the business succeed. Both the local franchisee and the large franchisor can profit from the arrangement.

On the other hand, a franchise has disadvantages, especially for the creative franchisee. In most cases, the franchisor hands the franchisee a business package and expects her to operate her business to the rigorous standards of the franchisor. There is no room for creativity. The franchisor believes that the success of the entire franchise business depends on customers finding consistent quality and service in every location. It will usually not, therefore, allow franchisees to exercise their creative judgment in response to local conditions or personal preference.

And, unfortunately, the franchisor often keeps for itself sweeping powers to cancel the franchise agreement. From time to

Minimizing Your Risk
Investigate Potential Franchisors Thoroughly

- Take advantage of disclosure requirements to conduct a thorough investigation of a franchisor's products, franchise terms, and financial situation.

- Investigate a potential franchisor's track record, and refuse to do business with franchisors who unexpectedly and unjustifiably revoke successful franchises.

time, it exercises these powers to the detriment of a blameless franchisee. For example, there have been cases where a franchisee has succeeded far beyond the expectations of the franchisor in a particular location, only to have their store taken from them. At the height of an outlet's success, some franchisors have used the powers given to them by the franchise agreement to revoke the franchise in order to take over the business and enjoy the profits themselves (or to give the franchise to someone to whom they are related).

Chapter Summary

In this chapter, we described the different methods of carrying on business, including sole proprietorships, partnerships, and corporations, and we compared the advantages and disadvantages of operating as each. We explored matters such as liability, the cost of setting up, the complexity of structuring the business, and various tax implications. Our purpose was to explore the circumstances under which business people might prefer to use one business structure in preference to another.

We compared the three types of partnerships (general, limited, and limited liability) and differentiated between the two types of corporations (private and public). We then described the agent–principal relationship and explored the practical implications of operating a business as an agency. Finally, we discussed joint ventures and the advantages and disadvantages of franchises.

KEY TERMS

agency agreement
agent
articles of incorporation
business structure
company
corporate seal
corporation
director
due diligence
fiduciary duty
franchise
general partnership
incorporator
joint venture
jointly and severally liable
limited liability partnership (LLP)

limited partnership
minute book
officer
partnership agreement
partnership or firm
pre-incorporation contract
principal
private corporation
prospectus
public corporation
ratify
share certificate
shareholder
shareholders' agreement
sole proprietorship
unlimited liability

REFERENCES

Bankruptcy and Insolvency Act, RSC 1985, c. B-3, as amended.
Business Corporations Act, RSO 1990, c. B.16.
Business Names Act, RSO 1990, c. B.17.

Canada Business Corporations Act, RSC 1985, c. C-44.

Canadian Charter of Rights and Freedoms, part I of the *Constitution Act, 1982*, RSC 1985, app. II, no. 44.

Constitution Act, 1982, RSC 1985, app. II, no. 44.

Irwin Toy Ltd. v. Quebec (Attorney General), [1989] 1 SCR 927.

Limited Partnerships Act, RSO 1990, c. L.16.

Partnerships Act, RSO 1990, c. B.17.

R v. Bata Industries Ltd. (1995), 25 OR (3d) 321 (CA).

Salomon v. A. Salomon & Co. Ltd. (1897), AC 22 (HL).

Steinman v. Snarey, [1987] OJ no. 2400 (Dist. Ct.); aff'd. [1988] OJ no. 2917 (HCJ).

Trade-marks Act, RSC 1985, c. T-13, as amended.

REVIEW AND DISCUSSION

True or False?

1. A sole proprietorship is a corporation with only one shareholder.

2. The name of a sole proprietorship must include the name of the owner.

3. A partnership is a legal entity.

4. A general partnership does not require a partnership agreement.

5. A corporation is a "person" in law.

6. Shareholders are liable for the debts and obligations of the corporation in which they hold shares.

7. A private corporation does not offer shares for sale to the public.

8. Many principals may work for one agent.

9. Before a company is officially incorporated, the incorporators often act as agents for the corporation.

Multiple Choice

1. Which of the following is not an advantage of a sole proprietorship?
   a. limited liability
   b. inexpensive to set up
   c. losses incurred by the business can be set off against the owner's income from other sources to reduce income tax
   d. changes to the owner's business plan can be made easily

2. The word "firm" is most appropriately used to describe which business structure?
   a. a limited partnership only
   b. a partnership of lawyers or accountants only
   c. any partnership
   d. a privately held corporation

3. Limited partners are best described as
- a. partners that make only a limited financial contribution
- b. partners in a general partnership
- c. partners that receive a smaller portion of the partnership's profits
- d. investors in a partnership

4. Which of the following activities may a corporation carry out?
- a. create other corporations
- b. buy or sell other business entities
- c. enter into contracts
- d. all of the above

5. Which of these statements is most correct?
- a. Shareholders report to directors.
- b. Directors report to officers, and officers report to shareholders.
- c. Directors report to shareholders, and officers report to directors.
- d. Directors report to incorporators.

6. Which of the following are responsible for the day-to-day operation of a corporation?
- a. shareholders
- b. directors
- c. officers
- d. incorporators

7. Which one of the following is not a characteristic of an agent–principal relationship?
- a. The agent's authority may be general, or it may be restricted in some way.
- b. The agent has a duty to fairly represent the principal and to act in the best interests of the principal.
- c. Any third party with whom the agent deals has the right to rely on the agent's authority and to hold the principal legally responsible for its dealings with the agent.
- d. The agent is an employee of the principal.

8. Which of these descriptions of a joint venture is false?
- a. It is a temporary relationship designed to allow participants to complete one or a series of projects.
- b. Participants may be individuals or businesses, including sole proprietorships, partnerships, and corporations.
- c. The joint venture must have a name that combines the names of all of its participants.
- d. A joint venture need not be registered with the government.

9. Which of the following is not an advantage to a franchisee?
- a. selling a known, popular product
- b. advertising and marketing support paid for by the franchisor
- c. business advice from the franchisor with a successful track record
- d. quick expansion into new territories

Short Answer

1. What are the legal requirements in creating a sole proprietorship?
2. Is it mandatory to register a name for a sole proprietorship?
3. Must a sole proprietor file a separate income tax return for her business?
4. Can two people co-own a sole proprietorship?
5. What are the three types of partnerships in Canada?
6. How are a sole proprietorship and a partnership similar?
7. What does "jointly and severally liable" mean?
8. A partnership agreement is a contract that sets out the rules that govern the partnership. What are some of the issues it may cover?
9. What are some of the rights that shareholders enjoy?
10. What is a comprehensive unanimous shareholders' agreement?
11. What is the main advantage of a public corporation over a private corporation?
12. Describe the contents and purpose of a prospectus.
13. What matters are covered in a franchise agreement?

Discussion and Debate

Corporations have enjoyed the status of "persons" under the law since the mid-1800s. In a recent film called *The Corporation*, filmmakers Mark Achbar, Jennifer Abbott, and Joel Bakan examine the "personality" of the corporate "person." Using psychiatric diagnostic criteria, they argue that corporate operating principles give corporations an extremely anti-social personality. They claim that, according to these criteria, many corporations are callous, self-interested, deceitful, and in breach of social and legal standards, yet oddly able to mimic the human qualities of empathy and altruism. Rent the film on DVD and, as a class, discuss the filmmakers' point of view. Do you agree with it? Why or why not?

Workplace Law

What Is Workplace Law?

Workplace law regulates the day-to-day relationships between you and the employees who work for your business. It affects all stages of these relationships, from the time you recruit employees until the time an employee resigns, retires, or is dismissed. Workplace law is an extremely broad branch of business law. It includes human rights law, contract law, employment standards law, health and safety law, equity law, privacy law, labour relations law, and tort law.

In order to deal with any of the following situations, you must be familiar with the laws that govern the workplace:

- An applicant for a secretarial job at your business is qualified and has excellent references; during his job interview, it is apparent that his vision is extremely poor and that he would need special equipment to do the work you require.

You are concerned that if you hire him, you may be required to purchase expensive equipment.

- Fearing that equipment is unsafe at your manufacturing plant, two certified members of the joint health and safety committee issue a stop work order. You need to get your staff back to work as quickly as possible to fulfill a significant contractual obligation.
- A manager confidentially advises you that certain of your employees are interested in forming a union to improve their benefits and working conditions. You consider speaking directly to these employees about their union activities until you remember that the *Labour Relations Act, 1995* prohibits you from interfering.
- You must restructure your operations quickly in order to remain competitive in the marketplace. It is necessary for you to dismiss a non-unionized long-term employee and several new recruits. You want to avoid the expense of being sued for wrongful dismissal. How do you begin to structure a severance package?

In Canada, laws governing the workplace rights of employers and employees are found both in statutes and in common law. Although both the federal and provincial levels of government can pass employment-related statutes, about 90 percent of employees in Canada are governed by provincial employment legislation. Federal employment laws cover the 10 percent of employees who work in national industries, such as airlines, broadcasting, banks, and interprovincial transportation. Since the majority of workplaces are provincially regulated, this chapter focuses on Ontario's employment legislation. (The employment laws in other provinces are often similar, although not identical, to the laws discussed below.) The key Ontario employment statutes that a business person needs to be aware of are the following:

- the *Human Rights Code*, which prohibits and provides remedies for discrimination based on specified grounds;
- the *Employment Standards Act, 2000*, which provides minimum working standards for employees, including minimum wages, overtime, hours of work, termination and severance pay, pregnancy and parental leave, vacation, and public holidays;
- the *Occupational Health and Safety Act*, which outlines requirements and responsibilities for creating a safe workplace and preventing workplace injuries and accidents;
- the *Workplace Safety and Insurance Act, 1997*, which provides a no-fault insurance plan to compensate workers for work-related injuries and diseases;
- the *Pay Equity Act*, which requires employers with 10 or more employees to provide equal pay for work of equal value; and
- the *Labour Relations Act, 1995*, which deals with the rights of employees to form unions and bargain collectively with their employer.

We also discuss the following federal statutes in this chapter because their requirements affect some Ontario employers:

- the *Personal Information Protection and Electronic Documents Act*, which establishes rules concerning how businesses may collect, use, or disclose personal information; and

- the *Employment Equity Act*, which requires employers with 100 or more employees to take measures to increase their representation of visible minorities, women, people with disabilities, and aboriginals to reflect the demographics of the available workforce.

Business people should also be familiar with certain aspects of the common law. The employment relationship between an employer and a **non-unionized employee** is contractual, and therefore the principles of contract law apply. The terms and conditions of employment for a **unionized employee** are set out in collective agreements, which we discuss later in this chapter in the section entitled "The Unionized Workplace."

The Importance of Workplace Law for Business People

The law of the workplace is diverse and can be complex. It is nevertheless essential for business people to understand and to be able to identify the key legal issues that can arise on a day-to-day basis. Why?

- Understanding *workplace law can help you reduce business risks and minimize time-consuming and costly legal problems.* If you are unaware of the laws that govern your workplace, your business is at a disadvantage. It may be subject to government fines and penalties for failing to comply with statutory employment, human rights, and health and safety standards of which you are unaware. It may also be sued by employees who are becoming increasingly knowledgeable and insistent about their rights and your obligations.
- *Infringement of workplace law can impair your business image.* Without knowing the prohibited grounds of discrimination under the *Human Rights Code*, for example, you may find—to your surprise—that your business is guilty of practising discrimination in the workplace. The costs to your reputation in the business community—and the community at large—of a well-publicized human rights complaint could be formidable.
- *A business's relationship with its employees can have far-reaching effects on an organization's public image, profitability, and survival.* If you comply with workplace laws, develop effective policies, and constructively manage disputes in your workplace, the resulting good relations with employees, unions, and the public can go a long way to ensuring the future success of your business and its place in the larger community.

Human Rights in the Workplace

The Ontario *Human Rights Code* states that it is "public policy in Ontario to recognize the dignity and worth of every person and to provide for equal rights and opportunities without discrimination." The Code, which applies to all stages of the employment relationship, aims to "create a climate of understanding and mutual respect for the dignity and worth of each person." The Code prohibits workplace **discrimination** and harassment on specified prohibited grounds.

non-unionized employee
employee whose terms and conditions of employment are based on an individual employment contract rather than a collective agreement negotiated between an employer and a union

unionized employee
employee whose terms and conditions of employment are based on a collective agreement negotiated between an employer and a union rather than on an individual contract of employment

discrimination
negative or singular treatment of a person or group on the basis of a prohibited ground of discrimination under the *Human Rights Code*

PROHIBITED GROUNDS OF DISCRIMINATION

The Ontario *Human Rights Code* prohibits discrimination in employment on the following grounds:

- race;
- ancestry;
- place of origin;
- colour;
- ethnic origin;
- citizenship;
- creed (religion);
- sex (male, female, or transgendered, and including the right to equal treatment without discrimination because of pregnancy);
- sexual orientation;
- age (where the person is at least 18 years old);
- record of offences (provincial offences or pardoned federal offences);
- marital status;
- family status (this ground covers parent and child relationships and includes biological parents, adoptive parents, and legal guardians); and
- disability (this ground includes physical, mental, and psychiatric disabilities; drug or alcohol addiction; perceived disabilities; and disabilities for which workers' compensation benefits were claimed or received; it excludes minor, temporary illness to which the general public is susceptible, such as the flu or common cold).

If your business makes an employment decision in which a prohibited ground plays *any* part, unless one of the exceptions described below applies, you have infringed the Code. It is irrelevant whether the prohibited ground was the only, or even the primary, factor that you took into account. It is irrelevant that you did not know you were discriminating or that the motives for your decision were not malicious. The crucial factor is the effect of the discrimination on the job applicant or employee. For example, in the case of *Smith v. Ontario (Human Rights Commission)*, a racist culture in the workplace led a court to determine that race was a factor in a discriminatory decision to dismiss an employee. (We discuss the *Smith* case in detail later in this chapter.)

DISCRIMINATION NOT COVERED BY THE HUMAN RIGHTS CODE

The Code's prohibited grounds now cover many, but not all, situations that involve discriminatory conduct. For example, an employee who suffers discrimination in the workplace on the basis of her political convictions or social status cannot file a complaint under the Code because neither political convictions nor social status are prohibited grounds of discrimination in Ontario.

The Code also sets out specific, narrow exemptions where discrimination on the basis of a prohibited ground is permissible. For example, a faith-based organization can stipulate that counsellors must be of that faith. However, it probably cannot insist that custodial staff be of that faith because such a requirement is not related to a custodial job. Similar exemptions from the Code apply in the case of sex discrimination in hiring. For example, a recreational club may hire only male attendants to work in the men's locker room.

There is also a **nepotism policy** exemption that allows an employer to give preferential consideration to, or to discriminate against, job applicants who are closely related to the employer or a current employee. In other words, as an employer, you may choose to have a hiring policy that gives preference to the close relatives of employees, or you may choose to have a hiring policy that prohibits the hiring of close relatives of employees (or, you may choose to have no such policy at all). The list of relatives that can be covered by a nepotism policy is short: spouse, children, or parents of an employee or of the employer.

nepotism policy
employment policy that allows an employer to discriminate in favour of, or against, her close relatives or the close relatives of employees

THE DUTY TO ACCOMMODATE

What constitutes "discrimination" has expanded greatly since Ontario enacted its first comprehensive human rights laws in 1962. Initially, discrimination meant intentional discrimination or discriminatory actions perpetrated on purpose. For example, if an employer advertises a sales position and states that only married men between ages 18 and 40 will be considered for the job, the discriminatory intent is obvious. The employer's hiring policy clearly discriminates on the basis of sex, age, and family status, and is a violation of human rights law. Such blatant instances of discrimination are unlikely today, although not unheard of. More commonly, discrimination is unintentional. Often a business can implement discriminatory policies without being aware of its error.

Today, the effect of an employer's behaviour matters as much as its intent. A workplace policy that unintentionally affects certain groups in a detrimental, or negative, way is called **adverse impact discrimination** (also known as constructive discrimination). For example, a security guard company whose hiring policy requires all applicants be a certain minimum height may not intend to discriminate against women or certain racial groups, but this will be the result. A retail store's requirement that all employees be available to work Saturdays may not intend to discriminate against members of religious groups who observe Saturday as a day of rest, but this will be the result. A business in an office building without a wheelchair ramp may not intend to discriminate against people in wheelchairs, but this will be the result.

adverse impact discrimination
workplace policy that unintentionally affects certain groups in a detrimental way

A rule or qualification that has a negative impact on a person or group based on one of the Code's prohibited grounds is generally considered to be discriminatory, and thus unlawful, unless a business can prove that it is a legitimate job requirement that cannot be modified or eliminated without creating a very severe burden for the employer. This type of qualification is called a **bona fide occupational qualification (BFOQ)**. For example, a trucking business would have no problem in proving that the absence of its rule against hiring blind truck drivers would create a severe burden; the qualification of sight is therefore a BFOQ for a trucking job.

bona fide occupational qualification (BFOQ)
reasonably necessary job qualification or requirement imposed because it is necessary for job performance

To be a BFOQ, a job qualification must be rationally connected to job performance, adopted in good faith, and reasonably necessary to accomplish a legitimate work-related purpose. To prove that a requirement is reasonably necessary, an employer must prove that it is impossible to accommodate a person who lacks this requirement without experiencing what the Code refers to as "undue hardship."

For example, an employer cannot refuse to hire someone with very poor eyesight for a clerical position if, by making certain workplace modifications such as purchasing a special computer screen or software program to produce large font size, that person could perform the job satisfactorily.

As an employer, you have an obligation to search for ways to assist a person in performing her work, which is called your "duty to accommodate." This duty describes your obligation as an employer to provide **accommodation** for special needs. It is based on the belief that it is unfair to exclude people from the workplace in a discriminatory fashion because their needs are different from those of the majority of workers.

The scope of the duty to accommodate has evolved over the years so that it now requires employers to consider differing needs when *designing* job requirements and workplaces. When building or renovating buildings, purchasing equipment, or setting up new policies and systems, employers should choose products or designs that do not create barriers for people with disabilities. For example, computer screens should be large, wheelchair ramps should be provided, and elevators should have Braille buttons. Similarly, an employer must be sensitive to its duty to accommodate people whose religious observances require a more flexible schedule, when designing and applying its attendance policy.

What is the scope of an employer's duty to accommodate? An employer must accommodate the needs of employees as far as it possibly can, short of creating undue hardship for the business, and it must do so in a way that respects the employees' dignity and privacy. The scope of the duty is in a continuous state of flux as a result of changing technologies and evolving legal standards. In the sections that follow, we present specific instances of the scope of the duty to accommodate in relation to disability, religion, and pregnancy.

Employees and their unions must cooperate in the accommodation process by taking reasonable steps to facilitate solutions to problems. In other words, accommodation is a shared responsibility. For example, it is up to the employee seeking accommodation to answer questions or provide information regarding relevant restrictions or limitations, including providing information from health care professionals. Similarly, unions have a legal obligation to help find solutions when accommodation potentially conflicts with the collective agreement. In one case a union was ordered to pay damages to an employee after it refused to allow a disabled employee to transfer his full seniority to a new accommodated position.

Undue Hardship

According to the Ontario Human Rights Commission's policy, **undue hardship** is the point at which the cost of accommodating an employee substantially affects the economic health of the business, or produces a substantial health and safety risk that outweighs the benefit of accommodation. In considering the economic impact, a business should try to obtain outside sources of funding to help pay for an accommodation, such as government grants. Tax write-offs may also be available.

To constitute undue hardship, the costs of accommodation must be quantifiable (not merely speculative). They must be substantial as well as directly related to a particular accommodation. Any business that claims it is unable to fulfill its obligation to accommodate is fighting an uphill battle. Inclusive workplaces are the order of the day.

---

accommodation
human rights concept that refers to making changes that allow a person or group protected by the *Human Rights Code* to participate in the workplace

undue hardship
difficulty beyond that which an employer is required to endure when accommodating the needs of an individual or a group protected under the *Human Rights Code*

Although they are not set out in Ontario's Code, the Supreme Court of Canada has also considered the following factors to be relevant in proving undue hardship:

- the potential for serious disruption of a collective agreement,
- severe morale problems among employees,
- the flexibility of a business's workforce and facilities, and
- the size of the business.

Minimizing Your Risk

Accommodate Employees in Good Faith

- Accept employee requests for accommodation in good faith and respond promptly.

- Obtain expert opinion or advice where necessary.

- Diligently investigate accommodation solutions.

- Where one solution would create undue hardship, investigate alternative approaches.

- Keep a record of accommodation requests, decisions made (with reasons), and actions taken.

- Maintain employees' confidentiality.

- Implement accommodation strategies in a timely manner unless they would create undue hardship.

- Where possible, seek grants and tax write-offs to fund accommodations.

Situations Commonly Requiring Accommodation

Disabilities

It is noteworthy that approximately 25 percent of all human rights claims filed in Ontario are based on disability in employment. The *Human Rights Code* states that employers may require an employee to perform only those duties that are "essential" to her job. For example, if a sales job depends on an employee's driving to customers' premises, then having a valid driver's licence is essential. On the other hand, if driving is necessary only to get to an occasional meeting, the requirement for a valid licence is not justifiable. Why? It unnecessarily disqualifies people who cannot obtain a driver's licence as a result of a disability.

Even if a job duty is essential, a business must tailor its workplace to meet the special needs of a disabled employee up to the point of undue hardship. This may require changing the layout of the workplace to make it barrier-free, modifying equipment and vehicles, providing stools and special computer hardware or software, modifying work hours, or reassigning disabled employees to vacant jobs that they are better able to perform. Employers have been ordered to create new positions for disabled employees by assembling physically undemanding duties from jobs currently performed by other employees.

The definition of disability includes alcohol and drug abuse, and therefore the Code requires businesses to accommodate employees who are disabled by a drug or alcohol problem, unless doing so creates undue hardship. This requirement usually obliges an employer to implement an employee assistance program or to allow an employee time off work to attend a rehabilitative program. However, it does not require an employer to accept lengthy, ongoing absences unrelated to rehabilitation, as demonstrated in the case of *Chopra v. Syncrude Canada Ltd.*

CASE IN POINT Alcohol Abuse and the Duty To Accommodate

Chopra v. Syncrude Canada Ltd., [2003] AJ no. 741 (QB)

Facts

An employee's performance was adequate for most of the 14-year period during which he worked for his employer. In the eight months preceding his retirement, however, the employee's alcoholism and depression created problems in the workplace. On one occasion he was found to have consumed so much alcohol while on the job that his supervisor had to escort him home.

The employee agreed to accept mandatory referral to the employer's assistance program, never again to violate the employer's drug and alcohol policy, and to attend supervisory and follow-up meetings as required. Both parties understood that failure to follow this plan would result in a termination hearing.

The employee attended a treatment program but was soon asked to leave for violating its policies. He was, however, admitted into a relapse prevention program to help him deal with his disability. Another disruptive incident occurred a short time later, resulting in the employee's absence from work because of intoxication. The employer then required the employee to submit to a medical tracking process, and random drug and alcohol testing. After he was again found to be under the influence of alcohol while at work, the employer dismissed him. The employee then filed a wrongful dismissal lawsuit against the employer.

Result

The court found that the employer had fulfilled its duty to accommodate the employee's disability. The employee was not entitled to any further accommodation, and the employer was justified in dismissing him.

Business Lesson

Before dismissing an employee for problems arising from alcoholism or drug problems, provide counselling services, necessary leaves of absence, and appropriate warnings in writing.

Religious Beliefs and Practices

The *Human Rights Code* refers to religious belief and practice as "creed." The requirement to accommodate an employee's creed may arise in a number of ways, including dress codes, break policies, work schedules, and religious leave. As a business person, you must implement flexible policies in your workplace. For example, break policies should be sufficiently fluid to accommodate daily periods of prayer for employees whose religion requires them. Employees who are unable to work on particular days of religious observance must be given the day off unless doing so would cause undue hardship for your business.

Pregnancy and Breast-Feeding

Your duty to accommodate a pregnant employee might include the need to relocate her temporarily from a work area that might endanger her pregnancy. For example, you might need to move her from an area that is close to chemical fumes. You may also need to provide her with a flexible work schedule, increase her break times, and, once she has the baby, give her a private and comfortable place to breast-feed her child or pump breast milk.

An employee who requires time off before or after her pregnancy or parental leave arising from pregnancy-related health concerns is entitled to benefits under an employer's workplace sick or disability plan.

Minimizing Your Risk
Accommodate Special Needs

- Design workplace policies and standards with everyone in mind, including those with special needs.

- Apply dress codes and other requirements in a way that is sensitive to people who have special needs for religious reasons.

- When assessing a disabled employee's or applicant's ability to do the job, consider only duties that are essential to the job and make reasonable adjustments to work processes and tools to accommodate the individual's disability.

- Implement and consistently apply a policy to assist in the rehabilitation of employees who suffer from substance abuse.

- Be prepared to provide pregnant employees with increased breaks, a temporary relocation, or a flexible work schedule if required.

- Be flexible with respect to breast-feeding requirements, including providing a comfortable, private place in the workplace for breast-feeding.

RECRUITMENT AND SELECTION

The Code's protections begin even before an employment relationship exists. Job advertisements, application forms, the interview process, and pre-employment testing all must comply with human rights law. You should remember that you are in violation of the Code if any of your reasons for making a hiring decision involve a discriminatory ground. In other words, you cannot claim in your defence that you based your decision mainly on non-discriminatory factors.

Job Advertisements and Application Forms

The intention of the Code is to have employers consider a broad range of qualified candidates in the early part of the recruitment process so that they do not eliminate suitable candidates inadvertently. The Code therefore prevents employers from advertising or requesting information in a discriminatory fashion. For example, in a job application form, employers can generally ask only for an applicant's name, address, education, and previous employment history.

Table 7.1, which is based on the Ontario Human Rights Commission's guidelines, sets out the prohibited grounds of discrimination and provides examples of questions that the commission believes should be avoided on application forms (including online forms) because they directly or indirectly touch on those prohibited grounds. In some cases, acceptable alternative wording is suggested.

Table 7.1   Job Application Forms

Prohibited Grounds	Examples of Unacceptable Questions	Examples of Acceptable Questions
Race/Colour/ Citizenship/ Place of origin/ Ethnic origin/ Religion	• Are you a Canadian citizen? • What is your social insurance number? (This may indicate place of origin or citizenship status, and employers should request it only following a conditional offer of employment.) • Where are you from originally? • What schools have you attended? (This may indicate a candidate's place of origin.) • Are you a member of any clubs or other organizations? (This could indicate sex, race, or religion.) • What is your height and weight? • What is your Canadian work experience? • Are there any days of the week you are unable to work? • What is your religion? • What religious holidays or customs do you observe? • Are you willing to work Saturdays?	• Are you legally entitled to work in Canada? • What is the highest level of education you have reached? • What professional credentials and diplomas have you received? • Are you fluent in English, French, or another language? (This question is acceptable only if fluency is a BFOQ.)
Sex	• What was your surname before marriage? • What form of address do you prefer: Ms., Mrs., Miss, or Mr.? • What is your relationship with the person to be notified in case of emergency?	None
Sexual orientation	• Is your spouse willing to transfer? • Are you a member of any clubs or other organizations?	None
Marital status	• Are you married? • What was your surname before marriage? • What form of address do you prefer: Ms., Mrs., Miss, or Mr.? • Is your spouse willing to transfer? • What is your relationship with the person to be notified in case of emergency?	• Are you willing to travel or relocate? (This question is acceptable only if travel or relocation is a BFOQ.)

Family status	• Are you married, divorced, single, or living in a common-law relationship?	• Are you willing to travel or relocate? (This question is acceptable only if travel or relocation is a BFOQ.)
	• What is your birth name?	
	• What form of address do you prefer: Ms., Mrs., Miss, or Mr.?	
	• Do you have children?	
	• How many children do you have?	
	• Do you plan to start a family soon?	
	• Are you pregnant?	
	• Do you have appropriate child care arrangements?	
	• Is your spouse willing to transfer?	
	• What is your relationship with the person to be notified in case of emergency?	
Record of offences	• Have you ever been convicted of a crime?	• Have you ever been convicted of a criminal offence for which a pardon has not been granted?
	• Have you ever been arrested?	
	• Have you ever spent time in jail?	
Age	• What is your date of birth?	• Are you 18 years of age or older? (As of December 2006, it is no longer acceptable to ask a person whether he or she is less than 65 years of age.)
	• Attach a copy of your driver's licence.	
	• Provide an educational transcript. (This could include dates that indicate the age of the applicant.)	
Disability	• Do you have any handicaps?	None
	• Have you ever claimed or received workers' compensation benefits?	
	• Do you have a history of substance abuse?	
	• Are you physically or mentally capable of performing this job?	
	• Do you require any accommodation to perform this job?	
	• This job requires heavy lifting. Will you be able to do it?	
	• Are you a member of Alcoholics Anonymous?	

Source: Compiled in part from information contained in Ontario Human Rights Commission, *Hiring? A Human Rights Guide* (Toronto: OHRC, 1997), pp. 3-6.

Job Interviews

At the job interview stage, the employer may expand the scope of job-related questions to include questions that touch on prohibited grounds where these relate to either

- one of the exceptions to the rule against discrimination, such as a nepotism policy or
- a BFOQ.

You should not ask any BFOQ questions that relate to a prohibited ground unless they are directly related to a candidate's ability to perform the essential duties of the job, and to the nature of any necessary accommodation.

The following interview questions are allowed in certain circumstances:

- What languages do you speak? (This question is acceptable if multi-lingualism is a BFOQ, as it is for a customer service job in a business that serves clients who speak languages other than English and French.)
- Are you a Canadian citizen? (This question is permitted only in limited circumstances such as where the job is a senior executive position.)
- Are you bondable? (Record of offences may be relevant where an applicant's capacity to be bonded is a BFOQ, as it is for a security guard job.)
- Do you have a valid driver's licence? (Driving may be an essential job duty, as it is for truck drivers, whose convictions under the *Highway Traffic Act* are relevant.)
- Do you have a spouse, parent, or child employed here? (The employer may have a nepotism policy that prevents or favours the hiring of these family members.)

Conditional Offers of Employment

conditional offer
offer subject to the fulfillment of one or more conditions

A **conditional offer** of employment is an offer subject to the fulfillment of one or more conditions. For example, a transport company may offer a truck driving job to a candidate and attach the condition that she provide a copy of a valid driver's licence or other documentation to prove that she is qualified and meets government criteria. Should the candidate fail to satisfy the condition, the company is justified in revoking its offer of employment.

If a candidate raises the issue of accommodation at the interview stage, or if a disability is obvious, you should address the issue of accommodation at that time. Otherwise, the Ontario Human Rights Commission suggests that a business person should discuss accommodation only after making a conditional offer of employment to a candidate. This is because, as an employer, if you become aware of a candidate's disability before making an offer of employment, and you do not offer employment to the candidate, the candidate may claim that his disability played a part in your decision. Therefore, in general, it may be better if you do not become aware of the candidate's disability until after you have offered him a job.

In order to address the question of a candidate's actual ability to do the job, you should make the employment offer conditional upon successful completion of a pre-employment medical examination, where appropriate to the type of work.

Once you have hired a candidate with a disability, your duty of accommodation, up to the point of undue hardship, applies in enabling him to fulfill the essential requirements of the job.

THE INCLUSIVE WORKPLACE

The same anti-discrimination and accommodation principles that apply during the recruitment and hiring process continue to apply throughout your workplace relationship with your employees. You must make all decisions concerning promotions, training opportunities, rewards, job assignments, discipline, layoffs, and terminations on a non-discriminatory basis.

For example, in the case of *Green v. Canada (Public Service Commission)*, a human rights tribunal found that the employer had discriminated against an employee by denying her entry into its full-time French language training program. The denial was based on testing and evaluation that revealed that she had a learning disability (dyslexia) in auditory processing. As a result of this decision, the employee was unable to obtain a bilingual management position and was instead placed in a consulting role. The tribunal ruled that use of this type of auditory testing to determine aptitude to learn another language inadvertently created a discriminatory practice. Further testing would have showed she could learn a second language if learning methods had been adapted. The tribunal ordered that the employee be immediately appointed to the position of manager and awarded her a lump-sum payment for lost wages and pension. It also ordered $5,000 for special compensation, interest, and legal costs. The Federal Court of Canada upheld this decision.

Minimizing Your Risk
Recruit, Select, and Hire Job Candidates Fairly

- Advertise jobs widely to draw candidates from diverse backgrounds.

- Follow the Human Rights Commission's guidelines when designing application forms.

- Standardize your interview questions to ensure consistent treatment of candidates.

- Accommodate job candidates who are unable to attend a job interview because of a disability.

- Train staff involved in the hiring process about the Code's requirements.

- Use interview teams to reduce the risk of individual bias.

- Document reasons for decisions made throughout the hiring process.

- Unless disability is obvious or the job candidate raises the issue, leave accommodation issues until after a conditional offer of employment is made.

- Where relevant to the job, have the candidate undergo a pre-employment medical examination after a conditional offer of employment is made.

ON-THE-JOB DRUG AND ALCOHOL TESTING

Under human rights law, substance abuse is viewed as a disability, and employment-related drug and alcohol testing is severely restricted. According to the Ontario Human Rights Commission's *Policy on Drug and Alcohol Testing*, pre-employment testing infringes the Code, and on-the-job testing is unjustified except in very limited circumstances—for example, where an employee is involved in a workplace accident that reasonably suggests impairment.

Courts and tribunals have made a distinction between testing for alcohol and testing for drugs. It is very rare for an employer to be able to defend a random drug-testing program since it is considered overly intrusive (a urine sample is required) and is not indicative of current impairment.

Random alcohol testing, which requires only a Breathalyzer test and does indicate a current level of impairment, may be acceptable in certain limited circumstances—for example, where a job such as driving heavy machinery must be performed soberly to avoid accidents, and where other ways of monitoring employees are impractical.

HARASSMENT

harassment
course of vexatious comment or conduct that is known or ought reasonably to be known to be unwelcome

In addition to outlawing workplace discrimination on the prohibited grounds, the Code also prohibits harassment, including sexual harassment, in the workplace. **Harassment** is defined as "a course of vexatious comment or conduct that is known or ought reasonably to be known to be unwelcome." The term "harassment" potentially includes a broad range of conduct, including verbal threats, intimidation, jokes, unwelcome remarks, and offensive pictures and posters.

sexual harassment
course of vexatious comment or conduct based on sex or gender that is known or ought reasonably to be known to be unwelcome

Courts have found that the term **sexual harassment** includes unwelcome expressions of sexual or romantic interest or physical contact, offensive remarks, ostensibly flattering remarks about physical appearance, inappropriate staring, offensive jokes, displays of offensive pictures or other materials, questions or discussions about sexual activities, and paternalistic comments that undermine the recipient's authority.

Businesses may be liable for the human rights infringements of their employees, so it is important to have clear policies in place with fair and effective complaint procedures. Businesses are wise to foster a corporate culture that encourages victims of harassment to come forward and have their complaints dealt with internally. Awareness gives companies the opportunity to fix problems before they become worse—and costlier.

poisoned work environment
workplace plagued with insulting or degrading commentary or actions related to a prohibited ground of discrimination under the *Human Rights Code*

Another type of prohibited harassment relates to creating or allowing a **poisoned work environment**. This term refers to a workplace that feels hostile because of insulting or degrading comments or actions related to a prohibited ground of discrimination. It is not necessary that a particular complainant is the target of offensive comments or actions to create grounds for a human rights complaint. A poisonous workplace may be one that, for example, tolerates the display of pornographic images or racial slurs that undermine and humiliate employees.

The employer must be alert to the atmosphere of the workplace, since ultimately the employer is responsible for keeping the environment inclusive and humane. For example, an employer who fails to erase offensive graffiti as quickly as possible may be liable for harassment for allowing a poisoned work environment. Where harassment is extreme and ongoing, a human rights tribunal may order systemic remedies aimed at changing a workplace culture. *Smith v. Ontario (Human Rights Commission)* below illustrates the range of direct and systemic remedies that are available for workplace harassment and discrimination.

CASE IN POINT Antidotes for Poison in the Workplace

Smith v. Ontario (Human Rights Commission), 2005 CanLII 2811 (SCDC)

Facts

An employee worked in a junior position for an employer for a year before being promoted to a supervisory position. There was ongoing friction between the employee, who was black, and the acting manager, who was white and made racial slurs against the employee. The business owner was aware of the tension between the two, but he stated that he was unaware of the particulars or that the workplace was tainted with racism. About a year after his promotion, the employee was fired for allegedly refusing to assist a junior employee in serving a customer. The business owner did not give the employee a chance to defend himself against the allegation.

The Human Rights Tribunal found that the employee had been subjected to a poisoned workplace, but that the owner did not wilfully or recklessly infringe his rights. It accepted the owner's contention that he was unaware of the discrimination and harassment when he decided to dismiss the employee, and that the dismissal was not racially motivated. The employee appealed.

Result

The court concluded that the business owner was at least reckless in infringing the employee's right to be free from a poisoned atmosphere. It awarded him $10,000 for mental anguish. It also found that the tribunal had incorrectly considered the motivation of the business owner, rather than the effect that the discrimination had on the employee, in deciding that race was not a motivating factor. If an employee is fired from a poisoned work environment, the dismissal must be examined in the context of that environment.

Because race was a factor in the dismissal, the employer was ordered to pay the employee compensation for lost income ($25,131) as well as his legal costs. It also ordered systemic remedies that required the business, under the supervision of the Human Rights Commission, to implement a workplace anti-harassment policy, undertake staff training, implement an internal complaint process, and educate management.

Business Lesson

Monitor the atmosphere in your workplace, and take immediate action to prevent any poisonous conduct.

ENFORCEMENT OF THE HUMAN RIGHTS CODE

The Ontario *Human Rights Code* is administered by the Ontario Human Rights Commission, which receives and investigates human rights complaints. The Commission publishes guidelines and policy papers that suggest how the commission would respond if a complaint about a particular issue were filed, but these are not legally binding.

Complaints that are not settled after the commission's investigation may proceed to a hearing by a human rights tribunal. If your workplace is unionized and

Web Link

The Ontario Human Rights Commission's guidelines and policy paper are available at www.ohrc.on.ca.

a complaint arises from a matter covered by a collective agreement, an arbitrator will usually hear the complaint under the grievance procedure established by the agreement. However, these complaints may eventually still be heard by a human rights tribunal, which remains the forum in which the commission can, as the tribunal in *MacKinnon v. Ontario (Ministry of Correctional Services)* put it, "seek to vindicate the overriding public interest in such matters."

Remedies for human rights violations may include orders such as the following against an employer:

- Pay compensation to the employee for actual lost earnings.
- Pay compensation to the employee for loss of dignity and self-respect, and mental anguish (up to $10,000 per violation).
- Pay the employee's legal costs.
- Hire or reinstate the employee.
- Undertake staff training, such as in cross-cultural communications or sexual harassment.
- Implement an anti-harassment policy.

Bill 107, introduced in spring 2006, proposes significant changes in the enforcement provisions of the Code. It would, among other things, give complainants direct access to the Human Rights Tribunal and increase potential damage awards to complainants.

REPRISALS FOR EXERCISING RIGHTS

Like other employment statutes, the Ontario *Human Rights Code* specifically prohibits reprisals, or actions taken against anyone who asserts his rights under the Code. Reprisals are a violation of the Code and subject to the same orders as above.

Minimizing Your Risk
Prevent and Eliminate Harassment

- Prepare an anti-harassment policy that explains the types of behaviour that are considered harassment.

- Communicate this policy to all staff—before they begin employment.

- Hold awareness programs to emphasize the policy's importance.

- Encourage employees to report instances of harassment.

- Train supervisors so that they will be able to recognize harassment and respond quickly.

- Clearly explain the process for making internal complaints as well as how these complaints will be investigated.

- Encourage complainants to bring their concerns to the employer's attention.

- Advise employees either to inform harassers that their behaviour is unwelcome or to inform their supervisor of the harassment.

- Treat complaints confidentially and inform employees in advance about the confidentiality policy.

- Maintain a written record of all complaints.

- Require a prompt and thorough investigation by an impartial person who is knowledgeable in human rights law.

- Post the anti-harassment policy in a prominent place.

Hiring and the Common Law

In addition to human rights concerns, there are a number of common-law issues that are of concern to business people before employment begins. When hiring employees, it is important to act with honesty and integrity and to check candidates' references thoroughly. It is also necessary to consider the legal relationship between your business and the person you are engaging to work for it. Not all workers need be "employees," as this term is interpreted in law. Finally, a carefully crafted contract of employment provides a solid basis for a successful employer–employee relationship. In the sections that follow, we explore these and related issues.

HONESTY AND GOOD FAITH IN THE HIRING PROCESS

During the hiring process, both business owners and job candidates should interact honestly with one another. Misrepresentations, including deliberate lies, can result in legal consequences.

Courts have held that misrepresentations by candidates for jobs may justify dismissal after they have been hired if the misrepresentations go to the root of a candidate's qualifications or if they suggest an inherent lack of honesty. This may be of particular concern where the job is one that requires a high degree of trust. For example, if an applicant for a nursing job claims that he has a nursing degree and the nursing home that employs him subsequently discovers that he has completed his first year only, the nursing home may be entitled to dismiss him, even if he is performing his job satisfactorily.

Similarly, if a business owner makes inaccurate statements to a job candidate during the hiring process, she may be legally liable if the candidate relies on the misrepresentation and suffers damages as a result. For example, imagine a situation in which a company recruiter states that the position being offered involves heading up a major new innovative project. However, the recruiter fails to mention that the project is still subject to final board approval. The candidate accepts the offer—leaving a secure job and relocating his family—only to be terminated shortly thereafter when final approval for the project is denied. In this situation the employer could be liable for the tort of negligent misrepresentation, with possible damages including loss of income, the cost of obtaining new employment and relocating, as well as general damages for emotional stress. The fact that the recruiter did not intentionally mislead the candidate is not relevant. The employer has an obligation to ensure that all material statements made during the recruitment process are accurate.

Employers must also take care not to be overly aggressive in "luring" prospective employees, especially ones that are currently in secure employment. For example, if the recruiter repeatedly calls a candidate, urging her to leave her current job, or makes inflated promises about what the new position will offer, that employee may be awarded a longer termination notice period if she is later dismissed from the new job without just cause.

RESTRICTIVE COVENANTS

restrictive covenant
clause in an employment contract that restricts an employee's activities, especially after employment ends; for example, a restrictive covenant might prohibit an ex-employee from disclosing confidential information about the employer

A **restrictive covenant** is a clause in an employment contract that restricts the legal right of employees to engage in certain types of activities during employment and after it ends, such as compete with the ex-employer, solicit customers from the ex-employer, and disclose confidential information about the ex-employer. Before hiring a candidate, determine whether there was an enforceable restrictive covenant in the employment contract that the candidate signed with her previous employer. The terms of such a covenant might affect the candidate's ability to do the job that you are offering.

Your business might be wise to include in employment contracts a clause in which a candidate verifies that she has no existing contractual obligations that prevent her from accepting a job at your business. We return to restrictive covenants in the context of employment contracts later in this chapter under the heading "Restrictive Covenants."

CHECKING REFERENCES

At the hiring stage, an employer must keep in mind potential obligations related to checking employment references. Although the law imposes no general obligation to check references, an employer may nevertheless be liable for "negligent hiring" if he fails to verify the references of applicants for jobs that could expose others to harm.

Employers who hire employees to fill positions of trust (such as daycare workers) or employees who may be required to use force (such as security guards) are required to exercise a high standard of care in checking references. We discuss an employer's liability for the actions of an employee in chapter 3 under the heading "Vicarious Liability."

Minimizing Your Risk
Check Candidates' References

- Obtain candidates' written permission to check references through a statement on the application form.

- Check references thoroughly, particularly if the job could result in harm to others.

- Make the same general inquiries about all applicants.

- Record details of all steps taken when investigating candidates, including references who did not respond and the information provided by those who did.

- Keep information confidential.

INDEPENDENT CONTRACTOR OR EMPLOYEE?

An increasingly popular alternative to hiring employees is to hire independent contractors. An **independent contractor** is a self-employed worker who accepts specific projects, usually from several businesses. Although it is sometimes difficult to distinguish an employer–employee relationship from a principal–independent contractor relationship, the two are treated very differently in law. For example, an independent contractor is not covered by employment standards legislation and therefore is not entitled to receive vacation pay, pregnancy or parental leave, or the termination notice specified in statutes. Independent contractors receive tax benefits that are not available to employees. For example, they may deduct business expenses, and income tax is not withheld and submitted by the business that hired them.

What makes an individual an independent contractor rather than an employee? Generally, courts and tribunals apply the common-law test: is the individual an independent entrepreneur in business for herself (an independent contractor), or is she under the control and direction of the hiring organization (an employee)? No single fact determines the matter; a court or tribunal will assess the substance of the relationship, including whether the business controls where, when, and how the work is performed and whether the individual is free to have other clients. A statement in the contract that the relationship is one of principal and independent

independent contractor
self-employed worker who accepts specific projects, usually from several businesses

contractor, rather than employer and employee, indicates the parties' intentions. However, it will not be the only evidence considered and does not bind courts or tribunals.

What is the significance of the difference between employees and independent contractors? There is a risk that a court or tribunal may recharacterize the relationship to your business's detriment. For example, if your business treats the individual as an independent contractor, you are justified in not paying him employment standards benefits and in not providing him with statutory notice of dismissal. However, if a court or tribunal subsequently determines that your independent contractor is, in fact, your employee, you may have to remit thousands of dollars to various government agencies for outstanding statutory premiums payable on behalf of employees (such as Canada Pension Plan and employment insurance). You may also have to pay your newly characterized "employee" significant amounts of money for employment standards benefits (such as vacation pay). And you may even be liable for wrongful dismissal damages, available to employees only. (We discuss wrongful dismissal later in this chapter under the heading "Wrongful Dismissal.")

Minimizing Your Risk
Respect the Independence of Independent Contractors

- Encourage independent contractors to work for other businesses, and never restrict their ability to do so.

- Specify in a written contract that both you and the independent contractor intend your relationship to be that of principal and independent contractor.

- Take no statutory deductions from the money you owe independent contractors, and make no income tax remittances on their behalf.

- Do not reimburse independent contractors for their expenses.

- Do not provide employee benefits such as vacations, holiday pay, or overtime pay.

- Avoid setting hours of work.

- Encourage independent contractors to work off-site as much as possible.

- Have independent contractors supply their own tools and equipment.

EMPLOYMENT CONTRACTS

Under the common law, the relationship between an employer and an employee who is not a member of a union is basically a contractual one. (We discuss an employer's relationship with unionized employees later in this chapter under the heading "The Unionized Workplace.") Subject to any statutory requirements, the terms and conditions that apply to non-unionized employees generally are those that the employer and the employee themselves negotiate. The essence of an employment contract is the following:

- the employer makes a job offer that the employee accepts, and
- the parties mutually promise to exchange wages for work.

A well-drafted written contract offers a number of advantages over an oral contract, including greater certainty about the terms of employment and reduced risk of misunderstanding. In most employment relationships, a written contract is not lengthy or formal. It often consists of a letter from the employer offering an employee a job and setting out the key terms, such as salary, benefits, starting date, title, job duties, and termination provisions. If your business has a policy manual—and it is a good idea to develop one if you are going to be hiring many employees—refer to this manual in your letter. Such a reference incorporates your policies about matters such as discipline, probationary periods, absence, safety, and harassment into the employment contract.

Sometimes a more formal employment contract is needed. If you are hiring a senior employee or one who will be doing a specialized job, ensure that you draft the contract carefully—perhaps seeking professional assistance—and customize it to reflect the issues that are important to both parties. If, for example, a job requires an employee's use of specialized knowledge, you might want to include a restrictive covenant to protect your business interests by limiting what an employee can do during, and especially after, employment. However, a prospective employee with specialized skills may be interested in negotiating terms that are as flexible as possible.

In the following sections, we examine some terms that are of particular interest to business people in drafting contracts: notice of termination, probation periods, and restrictive covenants.

Minimizing Your Risk
Customize Your Employment Contracts

- Ensure that all employees have written contracts of employment—even if they are only a one- or two-page letter of hire.

- Use plain, clear language.

- Customize the contract so that it reflects what is important to the parties involved.

- Seek legal assistance, if necessary, in negotiating and drafting more complex or specialized contracts.

- Make sure the contract is signed before work begins.

- Make sure the contract refers to the employee policy manual and that the employee receives a copy of the manual before starting work.

- Negotiate and include a notice of termination clause in the contract—even in fixed-term contracts.

- If hiring someone on a fixed-term contract, do not mislead that employee into believing that renewal is automatic or a mere formality.

- Include a probationary period clause in the contract.

- Use restrictive covenants where necessary, but limit restrictions to those absolutely necessary to protect your legitimate business interests.

Reasonable Notice of Termination

Typically, the most contentious clause in an employment contract relates to notice of termination. Without a termination provision, an employee who is dismissed without **just cause** (justification based on conduct) is entitled to "reasonable notice" of termination under the common law. Depending on the circumstances, reasonable notice may be very lengthy—as much as a month or more per year of service. If you, as an employer, fail to provide reasonable notice, you may be required to pay the employee an amount equal to the wages plus the benefits that the employee would have earned during this period of time.

just cause
justification for dismissal without notice based on an employee's conduct

If you address termination at the beginning of the employment relationship, while you and the employee are on good terms, you reduce the costs and uncertainty of relying on a court to determine what constitutes reasonable notice. The case of *Mesgarlou v. 3xs Enterprises Inc.* illustrates, from a business owner's point of view, the cost-effectiveness of a clearly worded termination clause.

CASE IN POINT Include a Clear Termination Provision in the Employment Contract

Mesgarlou v. 3xs Enterprises Inc., 2001 CanLII 6268 (ONSC)

Facts

A business hired an employee to manage its sales staff. Two weeks before the employee started work, the business sent him an employment contract that stated: "After the first three (3) months of employment, both parties shall give notice in accordance to the Ontario *Employment Standards Act, 2000* prior to terminating this employment agreement." The employee signed the contract. A year later the business fired the employee without just cause, and the employee sued for wrongful dismissal.

Result

The court found that the language of the contract of employment was sufficiently clear to rebut the common-law presumption that employees are entitled to reasonable notice of dismissal. In this case, reasonable notice would have been three months. Therefore, without a clear contractual provision limiting the notice period, the employee would have been entitled to three months' salary in lieu of notice, or $32,000. With the contractual provision, the employee was entitled to notice as provided in the Ontario *Employment Standards Act, 2000*, or $2,477.

Business Lesson

Negotiate a termination provision with your employee, and draft the term clearly in a written contract of employment.

Fixed-Term Employees

Employers may hire employees on a permanent basis or for a fixed term. Employees hired for a fixed term are sometimes called "contract workers," but they are not independent contractors: they are employees. They are entitled to all the rights conferred on workers under the Ontario *Employment Standards Act, 2000*, including the right to receive vacation pay. Because the date of termination is known in advance, an employer generally need not give the employee further notice of termination if the employee works for the entire fixed term. However, where the term is for 12 months or more, the *Employment Standards Act, 2000* requires statutory notice.

Employers should not use a series of fixed-term contracts to cover what is, in substance, an indefinite contract of employment in an attempt to avoid notice of termination obligations. In these circumstances, courts and tribunals have looked beyond the actual provisions in the contract and found that the employee is entitled to reasonable notice based on her total years of service.

Probation Periods

If you, as an employer, want to monitor an employee's suitability for a job by instituting a probationary period, you must provide for a probationary period in your contract of employment. Probationary periods typically last from three to six months, depending on the nature of the job. Business owners and managers usually determine the length of the probationary period based on how long it will take them to assess an employee's on-the-job ability.

Restrictive Covenants

There are three main types of restrictive covenants that are included in employment contracts:

- *non-competition clauses*, which restrict an ex-employee's ability to work in a competing business;
- *non-solicitation clauses*, which restrict an ex-employee's ability to solicit employees or customers of a former employer; and
- *non-disclosure clauses*, which restrict an ex-employee's ability to use a former employer's confidential information.

The key to creating enforceable restrictive covenants is to make them clear and no more restrictive than necessary to protect your legitimate business interests. They must be reasonable in duration and geographic scope. Courts are reluctant to enforce non-competition clauses unless you can show that the clause you have drafted is absolutely necessary to protect these interests. They will enforce a non-competition clause only if you can show that a non-solicitation clause is inadequate to protect your interests.

Enforceability of Employment Contracts

Like any other contracts, contracts of employment may be challenged because they are ambiguous or because they were made under duress. A party who is unhappy with the terms of an employment contract may also challenge its enforceability on the basis that it lacks consideration, is obsolete, or fails to meet minimum statutory standards.

Lack of Consideration

An employment contract lacks consideration when an employer fails to provide something of value in exchange for an employee's promise to work. Consider, for example, an employer who presents an employee with a contract that contains a non-competition clause *after* the employee has already started to work. The non-competition clause is unenforceable unless it is supported by consideration. *Kohler*

Canada Co. v. Porter is a case in which an employer attempted to impose such a clause on an employee who had been working for a business for many years.

As you can see from *Kohler Canada Co. v. Porter*, an employment contract that is fully enforceable at the time you hire an employee may become problematic in the future if you want to change your employment policies. If your proposed change is minor (for example, a small change in break times), it probably presents no legal problem. However, if the change is significant and the employee will not agree to it, it may constitute constructive dismissal (that is, a fundamental breach of the contract). To avoid this result you have two choices:

1. obtain your employee's consent and provide fresh consideration—in the form, for example, of a one-time bonus or raise in salary—or
2. provide your employee with reasonable notice of the change, which may be determined in the same way as reasonable notice of termination (unfortunately, this may be impractical if you have to make adjustments to the workplace in a hurry.)

CASE IN POINT Consider Consideration in Employment Contracts

Kohler Canada Co. v. Porter (2002), 17 CCEL (3d) 274 (Ont. SCJ)

Facts

The employee began work in 1988 as a customer service representative; by 1999, he occupied a management position. He did not have a written employment agreement until 2001, when the employer presented him with one and asked him to sign it. Believing it was a routine document, the employee signed it without obtaining legal advice. In fact, the agreement included a non-competition clause that prohibited him from working anywhere in North America for a period of one year after the termination of his employment in a business that competed with the employer's business. It also stated that the consideration for the agreement was the employee's "employment status with [the company] and payment of salary during such employment."

Result

The court held that the non-competition clause was unenforceable because it covered an overly broad geographic area. However, even had this not been so, the entire employment contract was unenforceable because the employee had received no new consideration for signing it. In these circumstances, continued employment did not constitute consideration.

Business Lesson

When making a significant change in the employment relationship, and you cannot provide reasonable advance notice, provide additional consideration that is acceptable to your employee.

Obsolescence

A court may decide that an employment contract is unenforceable because a job has changed so drastically since the employee initially accepted it that the contract no longer represents the employment relationship.

In *Lyonde v. Canadian Acceptance Corp.*, for example, an employee rose from an entry-level job to become vice-president of an organization over the course of 24 years without an updated contract. The court refused to enforce a termination provision in the original contract because the contract no longer reflected the job that the employee was performing.

Failure To Meet Minimum Statutory Standards

The terms of an employment contract must be at least as favourable to employees as the minimum standards set by legislation. We address some of these standards later in this chapter under the heading "Employment Standards: Pay, Vacation, and Working Conditions." If a contract fails to meet these minimum standards—in relation to wages or notice of termination provisions, for example—the relevant clause of the contract is void and unenforceable.

In this case, a court will not simply substitute statutory notice provisions; instead, it will apply the common law. This means that if the contract contains an inadequate termination notice provision, the employer must compensate an employee by providing reasonable notice of termination or pay in lieu of notice.

Minimizing Your Risk

Ensure Enforceability of Your Contract

- Have contract terms represent a reasonable balance between the interests of both parties.

- Avoid ambiguous wording.

- Point out complex or potentially contentious clauses and have the candidate initial them.

- Get the candidate to sign the contract before work begins.

- Give the candidate plenty of time to review the contract.

- Advise the candidate to seek independent legal advice before signing.

- If you want to introduce new terms that are disadvantageous to the employee after employment starts (for example, a restrictive covenant), give the employee reasonable notice of the change or provide additional consideration.

- Regularly review all contracts to ensure they are current.

- Update contracts whenever there is a promotion or other significant change in job duties.

- Ensure that the contract at least meets the minimum requirements of the *Employment Standards Act, 2000*.

Employment Standards: Pay, Vacation, and Working Conditions

The Ontario *Employment Standards Act, 2000* sets out minimum terms and conditions of work required for employees in provincially regulated businesses. An employer is free to create standards of work that are more favourable to employees than the statutory minimums, but, generally speaking, no employer can impose working conditions that are less favourable to employees than those imposed by the Act, even if an employee agrees to accept them.

Many employers provide employment conditions that are more favourable to employees than those in the *Employment Standards Act, 2000* to stay competitive in the market and to attract and retain talent. For example, the Act requires employers to provide only two weeks' paid vacation per year, regardless of an employee's length of service, but most employers offer additional vacation time, especially for long-term employees.

GENERAL STANDARDS

Web Link

A copy of the poster is available from www.labour.gov.on.ca. Click Employment Standards.

The *Employment Standards Act, 2000* requires employers to keep accurate and specific records about employees and to make them available to inspectors from the Ministry of Labour on request. Employers also are required to display, conspicuously in the workplace, a poster prepared by the Ministry of Labour that provides information about the Act and its regulations. This poster contains a brief summary of key standards and information about enforcement.

The Act also sets out specific requirements concerning the payment of wages, including the information that must be contained on each pay statement. As an employer, you may not make deductions from an employee's wages except in clearly defined and limited circumstances that are authorized by law, such as the deduction of employment insurance premiums. Even with specific written authorization from the employee, you may not make deductions for faulty workmanship or for cash shortages unless an employee has sole access and total control over the property or cash.

SPECIFIC STANDARDS

As a business person, you have the option of hiring various types of employees—for example, full-time, part-time, or temporary. Employment laws rarely distinguish between these different categories of employees, although their statutory benefits, such as vacation or holiday pay, reflect the number of hours worked.

The *Employment Standards Act, 2000* does make some distinctions based on occupations and industries. For example, managers and supervisors are not covered by the hours of work and overtime pay provisions. Some industries, such as construction, are exempt from certain employment standards as well.

Web Link

Regularly consult the Ministry of Labour's website at www.labour.gov.on.ca for up-to-date information. Click Employment Standards.

Employment standards is one of the most basic and stable areas of employment law; however, its particulars—such as the current minimum wage—are subject to frequent change. As an employer, you should ensure that you are complying with the current provision. Table 7.2 describes some of the current minimum employment standards set by the *Employment Standards Act, 2000*.

Table 7.2 Current Minimum Employment Standards

Standard	Particulars
Minimum wage	• Minimum wage is the lowest hourly wage that an employer can pay an employee. • Most employees are subject to minimum wage requirements, whether they are full-time, part-time, paid hourly, salaried, or paid by commission. • Special wage rates apply to some employees, such as students under 18 and workers who serve liquor.
Work hours	• The maximum number of hours that an employer may assign to an employee, or that an employee may agree to work in a given time period, is generally 48 hours per week. • Managers and supervisory employees are not covered (unless they perform non-managerial or non-supervisory functions on a regular basis).
Overtime	• Employers must pay non-managerial employees overtime pay at the rate of 1.5 times their regular rate of pay after they work 44 hours in a week. • Providing time off equal to the amount of overtime worked does not meet the law's requirements. The employee must receive 1.5 hours of paid time off for each hour of overtime worked.
Vacation	• Employees are entitled to 4 percent vacation pay and at least two weeks' vacation time after they have worked for 12 months. • An employer is entitled to decide when an employee can take vacation time; however, an employee is entitled to receive vacation time within 10 months of earning it.
Public holidays	• Most employees are entitled to eight paid public holidays per year. • Employees who work in industries such as hotels, restaurants, and hospitals may be required to work on a public holiday and take a substitute day off.
Statutory leaves of absence	• Employers are not required to pay employees while on statutory leave. • Employees may receive employment insurance benefits while on leave if they qualify. • Employees who take statutory leave have the right to return to the same job at the end of their leave period. • During leave, employees have the right to retain benefits, such as health insurance, provided that they continue to contribute to the benefit plan, and to accrue seniority. • Leaves include — pregnancy leave (17 weeks) — parental leave (35-37 weeks) — emergency leave (applicable only to employers with 50 employees or more—10 days per calendar year) — family medical leave (8 weeks).

ENFORCEMENT

The *Employment Standards Act, 2000* is typically enforced when an employment standards officer from the Ministry of Labour responds to a claim filed by an employee who believes that his employer has infringed his rights under the Act. In most circumstances, the maximum amount that an employment standards officer can order an employer to pay is $10,000 per employee. However, this $10,000 limit does not apply to certain violations, such as those involving statutory leave. In these cases, an employment standards officer can order an employer to reinstate an employee and/or to compensate the employee for, among other things, lost wages, job search expenses, and emotional pain and suffering as a result of the violation.

Health and Safety

The key health and safety statutes in Ontario are the *Occupational Health and Safety Act* and the *Workplace Safety and Insurance Act, 1997*. The *Occupational Health and Safety Act* has very broad coverage, including all workers and independent contractors. It sets the standards for employers in preventing workplace illness and injury. It requires employers to "take every precaution reasonable in the circumstances for the protection of a worker." The *Workplace Safety and Insurance Act, 1997*, on the other hand, addresses the financial consequences of workplace illness and injuries when they occur. It is essentially an insurance system paid for entirely by employers, which guarantees compensation to workers for work-related injuries or diseases. This is a no-fault system, and workers cannot sue employers for work-related injuries or disease.

THE OCCUPATIONAL HEALTH AND SAFETY ACT

Workers' Rights

The *Occupational Health and Safety Act* gives workers four key rights: the right to participate in the health and safety of their workplace, the right to refuse to do unsafe work, the right to stop unsafe work, and the right to know about workplace hazards. These rights encourage workers to take a proactive approach to their own health and safety, and are intended to encourage cooperation between employers and the people who work for their businesses.

Frontline workers are often the people most aware of the health and safety risks they face, and their knowledge and expertise is invaluable to business owners. Employers cannot penalize workers in any way for exercising their rights under the Act.

joint health and safety committee
committee composed of equal numbers of management and worker representatives generally required by the *Occupational Health and Safety Act* in workplaces with 20 or more workers

The Right To Participate

The *Occupational Health and Safety Act* places duties on everyone involved in the workplace, such as business owners, suppliers, workers, and supervisors.

The **joint health and safety committee** is one of the cornerstones of the system of internal responsibility created by the *Occupational Health and Safety Act*. The committee is an advisory group composed of equal numbers of worker and management representatives. Members meet regularly to discuss health and safety concerns, review progress, and make recommendations to the employer on health and safety issues. Every workplace where 20 or more workers are regularly employed generally requires a joint health and safety committee (special rules apply to construction projects).

The Right To Refuse Unsafe Work

Every worker has the right to refuse unsafe work, although this right is restricted for some occupations—such as police officers—where danger is an inherent part of the job. The statute sets out a specific procedure for both the employer and worker to follow when a worker chooses to exercise this right.

To refuse unsafe work, a worker must have a sincere belief that the equipment or physical condition of the workplace is "likely to endanger" her or another worker. To refuse work after a supervisor has investigated the safety issue, a worker must have reasonable grounds for believing that the work continues to be unsafe. This is an objective standard based on what a reasonable person would think or do in the circumstances. An inspector from the Ministry of Labour must be called in where the issue cannot be resolved between the workplace parties.

The Right To Stop Unsafe Work

The right to stop work is distinct from the right to refuse work. Only members of a joint health and safety committee who have undergone health and safety training and certification may initiate a stop-work order, according to the provisions of the statute. Where two certified committee members (one representing workers, the other representing management) have reason to believe that a contravention of the *Occupational Health and Safety Act* or its regulations poses a serious danger to a worker, they may jointly direct the employer to stop work, and the employer must comply immediately.

The Right To Know About Workplace Hazards

Under the *Occupational Health and Safety Act*, workers have the right to know about potential hazards to which they may be exposed. This includes the right to receive training about the safe use of machinery, equipment, and processes, as well as the right to know about hazardous substances at the workplace. Employers and workers also must comply with the requirements of **WHMIS** (the workplace hazardous materials information system), which is a nation-wide system designed to provide workers with essential information about using, handling, and storing hazardous materials in the workplace.

WHMIS
(workplace hazardous materials information system) national information system designed to provide essential information about hazardous materials in the workplace

Web Link

Check out workplace health and safety requirements at www.labour.gov.on.ca. Click Health and Safety.

Accident Reporting

The *Occupational Health and Safety Act* requires employers to report all workplace accidents to the Ministry of Labour. In the case of critical injuries or fatalities, the employer must notify the ministry immediately and provide a written report within 48 hours. Non-critical injuries must be reported within four days of the occurrence. Separate accident-reporting obligations exist under the *Workplace Safety and Insurance Act, 1997,* which we discuss below under the heading "The Workplace Safety and Insurance Act, 1997."

Minimizing Your Risk
Fulfill Your Health and Safety Obligations

- Designate a senior manager to be responsible for compliance with the *Occupational Health and Safety Act.*
- Prepare a written health and safety policy, as required by the legislation.
- Provide a safety orientation for all new employees and existing employees with new job assignments.
- Have senior executives actively support the joint health and safety committee.
- Identify workplace hazards through internal and external safety audits.
- Support and respond to concerns of the joint health and safety committee.

- Hold regular safety meetings to update workers.
- Discipline all workers and managers who fail to follow safety requirements.
- Implement a system of recognition and rewards for departments and individuals who reach safety goals.
- Keep equipment in good working condition.
- Investigate accidents promptly and thoroughly.
- Do not tamper with the site of an accident.
- Report accidents as required by the Act.
- Document all your efforts to ensure a healthy and safe workplace as part of proving due diligence.

Enforcement

Safety inspectors from the Ministry of Labour are available to provide specialized safety advice and expertise. In addition to investigating work refusals, work stoppages, and serious injuries or fatalities, inspectors also conduct random, unannounced inspections of workplaces. They have broad powers, including the power to enter any workplace without a search warrant, except where the workplace is also a personal dwelling.

strict liability offence
offence in which proof that an accused performed the prohibited act is sufficient to sustain a conviction, regardless of intention, unless the accused demonstrates that he took all reasonable care to avoid committing the prohibited act

Every offence under the *Occupational Health and Safety Act* is a **strict liability offence,** which means that the ministry does not need to prove that an employer intended to commit an offence in order to obtain a conviction under the Act. Once a prosecutor establishes that an offence occurred, the onus is on the employer to prove that he took every precaution that was reasonable in the circumstances to prevent the occurrence. This is called the **due diligence defence**. If, for example, a worker is injured by unguarded machinery, the employer may successfully defend himself by proving that he took all reasonable care to ensure that the machinery was guarded, including training employees about the importance of guards and disciplining employees who remove them. If, on the other hand, the employer cannot prove due diligence and is convicted, he may be fined up to $25,000 and imprisoned for up to 12 months. Corporations may be fined up to $500,000.

due diligence defence
defence to strict liability offence requiring accused to demonstrate that he took all reasonable steps to avoid committing a prohibited act

Canada's *Criminal Code,* a federal statute, was recently amended to impose duties on anyone who directs work to take "reasonable steps" to prevent bodily harm arising from that work. Failure to adhere to the duty may result in life imprisonment and unlimited fines.

THE WORKPLACE SAFETY AND INSURANCE ACT, 1997

In the following sections, we examine the Ontario *Workplace Safety and Insurance Act, 1997*. This Act is of particular interest to business people because it puts in place a scheme, funded entirely by employers, to compensate workers for injuries or diseases that they suffer on the job. In addition to examining eligibility requirements and benefits available to workers, we also consider methods by which businesses can reduce their costs under the scheme.

Employers can consider the workplace safety and insurance scheme as a method of managing risk. It eliminates lawsuits by workers who have suffered workplace injuries and illnesses in the course of their employment. Workers may no longer sue in tort for this type of harm. However, unlike most other risk management strategies, workplace safety and insurance is a government program in which most employers are required to participate.

Eligibility for Benefits

The *Workplace Safety and Insurance Act, 1997* insures workers against injuries or diseases that "arise out of and in the course of employment," such as injuries resulting from workplace accidents or diseases caused by exposure to toxic chemicals at work. The Act does not apply to non-occupational injuries or illnesses. Insurable injuries need not result from the performance of a worker's job, as long as the activities that result in the injury are related to the job. In one case, for example, an employee who hurt her back when she reached around to do up a button while in the washroom received compensation for her injury because going to the washroom was reasonably incidental to her employment.

The presumption that an injury incurred on the job is work-related does not apply to disability cases. For example, with a repetitive strain injury, the onus is on the worker to show a relationship between the disability and the work. However, it is not necessary that the work be the primary or dominant cause of a worker's injury, provided that it contributed to the injury in a significant way.

The *Workplace Safety and Insurance Act, 1997* compensates workers for occupational diseases if there is a causal relationship between the disease and the employment. Industrial diseases that are known to arise from specific industrial processes are set out in the schedules to the Act.

Types of Benefits

There have been many changes to the benefit structure over the past 15 years. As a result, three different schedules for monetary benefits are now in place. In the sections that follow, we discuss only the third system, which applies to workers who were injured after January 1, 1998.

Types of compensation available under the Act include the following:

- health care costs resulting from the injury,
- loss of earnings benefits,
- non-economic losses (such as loss of the enjoyment of life),
- loss of retirement income benefits, and
- death and survivor benefits.

Web Link

For more information on occupational diseases, go to www.wsib.on.ca. Click Resources, then WSIB Fact Sheets, then Occupational Disease Fact Sheets.

Workers are compensated for lost earnings after the day of the injury. The employer must pay the worker the wages and benefits she would have earned for the day or shift on which the injury occurred. Benefits for loss of earnings are calculated at 85 percent of net earnings—that is, earnings after income tax, Canada Pension Plan premiums, and employment insurance deductions are deducted.

Workers are encouraged to return to work as soon as they are safely able to do so, even if only on a part-time basis or with reduced responsibilities. Under the *Workplace Safety and Insurance Act, 1997*, employers have a duty to cooperate with injured workers and facilitate their return to work. The employer and the injured worker are expected to keep in touch throughout the worker's recovery period, sharing information as necessary to assist with rehabilitation. Employers with 20 or more employees have specific obligations related to re-employment of an injured worker with one or more years of service. An employer who dismisses a worker within six months of his returning to work must prove that the worker's claim for compensation played no part in the employer's decision to dismiss the worker.

Businesses are obliged to provide a safe environment for everyone who works in their workplace. The *Workplace Safety and Insurance Act, 1997* covers most industries in the province, both union and non-union, including manufacturing, construction, hospitals, hotels, restaurants, and theatres. Some industries, such as financial institutions and law firms, are not required to participate in the legislative scheme. However, many of these low-risk businesses choose to apply for coverage since it protects them from lawsuits for work-related injuries at a relatively low cost.

Funding the System

Employers pay the full cost of the compensatory system through premiums paid to the Workplace Safety and Insurance Board. These premiums are based on the employer's industry class and rate group. For example, low-risk industries, such as technical services, pay a low rate; high-risk industries, such as demolition, pay a high rate. The employer's assessment is calculated as a percentage of the employer's payroll, to a maximum amount per worker.

The *Workplace Safety and Insurance Act, 1997* provides financial incentives to employers to reduce the cost of injuries, with experience rating. This is a system that compares the claim rates and costs of businesses in the same or similar industries. Employers receive a refund or pay a surcharge on the regular premium rate, depending on how their claims measure up against those of other employers in the same rate group.

Web Link

Ensure that your workplace is a healthy and safe environment by checking out www .wsib.on.ca.

Minimizing Your Risk
Reduce Your Workplace Safety and Insurance Costs

- Participate in safety associations such as the Industrial Accident Prevention Association.
- Report work-related injuries and diseases to the Workplace Safety and Insurance Board as required.
- Effectively manage insurance claims: document all claims, even those that seem minor; keep notes of all contacts; establish a return-to-work plan; and make necessary accommodation short of undue hardship.

- Fully cooperate in efforts to return a worker to the pre-injury job or attempt to provide suitable work.
- Find out if your business is in the appropriate rate assessment group or whether all or part of your employees could be in a group with lower premiums.

Equity in the Workplace

Equity in the workplace refers to both fairness in terms of pay and fairness in terms of employment opportunities. While human rights legislation prohibits discrimination in the workplace, it depends on the lodging of complaints and usually focuses on individual instances of unfairness. In contrast, employment equity addresses the broad social problem of the under-representation of certain groups of people, such as visible minorities and people with disabilities, in most workplaces, especially in better-paid and higher-level jobs.

In this section, we discuss and distinguish between three related topics:

- equal pay for equal work, under the *Employment Standards Act, 2000*;
- equal pay for work of equal value under the *Pay Equity Act*; and
- fair and representative employment practices under the *Employment Equity Act*.

EQUAL PAY FOR EQUAL WORK

The Ontario *Employment Standards Act, 2000* requires that women and men receive **equal pay for equal work**. To fall within the scope of this law, the work need not be identical as long as it is substantially similar. For example, male and female cooks who work in the same restaurant must receive the same rate of pay. Different rates of pay can apply if based on factors unrelated to gender, such as merit and seniority.

EQUAL PAY FOR WORK OF EQUAL VALUE

The Ontario *Pay Equity Act* also addresses the issue of fair pay, but it goes further than the *Employment Standards Act, 2000* by requiring employers to provide **equal pay for work of equal value (pay equity)**. This is a relatively recent concept that requires employers to compare different jobs within a workplace to determine whether they are of equal value to the business. Pay equity legislation is intended to reduce—and eventually eliminate—systemic gender discrimination and the wage gap between women and men by requiring employers to compare job value, rather than job content.

For example, traditional "female jobs," such as secretary, are often paid substantially less than traditional "male jobs," such as janitor. Under the *Employment Standards Act, 2000*, this form of discrimination is not addressed because the content of the jobs is different. But how different is their value to an employer? Is a janitor's work more valuable than that of a secretary?

It can be very complex to quantify and compare the value of jobs usually performed by women with the value of jobs usually performed by men. The *Pay Equity Act* requires an employer to use a **gender-neutral job evaluation system**. This is a system that does not undervalue aspects of jobs traditionally performed by women—such as those requiring manual dexterity—when comparing them to aspects of jobs traditionally performed by men—such as those requiring physical strength. If the jobs are of equal value, an employer must raise the pay for the women's job classes to match that of comparable men's job classes. There are statutory exceptions to this obligation. For example, no pay adjustment is required if the pay differential results from a formal seniority system.

equal pay for equal work
concept obliging employers to pay female and male employees who perform substantially the same jobs in the same workplace at the same rate, unless a legislated exception applies

equal pay for work of equal value (pay equity)
concept obliging employers to pay female- and male-dominated jobs at the same rate based on an assessment of job value rather than job content

gender-neutral job evaluation system
system that evaluates the relative value of jobs in a manner that does not favour factors found in jobs traditionally performed by men

The *Pay Equity Act* applies to all Ontario public sector (government) employers, and all provincially regulated private sector (non-government) employers with 10 or more employees. Employers must keep the requirements of the *Pay Equity Act* in mind when making changes in the workplace that might affect the value assigned to a job or the job comparisons required under the Act (for example, eliminating or adding a job).

Fair and Representative Employment Practices

employment equity
range of measures promoting a representative workforce; federal employment equity legislation and programs focus on four designated groups: women, visible minorities, people with disabilities, and aboriginal people

The purpose of the Ontario *Human Rights Code* is to prevent discrimination. **Employment equity** legislation goes a step further: its purpose is to encourage fair and representative hiring and promotion practices by focusing on four designated groups: visible minorities, women, aboriginal people, and people with disabilities. Many workplaces do not reflect the external workforce from which they recruit with respect to these designated groups because some employment practices have the effect of excluding certain groups.

Today, many business people recognize that by failing to have a workplace that reflects their community, they may be alienating customers and clients, and failing to reap the benefits of a rich labour market. Nevertheless, there has been resistance to employment equity legislation because of the additional costs it imposes on businesses and the perception of "reverse discrimination." Ontario passed employment equity legislation in 1993, but it was repealed soon after when the party in power changed. There is currently no law in Ontario requiring employers to implement employment equity.

Canada does have the *Employment Equity Act*, which applies only to federally regulated companies—such as banks, railroads, airlines, and broadcasting companies—with 100 or more employees. It requires employers to implement employment equity programs to address the under-representation and lower job status of the four designated groups—women, visible minorities, disabled people, and aboriginals—in their workplaces.

The federal government has also implemented a federal contractors' program that affects some Ontario employers. Businesses with at least 100 employees that wish to bid on federal government contracts worth at least $200,000 must certify that they will develop and implement a formal employment equity plan. This plan includes collecting and analyzing workforce data; reviewing employment systems to identify barriers to hiring, promoting, and retaining members of the four designated groups; and adopting special measures to achieve employment equity. There are many different kinds of barriers. For example, when businesses need to hire additional staff, they often turn to current employees and ask them whether they know anyone who could do the job. This may be faster and less expensive than advertising a

---

Minimizing Your Risk
Ensure Equity in Your Workplace

- Review your pay equity responsibilities when there are changes in the workplace that may affect job comparisons (such as eliminating or adding a job, introducing new technology, a sale or merger, or a union certification).

- Review your recruitment practices to ensure there are no barriers to increasing diversity.

- Analyze workforce data to see if your employees reflect the diversity of the external workforce in the relevant occupational groups.

- Review employment systems to identify barriers to hiring, promoting, and retaining members of the designated groups.

- Implement proactive employment equity programs (for example, a mentoring program that makes the workplace more welcoming to diverse groups).

job in the newspaper or hiring a recruiting agent to do a thorough search. However, the candidates suggested by your current employees are likely to have backgrounds and cultures similar to theirs: they may have grown up in the same neighbourhood, gone to the same schools, or belong to the same social or sports clubs. Employers can avoid perpetuating a limited cultural demographic in the workplace by advertising jobs widely and considering candidates from diverse backgrounds.

Some provincially regulated employers in Ontario are implementing employment equity as a result of the federal contractors' program, while others are introducing it as a way of attracting and managing employees in a culturally diverse workforce.

In recent years, the concepts of **workplace diversity** and inclusiveness have gained prominence. These terms are now widely used to connote the importance of fairness in the workplace and the value of employing employees from different backgrounds in a workplace where all feel welcome, respected, and productive.

Web Link

For more information on pay equity, go to www.payequity.gov .on.ca/peo/english/ faqs.html.

workplace diversity employment of people from diverse backgrounds in a workplace where all feel welcome and respected

Privacy in the Workplace

New technologies have increased concerns about privacy. Computers allow personal information to be compiled and transferred in seconds. Employee monitoring is now possible by way of video cameras and e-mail monitoring. Employers have an interest in maintaining productivity as well as a duty to prevent the downloading of offensive material, as part of their effort to maintain a workplace free of discrimination and harassment. Balancing those interests is a challenge, and the right to privacy in the workplace is an area in which the law is evolving.

PIPEDA AND THE PROTECTION OF PERSONAL INFORMATION

Legislation such as the *Personal Information Protection and Electronic Documents Act* (PIPEDA) has been passed in recent years to address some concerns about privacy. PIPEDA's purpose is to balance an individual's right to have her personal information kept private with an organization's right to collect, use, and disclose this information when necessary, as it is, for example, when insurers require personal health information about employees for the purpose of insuring them.

As we have seen in chapter 5, PIPEDA is a federal statute that applies to federally regulated employers, such as banks, telecommunications companies, and airlines. Its requirements are based on 10 "fair information principles" that relate to the collection, use, protection, and disclosure of personal information. (We discuss the 10 information principles and the nature of personal information extensively in chapter 5.)

PIPEDA requires businesses to provide individuals with details about the personal information that they collect and are holding about them. For example, if a supervisor puts an informal note in an employee's file, the employee is probably entitled to see the note on request. Businesses should also give employees the opportunity to correct errors contained in any information that is held about them. If an employer provides personal information about employees to a payroll service provider, the employer should ensure that the payroll service provider commits to complying with PIPEDA—that is, the service provider should use the employees' personal information only for the purpose specified in its contract with the employer, and not for any other purpose, such as creating or selling mailing lists.

At present, provincially regulated businesses, such as restaurants, retail stores, and manufacturing companies, are not required to apply PIPEDA's provisions to their employees. (They are, however, required to comply with PIPEDA in relation to customers and clients, as we have seen in chapter 5.) However, PIPEDA is of interest to all Ontario workplaces for the following reasons:

- PIPEDA's principles are recognized as forming the basis of ethical practices concerning personal information.
- Quebec, British Columbia, and Alberta have already passed privacy laws related to employment, and Ontario will likely pass privacy legislation that is similar to PIPEDA.
- PIPEDA currently applies to personal information collected by provincially regulated employers about independent contractors.
- PIPEDA currently applies to personal information about employees when a provincially regulated employer outsources the administration of its benefits, payroll, training, or pension programs to another business.
- PIPEDA currently applies if personal information about employees is sold across provincial borders.

As an employer in Ontario, you should also be aware that disclosure of personal information that relates to a prohibited ground of discrimination under the *Human Rights Code*, such as religious affiliation or marital status, can be the subject of a human rights complaint.

EMPLOYEE SURVEILLANCE AND MONITORING

Concerns about privacy are increasingly being raised in the workplace as new technologies make it possible for employers to monitor employees' activities in unprecedented ways—for example, by maintaining video surveillance, recording Internet use, and monitoring email and keystrokes. We discuss these matters in the sections that follow.

Video Surveillance

In a non-unionized workplace, there is no legal restriction on video surveillance by provincially regulated employers. They may install video cameras in the workplace, and there is no government official comparable to PIPEDA's privacy commissioner to question the appropriateness of surveillance. The situation is different in federally regulated workplaces where PIPEDA applies to personal employee information. *Eastmond v. Canadian Pacific Railway* is a case that involves a federally regulated employer that installed surveillance equipment in its work yard. The case demonstrates the kinds of issues that can be raised under PIPEDA.

While surveillance for security reasons may be acceptable in some circumstances, an employer who tries to use video surveillance as a means of proving that an employee has engaged in misconduct may find that the videotaped evidence is inadmissible in court, especially if the employee is not aware that he is being monitored. The trend in legal decisions is for courts to apply a reasonableness

CASE IN POINT Video Surveillance Must Be Necessary To Be Lawful

Eastmond v. Canadian Pacific Railway, 2004 FCA 852

Facts

The employer installed video cameras in a work yard to reduce vandalism and deter theft, to reduce its potential liability for property damage, and to improve security for employees. An employee launched a complaint under PIPEDA on the basis that theft and security were not serious problems in the work yard and that the cameras could be used to monitor the performance and conduct of employees.

The privacy commissioner applied the following four-part test to determine the reasonableness of the placement of cameras:

1. Are the cameras demonstrably necessary to meet a specific need?
2. Are they likely to be effective in meeting that need?
3. Is the loss of privacy proportional to the benefit gained?
4. Is there a way of achieving this benefit that involves less invasion of privacy?

After applying these tests, the privacy commissioner recommended that the employer remove the surveillance cameras. Because thefts were relatively rare and lack of security was not a serious issue among employees, the employer failed to show a need for surveillance. It should have looked for alternatives, such as better lighting, that were less likely to invade the employees' privacy. Because the employer did not comply with these recommendations, the employee applied to the Federal Court for an order.

Result

The Federal Court applied the commissioner's four-part test, but concluded that the videotaping served a reasonable purpose. The cameras were not hidden from view, and they were placed in areas where employees had a low expectation of privacy. The tapes were reviewed only if there was a reported incident; otherwise, they were destroyed. The employer had considered alternatives, including fencing and security guards, but it had reasonably decided that these were not cost-effective.

Business Lesson

Use video surveillance only as a last resort after less intrusive methods have proven ineffective to secure your workplace.

standard: Did the employer have reasonable grounds for instituting the surveillance? Were less intrusive options for obtaining the information available? If so, the video surveillance evidence may be inadmissible.

In a unionized workplace, the collective agreement may restrict an employer's freedom to use video surveillance. For example, an agreement might contain a clause that requires an employer to notify the union and allow it to participate in discussions before conducting any video surveillance of its members.

Monitoring Email and Internet Use

An employee's right to privacy may conflict with an employer's need to manage the workplace, such as by monitoring the employee's email and Internet use. There are a number of legitimate reasons why employers may consider electronic monitoring. Computer misuse can adversely affect a business. It can reduce the productivity of employees who engage in excessive personal activity during company time. More important, an employer has a duty under the Ontario *Human Rights Code* to maintain a workplace free of discrimination and harassment. This means that employers must act proactively in preventing the intrusion of racist, pornographic, and other offensive materials into the workplace.

The owner of the business is legally entitled to monitor the use of its property, including electronic equipment. In fairness and as good business practice, however, employers who engage in electronic monitoring should forewarn employees in writing that they can have no expectation of privacy when using company computers. In order to rely on results of monitoring for discipline, employers should have a written policy so that employees are aware of the monitoring.

For more information on privacy law, go to www.privcom.gc.ca.

Minimizing Your Risk
Respect Privacy

- Limit collection of personal information to what is necessary.
- Obtain the consent of employees and independent contractors before collecting, using, or disclosing personal information about them.
- Use personal information only for the purpose for which the consent was given.
- Keep personal information safe from loss, theft, or unauthorized access.
- Dispose of personal information when it is no longer required.
- Unless certain statutory exceptions apply, allow employees access to personal information

about them and encourage them to correct any misinformation.

- If you use a third party payroll or other service provider, specify in writing that the service provider can use personal information only for the purpose of fulfilling its contract with you.
- Use video surveillance only as a last resort and make sure it is conducted in a reasonable manner.
- Prepare and broadly communicate a policy on email use that details what uses are, and are not, permitted. As always, be consistent in the enforcement of this policy.

The Unionized Workplace

union
organization of workers that negotiates wages and working conditions as a group with an employer

collective agreement
contract between a union and an employer that governs the terms and conditions of employment for union members

Canada, like many other democratic countries, has a long-established history of freedom for workers to form or join a **union**. Over the years, unions have significantly advanced the rights of workers by negotiating **collective agreements**—which set the terms and conditions of employment—and by providing collective representation for workers in dealings with their employers. Workers usually join unions with a view to bargaining with their employers for higher wages, more benefits, better working conditions, and greater job security than they are currently obtaining in their non-unionized workplace.

In the past, relationships between employers and unions have tended to be confrontational; however, in recent years, they have become more conciliatory in many instances. Unions and their members realize that unrealistic demands can drive employers into bankruptcy or cause them to move their businesses to places where labour is less expensive. A more cooperative approach has emerged, where employers and unions work together to improve the financial position of both employees and other stakeholders in the business.

Despite this trend, most non-unionized businesses prefer to stay that way. They do not want to assume the additional administrative costs of dealing with a union, and they prefer to retain maximum flexibility in communicating and dealing with employee relations. Many non-unionized employers offer pay and benefits that are comparable to those offered by unionized employers, in the hope that their employees will not seek union membership.

In Ontario, the statute that governs unionized workplaces is the *Labour Relations Act, 1995*. The Act allows most, but not all, employees to form unions; it creates exceptions for managers, human resources personnel, and professionals, such as architects and lawyers, who are employed in a professional capacity. The Act also sets out the process by which a group of employees may become unionized, and the rules for collective bargaining. Disputes arising from the application of the Act are heard by the **Ontario Labour Relations Board**, a government tribunal that specializes in labour law.

Once a collective agreement is negotiated between a union and an employer, it is ratified. **Ratification** involves approval by workers, as evidenced by a vote. The collective agreement then governs the employer–employee relationship in much the same way as an employment contract does for individual employees in a non-unionized workplace. Disputes arising from the application of the collective agreement are heard by an arbitration board, as described in the collective agreement itself.

UNION ORGANIZING

The *Labour Relations Act, 1995* strictly prohibits employers from interfering with the right of employees to join the union of their choice and to participate in its lawful activities. **Unfair labour practices** prohibited by the Act include the following:

- questioning employees individually about union activities,
- firing union organizers or other employees who are in favour of union activity,
- threatening (even subtly) that unionization will jeopardize employees' job security, and
- promising to increase wages if employees reject the union.

The Act prevents employers from disciplining, firing, or harassing employees for pro-union campaigning or activities. Any employer that the Ontario Labour Relations Board finds to have committed an unfair labour practice faces substantial damage awards. The board may also order automatic certification of the union without a vote (see discussion of certification below).

Typically, a group of employees, called a **bargaining unit**, becomes unionized when a union applies to the Ontario Labour Relations Board for **certification**. Certification gives the union the right to represent the bargaining unit by showing that it has the support of the majority of employees within the unit. When certified,

Ontario Labour Relations Board
tribunal that mediates and adjudicates labour relations (and other) matters arising in Ontario

ratification
approval by union members of a collective agreement

unfair labour practices
actions by employers that interfere with the formation and activities of a union, including intimidation

bargaining unit
a group of the employer's employees whom the trade union is entitled to represent

certification
approval by a labour relations board that gives a union the right to negotiate on behalf of a bargaining unit

the union has exclusive authority to bargain collectively with the employer on behalf of the employees in the bargaining unit. As an employer, therefore, you may not negotiate with your employees individually with respect to matters covered by collective agreements, such as raises, work hours, promotions, and job security. Instead, you must deal only with the certified union.

In Ontario, except in the construction industry, the process for applying for certification requires a vote. To hold a vote, a union must first show that at least 40 percent of employees in the proposed bargaining unit have signed union membership cards. The Ontario Labour Relations Board certifies the union if it wins the support, in an election by secret ballot, of more than 50 percent of the employees who vote. The vote is usually held within five to seven business days from the filing of the union's application for certification. If it occurs within your workplace, you must remember that it is your employees' right to join the union of their choice. You must be particularly careful about any communications you have with employees during this period to avoid any suggestion that you are interfering with the process and thus committing an unfair labour practice.

Unions can lose their right to represent a bargaining unit in several ways. Generally speaking, dissatisfied members of a bargaining unit may bring an application for decertification during the "open period" that occurs in the final three months of the term of every collective agreement. Alternatively, a union may succeed in convincing workers that they should join it instead; once it obtains certification, the first union is automatically decertified.

NEGOTIATING A COLLECTIVE AGREEMENT

Once a union is certified, you, as an employer, have a "duty to bargain" a new or renewed collective agreement as soon as you receive a "notice to bargain" from the union. Employers and unions are required to bargain in "good faith" and use "every reasonable effort" to reach a collective agreement. You may not negotiate terms and conditions of employment directly with any unionized employee. You must discuss all workplace changes that affect the terms of employment with the union, which will accept, reject, or negotiate them with you as your employees' certified bargaining agent. You may, of course, communicate with your unionized employees, but you must be careful not to do so in a way that reveals an attempt to bargain directly with them.

Generally, it is the responsibility of the parties—the employer and the union— to negotiate a collective agreement. However, with respect to the first collective agreement, the Ontario Labour Relations Board provides binding arbitration in the event that you and the union are unable to reach an agreement. In arbitration, a neutral third party (the arbitrator) makes decisions about the content of the principal terms of the agreement. One of the parties (usually the union) may ask the board to direct a settlement by arbitration if it can show that the other party is not making reasonable efforts to reach a first agreement. This removes the incentive some employers may have when faced with a newly certified union to "dig in its heels" and refuse to bargain. Arbitration of the first collective agreement has been a controversial development in Ontario labour relations because of the profound and lasting effects it can have on the agreement itself, as well as the future relationship of the parties.

Subject to the first contract provisions of the *Labour Relations Act, 1995*, you and the union are left to negotiate whatever terms and conditions of employment you both choose, as long as the terms are lawful. However, the Act does stipulate that you and the union *must* include the following matters in every collective agreement:

- recognition of the union as the exclusive bargaining agent of the employees in the bargaining unit,
- a term of at least one year during which the collective agreement remains in effect,
- a prohibition against strikes and lockouts during the term of the agreement,
- deduction of union dues from the wages of each bargaining unit employee if the union requests it, and
- grievance arbitration to resolve disputes that arise during the term of the agreement.

ADMINISTRATION OF THE COLLECTIVE AGREEMENT

A dispute arising from the administration of a collective agreement is called a **grievance**, and is resolved through **grievance arbitration**. For example, if you suspend a worker one day without pay for being late, she may file a grievance against you; her grievance will be heard through the grievance arbitration process that you negotiated with her union and specified in the collective agreement. If the grievance cannot be resolved through the internal grievance process, it may go to an outside arbitrator to decide how the grievance is to be resolved, based on the wording of the collective agreement.

Strikes, during which employees collectively refuse to work, and **lockouts**, during which employers refuse to allow employees to work, are prohibited while a collective agreement is in effect. These bargaining tactics are legal only after a collective agreement expires and serious attempts to negotiate a new agreement fail.

During a lawful strike or lockout, employers may hire replacement workers. However, it is illegal under the *Labour Relations Act, 1995* for employers to use strike breakers—outsiders who are brought in for the sole purpose of disrupting a lawful strike. Also, if a legally striking employee unconditionally applies in writing to an employer, within six months of the beginning of a strike, to return to work, the employer must reinstate the employee to his former job.

grievance
dispute arising in a unionized workplace with respect to matters covered in the collective agreement

grievance arbitration
an external process for resolving disputes that arise under the collective agreement

strike
collective refusal to work by a group of unionized employees that usually occurs while an employer and a union attempt to negotiate a new collective agreement

lockout
refusal by an employer to let unionized employees into a workplace; usually occurs while an employer and a union attempt to negotiate a new collective agreement

---

Minimizing Your Risk
Know Your Responsibilities as a Unionized Employer

- Understand and respect your employees' right to unionize.
- If you become aware of an organizing drive, speak to legal counsel before communicating with your employees about related issues.
- Once a union is certified, negotiate in good faith to reach a collective agreement.
- Treat the union with respect.

Web Link

To learn more about unions, visit the Ontario Labour Relations Board website at www.labour .gov.on.ca. Click Labour Relations.

RESPONSIBLE BUSINESS STRATEGIES TO AVOID UNIONIZATION OF YOUR WORKFORCE

Many business people find that day-to-day management and workplace relations can be much more flexible, informal, and collaborative in a non-unionized setting. As a business person, you may also want to save the time and money necessary to negotiate collective agreements and defend at grievance arbitrations. You may prefer to institute ethical hiring and firing policies on your own without having to follow job security provisions in a collective agreement. You are, of course, prohibited by the *Labour Relations Act, 1995* from participating in unfair labour practices during a union drive, and changing workplace conditions at such a time could amount to this type of practice.

By managing your workplace proactively, however, and engaging the loyalty of the people who work for you, your business may avoid a union drive. For example, if working conditions and wages in your place of business are comparable to those in unionized workplaces, employees are less likely to seek the benefits of union membership because they would be paying union dues for no purpose. If you want to reduce the likelihood that your employees will exercise their right to join a union, you might consider implementing the following strategies:

- Communicate openly and regularly with your employees about your business, their working conditions, and any other workplace issues that are important to them.
- Listen to your workers' concerns, and take their advice and recommendations seriously.
- Ensure that your employees' wages and benefits match those in similar types of businesses that have unions.
- Create an internal complaint procedure for employees. (You can use the same process to address human rights complaints.)
- Provide training and professional development opportunities for your employees.
- Promote your employees fairly.
- Foster an atmosphere in which your employees feel they are important members of the team.
- Introduce profit-sharing or share distribution plans so that your workers actually have a stake in the profitability of your business.
- Foster an atmosphere of fun and friendship by sponsoring social events for your employees.

Ending the Employment Relationship

In the following sections, we consider the three most common ways in which employment relationships come to an end: through resignation, retirement, or termination (dismissal). Each of these partings of the ways brings with it legal implications that you, as a business person, should consider. Our discussion focuses mainly on the obligations of employers in non-unionized workplaces because their employees have termination rights under the common law. Table 7.4, which appears later in the chapter, sets out an employer's obligations to both unionized and non-unionized employees under various circumstances.

RESIGNATION

Under the common law, employees have an obligation to provide notice of resignation, just as employers have a duty to provide notice of dismissal. However, in practice, employers rarely find it worthwhile to sue former employees for breaching this obligation.

One of the most common legal issues regarding resignation involves answering the following question: Did an employee quit, or was the employee fired? The answer is significant because employers who dismiss employees without cause—that is, without a reason based on the employee's conduct that is justifiable in law—must provide notice or pay in lieu of notice under the *Employment Standards Act, 2000* and the common law. Depending on the employee's length of service and the circumstances of the dismissal, an employer can owe a dismissed employee a substantial sum of money. If an employee gives an employer her resignation after the employer offers her a "choice" between resigning or being dismissed, a court or tribunal will probably find the resignation was not voluntary. The employer will therefore be obliged to provide pay in lieu of reasonable notice or to show just cause for dismissing the employee. Similarly, an employee who resigns from his job because an employer changes a fundamental term of his employment contract may be able to raise a successful argument that he was constructively dismissed. We discuss this concept later in this chapter under the heading "Constructive Dismissal."

To be effective, an employee's resignation must be intentional and voluntary. If a supervisor requires an employee to work through lunch and break times, and the employee in frustration walks off the job site saying, "I quit," it is unclear whether the employee resigned. Even the words "I quit" are not considered to be a voluntary resignation if an employee is provoked, obviously distressed, or acting in the heat of the moment. Depending on the circumstances, each of the following statements may fall short of an intentional and voluntary resignation:

- "That's it, I'm going to work for someone else."
- "You don't appreciate me, I'm leaving."
- "Maybe I should be looking for a new job."

Similarly, if an employee quits during a heated exchange but apologizes later that day, indicating that he did not intend to resign, in law there is probably no voluntary resignation.

RETIREMENT

The Ontario government has amended the Ontario *Human Rights Code* to prohibit employers from having a mandatory retirement policy at age 65. Effective December 12, 2006, the definition of "age" in the Ontario *Human Rights Code* was changed so that discrimination in employment because of age became illegal in Ontario for people over age 18. The previous definition allowed age discrimination against employees who were age 65 or older. This change will almost certainly require more accommodation of age-related disabilities.

Minimizing Your Risk
Know Your Obligations Regarding Resignations and Retirement

- Before acting on a resignation, consider all the circumstances in which it was given.
- Confirm your acceptance of an employee's resignation in writing as soon as possible after receiving it.
- Include a notice of resignation clause in the written employment contract (usually two to four weeks).
- Conduct "exit" interviews to get feedback on reasons for leaving and to ensure that company property is returned.
- Never fire an employee who provides notice of resignation. If you do not want that employee to stay in the workplace during the notice period, accept her resignation but tell her that while she will be paid throughout the notice period, she should not attend work.
- Implement a consistent performance review program, with relevant documentation, for all workers (not just older workers).
- Review pension and benefit plans to see if there is any impact from the abolition of mandatory retirement.
- Accommodate employees with age-related disabilities up to the point of undue hardship.

TERMINATION

In most situations, employers in non-unionized workplaces may dismiss employees by providing reasonable notice. If, however, an employer has just cause for dismissing an employee, no notice is necessary. Because of its potential cost, the termination of employment is one of the most important workplace issues facing all employers.

Only in unusual circumstances can you, as an employer, sever ties with an employee simply by saying, "You're fired." Usually employees are entitled to advance notice of their dismissal. If you do not want an employee to remain in her job during the notice period to which she is entitled, you are obliged to pay her the wages and benefits she would have earned during this time. This legal obligation is known as the duty to provide **pay in lieu of notice**.

pay in lieu of notice payment as a substitute for receiving adequate notice where an employee is dismissed without just cause

Employees are entitled to notice based on three possible sources:

- an employment contract that includes an enforceable provision that governs notice of dismissal;
- the *Employment Standards Act, 2000*, which provides fairly short notice based solely on length of service; and
- in the absence of an enforceable termination clause, the common law, which usually provides significantly longer notice.

The common-law reasonable notice period is based on several factors, including age and job type. The rationale behind both the statutory and the common-law notice obligations is to provide employees with an opportunity to obtain a new job before they are removed from a company's payroll.

Why are there two types of notice periods? The *Employment Standards Act, 2000* provides a minimum notice period that employers cannot override by contract. Employers and employees may, however, override the longer common-law notice obligations by clearly setting out an alternative notice period in a written employment contract. The contractual notice must meet the minimum standards provided in the *Employment Standards Act, 2000*, but a contractual notice period that is shorter than common-law notice binds the employer and the employee if the contract is otherwise valid. (We discuss employment contracts earlier in this chapter under the heading "Enforceability of Employment Contracts.")

The *Employment Standards Act, 2000* provides employees with a simple process for enforcing their rights. Rather than commencing a lawsuit for wrongful dismissal, they may simply file a claim with the Ministry of Labour, and the ministry will investigate. This is a much less expensive and less risky process for an employee than launching a lawsuit. Employees who wish to enforce their right to notice must choose between filing a complaint under the *Employment Standards Act, 2000* and commencing a lawsuit for wrongful dismissal. In Ontario, employees cannot do both.

Notice and Pay Entitlements Under the Employment Standards Act, 2000

Termination Notice or Pay in Lieu of Notice

Under the *Employment Standards Act, 2000* and its regulations, employees are entitled to receive notice of termination (or pay in lieu of this notice) unless the termination falls within one of several limited exceptions, some of which are listed below:

- the employee has engaged in *wilful* misconduct, disobedience, or *wilful* neglect of duty that is not trivial and has not been condoned by the employer;
- the employee has refused reasonable alternative employment with the same employer; or
- the employee is on temporary layoff (as defined in the Act).

Individual notice periods range from one to eight weeks, depending on an employee's length of service. It is up to the employer whether to provide the employee with advance notice of termination and let the employee work throughout the notice period, or to give the employee pay in lieu of notice. The employer may provide an employee with a combination of written notice and termination pay as long as together they equal the number of weeks set out in the Act. The employer must continue to pay the employee's benefits during the statutory notice period.

Mass Layoffs

In the unhappy event of a mass layoff, in which an employer dismisses many employees at once, different notice entitlements under the *Employment Standards Act, 2000* may apply. If an employer lays off 50 or more employees in a period of four consecutive weeks, the mass notice requirements under the Act generally replace the Act's individual notice requirements. Depending on the total number of employees laid off during the four-week period, workers are entitled to receive between 8 and 16 weeks' notice. No notice of mass termination is effective unless an employer notifies the director of employment standards at the Ministry of Labour and posts portions of a mass layoff form in a conspicuous place in the workplace.

Severance Pay

The terms "severance pay" or "severance package" are often used synonymously with "termination pay." However, under the *Employment Standards Act, 2000,* **severance pay** is a separate entitlement: it refers to a one-time lump-sum payment made in

severance pay
one-time lump-sum payment made to a terminated employee in circumstances set out in the Ontario *Employment Standards Act, 2000*

defined circumstances on the basis of an employee's years of employment. This payment is made in addition to any minimum termination notice or pay in lieu of notice requirements under the Act.

To qualify for severance pay under the *Employment Standards Act, 2000*, an employee must have worked for an employer for five or more years. In addition, the employer must have an Ontario payroll of at least $2.5 million or must have terminated the employment of 50 or more employees in a six-month period because all or part of the business closed. Qualifying employees are entitled to receive severance pay in the amount of one week's pay for each year's service (dating from their start of employment), to a maximum of 26 weeks.

As with termination pay, there are a number of exceptions to the obligation to pay severance. Employers are not required to pay severance to employees who engage in wilful misconduct, who refuse to accept a reasonable alternative position, or who are on temporary layoff.

Wrongful Dismissal

reasonable notice
period of time an employee should be given between notification of dismissal and end of employment

Over and above your responsibilities under the *Employment Standards Act, 2000*, you, as an employer, have a common-law duty to provide your non-union employees with **reasonable notice** of their dismissal, unless their employment contract specifies another notice period. This duty is based on the principle that an employee who is dismissed should have the opportunity to find new employment while still receiving an income.

How much notice is reasonable? This depends on the circumstances of each case, including factors such as an employee's length of service, his age, his job, his salary, and the conditions prevailing in the job market. Reasonable notice is usually a lengthy period under the common law, amounting to up to 24 months' pay in lieu of notice.

When firing an employee, it is important to act as decently as possible for financial, as well as humanitarian, reasons. If your conduct is abusive or harsh, a court may lengthen the notice period to which the employee is entitled. For example, an employer who falsely claims that he fired an employee for incompetence, and persists with these allegations until trial, may find that a judge adds several months to the employee's reasonable notice period. Consider the case of *Wallace v. United Grain Growers Ltd.* in this regard.

wrongful dismissal
dismissal without just cause in which an employer breaches her common-law duty to provide reasonable notice to an employee

The employee in *Wallace* took his employer to court in a **wrongful dismissal** lawsuit. Wrongful dismissal occurs when an employer fails to meet its implied contractual duty to provide reasonable notice of termination. If an employee decides to sue and is successful against his employer, a court will award the employee an amount equal to the wages and benefits that the employer would have owed him during the period of reasonable notice, as well as court costs. In practice, most employees and employers settle their cases without going to court for an amount that approximates what a court would order, because neither party wants to incur the expense of going to court.

In addition to damages for wrongful dismissal, an employee can also seek aggravated and punitive damages against an employer. These types of damages are discussed in chapter 3, Torts, under the heading "Non-Pecuniary Damages." The court refused to award these damages in *Wallace*. However, a judge may choose to

CASE IN POINT   Unfounded Allegations Increase the Notice Period

Wallace v. United Grain Growers Ltd., [1997] 3 SCR 701

Facts

The employer abruptly dismissed a 59-year-old employee with 14 years' service who had been its top salesperson for many years, without explanation or a separation package. When the employee sued the employer for wrongful dismissal, the employer falsely alleged that he was dismissed for cause. It withdrew these allegations only when the trial began. As a result of the unfounded allegations, the employee required psychiatric care.

Result

The employee was entitled to an award of 15 months' salary and benefits for reasonable pay in lieu of notice, extended to 24 months because of the employer's conduct, as damages for wrongful dismissal. Unfairness in the way an employer dismisses an employee may result in an extension of the notice period or damages in lieu of notice, to which an employee is entitled.

Employers have an obligation to deal fairly and in good faith when providing an employee with notice of termination. In this case, the employer's conduct breached this obligation. The rationale behind extending the notice period where an employer has breached its duty of fair play during the dismissal process was set out by Justice Iacobucci of the Supreme Court of Canada:

> The point at which the employment relationship ruptures is the time when the employee is most vulnerable and hence, most in need of protection. In recognition of this need, the law ought to encourage conduct that minimizes the damage and dislocation (both economic and personal) that result from dismissal ... . I note that the loss of one's job is always a traumatic event. However, when termination is accompanied by acts of bad faith in the manner of discharge, the results can be especially devastating. In my opinion, to ensure that employees receive adequate protection, employers ought to be held to an obligation of good faith and fair dealing in the manner of dismissal, the breach of which will be compensated for by adding to the length of the notice period.

Business Lesson

Exercise good faith and fair dealing when dismissing employees. This decision has had a major impact on subsequent wrongful dismissal cases, both in the way claims are put forward and the number of months' of pay in lieu of notice awarded.

make such an award against an employer whose conduct is particularly abusive. These awards are rare, and aggravated damages are limited to cases in which an employee can prove that the employer also committed an intentional tort such as intentional infliction of mental suffering. Recently, however, punitive damages of $100,000 were confirmed by the Court of Appeal in *Keays v. Honda Canada Inc.* The judge wanted to punish the employer for its harsh treatment of an employee who had a poor attendance record due to chronic fatigue syndrome.

Just Cause

One of the most common ways in which employers defend against wrongful dismissal lawsuits is by raising a defence of just cause. An employer has just cause to dismiss an employee when the employee's conduct is so serious that it fundamentally breaches the employment contract (whether written or oral) and thereby justifies dismissal without notice.

As an employer, if you can prove that you had just cause to dismiss an employee, you are no longer bound by the common-law obligation to provide reasonable notice or pay in lieu of notice. Proving just cause, however, is extremely difficult.

Some of the more common grounds of just cause include dishonesty, insubordination, disobedience, sexual harassment, and attending work while intoxicated. Some misconduct, such as premeditated theft, serious incidents of assault, or sexual harassment, may constitute just cause where the misconduct fundamentally undermines the employment relationship, even if it occurs only once. However, most other types of misconduct or performance-related incidents must usually occur more than once to justify dismissal. This is especially true in the case of a long-term employee who has an otherwise excellent performance and disciplinary record. It is also true in the event of extenuating circumstances that cause an employee to act out of character. Furthermore, courts are increasingly requiring employers to use progressive discipline before resorting to dismissal. (Progressive discipline is discussed below.)

While incompetence is one of the most common reasons for dismissing an employee, it is also one of the most difficult grounds to justify on the basis of just cause. An employer must show that the employee fell below an objectively determined level of performance and that the problem lies with the employee, not with other factors, such as lack of adequate training.

It is important in this regard for employers to have a consistent and objective performance appraisal process and to involve employees in the process. Performance reviews should be fair—never vindictive—and they should be accurate; they should neither ignore nor exaggerate problems. You would be wise to document performance reviews, including your employee's response to the review. You should be prepared to prove that you took all possible steps to facilitate an employee's improvement and to help the employee meet your expectations.

Table 7.3 provides a very brief summary of several cases so that you can get a sense of how Canadian courts interpret just cause. Keep in mind that the circumstances of every case are different, and that each case must be interpreted on its own merits.

Table 7.3   Interpreting Just Cause

Case Name and Allegation	Facts	Result
McKinley v. BC Tel (2001) Allegation: dishonesty	Employer argued just cause after finding out that, while on medical leave, employee deliberately withheld information that he could safely return to work if he took certain medication.	Employer lacked just cause for dismissal. Employee's dishonesty did not go to the root of the employment relationship.
Henry v. Foxco Ltd. (2004) Allegations: insolence and insubordination	Auto body shop employee quarrelled with supervisor who had said he took too long working on vans. During the confrontation, employee repeatedly challenged supervisor to "go ahead and fire" him.	Employer lacked just cause for dismissal. Given employee's length of service and previous work record, single incident did not warrant immediate dismissal. Employer should have observed a "cooling-off period" before deciding on an appropriate course of action.
Chaba v. Ensign Drilling Inc. (2002) Allegation: disobedience	Drilling rig employee was told to remove ice using a crowbar and pickaxe, but when this was unsuccessful he used and damaged a front-end loader that he knew he was not authorized to use.	Employer lacked just cause for dismissal. Employee's failure to follow instructions was an error in judgment, not a willful act of disobedience or defiance. Employee had experience using the equipment and had seen it used before to accomplish the same task.
Bannister v. General Motors (1994) Allegation: sexual harassment	Employee in supervisory position made unwanted sexual comments and gestures to a student employed for the summer. Five other employees lodged similar complaints about employee's conduct. Employee insisted his conduct was not harassment.	Employer had just cause for dismissal. Employee abused his power by condoning or creating a poisoned working environment for women. His repeated denial that his actions constituted misconduct raised a question as to whether he could change his behaviour.

Progressive Discipline

If you raise a defence of just cause in a wrongful dismissal action, you may be required to demonstrate that you first implemented progressive discipline. Increasingly, courts are requiring employers in non-unionized workplaces to use this form of discipline before resorting to dismissal.

Progressive discipline involves gradually increasing levels of discipline—for example, a verbal warning, a written warning, a final written warning, and finally dismissal. In unionized workplaces, progressive discipline steps are codified in the collective agreement and usually include an unpaid suspension after a written warning. However, progressive discipline can pose legal problems where the employee is not unionized, since it could constitute constructive dismissal, a concept that we discuss below.

progressive discipline
discipline imposed by an employer in steps that increase in severity

Progressive discipline allows an employer to respond to instances of misconduct or poor performance in a measured way. If an employee's misconduct or poor performance continues throughout the steps of the progressive discipline process, the employer has put herself in a strong position to defend a wrongful dismissal action by the employee. As an employer, it is very important that you meticulously document all disciplinary actions that you take so that there will be reliable written evidence of what occurred. You should also give your employees the opportunity to respond to any allegations that you make about them or their work before you take disciplinary action of any kind. Always act in a fair and even-handed manner.

If you apply progressive discipline, you can also prevent an employee from later arguing that you have condoned his misconduct by failing to respond to it within a reasonable period of time. **Condonation** of misconduct occurs when an employer overlooks misconduct or takes no action against it; it gives employees the impression that you will tolerate the misconduct in the future. If you condone a particular form of misconduct, you may be unable to rely on that incident in imposing discipline for future incidents.

condonation
implied acceptance by an employer of the conduct of an employee by permitting the conduct to continue without warning, discipline, or corrective action

Measuring Reasonable Notice

Employers can find themselves in a position where they want to dismiss employees for reasons that clearly do not constitute just cause, such as a restructuring of the workplace or changing business needs. If you find yourself in this position, you must provide your employees with reasonable notice (absent an enforceable termination provision in the employment contract) or a severance package so that they have time to look for a new job while they are still on your payroll. If you fail to live up to this legal obligation, your employees could successfully sue you for wrongful dismissal.

Even if an employee's conduct has been poor, unless the misconduct has been extreme, many employers choose to provide dismissed employees with a severance package rather than face the potential cost and uncertainty of a wrongful dismissal lawsuit. Unless you can prove that an employee fundamentally breached the terms of her employment contract through serious misconduct or performance problems, you owe the employee reasonable notice or payment in lieu thereof.

How do you determine the amount of an employee's severance package? From the employer's point of view, the package should be generous enough to eliminate an employee's incentive to sue. The actual amount will usually be less than the amount that a court might award, but large enough that the employee will still accept the discounted package because it will save him the cost of suing you.

Courts have considered a number of key factors when determining what notice period is reasonable. Other than length of service, many of these factors relate to the relative difficulty that an employee will face in finding a comparable new job. Older workers usually receive longer notice periods than younger workers. Higher-ranking employees usually receive longer notice periods than lower-ranking employees.

duty to mitigate
obligation to take all reasonable steps to lessen losses suffered

Courts also consider whether an employee has fulfilled his common-law **duty to mitigate** damages. Employees are required to take all reasonable steps to find comparable alternative employment during the notice period. Employees must undertake serious job searches or risk being awarded a shorter notice period by a court. If an employee is successful in finding new employment before the end of

Table 7.4   Summary of Employer's Legal Obligations to Employee When Employment Ends

Circumstances	Employer's Obligations
Unionized or non-unionized employee resigns.	• No notice or severance payment to employee required (unless otherwise specified in employment contract, which is rare).
Employer dismisses unionized employee with or without cause.	• Collective agreement and *Employment Standards Act, 2000* govern employer's obligations.
Employer dismisses non-unionized employee with legal just cause.	• No notice or severance payment to employee required.
Employer dismisses non-unionized employee with under five years' employment, without legal just cause.	• Minimum termination notice under *Employment Standards Act, 2000* applies. • Employer must provide reasonable notice under common law (or payment in lieu of notice) unless notice specified in employment contract.
Employer dismisses non-unionized employee with over five years' employment, without legal just cause.	• Minimum termination notice under *Employment Standards Act, 2000* applies. • Severance pay requirements under *Employment Standards Act, 2000* may apply if requirements are met. • Employer must provide reasonable notice under common law (or payment in lieu of notice) unless notice specified in employment contract.
Employer dismisses over 50 employees during four-week period.	• Mass termination provisions in *Employment Standards Act, 2000* with respect to notice apply.
Employer constructively dismisses non-unionized employee.	• Minimum termination notice under *Employment Standards Act, 2000* applies. • Employer must provide reasonable notice under common law (or payment in lieu of notice) notice specified in employment contract.

the notice period, his earnings from the new job are usually deducted from the wrongful dismissal award (but not from his entitlement under the *Employment Standards Act, 2000*).

Constructive Dismissal

Constructive dismissal occurs when an employer makes a fundamental change to an employment agreement without providing an employee with reasonable notice of the change. Fundamental changes include significant changes in job responsibilities or working conditions. When an employer makes such a change, the law treats the situation as if the employer had fired the employee from her old job and rehired her in a new job. Under these circumstances, the employee is entitled to reasonable notice of dismissal or payment in lieu of notice.

constructive dismissal fundamental breach by an employer of an employment contract that entitles an employee to consider herself dismissed and to sue the employer for wrongful dismissal

Although claims for constructive dismissal are relatively rare, employers should be aware of workplace changes that could initiate a constructive dismissal claim, including the following:

- significant changes to benefit packages;
- relocation of employees;
- alteration of duties and responsibilities of employees;
- changes in employees' reporting structure; and
- imposition of new obligations, such as restrictive covenants, on employees.

Employers may gain some protection by building flexibility into a written employment contract. If the employer anticipates changes to the job description over time, the employment contract should state that duties and responsibilities may vary in response to changing business needs.

Employers have an implied obligation to provide a workplace that is safe and non-hostile. Failure to protect an employee from workplace bullying, for example, could therefore also result in a constructive dismissal action.

Right to Reinstatement

The **right to reinstatement** is an employee's right to be returned to his job. In certain limited circumstances, a tribunal or court may order reinstatement. This extreme remedy is not available under the common law. It is available only in particular circumstances dictated by a collective agreement or statute. Unionized employees may be entitled to reinstatement if their employer dismisses them in contravention of the governing collective agreement. Non-unionized employees are also entitled to reinstatement if their employer dismisses them for exercising their rights under the *Employment Standards Act, 2000* or various other statutes.

Post-Employment Obligations

Two matters—letters of reference and confidentiality obligations—are discussed below in the context of post-employment obligations of employers and employees.

Letters of Reference

If you, as an employer, dismiss an employee, the law does not require that you provide the employee with a letter of reference. However, an employee who lacks a reference will probably find it more difficult to obtain a new job. If the employee successfully sues you for wrongful dismissal, your refusal to provide a letter could increase the damages that the court awards. An employer's refusal to provide a letter of reference, without good reason, has caused some courts to extend the reasonable notice period.

However, in one recent case, *Ashby v. EPI Environmental Products Inc.*, a British Columbia court held that, where there is no evidence of bad faith on the employer's part, there is no obligation to provide an employee with a positive reference letter. The rationale here is that the risk of increased damages could tempt employers to provide misleading references.

Minimizing Your Risk
Reduce the Potential for Dismissal Claims from Non-Unionized Employees

- Never dismiss or otherwise retaliate against an employee for exercising his legal rights.

- Include a notice of termination clause in the written employment contract.

- Include in the employment contract a clause allowing you some flexibility to make changes, such as to job duties.

- Make effective use of probationary periods by monitoring suitability and performance carefully.

- Provide employees with as much notice as possible of any significant changes to their duties and compensation.

- Carefully document any problems with employees as soon as they occur.

- Implement and consistently apply an objective performance evaluation program that provides employees with regular, balanced feedback on their performance, guidance on ways to improve, and a reasonable time in which to make these improvements.

- Apply progressive discipline in all but the most serious instances of misconduct.

- Allow employees an opportunity to respond to any allegations of misconduct.

- Do not appear to condone misconduct by failing to respond to it within a reasonable time.

- Put notice of termination in writing, clearly specifying the termination date.

- Unless you are certain that you have just cause for dismissing an employee (and this should be reviewed with expert legal counsel first), provide an employee with advance notice of dismissal.

- Ensure that advance notice of dismissal at least meets the mandatory minimum requirements of the *Employment Standards Act, 2000*.

- If there is no notice of termination clause in the employment contract, provide the dismissed employee with reasonable notice of termination.

- Consult an employment lawyer to determine the appropriate notice period and the best form of severance package for a particular employee.

- Be fair and courteous to dismissed employees.

- Obtain a written release from employees indicating their acceptance of your separation package and their agreement not to sue for more. Urge employees to obtain independent legal advice first.

- Provide job search support for employees where appropriate.

If you dismiss an employee for cause and provide the employee with too positive a reference, you are leaving yourself open to a lawsuit for negligent misrepresentation from a new employer who relies on your reference and suffers harm as a result. Moreover, if you take the position that you dismissed an employee for cause, you must be careful not to undermine that position by providing too glowing a letter of reference. One approach is to give the employee a letter that confirms his period of employment, position, and salary but does not comment on the employee's performance. This remains a difficult area.

Duty of Confidentiality

Under the common law, a former employee cannot use or disclose trade secrets or confidential information obtained as a result of his employment. For example, an employee cannot copy or memorize a list of an employer's customers to use after his employment ends.

Former employees who were **fiduciary employees**—that is, workers who held positions of trust and who could significantly affect an employer's financial interests, such as the vice-president of finance—have additional post-employment obligations to the employer under the common law. Even without a restrictive covenant,

fiduciary employee
employee who holds a position of trust, could significantly affect an employer's interests, and has special obligations to the employer

they may not solicit a former employer's customers or prospective clients for a period of time if they took part in developing a relationship with these clients while employed. Recent case law suggests that in some circumstances, this duty may extend to not being able to accept a contract with a client of a former employer, even without solicitation.

Minimizing Your Risk

Keep the Secrets of Your Success Within Your Workplace

◄ Include confidentiality clauses in your written employment contracts.

◄ Consider including non-solicitation and even non-competition clauses where special circumstances support their use. Check with a lawyer who is knowledgeable in this area since courts are reluctant to enforce them.

Chapter Summary

In this chapter, we explored some of the multi-faceted laws that govern workplaces in Ontario. Throughout, we concentrated on the responsibility of businesses to support and uphold the many rights conferred on employees by various statutes and by the common law. We devoted particular attention to the Ontario *Human Rights Code*, which sets out an employer's obligation to operate inclusive workplaces that are free of discrimination and harassment, and that accommodate special needs. We also addressed various types of equity in the workplace. In addition, we explored the relationship that exists between employers and non-unionized staff, including hiring and firing practices and terms commonly found in employment contracts. We briefly introduced the legislative requirements that govern unionized workplaces, including an employer's obligation to refrain from engaging in unfair labour practices. The chapter also examined provincial statutes that dictate minimum employment standards and requirements concerning the health and safety of employees. We also addressed the increasingly important, and still emerging, issues related to privacy in the workplace. The chapter concluded with a discussion of post-employment rights and obligations.

KEY TERMS

accommodation
adverse impact
  discrimination
bargaining unit
bona fide occupational
  qualification (BFOQ)
certification
collective agreement
conditional offer
condonation
constructive dismissal
discrimination
due diligence defence
duty to mitigate

employment equity
equal pay for equal work
equal pay for work of
  equal value (pay equity)
fiduciary employee
gender-neutral job
  evaluation system
grievance
grievance arbitration
harassment
independent contractor
joint health and safety
  committee
just cause

lockout
nepotism policy
non-unionized employee
Ontario Labour Relations
  Board
lockout
pay in lieu of notice
poisoned work
  environment
progressive discipline
right to reinstatement
ratification
reasonable notice
restrictive covenant

severance pay
sexual harassment
strict liability offence
strike
undue hardship
unfair labour practices
union
unionized employee
WHMIS
workplace diversity
wrongful dismissal

REFERENCES

Ashby v. EPI Environmental Products Inc., 2005 BCSC 1190.

Bannister v. General Motors (1994), 8 CCEL (2d) 281 (Ont. Gen. Div.); rev'd. 112 OAC 188 (CA).

Chaba v. Ensign Drilling Inc., [2002] AJ no. 1052 (Prov. Ct.).

Chopra v. Syncrude Canada Ltd., [2003] AJ no. 741 (QB).

Eastmond v. Canadian Pacific Railway, 2004 FCA 852.

Employment Equity Act, SC 1995, c. 44.

Employment Standards Act, 2000, SO 2000, c. 41.

Green v. Canada (Public Service Commission), [2000] FCJ no. 778.

Henry v. Foxco Ltd. (2004), 31 CCEL (3d) 174 (Sask. QB).

Human Rights Code, RSO 1990, c. H.19.

Keays v. Honda Canada Inc., 2005 CanLII 8730 (ONSC).

Kohler Canada Co. v. Porter (2002), 17 CCEL (3d) 274 (Ont. SCJ).

Labour Relations Act, 1995, SO 1995, c. 1, sched. A.

Lyonde v. Canadian Acceptance Corp. (1993), 3 CCEL 220 (Ont. HCJ).

MacKinnon v. Ontario (Ministry of Correctional Services) (No. 3) (1998), 32 CHRRD 1.

McKinley v. BC Tel, [2001] 2 SCR 161.

Mesgarlov v. 3xs Enterprises Inc., 2001 CanLII 6268 (ONSC).

Occupational Health and Safety Act, RSO 1990, c. O.1.

Pay Equity Act, RSO 1990, c. P.7.

Personal Information Protection and Electronic Documents Act, SC 2000, c. 5.

Smith v. Ontario (Human Rights Commission), 2005 CanLII 2811 (SCDC).

Wallace v. United Grain Growers Ltd., [1997] 3 SCR 701.

Workplace Safety and Insurance Act, 1997, SO 1997, c. 16, sched. A.

REVIEW AND DISCUSSION

True or False?

_F_   **1.** The Ontario *Human Rights Code* prohibits employers from discriminating against a job applicant with tattoos.

_T_   **2.** The obligations of employers under the Ontario *Human Rights Code* begin even before an applicant is interviewed.

_F_   **3.** If a business wishes to hire an independent contractor rather than an employee, a well-worded contract describing the nature of the relationship will always hold up in court.

_T_   **4.** The court views restrictive covenants strictly—if they are unclear or more restrictive than necessary, the court will not enforce them.

_T_   **5.** The principles of contract law apply to employment contracts, but not to unionized workers who are governed by a collective agreement.

_T_   **6.** The *Occupational Health and Safety Act* requires all employers with 20-plus employees to create a joint health and safety committee made up of both management and employee representatives.

_F_   **7.** Equal pay for equal work means equal pay for work of equal value.

_F_   **8.** The right of employees to form or join a union is governed by the *Human Rights Code.*

_T_   **9.** Employee incompetence is often successfully argued by employers to defend against wrongful dismissal claims.

_T_   **10.** Accident reports written immediately following the event will be useful evidence if you end up in court.

Multiple Choice

1. What is the duty to accommodate?
   a. the obligation to provide room and board to migrant workers
   b. the obligation to satisfy the demands of unionized workers
   c. the obligation to assist an employee who has special needs
   d. the obligation to help workers suffering from undue hardship

2. When are conditional offers of employment useful to the employer?
   a. when there is a bona fide occupational qualification
   b. when the employer anticipates dismissing the employee without cause
   c. when a union is about to be certified
   d. when a probationary period is appropriate

3. Which of these behaviours might be considered to be sexual harassment?
   a. holding a co-worker briefly by the waist while squeezing by a small space, such as behind a cash register
   b. pinning up in the lunch room magazine pictures of men in bathing suits
   c. asking a subordinate on a date
   d. all of the above

4. Why is addressing "reasonable notice" in an employment contract before work begins a useful strategy for employers?
    a. It permits the employer to circumvent the *Employment Standards Act, 2000*.
    b. It reduces the risk of human rights claims against the employer for acting unreasonably.
    c. It reduces the costs and uncertainty of relying on a court to determine what constitutes reasonable notice under the common law.
    d. It clearly demonstrates that the employee is a fixed-term employee.

5. Which of these issues is not governed by the *Employment Standards Act, 2000*?
    a. vacation pay
    b. wrongful dismissal
    c. minimum wage
    d. work hours and overtime

6. Which rights do employees have under the *Workplace Safety and Insurance Act*?
    a. The right to participate in the health and safety of their workplace, the right to refuse to do unsafe work, the right to stop unsafe work, and the right to know about workplace hazards
    b. the right to benefits in the event that a disability or illness makes it impossible for them to continue working
    c. the right to compensation for injuries and illness sustained at work
    d. both b and c

7. When may a worker refuse to do work according to the *Occupational Health and Safety Act*?
    a. when danger is an inherent part of the job
    b. when a worker has a sincere and reasonable belief that the equipment or physical condition of the workplace is likely to endanger her or another a worker
    c. when the joint health and safety committee has refused to initiate a stop-work order
    d. when a worker is aware that hazardous materials as described in the WHMIS (the workplace hazardous materials information system) are present in the workplace

8. Which of the following statements is false in regard to a union that has been certified?
    a. The union has the right to prohibit union members from communicating with other unions.
    b. The union has the right to negotiate a collective agreement with the employer.
    c. The union may apply to the Ontario Labour Relations Board for a remedy if the employer fails to bargain in good faith.
    d. The employer may not enter into employment contracts with new employees who would be part of the bargaining unit.

9. Factors that may be considered by a court when determining the common-law notice period include which of the following?
   a. length of employment, age of employee, progressive discipline, salary, and job market conditions
   b. length of employment, age of employee, disability of employee, salary, progressive discipline, and job market conditions
   c. length of employment, age of employee, intoxication, absenteeism, and insubordination
   d. length of employment, age of employee, salary, job market conditions, and manner of termination

10. Documenting your policies and your responses to particular incidents is important in which of the following contexts?
    a. progressive discipline
    b. harassment in the workplace
    c. workplace accidents
    d. all of the above

11. Which of the following is unlikely to result in a successful claim of constructive dismissal?
    a. significant changes to benefit packages
    b. relocation to a different city
    c. reconfiguration of the office cubicles
    d. change in duties or responsibilities

Short Answer

1. Your company offices are on the ground floor, but your operations and storage areas cover three levels, with two full sets of stairs. A candidate for an inventory clerk job mentions that she cannot climb more than three or four steps because of a long-term knee condition. She is well qualified for the job and most of the work can be done in the office; however, previous inventory clerks visited the other floors regularly to monitor supplies. What factors must you take into account in deciding whether to hire her?

2. An employee at your company has four years' experience in a manual labour job. During this time, he has twice required time off to participate in a drug rehabilitation program. Now he wants to apply for training to operate a lift truck. You have concerns about his taking on such a high-risk job. What should you do?

3. Since Ted started work in your plant, he has kept to himself. Some of the other employees have formed the impression that he is gay and have written derogatory messages to that effect outside the lunchroom. A supervisor had told you that, although Ted is doing a good job, "things would go smoother around here" if Ted found another job. What can you, as a business owner, do to address this situation?

4. Penny is an accounts payable clerk who has just returned from a pregnancy leave. During her leave, her employer hired a substitute, Zhang, who has mastered the job and has become a permanent employee. Without consulting

Penny, the employer assigns her to a different job that requires similar skills and has the same level of pay, hours of work, and general working conditions. What are the employer's legal obligations and workplace options in this situation?

5. Job applicants frequently list references on their application form, resumé, or covering letter. Should the employer construe this as permission to contact the references for information about the applicant's experience?

6. Chantal has been the manager of corporate communications for four years. Because her new boss feels that the "chemistry" is not right between them, she has hired a new person to head the corporate communications department, with the title "director." She tells Chantal that she values her talents and will use them on various special communications projects, with no reduction in her pay and benefits. What considerations does the employer need to take into account?

Discussion and Debate

1. Having reviewed the basic common and statutory laws that apply to the workplace, do you think that in general they represent a fair balance between the rights of employers and those of employees? If so, why? If not, what is one key change you would make?

2. As a future business owner, you may well occupy a position of power and assume the responsibility of exercising some degree of control over others, especially employees. Devise a bill of rights for the people who work for you. Make sure you address the issue of privacy in the workplace.

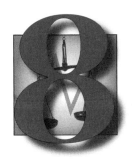

Property Law: Personal, Real, and Intellectual

What Is Property Law?

Property law confers rights over things. It allows the owners of these things to enforce their rights against others. Without laws to define property rights, people could not own things; they could merely possess them. Anyone who had or took possession of a thing could use it until she lost possession—until, for example, someone stole her property, or she gave it away, or she left it behind inadvertently. Because of the conflict and uncertainty that such a situation would produce, all societies have devised rules to govern property. In Canada, property ownership generally includes the right to

- possess and use property,
- prevent others from possessing it, and
- transfer property rights to others.

property law
collection of rules that confer rights of ownership, possession, and transferability over things

TYPES OF PROPERTY

public property
things owned by the government for the benefit of society

private property
things owned by individuals, businesses, or other organizations

tangible property
physical things

intangible property
things whose value does not arise from their physical attributes

goodwill
business's good reputation

real property
immovable things, including land, buildings, and fixtures

personal property
movable, tangible things, including physical objects that are not attached to land or buildings, and intangible property

intellectual property
things created by the mind or intellect, such as logos and inventions

Property may be classified as **public property**, which is owned by the government for the benefit of society as a whole, and **private property**, which is owned by individuals, businesses, or other organizations, to the exclusion of others.

Another important distinction is between tangible and intangible property. **Tangible property** consists of things that are physical—that can be seen and touched. Examples include a factory, a stapler, a painting, and a farmer's field.

Intangible property also has value, but its value does not arise from its physical attributes. Intangible property includes negotiable instruments such as cheques, intellectual property such as copyright and patents, and **goodwill**, which is a business's good reputation with its customers and others.

If, for example, Sam's Automotive Experts has spent 20 years building up a loyal customer base and establishing a reputation for doing solid work at fair prices, Sam's has created goodwill. When it comes time to sell the business, its value will include this goodwill. Since the new owner will benefit substantially from the reputation and customer base that Sam's has built, prospective buyers are willing to pay for them. Goodwill is not the only type of intangible property. Table 8.1 gives other examples, and distinguishes tangible from intangible property generally.

REAL, PERSONAL, AND INTELLECTUAL PROPERTY

Property is most commonly categorized into three types: real property, personal property, and intellectual property. **Real property**, commonly known as real estate, is immovable property and includes land, buildings, and fixtures that are attached to land or buildings.

Personal property includes movable tangible goods that are not attached to land or buildings. It also includes intangibles such as goodwill, negotiable instruments such as cheques, and **intellectual property**. Intellectual property is generally dealt with as a separate category of property because the rules, and the rationale behind them, are quite different from those that govern other types of property. In fact, intellectual property is broken down into numerous categories, including copyright, patents, and trademarks. Intellectual property, which is created by the mind or intellect, can be seen in designs, slogans, works of art, and inventions.

Table 8.1   Types of Property

Real Property	Personal Property	
	Tangible (chattels)	**Intangible**
• land • buildings (office towers, garages, fences) • fixtures (sinks, lighting fixtures, built-in shelving)	• automobiles • furniture • computers • inventory • office supplies • machinery	• shares in a corporation • goodwill • negotiable instruments (cheques, promissory notes) • intellectual property (copyright, patents, trademarks, industrial design, integrated circuit topography)

Each of the following situations requires some knowledge of real, personal, or intellectual property law.

- You are in the business of renting machinery to other businesses. An employee fails to inspect a forklift before it is delivered to a customer; the forklift malfunctions, injuring its operator. Who is responsible for the damages? How can you protect yourself from liability?
- The business that you work for rents office space from a landlord who takes no interest in the property: the lights are constantly dimming, the elevator is unreliable, the carpet is in need of repair, and the walls could use a paint job. Is your boss or your landlord responsible for fixing these problems?
- You have just discovered that the wonderful name you invented for your rapidly expanding restaurant business is practically identical to the name of a dog-grooming chain in your area. Should you continue using your name or think of a new one?

The Importance of Property Law for Business People

It is practically impossible to think of a business that could operate without property. Every day, businesses buy supplies and materials, manufacture goods, lease or own buildings, or develop new processes or products. The names of these businesses, their product names, and the goodwill they have built up are often very important and valuable assets. Property law affects all businesses that own or deal in property by defining the risks assumed by the ownership or possession of property.

Different types of property pose different risks of loss. Buildings and personal property may be destroyed by fire or storm damage. Personal property is at risk of being stolen or damaged. Intellectual property, such as patents and copyright, could be used without payment. The value of goodwill and trademarks may be diminished if your competitors use them without your authorization. Property law helps you manage these risks and offers several advantages:

- *It defines areas where your business may be vulnerable to loss.* For example, assume that you are in the business of storing other people's property. Property law defines the rights of both you and your customers in relation to this property. It indicates which of you is responsible if the property is damaged. It tells you when, how, and to what extent you need to protect yourself by purchasing insurance, for example.
- *It sometimes allows ownership and possession to be split.* Because property law distinguishes between ownership and possession, it is not always necessary to buy property: it is possible to rent an office or equipment from the owner. This frees your business from the capital outlay that owners are required to make.
- *It promotes the lending and borrowing of money.* Businesses need money to grow, and borrowing is an important source of capital. Ownership of property, including land, buildings, machinery, and inventory, facilitates borrowing, because lenders can take the property as security for the loan. In the case of land and buildings, this security is called a mortgage. For machinery and inventory, it is called a security interest.

- *It allows innovation to flourish.* By protecting creators and inventors from having their work expropriated by others, intellectual property law promotes artistic expression and encourages technological advancement. It allows your business to support projects and enterprises that can respond innovatively to challenges.

Personal Property

chattels
movable, tangible property

choses in action
intangible personal property, such as negotiable instruments and intellectual property

Personal property includes **chattels** and ***choses in action***. Chattels are movable items of property, or goods—distinct from land, buildings, and the fixtures attached to land and buildings. Your stapler, the paper you staple together, your pens and pencils, and the computer you use in your office are all chattels. They can be picked up and taken from one place to another.

Choses in action are intangible assets, including negotiable instruments, such as cheques, money orders, and promissory notes. Like other types of property, negotiable instruments are important assets that are included in the balance sheet of any business. They are discussed in detail in chapter 9. As mentioned earlier, intellectual property is also a type of intangible personal property; however, we deal with it below in a separate section. Here, we focus primarily on chattels, which are commonly called goods.

Personal property may be held as security for a debt. This means that if a business borrows money, the lender may require the business to secure the loan by giving the lender the right to seize and sell personal property if the loan is not repaid. For example, in the early days of doing business, Sam's Automotive Experts may need a bank loan to pay for tools and ensure a cash flow sufficient to pay its bills; a bank could take security in personal property, such as Sam's machinery. If the business fails to make the payments required by the bank, the bank could take possession of the machinery used to secure the loan and sell it to pay the unpaid debt. The rules governing this process are found in the *Personal Property Security Act*, and we discuss debt recovery in detail in chapter 9 under the heading "Debt Collection and Insolvency."

DISTINGUISHING OWNERSHIP FROM POSSESSION

Different people may have different property rights in the same piece of property. The primary distinction is between ownership and possession. For example, if a hardware store rents snow blowers to its customers, it continues to own the snow blowers while its customers have possession of them. The customers have the right to possess and use the snow blowers according to the terms of their rental agreement with the store. Similarly, a customer who takes his car to Sam's Automotive Experts for repair does not transfer ownership of the car to Sam's. Sam's has only temporary possession of the car.

Possession is a key ownership right, and owners of property may grant this right to others by giving them permission to possess their property. When ownership and possession of goods are split in this manner, the legal relationship between the owner and the possessor is called bailment.

Bailment

Bailment occurs when goods are borrowed, rented, stored, or found by a person other than the owner of the property. The owner is known as the **bailor**, and the person who is in temporary possession of the property—but who does not own it—is called the **bailee**.

The two key features of bailment are

1. the split between possession and ownership of goods and
2. the intention that the situation is temporary.

Every bailee has a duty to take care of the bailor's goods. In other words, the bailor may sue the bailee for the tort of negligence if the goods are damaged. In some cases, a defect in the bailed goods, such as a faulty braking system in a leased car, can result in the bailee suing the bailor. We discuss the elements of negligence, such as duty of care, standard of care, causation, and foreseeability in chapter 3 under the heading "Elements of Negligence." In a bailment, the standard of care—that is, the degree to which the bailee must be careful with the goods or the degree to which the bailor must be careful that the goods will not cause harm—varies depending on the type of bailment and other circumstances. We discuss the various types of bailment and their accompanying standards of care in the following sections. Table 8.2, on page 293, provides a summary. However, it is useful to keep in mind that when bailment occurs in a business context, it is usually governed by a contract, such as a rental agreement for a chainsaw. The common-law rules of bailment apply only to the degree that such a contract is silent, or in the absence of a contract.

LUCRATIVE BAILMENT

Lucrative bailment, which is also called "bailment for reward," is the most common form of bailment in the business world. It includes the following transactions:

- renting storage units or warehouse space,
- leasing vehicles,
- leasing postage meters,
- leasing photocopiers,
- renting water coolers, and
- using mail or couriers to send a package.

In each of these circumstances, both the bailor and the bailee receive a benefit.
Two other types of lucrative bailment are worth particular mention:

1. *Bailment for repair or service.* This is a form of bailment in which the bailor pays the bailee for repairing or servicing the bailor's goods. For example, suppose that Avery's necklace has a loose stone. She takes it to a jeweller to have the stone reset and leaves it there until the repair can be completed. Avery is not paying the jeweller to store her necklace but to repair it. Nevertheless, the situation qualifies as a lucrative bailment.

2. *Consignment.* This form of lucrative bailment is used by many antique and used clothing shops. Owners of clothing and antiques (bailors) approach these shops and ask if their goods can be sold there. Instead of buying the goods,

bailment
legal relationship that arises when personal property is borrowed, rented, stored, or found by a person other than its owner

bailor
party in a bailment that owns the personal property

bailee
party in a bailment that is in temporary possession of the bailor's personal property

the shops agree to display and sell them on behalf of the owners in return for a commission. The shops are never the owners of the goods: they are lucrative bailees. The compensation they receive for their services is the commission they earn if they sell the goods.

Liability for Lucrative Bailment

In most cases of lucrative bailment, there is a contract that dictates the terms of the bailment relationship and liability. The parties will resort to common-law bailment rules only if the contract is silent on an issue. Most standard contracts for the commercial rental of goods, for example, limit the bailor's liability by using a disclaimer clause, which provides that the bailee agrees to excuse the bailor from liability in the event that harm is suffered. (We discuss disclaimer clauses and their limitations in chapter 4 under the heading "Disclaimer.") These contracts may also impose obligations on the bailee for maintenance of the goods and return of the goods in a particular condition.

If you are involved in a lucrative bailment, it is wise to record your expectations in a written contract. This reduces the risk of misunderstanding, conflict, and lawsuits. Because the terms of a contract generally override common-law principles, a contract provides you and the other party with the opportunity to make your own rules. Where there is no contract and common-law tort principles prevail, the standard of care applicable to a lucrative bailment is usually the care that an ordinary or reasonably diligent person would take of the goods in the circumstances.

Effect of Payment to Bailee on Standard of Care

Under the common law, if the bailee receives payment to possess the bailed goods, he has a duty to preserve the value of the goods. The bailee is obliged to care for the goods at least as well as—and probably better than—he would if he owned them.

An even higher standard of care exists if the goods are particularly valuable (an antique necklace, for example), if they are easily damaged (glassware), or if they are perishable (fresh produce). It is reasonable to assume that all such goods require extra care. The bailee may be liable for even slight negligence. On the other hand, if the loss occurs as a result of a defect in the bailed goods (such as a defective clasp on the antique necklace), then the bailee may not be liable for the loss.

Liability of Bailor in Rental Situation

Suppose Martina's Equipment Rental Ltd. enters into a contract with Green Grow the Grasses-O Inc., a landscape company, to lease a riding lawnmower. Even if the contract is silent about the condition of the lawnmower, there is likely an implied term that the mower is in usable condition. If the mower is defective, Green Grow would have a claim, based on contract and on tort, against Martina's. Martina's could be liable for any damage caused by the defect. For example, Green Grow is no doubt relying on the lawnmower to perform work for its clients. Because of the defect, Green Grow might lose clients, damage lawns, and incur additional rental costs for a replacement mower. It can look to Martina's to compensate it for these losses.

Lien Against Bailor Who Refuses To Pay

Where there is a bailment for repair or service, the bailee has the right to a lien on the bailed property in the event that the bailor refuses to pay the bill. For example, if Avery took her necklace to the jeweller for repairs but then refused to pay for this service, the jeweller could refuse to return the necklace. Ultimately, the jeweller might have the right to sell the necklace in order to be paid from the money received from the sale. (The remainder of the money would go to Avery.) Businesses engaged in automobile repairs commonly exercise their lien rights if customers fail to pay them for their services.

CONSTRUCTIVE BAILMENT

A constructive bailment is involuntary. It usually arises when a bailor accidentally loses an item that the bailee finds. Suppose Avery goes to a restaurant wearing the necklace, but the catch on the necklace breaks and the necklace falls off. Avery eats her meal and leaves without noticing that the necklace has fallen under the table. When the restaurant is closing, Avery's waiter notices the necklace and turns it over to the restaurant manager. This is a constructive bailment because Avery did not intend to leave the necklace with the restaurant: she left it there accidentally.

Once the waiter finds the necklace, the restaurant has an obligation to return it to Avery, its owner. If the restaurant is unable to locate Avery, then it may keep the necklace, subject to Avery's right to claim it in the future. Avery's ownership rights do not end until she abandons her claim to the necklace. Purchasing a new necklace or stopping the search might be considered abandonment of her claim. If Avery claims her necklace and finds that it has been damaged, the restaurant will be liable only if it has been grossly negligent.

SPECIAL BAILMENT

A bailment relationship that is created by statute, rather than common-law principles, is called a special bailment. By statute, governments have imposed particular obligations on certain bailees, including those involved in the business of transporting goods (railway or trucking companies) and innkeepers. These businesses generally have special obligations in relation to the property in their charge. For example, an innkeeper, or hotel owner, must allow his guests to deposit their goods "for safe custody" with him. The $40 liability limitation contained in the Ontario *Innkeepers Act* is inapplicable to goods in safe custody, so if he loses them, he may be liable for an amount exceeding $40. The liability limitation is also inapplicable if a hotel refuses to accept a guest's goods for safe custody.

GRATUITOUS BAILMENT

Gratuitous bailment, in which no payment changes hands between bailor and bailee, is uncommon in the business world. However, we discuss this type of bailment briefly for the purpose of comparison with commercial bailments. In a gratuitous bailment, either the bailor or the bailee can receive the benefit of the bailment. For example, Avery might create a gratuitous bailment by leaving her necklace with her friend Yasmin while she goes on a trip, thus saving herself the cost of renting a safety deposit box. She might also create a gratuitous bailment by lending her necklace to Yasmin, who wants to wear it on a special occasion.

Liability When Bailor Benefits from Gratuitous Bailment

If a gratuitous bailment benefits the bailor—Avery, for example, when she stores her necklace with Yasmin—the standard of care expected of Yasmin is relatively low because the bailee is doing the bailor a favour. The bailee is liable only for gross negligence—or negligence that involves recklessness—such as leaving the necklace on a table beside the front door while hosting a party for 200 unknown guests.

The standard of care imposed on Avery, however, is high. If, for example, Avery's young nephew was playing with the necklace while eating peanuts and Yasmin suffered anaphylactic shock because of a peanut allergy that Avery knew about, Avery would probably be liable for the harm suffered by Yasmin.

Liability When Bailee Benefits from Gratuitous Bailment

If the gratuitous bailment benefits only the bailee—Yasmin, for example, when she borrows Avery's necklace to wear on a special occasion—the standard of care expected of the bailee is high. She is liable even for slight negligence, such as failing to notice that the necklace has slipped from her neck while she is dancing. If, however, the clasp was defective and Avery, the bailor, knew or ought to have known about the defect, she has an obligation to tell Yasmin before loaning the necklace. Avery has an obligation to check the necklace for obvious problems, such as a defective clasp, that could result in its loss. If she fails to do so, or fails to inform Yasmin, Avery is liable for any damage or loss that results. Avery's failure to notice the defect would not be considered reasonable in these circumstances.

Minimizing Your Risk
Be a Responsible Bailor and Bailee

- Ensure that all bailed goods are well maintained, safe, and in good repair.

- Describe the responsibilities of bailor and bailee in a written contract.

- Include disclaimer clauses where appropriate.

Real Property

fixtures
property, such as shelving or sinks, that is attached to buildings

Real property, also called realty or real estate, is generally defined as land, buildings, and fixtures. Land includes the minerals and water below its surface as well as the airspace above it. **Fixtures** are items such as shelving, sinks, or equipment that are attached to buildings. When real estate is sold, all fixtures are included in the sale unless specified otherwise.

Unless a business operates purely on the basis of a cell phone and laptop computer, it likely owns or rents real property. Offices, stores, factories, farms, parking lots, and even hot dog stands require real property to conduct business. There are a number of ways in which businesses can meet their needs for real property, and we discuss the legal implications of each below.

Table 8.2 Comparison of Different Types of Bailment

Type of Bailment	Description	Examples	Liability of Bailee	Liability of Bailor
Lucrative	Money or other payment changes hands.	The bailee pays the bailor for renting personal property, or the bailor pays the bailee for storing or repairing property.	The bailee must conform to the standard of care of a reasonably diligent person. A higher standard may exist if the bailed item is particularly valuable or fragile.	The terms of the contract may dictate the standard of care owed by the bailor. If the bailor rents defective equipment to the bailee, the bailor may be liable for harm suffered by the bailee as a result.
Constructive	The bailor loses personal property, which comes into the possession of the bailee.	A customer inadvertently leaves his keys behind at a grocery store.	The bailee has an obligation to return the property to the bailor, if possible.	A person who loses personal property is generally not liable to the finder of the lost object. However, liability could arise if the object is inherently dangerous, such as a loaded gun.
Special	Particular obligations are imposed by statute on certain bailment relationships, such as those undertaken in the hotel business	A hotel guest deposits jewellery in a hotel safe.	The bailee hotel is required to receive the jewellery for "safe custody" and is liable if the jewellery is damaged, lost, or stolen.	The bailor is required to deposit the jewellery in a fastened and sealed box or other receptacle if the hotel requires him to do so.
Gratuitous	No money or other payment changes hands.	The property may be borrowed, to the benefit of the bailee, or it may be stored, to the benefit of the bailor.	When the bailment benefits the bailor, the standard of care is low: gross negligence. When the bailment benefits the bailee, the standard of care is very high: slight negligence.	Even when the bailment benefits the bailee, such as where the bailor lends property to a friend, the bailor has an obligation to be aware of any defects or potential injury that could be caused by the property, and to caution the bailee.

OWNERSHIP OF LAND

Technically, only the government owns real property. What we commonly call ownership is really an interest in the property called a "fee simple," which provides rights that are similar to ownership. These rights include the right to possess the real property, exclude others from it, use it, build on it, sell it, give it away, and transfer it by will.

What is the significance of the government's right of ownership? The government retains the right to expropriate, or take land away from, private owners without their consent if it is in the public interest, providing them with monetary compensation. This may occur if, for example, the government wants to build a road or airport on someone's land. The government may also impose taxes on property owners, and an owner's failure to pay may result in the loss of his property to the government. The government also has the right to limit how an owner uses his land by imposing zoning bylaws, and to limit how an owner exploits his land through activities such as mining or forestry.

Despite the technical distinction between the terms "ownership" and "fee simple," we will use the term "ownership" in this chapter because it is commonly used.

TRANSFER OF OWNERSHIP

In Canada, there are two systems for transferring the ownership of real property: the traditional land registry system and the more modern land titles system. The land registry system requires buyers to search records of past transfers of the property to ensure that **title**, or ownership, has been uninterrupted. By contrast, under the land titles system, the government vouches for the title. Therefore, if there is a problem—such as a fraudulent transfer—purchasers who were unaware of the fraud may receive compensation from the government. The land registry system is still used in many provinces, including southern Ontario; however, Ontario is slowly switching over to the land titles system, which provides greater certainty for buyers.

title
ownership

The following example demonstrates the risk that buyers face under the registry system and the importance of doing a title search. Imagine that your business wants to buy a factory from Preston Ironworks. First, you need to search title to this property, and you can do so by going to the local registry office. Here, records of title, called **deeds**, are kept for the properties in your area. Assume that your search uncovers records that reveal that Preston Ironworks bought the property from Fred Snell in 1995, and Franken Developments bought the property from Mary Butler in 1990. However, the records give no indication of who sold the property to Fred Snell. Because the chain of title is broken, you have no assurance that Fred Snell was the legitimate owner when he sold the property to Preston Ironworks. If Fred did not have legitimate title, he could not transfer title to Preston; Preston, therefore, would have nothing to transfer to you. Figure 8.1 illustrates this broken chain of title.

deeds
records of title

Caveat emptor, or buyer beware, is the ruling principle of the land registry system. A business that pays for real property without a clear chain of title may, in fact, be paying for nothing. Anyone who can establish a better claim of title may successfully challenge its ownership of the land. To address this risk, buyers should consult a lawyer to conduct (or oversee) a title search and should consider purchasing title insurance, which provides some protection to innocent purchasers in the event that a problem with title is discovered.

In addition to revealing a broken chain of title, a title search may also disclose other problems. There may be unpaid mortgages or other charges,

---

Minimizing Your Risk

Check Your Title When Purchasing Property

- Hire a lawyer to do a title search if the property you want to buy is registered under the land registry system. (If the lawyer makes an error, her liability insurance will provide some protection.)

- Consider buying title insurance to protect your business against any unexpected claims against the title of land that it owns.

- If your business does renovation or other work on a client's property, register unpaid debts on the client's title.

such as construction liens (renovation or repair work), registered against the property by creditors. Registration of these charges provides notice to potential buyers that clear title cannot be transferred until the debts are paid.

The land titles system is similarly not without its problems. The current state of Ontario law, as illustrated in *Household Realty Corporation Ltd. v. Liu*, shows that title holders who are innocent of fraud are nevertheless vulnerable to fraudulent mortgages.

The Ontario Superior Court of Justice has followed *Household Realty* in *Lawrence v. Wright*. In *Lawrence*, a fraudster stole title to a homeowner's property, mortgaged it, and absconded with the funds. The mortgagee demanded possession of the property, but found itself under intense public scrutiny and eventually abandoned its eviction action. The court returned title to the homeowner but was unable to offer her any relief under the mortgage because it claimed to be "unfortunately" bound by *Household Realty*. *Lawrence* is currently under appeal to the Court of Appeal, with the Ontario government intervening in the case on the side of the homeowner.

Figure 8.1 Broken Chain of Title

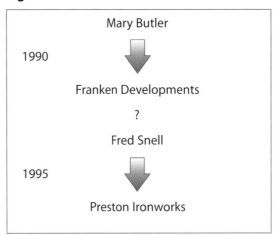

CASE IN POINT Fraudulent Mortgage Prevails

Household Realty Corporation Ltd. v. Liu, 2005 CanLII 43402 (Ont. CA)

Facts

A wife forged her husband's signature on a power of attorney and used this document to finance her gambling addiction by obtaining mortgages on the couple's home. She registered the fraudulent mortgages under the Ontario *Land Titles Act*. When the mortgages went into default, the mortgagees sued for the principal and interest owing. The husband, who was unaware of his wife's forgery, claimed that the mortgages were invalid because they were fraudulent. The judge found that the fraudulent mortgages were valid, and the husband appealed.

Result

The Ontario Court of Appeal, faced with deciding which of the innocent parties—the husband or the mortgage companies—would bear the loss, concluded that the fraudulent mortgage was valid. Quoting the judge in the court below, the Court of Appeal stated, "the two mortgages in this case, having been given for valuable consideration and without notice of the fraud are, once registered, effective and can be relied on."

Business Lesson

This case sets a dangerous precedent. As the law now stands, an innocent victim of a mortgage fraud has no defence against an eviction action under a fraudulent mortgage. Purchasing existing owner title insurance is the only way to obtain some measure of protection.

AGREEMENTS OF PURCHASE AND SALE

Land is bought and sold under sales contracts called agreements of purchase and sale. These contracts must be in writing to be enforceable. Like any contract, an agreement of purchase and sale may be negotiated to suit the needs of the parties. It includes terms such as the selling price and the closing date, and it may also include conditions and warranties, which usually protect the buyer.

Conditions Precedent

In chapter 4, we discussed conditions precedent in the context of standard form contracts. These conditions—which specify that something must happen before a party is required to fulfill her contractual obligations—often arise in agreements of purchase and sale. The following are examples of conditions precedent that you are likely to encounter when buying and selling real property.

1. *Conditional on financing.* The agreement of purchase and sale may provide that the buyer is not required to complete the sale unless she is able to arrange a mortgage or other financing by a specified date. (We discuss mortgages in detail later in this chapter.)
2. *Conditional on zoning approval.* The agreement of purchase and sale may provide that the buyer is not required to complete the sale unless she is able to obtain the zoning approval required to use the land in the manner intended.
3. *Conditional on inspection.* The agreement of purchase and sale may provide that the buyer is not required to complete the sale unless a building inspection indicates that there are no hidden structural problems with the building.
4. *Conditional on environmental audit.* The agreement of purchase and sale may provide that the buyer is not required to complete the sale unless an environmental audit indicates that there are no hidden environmental hazards on the property. This condition is particularly important to protect buyers of industrial land. Environmental laws can hold buyers responsible for the high costs of cleaning up toxic wastes, even if they were unaware that environmental problems existed at the time of purchase.

As we discussed in chapter 4 under the heading "Breach of Condition or Breach of Warranty?" the breach of a condition brings all contracts—including agreements of purchase and sale—to an end.

Warranties

Unlike the breach of a condition, the breach of a warranty does not terminate an agreement of purchase and sale. The non-breaching party is not excused from his obligations under the contract; however, he is entitled to sue the breaching party for damages. The following are warranties commonly found in agreements of purchase and sale:

1. *Warranting no toxic wastes on property.* The vendor may warrant that there are no toxic wastes, such as oil tanks, buried under the surface of the property. If toxic waste is found years later, the buyer can sue the vendor for

breach of contract. The vendor would likely be required to reimburse the buyer for the costs of restoring the environment to a non-toxic state.

2. *Warranting no asbestos in buildings.* The vendor may warrant that there is no asbestos in the building. If asbestos is later discovered to be present, the buyer's remedy is to sue the vendor for damages.

Of course, depending on whether the vendor can be found years later, and depending on whether the vendor has money to pay damages, the buyer may be limited in its ability to enforce the warranty.

Closing

Real property is not legally transferred when the parties sign an agreement of purchase and sale; rather, it is transferred at a time specified in the agreement, called the "closing date." On closing, the buyer pays the vendor the purchase price, and title is transferred. Under the land registry system, title is transferred by registering a deed. Under the land titles system, title is transferred by filing a transfer form. On closing, the buyer takes possession of the property.

> ### Minimizing Your Risk
> **Protect Yourself Against Environmental Clean-up Costs**
>
> - Ensure that the land you buy does not subject you to unexpected liability for environmental clean-up—by inserting appropriate conditions in your agreement of purchase and sale and by carrying out appropriate inspections and environmental audits.
>
> - Ensure that if you discover environmental or health issues associated with the property, you have the right to seek reimbursement of the clean-up costs from the vendor by having inserted appropriate warranties.

MORTGAGES

A **mortgage** is a loan secured by property; it gives the lender the right to sell the property, and recoup any loss, if the borrower fails to repay the loan. Mortgages therefore operate in relation to real property the way security agreements operate in relation to personal property. (We discuss security agreements in chapter 9 under the heading "Unsecured and Secured Credit.")

It is helpful to remember the terminology: the owner of the property who borrows funds is the **mortgagor**, and the lender (usually a financial institution) is the **mortgagee**. While the mortgage is in effect, the mortgagor keeps possession of the real property and may make full use of it, provided that he fulfills the following obligations, which are included in all standard mortgage agreements. The mortgagor must

- make periodic mortgage payments (usually monthly or bi-weekly),
- pay all property taxes,
- insure the property against loss, and
- make all repairs necessary to ensure that the property does not lose value.

Failure to fulfill any of these obligations results in **default**, which allows the mortgagee to take possession of the property and avail itself of other remedies, which we discuss below.

Like most loan payments, mortgage payments consist of a combination of principal (the amount of money loaned) and interest. The **amortization period** is the length of time it will take to pay off the debt entirely, based on the regular payment of a fixed amount. The amortization period is usually long—20 years perhaps.

mortgage
loan secured by real property

mortgagor
owner of real property who borrows funds from a mortgagee

mortgagee
party who loans funds to a mortgagor; usually a financial institution

default
mortgagor's failure to fulfill her obligations under a mortgage

amortization period
length of time required to pay entire mortgage debt

mortgage term
period, usually between one and five years, during which a stipulated interest rate applies

However, the **mortgage term** is considerably shorter, usually between one and five years. The negotiated interest rate applies only during the term of the mortgage. At the end of the term, the mortgagor and the mortgagee must negotiate a new interest rate. If another lender is offering lower rates, the mortgagor can switch lenders. Once the debt is paid in full, the mortgagor takes clear title.

Purchasers often obtain mortgages to finance the purchase of real property. Sometimes, however, property owners mortgage the property they already own as a method of raising funds for some other purpose. For example, a small business owner might mortgage her own home in order to finance the growth of the business. A large corporation with numerous real estate holdings, such as factories and office buildings, might mortgage some of these properties to raise needed capital.

It is possible to have several mortgages on the same property. Mortgagees, like personal property security holders, hold their interests in a priority sequence. In the event of a default, a first mortgage takes priority over a second mortgage, which takes priority over a third mortgage, and so on. The terms "first," "second," and "third" refer to the time when the mortgages are registered. Also like personal property security holders, mortgagees must register their mortgages in order to preserve their position in the priority sequence.

Default

acceleration clause
contractual term providing that payment of the entire debt becomes due on default

What happens if a mortgagor defaults by failing to make her mortgage payments, pay her property tax, insure her property, or make necessary repairs to the mortgaged property? Most mortgage agreements include an **acceleration clause**, which provides that full payment of the entire debt becomes due on default.

If the mortgagor defaults, the mortgagee may simply sue the mortgagor for payment of the debt. Alternatively, the mortgagee may seek an order for possession of the property, and then obtain relief in three different ways:

1. *Sell the property under the power of sale authorized by the mortgage.* Most mortgage agreements give the mortgagee the power to sell the property in the event of default by the mortgagor. This form of sale is the most commonly used remedy because it is relatively quick and easy. In less than two months from the date of default, title to the property may be transferred directly to a new purchaser, who receives clear title, free of the mortgage. The mortgagee uses the proceeds of sale to pay the debt that the mortgagor owes him. Any surplus goes to subsequent mortgagees and other registered creditors in priority based on the dates that the subsequent mortgages and interests were registered. Finally, anything left over is returned to the mortgagor. If the proceeds of sale are insufficient to satisfy the entire debt, the mortgagor is liable for the shortfall.

2. *Obtain title in a foreclosure action.* An action for foreclosure is more complicated than a sale under the power of sale clause in the mortgage agreement because it involves transferring legal title to the property from the mortgagor to the mortgagee. Once title is transferred, the mortgagee has the choice of selling or keeping the property. Some mortgagees may choose to keep the property, renting it to a tenant and recouping their losses over time.

Unlike a sale under the power of sale, a final order of foreclosure extinguishes the debt owed by the mortgagor to the mortgagee. The mortgagor is not liable for any shortfall, nor is it entitled to any of the proceeds of sale, even if they exceed the amount owed under the mortgage.

3. *Sell the property in a judicial sale action.* A judicial sale is a sale by court order. The sheriff sells the property by tender or public auction, and the proceeds are distributed in the same manner as a sale under power of sale. The mortgagees and other registered creditors are entitled to payment of the debts owed to them, in priority sequence, and anything left over is returned to the mortgagor.

> **Minimizing Your Risk**
> **Fulfill Your Mortgage Responsibilities**
> - If you are a mortgagor, make your payments on time, pay your property taxes, and insure your property and keep it in good repair.
> - If you are a mortgagee, search the registry for prior mortgages and liens and register your own mortgage without delay.

COMMERCIAL LEASES

Many businesses choose to rent the commercial property they occupy, rather than buy it. There are many reasons for this choice. For example,

- renting does not tie up capital,
- renting increases a business's flexibility to change locations, and
- renting may decrease maintenance responsibilities (depending on the terms of the lease).

Some businesses, such as property management companies, make their living from renting properties to others. Our focus here, however, is primarily on the needs and risks of the commercial tenant. It is also very important for business people to remember that the law governing commercial tenancies is significantly different from the law governing residential tenancies. Legislation such as the *Residential Tenancies Act* provides protection for residential tenants that greatly exceeds the protection provided for commercial tenants. Our discussion is limited to commercial tenancies.

Just as a bailment separates possession from ownership of personal property, a lease separates possession from ownership of real property. Under a commercial lease, a commercial tenant enjoys possession of property for the purpose of conducting business there, while the landlord continues to own the property. The **lease** is the contract that sets out the rental terms that the parties have agreed to, such as the length of the lease, the amount of rent to be paid, the timing of rental payments, obligations of maintenance and repair, and any restrictions on the tenant's use of the premises. When the lease comes to an end, the right of possession reverts to the landlord.

While the lease is in operation, the tenant is entitled to **exclusive possession** of the property. This means that the tenant may exclude all others from the property, including the landlord, except in unusual circumstances such as emergencies. The tenant may also use the property without interference by the landlord, subject to any agreed-upon restrictions provided in the lease. For example, a lease agreement may prevent a tenant from doing major renovations or making changes to the structure of a building.

lease
contract that sets out terms of property rental

exclusive possession
possession of real property to the exclusion of others

Common Lease Provisions

Term of the Lease

fixed tenancy
right to rent real property for a specified period of time

periodic tenancy
right to rent real property for an indefinite period of time, where both landlord and tenant have the right to terminate the tenancy after providing notice

In a **fixed tenancy**, a lease exists for a fixed term, such as 1 year, 5 years, or even 99 years. At the end of the term, the landlord and tenant have no obligation to each other to continue the lease arrangement. They may part ways without legal consequence or they may negotiate a new term. In a **periodic tenancy**, the lease does not specify a rental term or a termination date. Instead, the lease continues to operate indefinitely, unless one of the parties gives notice to the other to terminate the lease.

Both fixed and periodic tenancies require the periodic payment of rent. The notice period for termination of a periodic tenancy is generally one rental period. Therefore, if your business pays rent monthly, either you or your landlord—depending on which of you wants to terminate the lease—must provide the other with one month's notice. A full month's notice must be given the day before rent is due in the prior month. Fixed tenancies may become periodic tenancies if, after the termination date, no new term is negotiated, but the tenant continues paying rent and the landlord continues to collect it.

Rent

The amount of rent payable under most commercial and industrial leases is determined on the basis of the square footage of the space leased. The rate charged per square foot varies depending on the building's attributes and location, and is negotiated by the parties. Because the term of commercial leases is often long, and market rates for commercial premises change unpredictably over time, most long-term commercial leases provide for renegotiation of the rate at specified intervals—every five years, for example. If the parties are concerned about their ability to renegotiate a mutually agreeable rate, they may include an arbitration clause in the lease agreement.

Under the common law, a tenant's obligation to pay rent continues even if the property is rendered unusable by, for example, a devastating fire. The principle of frustration of contract that we discussed in chapter 4 does not apply to lease agreements. This is a serious concern for tenants. If you lease premises, it is important that you include a provision in your lease that permits you to stop paying rent under certain circumstances. Otherwise, you may find yourself paying rent for premises that your business cannot use.

If a tenant fails to pay his rent, a landlord has several remedies available. The landlord may sue for payment of the debt, most likely in Small Claims Court. This procedure is fairly simple, as described in chapter 2 under the heading "The Litigation Process in Small Claims Court." Once the landlord obtains a court order, he still must have the order enforced using one of the procedures described in chapter 9 under the heading "Debt Proceedings in Superior Court."

distress
remedy allowing landlord to seize and sell tenant's personal property when rent is unpaid

Commercial landlords also have the right of **distress** against their tenants' goods. This means they may seize and sell a tenant's personal property—such as computers and office equipment—that is located on the leased premises to cover the amount of the tenant's debt. (The right of distress is not available to residential landlords.)

Finally, commercial landlords have the right of re-entry, or **forfeiture**, which allows them to regain possession of the premises when a tenant fails to pay her rent. Changing the locks is the most common method of regaining possession. A tenant that has been locked out has the option of applying to a court to reinstate the lease after she pays the full amount of rent owing. Once a landlord uses the forfeiture remedy, he no longer has the right of distress. Therefore, landlords should consider their options carefully before changing the locks. If a tenant has enough personal property on the leased premises that can be sold to cover her debt, a landlord may be wise to use the distress remedy before resorting to forfeiture.

forfeiture
remedy allowing landlord to regain possession of leased premises when rent is unpaid

Repairs and Maintenance

A well-drafted lease sets out both a landlord and a tenant's responsibilities for repairing and maintaining the premises. Apart from a lease, commercial tenants have very little protection because legislation requires landlords only to maintain basic safety. The common law does not oblige a landlord to make repairs, only to warn tenants of any dangers.

Commercial tenants are generally not entitled to withhold rent for any purpose, even if their landlord breaches a provision in a lease. So, if your landlord refuses to make repairs according to the requirements of the lease, your business must seek other remedies, such as suing the landlord for breach of contract. If you are successful in such a suit, your business may be awarded a rent abatement, which is a reduction in the amount of rent payable.

Use of Premises

Tenants have the right to **quiet enjoyment** of the premises. This means that a tenant is entitled to use the property for its intended purpose, without interference from the landlord or others that are under the control of the landlord (such as other tenants). To avoid a misunderstanding about the tenant's intended purpose, the lease agreement should specify this purpose in the clearest terms.

quiet enjoyment
tenant's right to use leased property for intended purpose without interference from landlord or others under his control

For example, if your business wants to use the premises for heavy manufacturing—which involves noise 24 hours a day and will probably damage the interior of the building—it is important that you draw your landlord's attention to your intended usage and that your landlord accept this usage in the lease. The lease should also clarify both your landlord's and your business's responsibilities for maintaining the premises in a condition agreeable to you both. In addition, the lease should set out your business's responsibilities for its potential interference with the quiet enjoyment of the premises by other tenants.

Sublets

Tenants have the right to sublet the premises unless the lease states otherwise. This means that a tenant may find a new tenant to take possession of the premises. However, the original tenant remains responsible for fulfilling all of the obligations under the lease, such as paying the rent and maintaining the property. The new tenant, or subtenant, is responsible only to the original tenant; the subtenant has no contractual obligations to the landlord.

If a tenant has a long-term lease and it wants to change locations, it may find a subtenant. The original tenant will collect rent from the subtenant and pay the landlord. The sublet allows the original tenant to move out without losing money.

A tenant may charge as much rent as the market will bear; it need not be the amount specified in the lease. If a subtenant is willing to pay a higher rent, the tenant may be able to make a profit—that is, the difference between the amount the subtenant pays to the tenant and the amount the tenant pays to the landlord under the lease.

Assignment

Tenants also have the right to assign the lease, unless the provisions of the lease provide otherwise. In an assignment, a new tenant becomes a party to the lease and deals directly with the landlord according to the terms of the lease. However, unless the landlord releases the first tenant from its obligations under the lease, the landlord may still sue the first tenant in the event that the new tenant fails to pay the rent or otherwise abide by the lease.

Fixtures

If a tenant adds fixtures to the rented premises, what happens to the fixtures when the tenant leaves? Generally, fixtures stay on the premises and tenants are not permitted to remove them. The law creates an exception for trade fixtures, which are specific to the tenant's business—for example, washing machines in a laundromat, machinery in a factory, shelving in a store, or dental chairs in a dentist's office. It is wise to specify when signing the lease which fixtures the parties intend to be trade fixtures to avoid confusion and disagreement later.

Minimizing Your Risk

Customize Your Commercial Lease

- Include an arbitration clause in long-term leases to avoid rent hikes that exceed market rates.

- Specify the tenant's intended use of the property and the landlord's agreement to this use.

- Include a provision exempting the tenant from paying rent if the premises become unusable.

- Include detailed provisions about maintenance and repair obligations of both landlord and tenant.

- Specify which party will keep any fixtures installed by the tenant.

Shopping Centre Leases

Shopping centre leases are complicated because they include space that is shared among many tenants, such as space for parking, storage, and shipping, as well as public space for shoppers. The common interests of the tenants and landlord are reflected in the special obligations that they both assume under shopping centre leases. For example, a lease may require the landlord to promote the shopping centre with advertising. Tenants may be required to keep their stores open during specified business hours for the convenience of shoppers, which provides a benefit for all tenants. Also, because of the parties' shared interest in the shopping centre's success, rental payments are usually arranged so that the landlord shares in the profits of the tenants. The lease may require a minimum monthly rental payment, but it also usually requires the tenant to pay the landlord a percentage of gross sales.

LICENCES

Some uses of real property involve licences, such as:

- a licence from a municipality or an amusement park owner to operate a hot dog stand on a city street or on the grounds of the amusement park,
- a licence from a hotel to hold an office party in a banquet hall,
- a licence from a provincial government to extract oil or minerals from real property, and
- a licence from a building owner to attach an antenna or satellite dish to a building.

A licence does not create an interest in land; rather, it creates a contractual right. The rights of both parties are entirely dictated by the terms of the contract. Unlike a lease, there are no additional common-law principles (such as the right to exclusive possession) or special statutes to govern the relationship.

Insurance

Every business owner and most people have had some experience with insurance because it is an important part of any risk management plan. Car insurance, home insurance, life insurance, tenants' contents insurance, and liability insurance are all commonly obtained for prevention of loss. Insurance limits the risk of future loss by spreading the risk among a large group.

Suppose, statistically speaking, one house in your neighbourhood will sustain damages of $200,000 as a result of fire or water damage in the next year. There are 2,000 houses in your neighbourhood. Each household may choose to contribute $100 to a fund, with the understanding that the $200,000 collected will go to the household that sustains the damage. The result is that everyone enjoys peace of mind for the price of $100, and the owners of the damaged house will have the money they need for repairs. Insurers manage the pooled fund, which is called the "float." The float is the total of all premiums paid by those who are insured, less administrative expenses.

A person or business that seeks insurance typically applies to an insurer for insurance coverage. Once the insurer approves the applicant and after the applicant pays a premium, the insurer issues an insurance policy. The **policy** is a contract that describes the types of losses covered as well as the reasons why the insurer may deny coverage. If a loss occurs, the insured obtains compensation from the insurer according to the terms of the policy.

policy
insurance contract describing the rights and obligations of an insurer and an insured

TYPES OF INSURANCE

There are different types of insurance, which are generally divided into two main categories: (1) life and health, and (2) property and casualty. Life and health insurance may be of interest to businesses that create benefit plans for their employees. Beneficiaries of this sort of insurance are generally the employees and their families. Property and casualty (or liability) insurance protects against the loss of both real and personal property and against the costs of being sued for negligence, including professional negligence. (We discuss the tort of professional negligence in chapter 3. Businesses that employ professionals, such as architects or lawyers, should ensure that their professional employees are covered by appropriate levels of errors and omissions insurance.)

Below we list the types of property-related insurance that sensible businesses usually carry:

1. *Property loss.* Businesses carry property loss insurance to protect themselves against the risk of loss from catastrophes such as fire, flood, theft, accident, and extreme weather. Property loss insurance protects businesses against losses of real property, such as factories, and personal property, such as machinery and equipment inside these factories.

2. *Liability for property loss.* Businesses carry property liability insurance to protect themselves against the financial consequences of failing to take adequate care of the property of customers and others. This form of insurance is particularly important for businesses that act as bailees. For example, if a bailor leaves her dress for cleaning at a bailee dry cleaner, and the dress is ruined when the dry cleaner's machinery malfunctions, the dry cleaner is liable for damages for the ruined dress unless he has purchased property liability insurance.

   Bailment is not the only situation in which liability insurance protects a business against damage to the property of another. If, for example, a delivery driver rear-ends another vehicle, the business that employs the driver can look to its liability insurance for protection.

3. *Occupiers' liability.* The occupier of real property—that is, the owner or tenant, depending on who is using the premises—owes a duty of care to customers and others who venture onto the property. (We discuss the tort of occupiers' liability at length in chapter 3.) An occupier who is found to be negligent because she has, for example, failed to shovel snow or to clean up a spill quickly is liable for injuries sustained by those on the premises. Occupiers' liability insurance protects an occupier against negligence lawsuits by covering her legal costs and any damage awards. Business tenants of shared spaces, such as shopping malls, should review their leases carefully to determine the extent of their responsibility for maintenance and insurance.

4. *Business interruption.* After suffering the loss of real or personal property, a business may find that its operation is seriously impaired or shut down entirely. If, for example, a business is temporarily shut down when a fire devastates its premises, business interruption insurance compensates it for the loss of its operating income.

INSURABLE INTERESTS

insurable interest
interest that causes insured to benefit from the existence of property and to suffer from its loss

To obtain insurance for property, you must have an **insurable interest** in that property—that is, an interest that causes you to benefit from the existence of the property and to suffer from its loss. This is unlike insurance against liability for property loss. For example, only a tenant, not the landlord, can insure the tenant's computers. This is because the landlord does not have an insurable interest in the tenant's computers. However, the landlord could purchase liability insurance that would cover the cost of replacing the computers if they were stolen due to the landlord's negligence.

The insurable interest is limited by the fair market value of the property. For example, a computer system worth $50,000 may not be insured for $60,000.

Web Link

Visit the Insurance Bureau of Canada's website at www.ibc.ca for detailed checklists about how businesses can manage their insurance risks.

Where ownership and possession are split—as they are in situations involving tenancy and bailment—it is not always clear who should insure real or personal property. Generally, the party whose property is at risk should obtain insurance. In a tenancy, for example, the landlord usually insures the real property and the tenant usually insures the personal property. However, a landlord with obligations to repair the premises would be wise to obtain liability insurance to protect against a loss to a tenant's property that results from the landlord's negligence. For example, a roof that leaks because a landlord neglects to maintain it could damage a tenant's valuable computer system, and an insured landlord could look to her insurer for protection from the financial fallout.

Following the risk principle, a bailor usually insures against loss or damage to the goods that he rents to a bailee. However, the bailee is liable if the bailed goods are damaged or lost as a result of the bailee's negligence. Therefore, a bailee might want to obtain liability insurance to protect against such a loss. In some instances, to avoid double insurance of the same goods, bailors and bailees may want to include a term in their contract that assigns the responsibility for obtaining insurance to one party or the other.

COVERAGE

When deciding on the insurance coverage appropriate for your business, it is wise to consider

- the types of loss that you want to insure against and
- the value of coverage that you are willing to pay for.

Not all losses are necessarily covered by standard insurance policies. For example, property insurance may cover losses that arise from a variety of events, such as fire, flood, accident, and theft, but each type of loss must be specified in the policy. This issue was recently highlighted in New Orleans after Hurricane Katrina, when some insurers denied coverage by taking the position that storm coverage does not include floods, thereby leaving policyholders with no protection. As a business person, you should review your insurance contracts carefully to ensure that they specify all of the losses that you intend to insure against. If necessary, you may need to purchase additional coverage.

The value of insurance coverage may not exceed a business's insurable interest in its insured property. However, it is possible to insure your property for less than its market value and thereby partially self-insure your property. Businesses use this strategy as a cost-saving method because it reduces the premium payable to an insurer. When partially self-insuring, a business buys enough insurance to cover part—but not all—of a potential loss. For example, a business that owns a factory worth $800,000 might insure the factory for $600,000. In the event that the factory is completely destroyed by fire, the business receives only $600,000 in compensation. It bears the additional $200,000 loss itself.

Minimizing Your Risk
Purchase Adequate Insurance

- Carefully assess all your real and personal property risks.

- Check that your insurance policies specifically mention these risks and cover them adequately.

- Consider partial self-insurance or high deductibles to reduce premiums.

- Comply with building and safety codes.

- Inspect your premises and equipment regularly, and keep them in good repair.

- Train employees with respect to fire, safety, and emergency procedures.

deductible
out-of-pocket payment
that an insured must make
that is deducted from the
insurance payment

Another method of reducing insurance premiums is to include a higher deductible in your policy. The **deductible** is an out-of-pocket payment that an insured must contribute and that is deducted from the insurance payment. For example, if your deductible is $500, you must pay the first $500 of any claim yourself. Therefore, if you suffer property damage in the amount of $1,500, your insurer is obliged to contribute only $1,00 0, not to compensate you for your $1,500 loss. The higher your deductible, the lower your premium payment because the insurer takes less of a risk in insuring your interest.

Intellectual Property

Because Canada's economy thrives on creativity, new ideas, and advances in science and technology, it makes sense to encourage innovation by businesses and individuals. Society protects and promotes innovation with intellectual property law.

As we discussed at the beginning of this chapter, intellectual property is intangible—that is, its value is distinct from any physical object. Although an object may be associated with intellectual property, the real value of intellectual property lies in its owner's right to prevent others from copying it. For example, when you buy a CD or a prescription drug, you get a copy of the music or a bottle of pills, but you do not get the right to copy the CD or to manufacture a version of the pills and sell them to others. These rights belong to those who own the intellectual property rights that are associated with the CD and the drug.

Intellectual property rights can be claimed by creators, such as inventors, authors, engineers, and scientists, or—more commonly—by the businesses that employ them. Intellectual property law recognizes the value inherent in creating software programs, books, photographs, and scientific inventions, and it provides remedies for those who own the property rights in these things. There are laws that protect copyright, trademarks, patents, and industrial designs by preventing the unauthorized copying of a protected work, invention, design, or brand.

We discuss below the major types of intellectual property and the legislation designed to protect a business's property rights. Table 8.3, on page 321, provides you with a summary. In the commercial world, there are many types of intellectual property, including formulas or designs for products, logos, advertising slogans, brand names, and trade secrets. It is fair to say that virtually every business has some type of intellectual property to protect.

COPYRIGHT LAW

copyright law
branch of law that protects
the exclusive right to copy
creative work

Copyright law protects the exclusive right to copy. It prevents people other than the copyright holder from reproducing a creative work without the permission of the copyright holder. Illegal reproduction includes copying or plagiarizing part or all of a work. The *Copyright Act* is a federal statute, applicable across the country. It protects a broad range of works, including

- books, magazines, and newspapers;
- tables, charts, and maps;
- music, both recorded and written;
- computer programs;
- plays and movies;

- paintings, drawings, and photographs; and
- sculptures and architectural works.

The various types of works protected by copyright have different rights attached to them. Generally, however, copyright law gives the copyright holder the exclusive right to produce or reproduce the protected work in any form. This includes photocopying, file sharing, and other modes of copying. Additional rights—such as the right to translate a work or to convert it to another medium—are also protected by copyright law.

Canadian copyright law is enforceable outside Canada in countries that are signatories of the *Berne Convention*, a multinational treaty. Therefore, an international bestseller written by Canadian author Margaret Atwood is protected not only in Canada but also in other countries where her work is published, provided that these countries have signed the *Berne Convention*.

Recently in England, the publishers of the novel *The Da Vinci Code* were unsuccessfully sued for copyright infringement. The court held that the author of this book did not plagiarize a non-fiction historical work written by the plaintiffs in the action. Had the decision gone the other way, the publisher of *The Da Vinci Code* would likely have had to pay substantial damages to the plaintiffs, thus significantly lessening the profit it made from the work. In some cases, infringers of copyright have been required to pay all of the profits made by infringing the works of copyright holders.

Copyright holders may, of course, agree to permit others to reproduce their works. Authors, for example, can profit financially when their books are made into movies because film companies are required to compensate them for giving their permission to produce their work in film. Consider the position of the film company that was about to release a film version of *The Da Vinci Code*. Had the court found that the author of the novel had infringed copyright, the film company would certainly have inherited the copyright problems of the novelist.

Scope of Copyright Protection

Copyright protection does not last forever, and certain conditions must exist for it to apply. Where it does apply, the *Copyright Act* provides a number of exceptions and defences to infringement. We discuss these matters in the sections that follow.

Length of Protection

Copyright law protects copyright for a fixed period of time. Once copyright protection expires, a work is said to be "in the public domain." This means that the public is free to use it. Anyone may exercise the rights that were formerly exclusively held by the copyright owner.

In general, unless the *Copyright Act* contains a specific provision to the contrary, a work becomes part of the public domain 50 years after the calendar year following the author's death. This explains why the music of Mozart may be freely used and copied, and why new versions of fairytales by Hans Christian Andersen and the Brothers Grimm may be freely published and adapted into movies and plays.

Originality and Fixation

Two requirements must be met before the creator of a work may enjoy copyright protection: originality and fixation. Originality demands that the work be new in some way and come from the creator. If a work is not original, it cannot be protected by copyright. In other words, a work that is a copy of another work is not protected. The legal test for originality is not stringent. The work need not be a masterpiece or a great literary achievement. It can be similar to other works, but it must come from the author, rather than from another work.

Fixation demands that the work be more than simply an idea. Ideas themselves are not protected by copyright. To enjoy copyright protection, ideas must be fixed in a material form, such as written pages, digital data, or a video or audio recording. For example, a speech given at a conference may not be protected unless it is written down or recorded. Text on a computer monitor may not be considered fixed until it is saved. If a film company has an idea for a movie but never commissions a script or produces a film, copyright law will not protect the unrealized idea.

Copyright Symbol

The copyright symbol © is usually used by authors of works who are aware of their copyright and wish to assert it. The symbol has no significance in Canadian law, and there is no requirement to use it. However, it is internationally recognized, and if you are concerned about having your copyright respected outside Canada in countries that have signed the *Berne Convention*, you would be wise to attach the symbol to the work. The copyright symbol also functions as a reminder to potential copyright violators that copying the work is illegal.

Registration

Copyright in a work is protected automatically when a work is created, even if the work remains unpublished. You can, however, register your copyright with the Copyright Office, which is part of the Canadian Intellectual Property Office. The advantage of registration is that you obtain a certificate, which is evidence that you own the work. If a competitor ever infringes your work, registration creates a presumption that you are the owner; the infringer carries the burden of proving that you are not. Although unregistered rights are protected, there may be practical difficulties in demonstrating infringement; registration minimizes that risk.

Fair Dealing Exception

The *Copyright Act* sets out a long list of exemptions or defences to infringement. The chief defence to infringement is fair dealing. The fair dealing defence provides that there is no infringement if the purpose of copying the work is to research, privately study, criticize, review, or report on the work. The statute does not set out specific limits as to how much of a work may be copied. However, if all or substantially all of a work were copied for the stated purpose of making a report, for example, this thinly disguised means of distributing the work might constitute infringement.

Other Exceptions

Private copying of certain works is permissible, so that a child singing a song with her friends in her own home is not infringing copyright in the song. Other exemptions apply to the perceptually disabled, educational institutions, museums, archives, and libraries. There is also an exemption for copying computer programs. If you own a copy of a program, you are entitled to make one copy of it for backup purposes or to modify it for use on another computer.

Ownership and Assignment of Copyright

Generally, it is the author or creator of a work who is entitled to the protection of copyright law. However, where works are created in the course of employment—where, for example, a staff writer produces newspaper articles for the newspaper that employs her—the employer usually holds the copyright in the work. Likewise, the copyright for code produced by computer programmers is usually held by the businesses that employ them.

It is also possible for a creator to assign (transfer or sell) copyright in a work—that is, transfer copyright to a publisher or other business—and this is frequently done. Businesses that hire independent contractors, such as freelance writers or consultants, should be aware of this issue and ensure that the agreement between them addresses intellectual property rights.

Copyright Collectives

The *Copyright Act* permits copyright holders to form collectives for the purpose of administering their rights. Several collectives operate in Canada to administer rights to music, dramatic works, and published works. These collectives negotiate licences with users, collect fees, and distribute royalties to the copyright holders. A business that wishes to use copyright materials belonging to others, such as a nightclub that wants to play music or a school that wants to distribute photocopies from a textbook, may contact the appropriate copyright collective to arrange for a licence and pay a fee.

Moral Rights

Moral rights are separate from copyright. They belong to the creator alone. Moral rights may not be assigned to anyone, including an employer or publisher. The following are moral rights:

- the right to be identified as the author or creator and, if preferred, the right to remain anonymous or use a pseudonym;
- the right to prevent changes to the work that might dishonour the creator's reputation, such as drawing a moustache on a portrait; and
- the right to prevent the work from being used in association with a product, service, cause, or institution where the association might dishonour the creator's reputation.

While moral rights may not be assigned, they may be waived. In other words, a creator can agree not to enforce her moral rights. If a creator waives the enforcement of her moral rights in a business dealing with you, it is wise to record this agreement in a written contract. Consider an architect's moral rights to a building that is constructed according to the architect's plan. What happens if the owner of the building later decides to renovate and build an addition? If the change dishonours the architect's work, the owner may be prevented from renovating. To preserve future options, business people who hire architects should negotiate a waiver of moral rights.

Minimizing Your Risk
Respect and Protect Copyright

- Obtain permission to reproduce copyrighted work, either directly from the copyright holder or by paying a licensing fee to a copyright collective.
- Fix your creations—for example, by taping your conference speech.
- Ensure that those who create works on behalf of your business assign their copyright in writing.
- Ensure that those who create works on behalf of your business waive their moral rights in writing.
- Use the copyright symbol to remind others to respect your copyright.
- Consider registering important works with the Copyright Office to establish a presumption that your business is the owner of the work.

PATENT LAW

A pharmaceutical or technological company would not be willing to invest millions of dollars in research and development if its competitors were free to use and sell the new drugs or technology that it produced. Patent law protects the rights of inventors and the companies that employ them. It encourages individuals and businesses to invest in the research and development necessary to pursue ideas, innovate, and invent.

patent law
branch of law that protects the unauthorized manufacture, use, and sale of inventions

Patent law protects inventors by preventing others from manufacturing, using, or selling the inventions without the permission of the patent holder. However, permission is commonly granted pursuant to licensing agreements, which allow others to use the patentable invention in return for a fee. Like the *Copyright Act*, the *Patent Act* is a federal statute enforceable across Canada. Unlike the *Copyright Act*, the *Patent Act* requires that an application be made to the government before it will grant a patent for an invention. In order to protect your patents in other countries, you must make separate applications in those countries as well. Patent protection demands more effort than copyright protection. It is not automatic.

Scope of Patent Protection

The *Patent Act* contains numerous restrictions and complex procedures for obtaining a patent. An expert, such as a patent agent, is generally indispensable in helping a business through the patent application process.

Length of Protection

A patent is protected for 20 years from the day on which the patent application is filed. Since a patent application becomes public 18 months after it is filed, competitors and others are free to make, use, or sell a previously patented invention once the patent expires.

Physical Form

To be patentable, an invention must either have a physical form or be capable of having a physical form. Theories and mathematical formulas may not be patented. For example, your business cannot obtain a patent for its new theory of aeronautics. However, it can obtain a patent for the design of an aircraft, the product that results from the practical application of the theory. The invention of a process for manufacturing cheese or wireless communication devices, and the development of a new drug are other examples of patentable inventions.

New, Useful, and Not Obvious

To be patentable, an invention must be new in relation to what was known or used previously. This does not mean it must be entirely new. In fact, most inventions build on earlier inventions. This is why the *Patent Act* provides that "improvements" are patentable. Of course, if your business invents an improvement to a previously patented process or machine, you are required to negotiate a licensing agreement with the owner of the earlier patent. To be considered new, the invention must not have been published by the applicant more than one year before the applicant submits the patent application. Publicizing the invention includes displaying it at an invention convention or giving media interviews about it more than one year before filing the patent application.

Unlike a work in which copyright can exist, a patentable invention must be useful in a practical sense. It must have a purpose beyond an artistic one, and it must actually do what the patent application says it does. It must function when put together according to the specifications submitted with the application. If your invention is a device that emits a high-frequency signal to keep animals away from highways, it must fulfill the claims you make for it.

It is important to note that usefulness is not measured in market value. For example, a digital salt shaker that measures the portion of salt dispensed to the exactness of a grain could be patentable. The fact that the general public is not ready to accept your visionary invention does not prevent it from passing the "useful" test.

In addition to being new and useful, an invention must also not be obvious. Many patent applications fail this test. For example, in order to be patentable, an improvement in the manufacturing of maple syrup must not be obvious to someone skilled in maple syrup manufacturing.

Higher Life Forms

Although Europe, the United States, and Japan allow businesses to patent "higher life forms"—including the genetic material of animals—Canada does not. The leading Canadian case in this area is *Harvard College v. Canada (Commissioner of Patents)*. In June 2006, the Canadian Patent Office issued a practice notice in which it declared its position that "animals at any stage of development, from fertilized eggs on, are higher life forms and are thus not patentable subject matter." The Patent Office also maintains that organs and tissues are similarly incapable of being patented. However, the office is willing to consider issuing patents, on a case-by-case basis, for "artificial organ-like or tissue-like structures," provided that they have been "generated substantially" by human beings.

CASE IN POINT The Harvard Mouse

Harvard College v. Canada (Commissioner of Patents), [2002] 4 SCR 45, 2002 SCC 76 (CanLII)

Facts

Harvard College applied to patent a mouse that was genetically altered to increase its susceptibility to cancer and, therefore, its usefulness to scientists engaged in cancer research. The application claimed to extend to all non-human mammals that had been similarly altered. The patent examiner refused to grant the patent. This decision was upheld by the commissioner of patents and the trial division of the Federal Court, but was overturned by the Federal Court of Appeal. The commissioner of patents appealed to the Supreme Court of Canada.

Result

The Supreme Court allowed the appeal. The mouse was not patentable because it—like all higher life forms—is not an "invention" within the meaning of section 2 of the *Patent Act.* Justice Bastarache, who wrote the decision for the majority of the Supreme Court, stated:

> In my opinion, Parliament did not intend higher life forms to be patentable. Had Parliament intended every conceivable subject matter to be patentable, it would not have chosen to adopt an exhaustive definition that limits invention to any "art, process, machine, manufacture or composition of matter."

Business Lesson

Businesses engaged in biotechnology must respect the limits imposed by Canadian patent law.

Application for a Patent

Unlike copyright law, patent law does not automatically protect an invention once the relevant criteria are met. Instead, a business person who wants to patent an invention must file an application with the Patent Office, which is part of the Canadian Intellectual Property Office.

The Patent Office grants a patent to the party who is first to file an application. For example, assume that Lydia and Padma are independently working on a design for a garbage can that has a childproof locking mechanism that releases automatically when an adult passes his hand over the bin in a particular manner. The businesses for which Lydia and Padma work each test prototypes of the products. Lydia's company files a patent application on June 13, 2007, and Padma's company files a patent application two days later on June 15, 2007. Since Lydia's company was first to file the application, Lydia's invention is entitled to patent protection, and Padma's is not. This is the case even though Padma actually invented her garbage can several months before Lydia did. However, Lydia's company consulted a patent agent, while Padma's decided to muddle through the application process on its own. Consulting a patent agent can help you minimize the extensive delays that you may encounter when filing a patent application. Efficient filing is often essential if you want to avoid having a competing invention take priority over your own.

Patent agents first conduct searches using the Canadian Patents Database, which is available at the Canadian Intellectual Property Office website, to determine whether there is already a patent application on file in Canada for the product.

A patent application contains an abstract and a specification describing the product or process in detail and the utility of the invention; it may also contain drawings or illustrations of the design of the invention.

Within five years of the date of the application, the applicant or her agent must formally request an examination by the Patent Office staff. The examination determines that the invention is not already in existence and that the application meets all of the statutory requirements for a patent—for example, the requirement that the invention is useful. It can take several years to complete an examination. Once the invention passes the examination stage, the Patent Office issues a patent. Publicizing the patent application gives potential objectors the opportunity to oppose the granting of a patent by arguing, for example, that the invention is not new or useful. An opponent of Lydia's invention might, for example, argue that garbage cans that open when people pass their hands over them currently exist.

Web Link

Check the Canadian Intellectual Property Office's website at http://patents1.ic.gc .ca to study a database containing patent descriptions and images compiled from over 75 years of patents.

Ownership of Patent Rights

Generally, it is the inventor of the process or product who is entitled to the protection of patent law. Even where works are created in the course of employment, the inventor may be the owner of the patent unless there is a contract in place that specifies that the inventor's employer is the owner. If your business is funding research, it should ensure that its employment contracts specifically address the issue of ownership of patents for products developed by employees in the course of their employment.

Infringement of Patent Rights

A patent right is infringed when anyone produces, uses, or sells a patented invention without the permission of the patent holder. Therefore, if Padma's company decides to go ahead and market the garbage bin that Padma created, it is infringing the patent held by Lydia's company. Lydia's company could sue for all damages, such as lost sales, incurred by Padma's company.

Minimizing Your Risk
Respect and Protect Inventions
- Negotiate licensing agreements with patent holders if you intend to use their inventions.
- If you determine that your invention is viable, file a patent application without delay.
- Consult a patent agent because the application process is complex and the stakes may be high.
- Negotiate contracts with employees and independent contractors that specify that their inventions may be patented only by your business.

TRADEMARK LAW

Trademark law protects the words, symbols, and pictures that are associated with a business's name, brand, or product. It protects the trademark owner's name, its brand recognition, and the reputation that accompanies its name and brand recognition. Consider a successful fast food, or a soft drink, and the slogans associated with it. As you think of the slogans connected to these products, an image may also come to mind. Maybe it is an advertising device, such as Ronald McDonald, or the distinctive

trademark law
branch of law that protects words, symbols, and pictures associated with a business's name, brand, or product

colour and design of a soft drink can. Each of these marketing symbols or logos can be protected by trademark law.

Arguably, trademark law is not "intellectual." It does not protect creativity so much as it protects marketing and advertising clout. Trademark rights have more to do with who uses a trademark, and how this leads to brand identification, than with who creates the trademark. Unlike the purpose of other types of intellectual property law, the primary purpose of trademark law is to facilitate commerce, not to promote innovation.

Trademark law is based largely on the tort of passing off, an intentional tort that we describe in chapter 3. Passing off involves the misrepresentation of a product or business by using a name or mark that is associated with another similar product or business. To succeed as a plaintiff in a lawsuit based on passing off, you must prove each of the following elements:

- use of the trademark for sufficient time to demonstrate a market association between the mark and your product or business;
- confusion between your trademark and the use of it by a competitor, or misrepresentation by your competitor in connection with your trademark; and
- damage to your reputation or a loss of sales.

The *Trade-marks Act*, a federal statute like the *Copyright Act* and the *Patent Act*, provides greater protection for trademarks than tort law does. Under the statute, if a trademark is properly registered, the owner can automatically prevent others from using the mark. Canadian trademark protection, like patent protection, does not apply in other countries. Therefore, if you own a Canadian trademark and want to protect it in Mexico, for example, you must obtain protection in Mexico as well.

Types of Trademarks

The following types of marks are covered by the *Trade-marks Act*:

1. *Ordinary or classic marks.* Trademarks may include the names of products, product lines, businesses, and slogans. The key feature of these, and every other trademark, is that the name or slogan must distinguish the product or business from its competitors. Generally used descriptive words, such as "fast" or "fresh," may not be accepted. However, if such a word has become associated over time with a certain product or business, registration may be possible.

    A business or trade name can have great value to a business by linking the business's reputation with the quality of its goods or services. Trademark law protects business names, provided that they are used to identify wares or services. For example, a business name such as Sony is protected because it is used in this manner.

2. *Service marks.* Service marks protect services rather than products. Service industries are numerous and include banking, insurance, transportation, restaurants, and professional services such as legal, accounting, and engineering. For example, if Elinor is marketing tax preparation services, she does not have a product or packaging to mark with a brand name. However, she can advertise on a local radio station, for example, with the slogan, "Take a tax break. Let me do the job." If this slogan is associated with her services, she can register it as a trademark.

3. *Distinguishing guise.* The appearance, shape, colour, and packaging of a product can be characterized as a trademark if these attributes distinguish the product from that of a competitor. Examples of distinguishing guise include a bell-shaped bottle of scotch, gold foil-wrapped chocolates, or pink insulation.

4. *Certification marks.* This type of mark labels a product or service as having met a particular standard, be it the safety or quality of the goods, the place where the goods were produced, or the working conditions of the workers who made them. For example, a product approved by the Canadian Standards Association may be labelled as such. Unions may also permit the labelling of products to indicate that they were produced by unionized labour only. Similarly, certification marks may be used by franchisors to label the products sold by franchisees.

Scope of Trademark Protection

In the following sections, we consider the protection of marks registered under the *Trade-marks Act.* (As mentioned previously, to protect an unregistered mark, it is necessary to prove all of the elements in the tort of passing off.)

Length of Protection

Unlike copyright and patent law, the law governing trademarks provides no cutoff time for protection in Canada. You can protect a trademark indefinitely; however, to keep it registered, you must renew it every 15 years and continue to use it.

Mark, Distinctive, and Used

To qualify for registration, a trademark must be a mark, it must be distinctive, and it must be used. A mark generally means something that is visible and separate from the product itself. A chocolate bar would not be subject to trademark protection; however, its name and the logo on the wrapper probably would be.

What is distinctive? It is easy to argue that made-up words, phrases, and symbols are distinctive. However, more common words and even colours can be subject to trademark protection if their use over time has associated them exclusively with a particular product or brand.

If you do not use a trademark, you can lose it. Even if registered, an unused trademark may be expunged, and then used by someone else. This makes sense when you consider the purpose of trademark protection: to facilitate commerce and marketing.

Registration

Failure to register a trademark may invite a challenge from competitors. To minimize the risk of losing your mark to a challenger, register any trademarks your business considers valuable. A trademark owner who has registered her trademark will use the symbol ® to indicate that she is the owner of the mark. (If she has not registered her trademark, she will use the symbol ™.) A trademark can be registered by a business, a trade union, or an individual at the Trade-marks Office, which is part of the Canadian Intellectual Property Office. Applications for registration are processed by the Trade-marks Office examiner, who ensures that there are no other applications for a similar trademark and that the mark is registrable—that is, the mark is not any of the following:

- an official government symbol;
- offensive;
- the first or last name of someone who is living or has died within the previous 30 years (made-up names are acceptable);
- a deceptive or misleading description of the product or its place of origin;
- a generic descriptive word that is regularly used to describe the type of product (such as "firm" mattress) and that does not distinguish it from competitive products; or
- the name of the product in a language other than English or French.

If the examiner accepts the application for registration, the public is provided an opportunity to object. The application is listed in the *Trade-marks Journal*, and any person—such as the owner of an unregistered trademark or a registered trademark that is similar to the proposed mark—may file an objection within two months. The grounds for objection may be a prior use of the trademark in Canada or an association of the trademark, or something similar, with the objector's product. Other grounds of objections are that the trademark is not distinctive, is confusing, or is not registrable for one of the reasons listed above. If there are no objections, or if objections are addressed or dismissed, the trademark will be registered.

Consider the example of Elinor's tax preparation business. What steps would Elinor take to register her slogan?

Web Link

Check the Canadian Intellectual Property Office's website at http://patents1.ic.gc .ca to search the Canadian Trade-marks Database.

- *Step 1: Conduct a search.* Elinor must show that the public will not confuse her slogan with other slogans. To do this, she should conduct a preliminary search to ensure that a similar trademark is not registered. This search can be done using the Canadian Trade-marks Database.
- *Step 2: Consider the potential for confusion.* Elinor's slogan must be distinctive or unique, and distinguish her services from similar services offered by others. If an accountant has used a similar slogan previously, Elinor's slogan could confuse potential customers. It could mislead them into believing that they were hiring the other accountant, or that they were hiring someone with a connection to the other accountant. If, however, a travel agency were using a slogan like "Take a break," which is similar to Elinor's slogan, "Take a tax break. Let me do the job," Elinor's slogan might still be registrable. It is unlikely that potential customers would confuse accountancy services with the services of a travel agency.
- *Step 3: Include a list of services.* Elinor's application must include a detailed list of the services associated with her trademark.
- *Step 4: Submit the application.* After Elinor submits her application, an examiner reviews it to determine whether her proposed trademark is registrable.
- *Step 5: Wait for objections.* If Elinor's application passes the examiner's test, her trademark will be advertised in the *Trade-marks Journal*. This provides an opportunity for other businesses to object. If there are no objections, Elinor's trademark will be registered.

Ownership Rights

If you own a trademark, you are entitled to the exclusive use of it. You are protected from misuse and imitation of the mark by others. You are also entitled to prevent another business from registering any trademark that is so similar to your own that it would create confusion for members of the public. It is important to remember, however, that not all similar marks will result in a successful action for trademark infringement. Consider the result in *Mattel, Inc. v. 3894207 Canada Inc.*

> ### Minimizing Your Risk
> **Respect and Protect Trademarks**
> - Be original in your packaging, brand names, and slogans to avoid infringing the trademarks of others.
> - Register all trademarks that are valuable to your business.
> - Keep your trademarks in use.

Infringement

Use of a trademark without the owner's consent constitutes trademark infringement. Infringement includes use of a trademark that is confusingly similar to a registered trademark. Where

CASE IN POINT   Barbie Doll or Bar-bie-Q?

Mattel, Inc. v. 3894207 Canada Inc., 2006 SCC 22

Facts

A toy manufacturer who produced a well-known doll with the trademark "Barbie" opposed the application of the owner of a small chain of restaurants in the Montreal area to register its "Barbie's" trademark and a related design. The restaurant owner had used "Barbie's" as a trademark since 1992 to designate its restaurant, takeout, catering, and banquet services. The Trade-marks Opposition Board allowed the registration on the basis that use of the trademark "Barbie's" was unlikely to create confusion in the marketplace. Both the trial and appeal divisions of the Federal Court upheld the board's decision. The toy manufacturer appealed to the Supreme Court of Canada.

Result

The Supreme Court dismissed the toy manufacturer's appeal. Although trademarks are now recognized as among the most valuable of business assets, their legal purpose is to distinguish their owner's wares or services from those of others. A mark is both a guarantee of origin and an assurance to consumers that the quality of goods or services will be what they have come to expect. In the circumstances, the board acted reasonably in deciding that there was no possibility that a hypothetical purchaser—that is, a casual consumer somewhat in a hurry—would be confused by the marks in the marketplace.

Business Lesson

Be aware that trademarks that resemble those of famous products may be open to expensive challenges before the courts. However, also consider that the relevant test is confusion and that the use of even famous trademarks is open to analysis on a case-by-case basis.

an action for trademark infringement is successful, a court may make any order "appropriate in the circumstances" including an order for damages and an order for destruction of the goods.

INDUSTRIAL DESIGN LAW

Industrial design law protects the visual appearance of a product, including its shape, patterns, and ornaments. The law that governs industrial design fills a gap left by copyright law, which does not generally cover mass-produced goods, such as lamps and lawnmowers. The *Industrial Design Act* offers creators of mass-produced goods an opportunity to protect their designs from use by others. It, like the other intellectual property statutes we have discussed in this chapter, is a federal statute, enforceable across Canada.

Scope of Industrial Design Protection

Like patents, industrial designs must be registered, and protection is time-limited.

Length of Protection

An industrial design cannot be registered until six months after the application is filed. A registered industrial design is protected for 10 years.

Non-Functional Visual Appeal

Because industrial design is based on visual appeal, it contains a non-functional element. For example, the basic shape of a potato peeler is dictated by its function and does not create an industrial design. However, the distinctive curves, angles, and other decorative features of the particular potato peeler designed by your company may qualify for protection as an industrial design if these features are sufficiently novel. Similarly, a standard rectangular swimming pool may not qualify as an industrial design, but a pool shaped like a poplar leaf might.

Applied to a Finished Product

To be registered, an industrial design must be applied to a finished product. The application must describe not only the design but also the product or products to which the design is applied. For example, if you want to register a poplar leaf design for a swimming pool as an industrial design, your application must also describe the pool. Registration will apply to a pool only. It will not prevent another company from manufacturing plates shaped like a poplar leaf.

Registration

To protect your industrial design, you must register it with the Industrial Designs Office, which is part of the Canadian Intellectual Property Office. The office will not register industrial designs that have been previously disclosed or used before the one-year period preceding your application. As we noted above, your application must include a description and drawings of the industrial design, as well as the product to which the design is applied. Your design must be original and not similar to a previously registered design.

Ownership of Rights

As the owner of a registered industrial design, you have the sole right to use it when manufacturing the product that you registered with your design. This means that you can prevent others from copying or imitating your design when they manufacture a competing product. A business that wants to own the industrial designs created by its employees and consultants can establish its ownership rights contractually. Such a contractual arrangement eliminates the risk that an employee or consultant will later claim ownership of a design that the company believes to be its own.

Infringement

If anyone copies, sells, imports, manufactures, or rents your registered industrial design without your permission, they have infringed your industrial design. If you are successful in an action for infringement, the court may make an order "as the circumstances require," including an order for damages and an order for an injunction.

> ### Minimizing Your Risk
> **Respect and Protect Industrial Designs**
> - Be original in your industrial designs.
> - Employ consultants and staff who prefer to work creatively than to recycle thinly veiled copies of the work of others.
> - Register your industrial designs: it is your only way to protect them.

INTEGRATED CIRCUIT TOPOGRAPHY

Integrated circuit topography involves the design of microchips, which are found in computers and many types of appliances, such as televisions and ovens. Canada has a statute, the *Integrated Circuit Topography Act*, to protect the rights of the creators of topographies from having them copied or integrated into another product. To be protected, a topography must be registered.

CONFIDENTIAL INFORMATION AND TRADE SECRETS

Confidential information is information that a business does not want its competitors to have and that it takes steps to protect. (Unless your business makes an effort to protect its confidential information, the law will not protect it for you.) Confidential information includes supplier pricing, customer names, accounts receivables, and advertising slogans before they are launched. A trade secret is often a formula or manufacturing process, and trade secrets are classified as confidential information.

Confidential information, including trade secrets, has value to a business. Its value is often monetary and is dependent—at least in part—on it remaining confidential. For example, your customer list is valuable to your business even if your competitor gets a copy of it; however, the list has less value to you once it is in the hands of your competitor because your competitor can use your list to systematically entice your customers away.

You may decide that it is advantageous to your business to disclose some confidential information; however, such a decision has its consequences. Consider the case of Sam Cram, a retailer who maintains a business website. His key salespeople have all signed employment contracts that prohibit them from disclosing Sam's customer lists to competitors. However, Sam decides that he wants to disclose the names of several prominent customers on his website in order to promote his business. Once he satisfies his obligations to his customers under the *Personal Information Protection and Electronic Documents Act* (PIPEDA, which we discuss in chapter 5), he posts the names of a few of his customers on his website. Because this information is now public, Sam may no longer claim that it is confidential. He may not enforce his confidentiality agreements concerning these customers with his employees. Sam has decided to reveal this information because he believes that the risk of losing confidentiality over part of his customer list is outweighed by the promotional benefits for his business. Wisely, however, Sam has balanced the risk by preserving the confidentiality of the identities of 80 percent of his customers.

Protection of Rights

Confidential information—unlike copyright, patents, trademarks, and industrial designs—is not protected by legislation. There are common-law principles that prevent employees from revealing confidential information; however, businesses that are truly concerned about confidentiality should protect themselves with contracts.

Many businesses have confidentiality clauses in employment contracts and in contracts with external organizations or independent contractors, such as advertising agencies or management consultants. Employees inevitably acquire certain skills in the course of their employment and transfer those skills to other jobs. However, this situation is vastly different from one in which an employee reveals a "secret ingredient" of a dye, for example, to a subsequent employer and thereby allows it to corner a waiting market. We explore these and similar clauses in chapter 7 under the heading "Restrictive Covenants."

Summary

We opened this chapter with a general discussion of property law, a collection of rules that makes possession merely one attribute of property and not its governing principle. The majority of the chapter has been devoted to an examination of the three major types of property law: personal, real, and intellectual. Our discussion of personal property focused on the law of bailment. We examined the ownership and transfer of real property, as well as other practical aspects of real property law, such as mortgages and commercial leases. Because insurance is crucial to businesses in managing the risks involved in owning and using real and personal property, we also included a brief examination of this topic.

Our discussion of intellectual property included copyright, patents, trademarks, industrial designs, and integrated circuit topography. We examined the methods by which business people can protect their valuable inventions and imaginative creations from exploitation by others. Finally, we concluded the chapter with information about protecting trade secrets.

Table 8.3   Comparison of Copyright, Patents, Trademarks, and Industrial Designs

	Types of Property Protected	Essential Qualities of Property	How To Protect Your Business's Property
Copyright	Creative works: written, dramatic, musical, artistic	Original and fixed	• Ensure that employees and consultants who create works on behalf of your business assign their copyright. • Use the copyright symbol © to remind others to respect your copyright. • Consider registering important works with the Copyright Office to establish a presumption that your business owns the work.
Patents	Physical invention or process	New (or improved), useful, and non-obvious	• If your invention is viable, file a patent application immediately. • Consult a patent agent because the application process is complex. • Specify in contracts with employees and consultants that patents belong to your business, not to the inventor.
Trademarks	Brand names, logos, symbols, and pictures	Visible mark separate from product, distinctive, and used	• Register all trademarks that are valuable to your business. • Keep all registered and unregistered trademarks in use to avoid losing them.
Industrial designs	Visual appearance, including shape, pattern, and ornament	Non-functional visual appeal applicable to specific product	• Register all industrial designs that are valuable to your business. • Specify in contracts with employees and consultants that designs belong to your business, not to the designer.

KEY TERMS

acceleration clause

amortization period

bailee

bailment

bailor

chattels

choses in action

copyright law

deductible

deeds

default

distress

exclusive possession

fixed tenancy

fixtures

forfeiture

goodwill

industrial design law

insurable interest

intangible property

intellectual property

lease

mortgage

mortgage term

mortgagee

mortgagor

patent law

periodic tenancy

personal property

policy

private property

property law

public property

quiet enjoyment

real property

tangible property

title

trademark law

REFERENCES

Berne Convention for the Protection of Literary and Artistic Works, September 9, 1886, amended S. Treaty Doc. No. 99-27 (1986).

Canadian Patent Office, *Office Practice Regarding Fertilized Eggs, Stem Cells, Organs and Tissues*. Canadian Patent Office Record, Practice Notice, June 20, 2006.

Copyright Act, RSC 1985, c. C-42.

Household Realty Corporation Ltd. v. Liu, 2005 CanLII 43402 (Ont. CA).

Industrial Design Act, RSC 1985, c. I-9.

Inkeepers Act, RSO 1990, c. I.7.

Integrated Circuit Topography Act, SC 1990, c. 37.

Lawrence v. Wright, 2006 CanLII 24129 (Ont. SC).

Mattel, Inc. v. 3894207 Canada Inc., 2006 SCC 22.

Patent Act, RSC 1985, c. P-4.

Trade-marks Act, RSC 1985, c. T-13.

REVIEW AND DISCUSSION

True or False?

___T___ **1.** Real property is the same as real estate.

___F___ **2.** Chattels are fixtures attached to real property.

___F___ **3.** Bailors are always responsible for insuring the bailed property.

___F___ **4.** Businesses are required to obtain patents for all inventions of their employees and independent contractors.

___T___ **5.** Property loss insurance can protect businesses against fire, theft, accident, and weather damage.

___T___ **6.** Breach of environmental audit conditions terminates agreements of purchase and sale.

___F___ **7.** Patent holders, but not copyright holders, can assign moral rights in their property.

___F___ **8.** Provincial statutes govern all lucrative bailments.

Multiple Choice

1. Intangible property does *not* include which one of the following?
   a. copyright
   b. trademarks
   c. share certificates
   d. goodwill

2. Lucrative bailments do *not* include
   a. bailment for repair or service
   b. consignment
   c. lease of a photocopier
   d. lending of money

3. To obtain insurance, you must have which one of the following?
   a. an insurance policy
   b. an insurable interest
   c. sufficient float
   d. possession of the insured property

4. Which is the most complete and correct list of types of property that may have copyright?
   a. written text, music, movies, drawings, photographs, architectural works, and computer programs
   b. written text, music, movies, drawings, photographs, and architectural works   — missing
   c. written text, music, movies, drawings, photographs, architectural works, computer programs, and computer circuits
   d. written text, music, movies, drawings, photographs, architectural works, computer programs, and ideas

5. Which statement is incorrect?
   a. Industrial designs are decorative, not functional.
   b. Inventions that are improvements to other inventions may be patented.
   c. Patents must be useful and have market value.
   d. Trademark law is based on a tort.

6. Which of the following statements about integrated circuit topography is correct?
   a. Copyright in it is protected without registration.
   b. It is governed in Canada by the *Berne Convention.*
   c. It relates to geographic circuit polarities.
   d. A federal statute allows creators to protect their designs from unauthorized copying through registration.

7. Which of the following objects in a hair styling salon is not personal property?
   a. a shelving unit on wheels
   b. the mirrors and combs contained in the unit
   c. a chair bolted to the floor
   d. mousse, razors, and hair gel

Short Answer

1. In Canada, what rights do property owners have?

2. What is bailment?

3. What is the key component of any risk management plan involving a business's real and personal property?

4. If copyright law applies to sculptures, what is the point of industrial design law?

5. Explain whether the law protects confidential information in the following situations.
   a. Uncle Bill's Bonbons is a family business that uses secret recipes passed down from the founder's grandmother. Its employees know that these recipes are not to be disclosed to customers or competitors. One of the chefs leaves to found her own company that produces strikingly similar products using identical ingredients.
   b. Uncle Bill's holds a contest, asking its customers to submit their best recipe for cookies, and posts the winning recipe in its store. A competitor begins to sell cookies based on the recipe.
   c. Emily's Edibles independently arrives at a manufacturing process that exactly duplicates the creamy texture of Uncle Bill's chocolate pudding.

6. Karl, a potter, owns property in the country where he has a workshop and two large kilns. He supplies his high-quality pottery to various shops across Canada and also fills orders directly from people who order on his website. The stores that sell Karl's pottery do so on a consignment basis. When an item is sold, Karl receives payment, less the store's selling fee. Karl stores his pottery in his friend Larry's barn before it is shipped to stores or Internet customers.
   a. Describe the legal relationship between Karl and the stores that sell his work.
   b. Explain the legal relationship between Karl and Larry.
   c. What risks might Karl want to insure against?
   d. What risks might Larry want to insure against?
   e. Do the stores need to insure Karl's pottery? Why or why not?

Discussion and Debate

How have computer technology and the Internet changed the music industry? Who has been hurt and who has gained? Do copyright laws adequately address the issues raised by the new technologies? How should the competing interests of corporations, artists, and the general public be balanced?

Banking, Financing, and Debtor–Creditor Law

LEARNING OBJECTIVES

After reading this chapter, you should be able to:

- Understand how financial institutions can assist business people.

- Describe the different types of negotiable instruments and their uses.

- Define an account agreement and describe its main provisions.

- Explain how and why a business might borrow for the short and long term.

- Understand how to negotiate a credit agreement.

- Describe how businesses use equity financing.

- Explain the remedies available to secured and unsecured creditors.

- Explain a debtor's options under bankruptcy legislation and the *Companies' Creditors Arrangement Act*.

- Describe bankruptcy requirements and proceedings under the *Bankruptcy and Insolvency Act*.

What Are Banking, Financing, and Debtor–Creditor Law?

Banking, financing, and debtor–creditor law concern the borrowing and lending of money, the types of loans available, and the consequences of failure to repay these loans. All of these areas of law are governed principally by statutes, which have been passed by both the federal and the provincial governments.

The federal government regulates chartered banks. Much of the governing legislation relates to inspecting and auditing bank operations and ensuring that banks do not fail or go bankrupt. The provinces regulate other financial institutions, such as provincially chartered trust companies and credit unions; much of this legislation also concerns inspections and audits. Recently, regulators have also begun to focus on maintaining adequate levels of service to consumers.

Financial institutions operate by taking deposits from customers and then lending the funds to others. Rather than simply handing over bags of coins and bills, they make and receive payments by using negotiable instruments. There are three types of negotiable instruments currently in use in a business context: cheques, bills of exchange, and promissory notes. Your business will no doubt choose to conduct its day-to-day financial affairs through a bank or provincially chartered financial institution.

When it comes time to raise money, you will have additional financing decisions to make. Whether you need capital to start up your business or to enlarge its operations, you will have to consider whether you want to use debt or equity financing. If you decide to raise money with debt, you will be borrowing money and paying it back over time. If you decide to use equity, you will be attracting investors to invest in your business. You will probably need expert advice in deciding which type of financing is best for you.

If your business borrows money, it becomes a debtor and the lender becomes a creditor of your business. This debtor–creditor relationship becomes particularly important if your business ever suffers serious financial setbacks—that is, becomes insolvent or goes bankrupt. Depending on the type of loan your business has taken out, the creditor must consider its options. These may include assisting your business by extending further credit in the expectation that it will again become profitable. However, if your business is insolvent and unable to pay its creditor, the creditor may petition your business into bankruptcy under the *Bankruptcy and Insolvency Act*. It can also sue your business for the amount that it owes. Businesses that are heavily in debt, and unlikely ever to recover, may also choose to voluntarily make an assignment in bankruptcy.

Familiarity with banking, financing, and debtor–creditor law will assist you in dealing with many business problems. A few are set out below.

- The manager of the bank where you would like to do business has just presented you with a general account agreement. The agreement includes a clause absolving the bank of all responsibility for errors or machinery malfunctions that may affect your business interests—even those resulting from its own negligence. You are reluctant to sign the agreement. What are your options?
- Your company, which sells garden supplies and landscaping services, runs a seasonal business. You have a lot of income during the spring and summer, when gardeners buy your wares and there is a high demand for your services. You have a lot of expenses during the fall and winter, when you attend shows, buy supplies, produce designs, and nurture samples in greenhouses. You need to borrow funds on a short-term basis from your credit union to cover your operating expenses when your income is low. What documents should you present to your credit union to ensure that you get the best possible interest rate?
- You work for a computer-servicing firm that has been waiting to be paid for three months on a $20,000 contract. Rumours in the industry tell you that your client is falling into arrears on other accounts and is having trouble keeping staff. Your client tells you that everything is fine and that you will be

paid shortly. What factors should you take into account before petitioning your client into bankruptcy?

The Importance of Banking, Financing, and Debtor–Creditor Law for Business People

Banking, financing, and debtor–creditor law provide the legal framework for the financial operations of businesses. These branches of law not only provide the rules under which money changes hands; they also address the assignment of economic risk by providing schemes under which losses are allocated between businesses and their creditors when businesses find themselves in financial ruin. There are many reasons why business people should familiarize themselves with these areas of law, three of which are set out below:

- *Knowledge of how financial institutions work can strengthen your position when dealing with them.* Understanding that there is room for negotiation with banks and other financial institutions when, for example, signing account and loan agreements may assist you in obtaining the services of these institutions on the terms most favourable to your business.
- *A sound mixture of debt and equity financing may be your business's recipe for success.* At some point your business will very likely need to acquire funds for operations or expansions. Should you borrow? Should you seek investors? There are advantages and disadvantages to both. Knowledge of your options will help you obtain the financial balance that you need, both in the short and the long term.
- *If your business falls on hard times, sensible treatment of your creditors may keep you out of bankruptcy.* Bankruptcy is not the only option if times get tough for your business. The law provides you with various opportunities, such as the relatively inexpensive procedure of making a proposal to your creditors in order to restructure your debt. You may have much more leverage than you think because banks like to avoid suing their customers and spending money on enforcing their rights, if possible.

Banking

In practical terms, it is not possible to operate a business without the backing of a financial institution to help meet the business's monetary needs and to provide the financial services required on a day-to-day basis. During any single week, your business may need to borrow operating funds, finance sales by extending credit to customers, facilitate credit card transactions, deposit sales receipts, make payments by cheque, or convert foreign currencies into Canadian dollars. To accomplish any of these goals, your business—or the business that you work for—needs an ongoing relationship with a financial institution. In Canada, that institution is likely to be a federally chartered bank, a federally or provincially chartered trust company, or a provincially chartered credit union or ***caisse populaire***.

caisse populaire
credit union based primarily in Quebec but also operating for francophone clientele in other parts of Canada

NEGOTIABLE INSTRUMENTS

In the modern business world, most people use negotiable instruments to make and receive payments for goods and services. A **negotiable instrument** is a document that promises to pay the bearer a specified amount, and that can be transferred to a third party. Negotiable instruments in Canada take three forms: cheques, bills of exchange, and promissory notes.

Negotiable instruments have certain advantages over money. They are more portable than large sums of cash, and they reduce the risk of theft because only the named payee can cash them. They can create credit by deferring the payment of funds from the date the instrument is created to another date specified in the instrument (consider a postdated cheque, for example). They can also be transferred to third parties.

In Canada, negotiable instruments are regulated under the federal *Bills of Exchange Act*. The rules that govern negotiable instruments in Canada are similar to those in the United States and the United Kingdom, which is important when enforcing rights to payment in international markets.

> **negotiable instrument**
> financial document, such as a cheque, that promises to pay the bearer a specified amount, and that can be transferred to a third party

Cheques

The parties involved in writing a **cheque** consist of a drawee, a payer, and a payee. The **drawee** of a cheque is always a financial institution. The **payer** is always an account holder at that institution. The payer uses the cheque to direct the drawee bank to pay the payee, who is the person named on the cheque. However, the drawee bank is required to pay the **payee** only if there are sufficient funds in the payer's account to cash the cheque. If there are insufficient funds in the account, the drawee bank may refuse to honour the cheque by returning it to the payee. The drawee bank is not liable to the payee for the amount of the cheque; the payee's only recourse is against the payer.

For example, suppose Woodhouse Ltd., a house-building business, buys a load of lumber from Little Axe Inc. Little Axe carries on business in North Bay and Woodhouse is located in Toronto. If Little Axe requires payment before it ships the lumber, Woodhouse can write a cheque, in which Woodhouse is the payer, the bank is the drawee, and Little Axe is the payee. Little Axe will deposit the cheque with its bank. This bank, acting on Little Axe's behalf, will present the cheque for payment to Woodhouse's bank. If there are sufficient funds in Woodhouse's account, Woodhouse's bank will pay Little Axe's bank, which will pay the amount into Little Axe's account; if not, it will return the cheque to Little Axe's bank marked NSF (non-sufficient funds). Such an event will alert Little Axe to the risk that it might not be paid if it ships the lumber to Woodhouse. Figure 9.1 is a copy of Woodhouse's cheque.

Cheques are payable on demand any time after the date that appears on the cheque, provided that the cheque is presented for payment within a reasonable time. In Canada and the United States, the time is usually six months, after which the cheque is stale-dated and therefore no longer negotiable.

While most businesses accept company cheques, some do not. If Little Axe does not want to accept Woodhouse's cheque, Woodhouse may have to provide cash, use a bank cheque, or use a bank money order. These methods of payment are more

> **cheque**
> negotiable instrument under which the drawee banking institution pays the payee from the bank account of the payer
>
> **drawee**
> the person or institution to whom a negotiable instrument is sent for payment
>
> **payer**
> person who pays, or honours, a negotiable instrument
>
> **payee**
> person who receives payment on a negotiable instrument

Figure 9.1 Negotiable Instruments: Woodhouse's Cheque to Little Axe

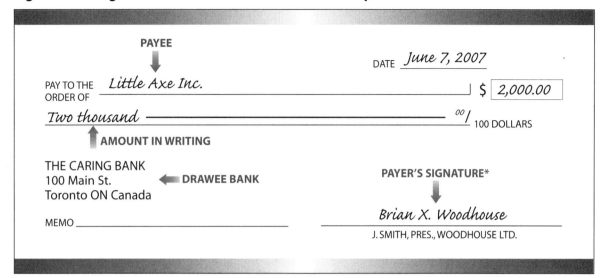

* Signature of authorized signing officer for payer, Woodhouse Ltd.

secure than a simple company cheque because, in our example, Woodhouse must pay the required funds to the bank before the bank will issue the cheque or money order. A certified cheque offers similar security, because the bank certifies it only after withdrawing the funds from the customer's account.

Once the drawee bank honours Woodhouse's cheque, Woodhouse's debt to Little Axe is extinguished. Woodhouse, or any payer, may choose to note details about a transaction on a cheque so that there is clear evidence that the debt has been paid. For example, Woodhouse may write "payment for lumber ordered May 2, 2007, invoice 1234" for the purpose of its own records. Banks either retain cancelled cheques for a period of time or return them immediately to the customer.

Since a cheque is a negotiable instrument, the payee may assign or transfer the right of payment to someone else. Little Axe, for example, might wish to transfer its right to payment to Rusty Saw Ltd., one of its creditors. In this case, Rusty Saw becomes the holder and may present the cheque to Woodhouse's bank for payment. To transfer its right to payment to Rusty Saw, Little Axe must endorse the cheque. Endorsement can occur in either of the following two ways:

1. *In blank.* Little Axe signs the back of the cheque and passes it to Rusty Saw, in which case not only Rusty Saw but anyone else can cash it.
2. *By restrictive endorsement.* Little Axe writes "pay to Rusty Saw Ltd. only" and signs the back of the cheque. In this case, only Rusty Saw can cash the cheque.

Bills of Exchange

Bills of exchange are less common in commercial transactions than they once were. The widespread use of cheques, the availability of other forms of credit, and the ease with which funds may be electronically transferred from one financial institution to another have reduced the need for bills of exchange. However, these instruments may still be of use to your business by allowing it to buy goods or services from a seller on credit; a bill of exchange provides the seller with some assurance that your business will pay its debt at a fixed time in the future.

bill of exchange
document signed by a drawer ordering a drawee to pay a specified sum to a payee immediately or on a later fixed date

A **bill of exchange** involves three parties: the **drawer**, the drawee, and the payee. Imagine that Little Axe is willing to extend credit to Woodhouse for one month on a shipment of lumber. Little Axe, the drawer, makes out a bill of exchange that states that Woodhouse, the drawee, will make payment in full 30 days from the date of sale. In the simplest example of a bill of exchange, the drawer is also the payee. That is, Little Axe is both the drawer (maker of the bill of exchange) and the payee (the party entitled to receive payment under the terms of the bill). In a more complicated example, Little Axe could direct that another party—such as its bank or any of its creditors—become the payee.

drawer
person who drafts and sends the bill of exchange to the drawee for acceptance

If Woodhouse agrees to the terms in the bill of exchange, it accepts the bill by signing it and returning it to Little Axe. Little Axe may then send the bill to Woodhouse's bank for payment on the date set out in the bill. Little Axe could also deposit the bill in its own bank account, so that its bank would present the bill to Woodhouse's bank for payment. Either way, the bank treats the bill of exchange as a cheque and pays Little Axe out of Woodhouse's account when the bill is presented for payment.

A valid bill of exchange has the following features:

- It is in writing.
- It is an unconditional order to pay, usually framed in the terms "pay to the order of."
- It is addressed from one person (the drawer) to another (the drawee), requiring the drawee to pay a named person (the payee) by the date indicated on the bill.
- If no payment date is specified in the bill, the bill is payable on demand when presented for payment.

For the bill to be negotiable, the drawee must write "accepted" on the bill, date it, and indicate the place where it is signed. The drawee then signs her name. The bill thus becomes a promise to pay, and the drawee can be sued if she fails to live up to her promise. If there is a payment default on a bill of exchange, the law in Canada creates a three-day grace period on most bills to allow the defaulter to make the payment without penalty. Figure 9.2 is an example of a bill of exchange.

Promissory Notes

promissory note
document in which the maker, or promisor, promises to pay the promisee a sum indicated in the note, either on demand or on a fixed date in the future

While bills of exchange and cheques are orders to pay, a **promissory note** is simply an unconditional written promise to pay a specified amount to a certain person on the date set out in the note. The promissor—that is, the person who makes the promise to pay—must sign the note. Once the promissor has signed the note, the promise to pay is enforceable without anyone having to do anything further.

holder
person who is assigned the right to be paid on a promissory note by the creditor originally entitled to be paid

The debtor on a promissory note is called the "maker." He is liable to the creditor for the amount specified in the note, plus interest in accordance with the terms of the note. However, because a promissory note is a negotiable instrument, the creditor may endorse the note to another person, called the **holder**. The holder has the same rights that the creditor originally had to enforce the right to payment. Figure 9.3 is an example of a promissory note.

Figure 9.2 Negotiable Instruments: Woodhouse's Bill of Exchange

① DATE *June 7, 2007*

② *North Bay, Ontario*
July 7, 2007

PAY TO ORDER OF
③ *Little Axe Inc.*

Two thousand ———————————————————— 00/100 DOLLARS

2,000.00

④ TO
Woodhouse Ltd.
800 4th Ave.
Toronto, ON

⑤ *Little Axe Inc. per B. Jones*

① Drawer accepts bill by writing "accept," the date and place of payment, after which drawee signs his name.

② Payable at a specific place and fixed or determinable time.

③ Payee.

④ Drawee, who is expected to accept the bill.

⑤ Drawer of the bill.

Figure 9.3 Negotiable Instruments: Woodhouse's Promissory Note

DATE *January 5, 2007*

I promise to pay Little Axe Inc. the sum of

Two thousand ———————————————————— 00/100 DOLLARS

2,000.00

At the offices of Little Axe Inc., North Bay ◀ PROMISSEE OR PAYEE
on or after Sept. 27, 2007, with interest of 8% ◀ MATURITY DATE WHEN PRINCIPAL
per year both before and after maturity. AND INTEREST DUE

Value Received   *Woodhouse Ltd. per Brian X. Woodhouse*

▲ PROMISSOR OR MAKER

Consumer Bills and Notes

Businesses often use promissory notes when their customers purchase expensive consumer items, such as cars or large appliances, on installment. The notes are documents that set out the terms and conditions for repayment of the loan. Like other bills of exchange, promissory notes often provide for the payment of interest after their due date; they may also require the payment of interest before the due date.

In the past, the use of negotiable instruments in consumer purchases sometimes created problems. The fact that a promissory note is a negotiable instrument that can be transferred to a third party meant that consumers who bought defective goods could sometimes be held responsible for paying an innocent third party who had purchased the note. For example, Fred might give a promissory note for part of the purchase price of a used car to Ed's Car Lot. Ed might sell the promissory note to his bank at a discount, in return for cash. The bank now holds the note and is entitled to enforce it against Fred. What if the car is defective? The bank still has the right to collect the debt from Fred. To address this problem, Parliament amended the *Bills of Exchange Act* in 1970 to provide consumers with some protection. The legislation modified the rules governing traditional bills and notes, requiring that a consumer bill or note be marked "consumer purchase."

Minimizing Your Risk
Use Bills of Exchange Wisely

- Try to negotiate the interest rate and the timing of payments for large purchases.

- If you default on a demand for payment on a note, take advantage of the short grace period that you are allowed to find the money.

- Check whether you can obtain more favourable interest and repayment terms by using a line of credit with a bank for ongoing business operations than by using a promissory note or other bill of exchange.

- In a non-consumer purchase, negotiate terms that prevent or limit the creditor from assigning or transferring payment rights to a third party.

- Negotiate to pay a lesser sum than owed if you are in default. Creditors are usually not interested in lawsuits.

CREDIT CARDS

The use of credit cards has increased astronomically since the cards were first introduced in the 1960s by banks and some businesses. Credit cards are not negotiable instruments. Neither can they be construed as money in the ordinary sense because they do not necessarily bear any relationship to currency in the hands of the cardholder. Rather, they are a form of money substitute that allows purchasers to buy now and (presumably) pay later.

General card issuers such as Visa or MasterCard sometimes charge an annual fee. In addition, they charge participating businesses a fee on each transaction and may charge other fees as well. Their biggest profits, however, come from cardholders who do not pay their monthly balances in full. Those who have unpaid balances may pay anywhere from 10 to 20 percent interest. This easy but expensive credit, critics say, has led to an increase in consumer bankruptcy and a decline in consumer's personal savings rates.

Businesses also use credit cards, but not in the way consumers do. They would not use a credit card to purchase a major asset where they could make this purchase by obtaining a loan from a financial institution or by using a bill of exchange. The reason for this is that the interest rate on the purchase is much higher on a credit card than on a negotiable instrument or almost any other type of business credit. Businesses use cards for small purchases and to cover employees' business-related expenses. For example, employees who travel on business often use a company credit card to cover hotel and meal expenses on the road. The monthly statement goes directly to the business, which usually pays the account promptly to avoid high interest charges. It is a convenient way of paying for expenses.

ELECTRONIC BANKING

Electronic banking is a term that describes the use of computers, public automated teller machines (ATMs or bank machines), and telephones by bank customers to perform many of their banking transactions, instead of having to complete paper documents and attend bank branches in person. Electronic banking, particularly online banking and ATMs, has had a great impact on consumers.

Businesses can conduct day-to-day transactions by bank machine, online, or by telephone. Businesses can also monitor their accounts, including payments on loans. Many use telephones or computers for receivables when customers pay by credit cards. However, in more complex arrangements—such as negotiating business loans—face-to-face transactions prevail. And electronic banking is of limited use to businesses such as convenience stores and coffee shops, because cash deposits still require that businesses physically take the cash to the bank.

THE ACCOUNT AGREEMENT

Before the government made changes in the financial services sector, when your business opened a bank account, you signed an account agreement that set out the bank's rules about the operation of the account and apportioned risk resulting from errors or negligence between your business and the bank. Account agreements, which were drawn up by the bank, were often composed in legal language and were not negotiable. Not surprisingly, they usually favoured the bank and required a business to accept most of the risk and liabilities that could arise from the use of its account.

Since 2001, the Financial Consumer Agency of Canada (FCAC) has been encouraging banks to establish codes of conduct and to become more customer friendly, both to businesses and consumers. One of the results of the agency's work is a reshaping of the old account agreement into a general financial services agreement. This general agreement, usually drafted in everyday language, covers all of the services that a bank offers to its customers. However, these terms often still favour the interests of the bank over those of its customers, both businesses and consumers. General agreements often contain terms such as the following:

- The agreement covers all services that the bank offers at the time the business signs the agreement, whether or not the business uses them. Should the business decide to use these services in the future, it is bound by the terms applicable on the signing date.

- The bank may hold cheques—that is, refuse to make money available—for a specified period of time or until the cheque has been honoured by the drawer's bank.
- The bank can require seven days' notice of a withdrawal from any account.
- The bank takes no responsibility for verifying signatures on a business's cheques. It will cash all cheques, even if they are fraudulent, unless the business can show that it took reasonable care to safeguard them and checked its transactions against its statement or passbook. The business must report all errors or incidents of fraud within 30 days of receipt of the bank statement.
- If the bank makes an error, or its account machinery malfunctions, or if a business suffers loss through any failure in the bank's service—even if the bank knew the loss was likely and even if the loss resulted from the negligence of the bank or its employees—the bank is not liable for any damages.
- The business is responsible for reimbursing the bank for any legal or other costs it incurs in recovering money owed by the business.
- The bank can close all of a business's accounts and can terminate the agreement without notice to the business.

Web Link

Check TD Canada Trust's website at www.tdcanadatrust.com/accounts/fst.jsp for an example of a financial services agreement.

RESOLVING PROBLEMS WITH YOUR BUSINESS'S BANK

What, as a business person, can you do if you have a complaint about a bank's treatment of your financial affairs? The answer depends on whether the financial institution you are dealing with is federally or provincially regulated. If you wish to complain about a bank, particularly if it has breached a regulatory requirement, go to the federal Financial Consumer Agency of Canada. If the financial institution operates under provincial regulation, complaints may be made to a provincial body; in Ontario, these complaints are handled by the Financial Services Commission of Ontario.

In the past decade or so, regulators have been paying attention to the growing friction between consumers of financial services and the financial institutions that supply them. Regulators have made provision for informal resolution of disputes and for review of decisions by banks to reduce customer services, particularly in rural areas. These services are designed for individual consumers, however, not for businesses. Businesses are basically on their own.

This is not a problem for large corporations. Because they are major customers, and a source of great profit for financial institutions, the institutions are responsive to their needs. But small businesses are more like individual consumers from the bank's point of view: it is more expensive to provide them with services than it is to provide these services to large corporations, and small businesses generally pose much higher risks as borrowers than large corporations. Many small businesses complain about the cavalier treatment they receive from banks, the complicated procedures and red tape, and the resistance to extending credit on acceptable terms. If a business finds itself in a dispute with the bank, existing government agencies are of little use in the absence of outright fraud by the financial institution. The only real recourse if a business cannot work out its problems with the bank is to sue, either for negligence if the bank has been derelict in its duty, or for breach of contract if the bank is in breach of its account agreement.

Minimizing Your Risk
Get the Best Possible Deal from Your Financial Institution

- Try to negotiate some of the terms of your account agreement, despite the fact that the agreement is a standard form. If, after signing the agreement, the bank offers more favourable terms on a particular service, renegotiate.

- Ensure you understand the terms of your account agreement before you sign it; consult a lawyer if necessary.

- Train your employees, particularly those responsible for accounts payable and receivable, so that they understand what the bank requires from your business.

- Be vigilant about checking your monthly statements and accounts for errors.

- Report all errors immediately in order to hold the bank responsible for them. This can be done online.

- Shop around. Financial institutions offer a variety of services, at a range of costs, and on different terms.

Financing a Business

All successful businesses ultimately meet their expenses out of the income that they generate from the sale of their goods or services. However, circumstances may require a business to borrow funds to finance or expand its operations, either on a short- or a long-term basis. Most business people arrange for short-term financing by means of loans secured through banks or other financial institutions. There are a number of ways in which businesses obtain long-term financing: arranging loans from financial institutions, issuing and selling long-term company bonds with fixed interest rates, or selling shares in the business to investors.

Generally, in making a decision about how to finance a business, a business person must decide between two forms of financing: equity and debt (or a combination of the two). With **debt financing**, the business borrows capital, usually from a financial institution. The business's obligation is to repay the loan, including interest, in accordance with the terms of the loan agreement. Debt financing may also be accomplished through the sale of bonds. Individual investors buy a business's bonds, thereby providing the business with capital in exchange for a fixed or variable rate of return over a number of years.

debt financing
borrowing money from a lender

Equity financing, on the other hand, is arranged through the sale of shares in a business corporation. The shares give investors an interest in the business in exchange for providing capital. The value of a company's shares generally depends on how successful the business becomes. Shareholders must accept the risk that their shares may turn out to be valueless if the business fails. They cannot sue a company for the return of their capital in the same way that a lender can sue for repayment of a loan.

equity financing
raising money by issuing and selling shares in a corporation or using retained earnings to meet short- or long-term financial needs

A business person who is considering debt financing must also consider whether the debt is to be secured or unsecured. An unsecured debt is a simple promise by the debtor to repay the loan. If a debtor breaches her promise by failing to repay a loan, the lender must first sue the debtor and then enforce the judgment.

If the debt is secured, the debtor—in addition to promising to repay the debt—backs up the promise by giving the lender a security interest in something of value owned by the debtor. The right or thing given as security is called **collateral**, and if the debtor fails to repay, the lender has the right to seize and sell the collateral and

collateral
property that a borrower makes available to a lender to sell, in order to repay the amount due on a loan if the borrower defaults

use the sale proceeds to pay down the loan. Examples of collateral include land, machinery, the right to collect on account receivables, royalties, and inventory.

Where a creditor has an interest in collateral owned by the debtor, the creditor is known as a **secured creditor**. A secured creditor can often register his interest in a public registry system. Registration gives notice to the world that the secured creditor has an interest in property owned by the debtor. This means that others who have no collateral interest in the debtor's property—or who have an interest but who registered or acquired it after the secured creditor acquired and registered his—cannot interfere with the secured creditor's right to seize and sell the collateral to pay down the debt. The secured creditor in this example is said to have **priority** over secured creditors who acquired or registered interests at a later date, or who had no security interest at all. In situations where there are multiple creditors and few valuable assets, a creditor's place in the priority sequence can make the difference between collecting on the debt and being out of luck.

DEBT FINANCING

Borrowing money from a lender is called debt financing, a concept that can include both short- and long-term borrowing. Suppose you are the president of Woodhouse Ltd. You will need to decide how to finance your house-building business by meeting both its short- and its long-term needs as they arise. Woodhouse's income is likely to be cyclical. It can expect to have large income receipts at the end of the building season, when it sells its stock of recently built houses. But in the early spring, when Woodhouse is buying supplies, it may have very little income. As president of Woodhouse, you will likely need to borrow money in the spring on a short-term basis to cover Woodhouse's operating expenses, and repay the loan out of the profits that Woodhouse generates later in the year.

You may also wish to expand Woodhouse's operations by buying more capital property, such as construction machinery. For these capital expenditures, you may need long-term financing—that is, you may need to incur debt that Woodhouse will repay over several years. If this is the case, you should be knowledgeable about secured and unsecured credit, general credit agreements, and corporate bonds. We examine each of these types of debt financing in the sections that follow.

Unsecured and Secured Credit

As we have already noted, a lender can extend credit to a business on either a secured or an unsecured basis. In an **unsecured loan**, a lender advances funds to a borrower in exchange for a simple promise to repay the loan. If the borrower does not repay the loan, the lender's only legal recourse is to sue the borrower on his promise to repay. With a **secured loan**, the borrower promises the lender that he will repay the loan *and* provides the lender with rights in collateral. If the borrower does not repay the loan, the lender can still sue the borrower, but the lender may also seize the collateral and sell it, using the money from the sale to pay down the loan.

A lender rarely provides unsecured credit unless there is

- an ongoing relationship between the parties,
- a high degree of trust,
- a small loan,

secured creditor
lender who has the right to sell an asset owned by the borrower to pay the loan if the borrower defaults

priority
position in a ranking system that creates the order in which competing creditors can satisfy their claims against a debtor's property

unsecured loan
loan given without collateral in exchange for a simple promise to repay

secured loan
loan for which a borrower provides collateral that the lender may sell to pay the loan if the borrower defaults

- a short repayment period, and
- a high expectation that the loan will be repaid.

If one or more of these criteria is absent, the lender is likely to insist that the loan be secured because security increases the likelihood of repayment. If the lender's only recourse is to sue a defaulting borrower on his promise to repay his debt, the lender may never get her money back. She can obtain a judgment—that is, a court order that the borrower repay her—however, collection of the debt can quickly become very costly, and unsatisfied lenders often have little to show for all their collection efforts. Furthermore, if a borrower goes bankrupt, a lender cannot enforce the judgment at all, but must claim against the bankrupt's estate along with all of the other unsecured creditors. If the lender is lucky, she will collect 25 cents on each dollar owed.

However, if the loan is secured, the lender has additional remedies at her disposal. On default, most secured loan agreements permit the lender to seize control of the collateral and sell it without having to obtain a court order. The lender may recover the funds that she loaned the borrower—and the money she spent on selling the collateral—from the proceeds of the sale. If the funds obtained from the sale do not cover the loan, the lender can then sue the borrower for the balance still owing. If the funds obtained from the sale exceed what is owed to the lender, the borrower is entitled to the excess amount.

Declaring bankruptcy constitutes a default under the terms of most secured loan agreements. Therefore, if a borrower goes bankrupt, the lender is entitled to take steps to recover her investment by seizing the collateral, which gives her interest in the bankrupt's property priority over the interests of the unsecured creditors of the bankrupt. This is why an unsecured creditor often recovers little or nothing from a bankrupt: the secured creditors get in ahead and take the bankrupt's most valuable assets.

Negotiating a Credit Agreement

The decision of a financial institution to advance credit to a business will depend on the institution's assessment of the business's prospects for making a profit. It is therefore important for business people to consider their credit options in relation to their business's projected profitability, and to prepare carefully to negotiate a credit agreement.

You must first determine which institution you want to deal with. In making your choice, you should consider the following factors:

- *How willing is the financial institution to assume risk?* If an institution is willing to assume some risk, it will be more likely to grant a loan, but the risk that it assumes may be reflected in a relatively high interest rate.
- *Can the institution give you useful financial advice?* Some financial institutions offer financial analysis, provide assistance with cash flow planning, and make helpful suggestions based on their experience with businesses similar to your own.
- *Does the institution understand your business and your market?* It is helpful to have a bank manager, or loans officer, who is familiar with your type of business and who understands its particular needs.

- *Does the institution have loan limits?* Many new businesses fail because they are inadequately financed. The ability to obtain adequate funding when you need it is important to your business's ultimate success.

In order to persuade a bank to finance Woodhouse, you will need a written business plan. An effective plan accomplishes the following:

- *It tells potential lenders why the business needs money.* For example, explain that the types of houses the business is building have become very fashionable and demand for them has surged across Canada. You seek to expand the business by opening new operations in key cities.
- *It explains how you intend to use the money to improve operations and profitability.* Describe your intention to use the capital to hire staff for new branches, buy machinery, and purchase raw materials to meet the increased market demand.
- *It describes the competence and industry experience of key company employees.* Identify key managers and employees in terms of their skills, experience, and the length of time they have been with the company. Resumés for each may be attached.
- *It sets out the amount of money you need.* Set out your capital needs, estimating the amount required for new equipment, staff, staff training, and inventory. Also provide projected revenue estimates.
- *It describes the sources and types of collateral that are available.* Identify those assets that are available as collateral and provide an estimate of the value of each asset. Arrange the assets by class: land, buildings, machinery, vehicles, inventory, and accounts receivable, for example.
- *It states when you will repay the loan.* On the basis of revenue estimates, present several options for repayment. To do this, calculate various credible estimates, based on different installment amounts and payment dates.

In addition—particularly if Woodhouse is an established company—you should provide the financial institution with a cash flow analysis, which shows the times in the fiscal year when income exceeds expenses and when expenses are higher than income, and provides an explanation for this cycle. An intelligent analysis is especially important in a seasonal business such as Woodhouse's, which will need short-term loans to cover some of its slow periods.

The financial institution will also expect to see that Woodhouse has a risk management program to safeguard its investment in the company. It may require that you carry risk management insurance as well as life insurance for key personnel.

Once you have gathered the necessary information, you are ready—on Woodhouse's behalf—to negotiate a credit agreement. Your mission is to obtain the highest possible credit limit at the lowest possible rate of interest. The more solid Woodhouse appears to be, and the better its profit record, the more likely the financial institution will be to offer terms that it gives to its most creditworthy commercial borrowers.

General Security Agreements

A financial institution will often require a borrower to enter into a general security agreement. Such an agreement, whose purpose is to secure the institution's loan, is usually required before financial institutions will extend short-term credit to cover operating expenses and cash flow fluctuations, and in some cases before they will extend credit to cover capital loans. In a **general security agreement**, a borrower pledges all or most of its assets as collateral or security for a loan. Financial institutions may also require that the officers and directors of small businesses pledge their personal assets—their homes, for example—as security for the business's loan.

Because loans may be advanced in the future and may be in amounts not yet known, the general security agreement requires that Woodhouse—and possibly its officers and directors—pledge a pool of assets sufficiently large to cover its future debt. This pool of assets will vary from time to time. This pledge is called a **floating charge**. It is created because Woodhouse needs to be free to use its assets to earn income. For example, Woodhouse may pledge its heavy machinery, inventory of supplies, and accounts receivable as collateral. However, it may need to sell or replace machinery. Supplies will be used up, inventory will be sold, and customers will pay their bills, thus replacing accounts receivable with company income. The floating charge permits individual assets in the listed categories to be used up, sold, or replaced.

If Woodhouse defaults on its loan, the floating charge over all of these assets "crystallizes"—that is, the charge attaches to all of the specific assets in the various pledged classes at the time of default. The charge, of course, crystallizes only to the extent of the debt, because the financial institution is not able to recover more than Woodhouse owes it.

Potential lenders often want to know if other lenders already have a security interest in a business's assets. For this reason, a security agreement can be registered under provincial legislation. Registration is notice to the world of a creditor's security interests. If Woodhouse pledges assets as security for one loan when it has already pledged these assets as security for another loan, the earlier lender takes priority over the later lender in seizing and selling the collateral, provided that the earlier lender has registered its security agreement.

In practical terms, this means that the later lender must stand back and allow the registered lender with a prior interest to seize and sell the collateral. In practical terms, this means that regardless of which lender seizes and sells the collateral, if there is nothing left after the earlier lender is repaid, the later lender is out of luck. Whoever registers first has priority, and it does not matter that the second lender did not search the registry before advancing funds. Registration is notice, whether you check the registry or not.

Corporate Bonds

A **corporate bond** is a company's written promise to repay the buyer of the bond—who is also the lender—both principal and interest at a fixed rate at specified intervals. Bonds are often used by large public companies to raise capital, with repayment periods spread over long periods—for example, 10, 20, or 30 years. Should the company become bankrupt, bondholders are entitled to recover their capital investment in a company ahead of all of the company's shareholders.

A company may use more than one class of bond to raise money. Differences in the terms of individual bonds—for example, the interest rate payable on the bond—

general security agreement
pledge, often used by a debtor's bank, of most of a debtor's assets to cover short-term loans made over an extended period

floating charge
class of collateral, such as inventory, where a creditor allows a debtor to dispose of items in the class

corporate bond
company's written promise to repay the buyer of the bond both principal and interest at specified intervals

may affect both the bond's initial price and its price on resale. In general, secured bonds (bonds backed by collateral) make safer and more expensive investments than unsecured bonds. Unsecured bonds issued by a company in poor financial condition are often called junk bonds, and the interest rates offered are higher to compensate for the increased risk.

Although bonds are a form of debt financing, they are not arranged between a business and an individual lender, as a loan is. Bonds are often issued in amounts far too large to be attractive to an individual lender, and a successful bond issue needs to attract many investors. For these reasons, bonds are issued in a manner that is similar to the way that shares are sold. Several financial institutions or a brokerage house may be given the task of marketing a company's bonds to the general public or to institutional investors. Those who wish to invest may buy units of the bond offering. After bonds have been initially offered to the public, investors who buy them may also sell them to other investors, in the same way that share-holders may sell their shares.

Once a bond has been issued, its resale value will be governed by its rating and also by the economy generally. If interest rates are rising, the value of bonds tends to fall. To minimize risk, bond investors scrutinize a bond's terms, the bond market generally, future market trends, and the performance of the company that issued the bond. To assist investors, there are bond-rating services, such as Moody's, Standard & Poor's, and Canadian Bond Rating Services, which rate both government and corporate bonds, assessing them as high grade, medium grade, speculative, or poor grade investments. These assessments are often expressed in letter grades: AAA is a high grade bond and a grade of C or D is considered a poor investment risk.

Minimizing Your Risk
Use Debt Financing Wisely

- Distinguish between the amount you want to borrow and the amount you can afford to repay. They may not necessarily be the same. Your object is to borrow capital, not to end up in bankruptcy.

- Estimate projected income and profits conservatively to ensure that you can meet the debt obligations you are incurring.

- Consider whether you can get someone to guarantee your loan. If someone who is creditworthy guarantees repayment, a lender may extend funds to you on more favourable terms or may forgo security.

- Decide whether you have collateral that you wish to give as security for the loan. Collateral may increase the amount of the loan and lower your interest rate.

- In giving security, try to use valuable assets that are not closely tied to production. If, for example, a business owns land that is not central to its operations, the land could provide valuable security for a lender, the seizure of which would not hamper the company's operations.

- Try to avoid giving inventory or accounts receivable as collateral because both directly affect cash flow and the ability to repay debts.

- If you default on a loan, try to renegotiate to extend the time for payment or reduce or defer the interest. Your lender may be amenable if there is any prospect that your fortunes will improve.

EQUITY FINANCING

So far, we have been talking about debt financing—that is, borrowing funds from financial institutions and bondholders. A second approach is equity financing. Equity financing involves the contribution of funds by the shareholders. In the case of a privately held corporation, this may involve a contribution by the founders or it may involve an "angel investor" who invests in the business but does not get involved otherwise. In the case of public companies, equity financing involves issuing and selling shares to institutional investors and the public.

Shares

Suppose Woodhouse wishes to raise funds by issuing shares and selling them to members of the public. If Woodhouse is issuing new shares, it will sell them by making an **initial public offering (IPO)** on a stock exchange. To do this, Woodhouse will enter into a contract with a brokerage house. Often the brokerage house, either alone or in combination with investment banks, will buy the shares—thus providing Woodhouse with capital—and will then sell them to the general public. Before Woodhouse's shares can be sold to the public, Woodhouse will have to issue a detailed prospectus, providing information about ownership of the company, its assets, performance, the purpose for which the shares were issued, and any other data that will allow purchasers to make an informed decision about whether to buy the shares. We provide further information about the contents of prospectuses in chapter 6 under the heading "Public Corporations."

Common shares are the most widely traded shares. They can produce a return on investment for shareholders in two ways:

1. through dividends—that is, a company's distribution of its profits to its shareholders—and
2. through resale by shareholders to new investors at a higher price than originally paid.

Unlike interest that is paid to a bondholder, payment of dividends is always at the discretion of the corporation. Some shares, called **preferred shares**, provide that, should the corporation choose to distribute dividends, the preferred shareholders must be paid before the common shareholders. This makes the price of preferred shares less volatile than the price of common shares and makes them somewhat more certain of producing some benefit for shareholders. However, shareholders will pay a premium price for preferred shares.

initial public offering (IPO)
first offering of shares by a corporation to the public through a brokerage firm to raise capital for use by the company

common shares
shares whose dividends are paid at the discretion of a corporation's management on the basis of the company's profits after dividend payments have been made on preferred shares

preferred shares
shares for which dividends are paid before any dividends are paid on common shares

> ## Minimizing Your Risk
> ### Use Equity Financing Wisely
>
> - Calculate your capital needs, and analyze the reasons you need this amount and your company's prospects.
>
> - Take great care in preparing a fair and accurate prospectus to avoid lawsuits for fraudulent or negligent misrepresentation and prosecution by securities commissions.
>
> - Because the brokerage house or financial institution that is managing the sale stands to make a large commission on sales, negotiate the terms of an initial public offering.
>
> - If you are concerned about restless shareholders or hostile takeovers, remember that common shares have voting rights, but preferred shares do not.

THE PROS AND CONS OF EQUITY VERSUS DEBT FINANCING

A company's "capital structure" refers to its mix of debt and equity financing. Achieving an appropriate capital structure usually requires consideration of a number of factors, some of which are listed in table 9.1.

Table 9.1   Equity Versus Debt Financing

	Debt Financing	Equity Financing
Timing of repayment	Accurate prediction of a company's future performance is required to meet a repayment schedule.	No payment plan is required.
Cost of financing	Regular principal and interest payments are required.	Payments are made in the form of dividends only when the company generates profits and when other financial needs (that is, growth) are not considered a priority.
Effect on company's assets	Assets are usually required as collateral and will be sold in the event of default.	Shareholders accept the risk of loss if the company does poorly and take assets only after all creditors are paid.
Tax implications	Interest payments are deductible from business income.	Dividends paid to shareholders are not tax-deductible.
Control of the company	Lenders have no direct influence over the management of the company, but payment of principal and interest at regular intervals reduces the amount of profit available for such things as new equipment and advertising. In case of default, secured creditors can seize assets and may be able to take over management.	Profits can be used for growth rather than dividends, subject to shareholders' right to remove directors and seize control or influence management. One company can take control of another by buying up shares on the stock market. This may be friendly (encouraged by management) or hostile (not encouraged by management, and a bidding war for shares may occur).

From this discussion, it might appear that a business can minimize its risk by preferring equity financing over debt financing. However, a company may need to sell a lot of shares—thereby greatly expanding its ownership base—in order to raise the funding that it needs. If key shareholders control the management of a company, they will not be willing to share control with a group of dissatisfied shareholders, nor do they wish to set the scene for a successful takeover of the company. For these reasons, most companies opt for a mix of both debt and equity financing.

Debt Collection and Insolvency

In the sections that follow, we examine the legal relationship between creditors and debtors. How do creditors go about assessing risk before they extend credit? What do they do when a debtor fails to pay them back? When do they send a defaulting debtor into bankruptcy?

CREDITOR PROTECTION

When a creditor extends credit, he is concerned about making a profit and avoiding a loss. The interest rate he will decide to charge is dependent on both market rates and his assessment of the risk he is taking by lending money to a particular debtor in particular circumstances: the higher the risk, the higher the interest rate.

If, for example, Woodhouse seeks to raise capital by obtaining credit from a credit union, the credit union will examine Woodhouse's business plan to see if Woodhouse's proposal makes economic sense. The lender may also assess Woodhouse's credit application against economic trends and other factors relevant to the house construction industry in which Woodhouse is active. The lender will also examine Woodhouse's credit history to see how diligent it was in repaying past debt. If the company has a good track record, both as debtor and as participant in a profitable industry, the credit union will likely advance the loan at a relatively low interest rate. If Woodhouse's credit record is bad, if the housing industry looks shaky, or if Woodhouse's business performance has been less than stellar despite a generally profitable market, the credit union will likely demand a higher interest rate, or may refuse to lend Woodhouse money.

Credit History

The credit union can inquire into Woodhouse's credit history in a number of ways: through credit-reporting agencies and through bankruptcy, execution, and secured transaction searches. We examine each of these methods in the following sections. Here, we also take a detailed look at the ranking of interests of both secured and unsecured creditors.

Credit-Reporting Agencies

If Woodhouse has ever issued corporate bonds, potential lenders can check indexes such as Canada Bond Rating Services to see how these bonds have been rated. (We discussed bonds and their rating above under the heading "Corporate Bonds.") Let us assume, though, that Woodhouse is a relatively small company with a relatively small amount of capital, and therefore is unlikely ever to have issued bonds as a means of raising funds.

In this case, the credit union can look to its own informal information networks based on information gathered by its loan officers, or it may use a commercial credit-reporting agency, such as Equifax. These agencies are clearinghouses for information about credit transactions, and they can provide Woodhouse's credit transaction history. The credit union can use this information to contact other creditors and obtain details about Woodhouse's repayment of debt. Some credit-reporting agencies have inexpensive online search facilities, where clients either pay on a per-search basis or pay an annual fee to use an agency's database.

All credit-reporting agencies have an obligation to correct inaccurate information about a debtor if the debtor demands it. Businesses who become aware that inaccurate information is being held about them may call the agency and provide the correct information, or file a complaint with the relevant regulatory agency, such as a provincial consumer and business relations ministry. Publishing inaccurate and negative information is defamatory and may provide the basis of a lawsuit against the agency for the tort of libel.

Bankruptcy, Execution, and Secured Transaction Searches

Public databanks may also be searched for information about a debtor's past repayment performance. Potential creditors can conduct any of the following inexpensive searches:

1. *Bankruptcy searches.* A lender can search online at www.strategis.gc.ca to determine if the debtor has gone bankrupt in the past, is about to go bankrupt, or is currently involved in the bankruptcy process.
2. *Execution searches.* Anyone who has obtained a judgment against a defendant (in a lawsuit concerning debt or anything else) is likely to have filed a **writ of seizure and sale**. (These writs are also referred to as "writs of execution.") Such a writ directs a sheriff to seize and sell a defendant's assets and to use the money from the sale to pay the judgment that a plaintiff has obtained against the defendant. An execution search would tell the credit union whether there are any judgments against Woodhouse, and if so, it would identify Woodhouse's judgment creditors, as well as specify the amount of the judgments and how much remains to be paid.
3. *Secured transaction searches.* The credit union will likely be asking Woodhouse for security in the form of collateral. It needs to know that any property that Woodhouse offers as collateral is not already pledged to other creditors. It also needs to know that Woodhouse actually owns the collateral that it will be pledging as security. Secured transaction searches will show whether Woodhouse is the owner of the collateral, whether there are others with an interest in it, and the nature and extent of these interests. It is essential that the credit union perform these searches because, if another creditor has already registered an interest in Woodhouse's collateral, the interest of the earlier-registered creditor will take priority over any later-registered interest of the credit union. Important registries include the following:

   a. *Land titles or registry search.* In Ontario, registries maintained under the *Land Titles Act* and the *Registry Act* contain a record of interests in land—for example, ownership interests, mortgage interests, and construction liens (a security interest that can be taken by contractors for unpaid work).
   b. *Personal property security registry search.* In Ontario, a registry maintained under the *Personal Property Security Act* allows a creditor to register its interest in any personal property (property other than land) that a debtor has pledged as collateral. Registered security agreements will describe the collateral that a debtor has pledged and the amount of the loan at the time the agreement was registered. Potential creditors may contact existing security holders to obtain details about their security interests.
   c. *Bank Act search.* Certain Canadian businesses—usually large ones in specific commercial sectors, such as mining and manufacturing—

---

writ of seizure and sale court order directing a sheriff to seize and sell assets belonging to a judgment debtor and pay the money from the sale to a judgment creditor; also called a "writ of execution" can obtain long-term loans from chartered banks to finance their operations. Under section 427 of the *Bank Act*, if the business gives the bank a collateral interest in an asset to secure continued financing, the bank acquires an ownership interest in the asset. The bank keeps title to the asset until the business repays the loan. The business retains possession of the asset and can use it in the usual course of its operations, as long as it keeps making payments on its loan. A potential creditor can conduct a search to determine the extent of a bank's interest in the property of a potential debtor.

Priority Among Creditors

Suppose Fly by Night Bank gave credit to Woodhouse last year, and Venture Fund gave it a loan this year. If Woodhouse cannot pay either of its creditors in full, because it has insufficient assets to cover its debts, which creditor has the right to be paid first? The answer depends on which creditor's debt was secured, whether the security interest was registered, and when.

Unsecured Creditors

As we have discussed earlier in the section entitled "Unsecured and Secured Credit," unsecured creditors are those who extend credit in exchange for a simple promise by the debtor to repay the debt. If the debtor fails to repay the debt, the creditor's only remedy is to sue the debtor for repayment. Suppose that Woodhouse defaults on a debt and Little Axe, one of its unsecured creditors, obtains a judgment against it for $50,000. If Little Axe takes action to enforce the judgment—that is, finds one of Woodhouse's assets that is valuable and has the sheriff seize and sell the asset—Little Axe will use the proceeds of the sale first to pay the costs of the sale and then to pay Woodhouse's debt.

But what happens if more than one unsecured creditor obtains a judgment against Woodhouse? If other judgment creditors have filed writs of seizure and sale with the sheriff against Woodhouse—and have thereby become **execution creditors** of Woodhouse—the sheriff must pay them all on a pro rata basis. Figure 9.4 demonstrates such a payment.

execution creditor
creditor who has obtained a judgment and seeks to enforce (execute) it

Secured Creditors

How does a secured creditor get priority over another secured creditor? The rule is that the secured creditor with the earliest registered interest in a particular item of collateral takes priority over other secured creditors with interests in the same collateral. This means that if the debtor defaults, any secured creditor can seize and sell the collateral, but money from the sale must be paid out to the creditor with the earliest registered interest first, after which the next most senior secured creditor is paid, and so on. If there is not enough money from the sale to pay all of the secured creditors, the most junior creditor may end up not being paid anything.

The earliest creditor establishes his priority rights by giving **notice** of his interest in the collateral by means of registration. Because subsequent creditors know that there may be nothing left for them if the earliest registered creditor seizes and

notice
verification, under a registration system, that a creditor has an interest in the property of a debtor

Figure 9.4   Pro Rata Payment of Unsecured Execution Creditors

Woodhouse has three execution creditors:

- It owes creditor A $50,000.
- It owes creditor B $20,000.
- It owes creditor C $10,000.

Woodhouse's total judgment debt is therefore $80,000.

Creditor C is successful in having the sheriff seize and sell one of Woodhouse's assets, recovering $30,000.

Each creditor is entitled to payment in accordance with the following pro rata payment formula:

$$\frac{\text{amount recovered in sale} \times \text{amount owing to creditor}}{\text{amount owing to all creditors}} = \text{share paid to creditor}$$

Therefore:

Creditor A receives $\dfrac{\$30,000 \times \$50,000}{\$80,000} = \$18,750$

Creditor B receives $\dfrac{\$30,000 \times \$20,000}{\$80,000} = \$7,500$

Creditor C receives $\dfrac{\$30,000 \times \$10,000}{\$80,000} = \$3,750$

sells the collateral, they may be unwilling to extend credit. If they do extend credit, they may demand a much higher rate of interest to compensate them for the risk they take in being unable to recover their loan from the sale of the collateral if the secured debtor defaults.

The priority right of one secured creditor over another depends not only on who extends credit first, but also on whether subsequent creditors had adequate notice of the prior interest. As we noted earlier, the various statutory registration systems for real and personal property has made it easier to give effective notice to creditors. Registration of a right in collateral is effective notice to all creditors, whether they search the register or not.

It is simple enough to determine priority rights by searching a register. However, when a business defaults on its credit payments, there are often competing claims by various creditors, both secured and unsecured. The situation can become quite complex, as demonstrated in the example that follows.

Woodhouse owes $40,000 to Sun Equipment Ltd. on a conditional sale contract for machinery that Sun registered under the *Personal Property Security Act* in 2002. Under this contract, Sun has the right to seize the machinery if there is a default ahead of and with priority over other creditors that have later-registered interests in the machinery and over unsecured creditors. In 2000, Woodhouse had bought supplies from Bulk Out Ltd. for $10,000. Woodhouse did not meet its payments, and Bulk Out sued Woodhouse for the debt in 2000. After obtaining judgment, Bulk Out filed a writ of seizure and sale against Woodhouse in 2001. In 2004, Woodhouse obtained a $20,000 loan from EasyCredit, pledging the machinery that Sun has a security interest in as collateral. EasyCredit registered this credit arrangement under the *Personal Property Security Act* in 2004.

The claims of Woodhouse's creditors rank in the following order:

1. Sun, having registered its interest in 2002, has top priority with respect to a claim against the machinery.

2. EasyCredit, having registered its interest in the same collateral, occupies the second priority position with respect to any claim on the machinery. After Sun seizes and sells the machinery, it will satisfy its own debt. It must then pay any remaining sale proceeds to EasyCredit, to the extent of EasyCredit's debt.

3. Bulk Out is an unsecured creditor. Although Bulk Out's claim is earlier than EasyCredit's, EasyCredit has priority with respect to a claim against the machinery. Bulk Out can be paid out of the money from the sale by Sun only after both Sun's and EasyCredit's claims have been satisfied. Bulk Out may, however, have the sheriff seize and sell other property belonging to Woodhouse, on which no secured creditor has priority.

Minimizing Your Risk
Extend Credit Judiciously

- Conduct a credit bureau search to check the credit history of the potential debtor.

- Do a bankruptcy search to determine whether the debtor has been or is bankrupt.

- Do a personal property security search to see whether assets have been pledged as collateral so that you can determine whether there are any unencumbered assets that could be pledged as security.

- If the debtor owns land, do a land registry search to see if the debtor has mortgaged the land.

- Do a search of writs of seizure and sale to see if there are outstanding judgments against the debtor that are unsatisfied.

- Ask to see company financial statements and a business plan.

- Consider whether the loan should be co-signed, making the co-signer directly liable.

- Consider repaying a guarantee so that the guarantor would be liable if the debtor defaults.

- Consider whether the debtor should be required to carry loan insurance, so that the loan is repaid if the debtor dies.

- Register all security interests immediately upon acquiring them.

CREDITORS' REMEDIES

What should you do if your business becomes an unpaid creditor—if, for example, your business has supplied goods to a retailer who seems unlikely to pay for them? Most creditors are wise in pausing a moment before they seize and sell collateral, or proceed with a lawsuit against the debtor. These proceedings are expensive and may not yield the desired result. Creditors who have existing relationships with defaulting debtors may want to preserve these relationships if they can.

demand letter
letter, usually written by a
creditor's lawyer, stating
that the debtor to whom
the letter is addressed has
defaulted, and that the
debtor must pay the full
amount, including interest
on the principal sum
owing, by a given date, or
face legal action

Rather than taking aggressive action immediately, your business may choose to send a payment reminder to the debtor and, if that fails, a demand letter. A **demand letter** is a document that states that the debtor has defaulted and that he must pay the full amount owing, including interest, by a given date, or face legal action. You must take care to phrase such a letter carefully. Do not threaten criminal proceedings for fraud or theft if the debtor does not pay; threatening to bring criminal proceedings to collect a debt constitutes the criminal offence of extortion.

A debtor may respond to your demand letter by offering to pay you all or some of the amount owing. You should consider this offer carefully. If the debtor is in financial difficulty, a negotiated settlement in which you agree to accept less than the amount you are owed may be preferable to an expensive lawsuit followed by a failed attempt to enforce a judgment after the debtor has gone bankrupt. This is particularly important for an unsecured creditor, whose interests might be near the bottom of a lengthy list of other creditors' interests. If demand letters or attempts to negotiate a compromise are unsuccessful, however, you may choose to take legal action to collect the debt.

Debt Collection for Unsecured Creditors

If your business is an unsecured creditor and a debtor does not pay you what it owes, your only remedy is to sue the debtor for failure to pay the debt, and then to enforce your judgment. Depending on the amount of the debt, you can sue the debtor either in the provincial Superior Court or the Small Claims Court.

Debt Proceedings in Superior Court

In Ontario, if the debt is significantly more than $10,000, you would commence legal proceedings in the trial division of the Superior Court. Your legal costs could be anywhere from $20,000 to $100,000. Furthermore, if you lose the case, you might have to pay some of the debtor's legal costs. The procedures followed in the Superior Court are described in chapter 2 under the heading "The Litigation Process in Superior Court Trial Division."

Most cases do not go to trial. Instead, the parties settle by way of compromise. Even if there is no formal settlement, it is common for a debtor to choose not to defend the case. If the defendant fails to file a statement of defence, after a brief period the plaintiff may ask the court for a **default judgment**. In a debt case, where the amount owing is easily calculated, a court official will give judgment without a hearing.

default judgment
a judgment based on the
plaintiff's claim if the
defendant has failed to file
a statement of defence

If a defendant does choose to defend the case, you should be aware that the courts are introducing various procedures to speed up their process. Ontario has introduced a simplified procedure that streamlines the pre-trial process to save time and legal expenses when the amount sued for is $50,000 or less.

By obtaining judgment, you receive an order from the court requiring the defendant debtor to pay the amount of the judgment, which generally includes the amount of the original debt, pre- and post-judgment interest, and some of your legal costs. The debtor is usually unable to pay the judgment—after all, he was unwilling or unable to pay you when the amount he owed was simply a debt. At this point, you must take steps to enforce the judgment. A common first step is to request a **judgment debtor examination**. This is a procedure in which you have an opportunity to ask the debtor questions under oath about his financial situation. A judgment debtor examination can sometimes lead to a settlement between you and the judgment debtor. If not, you must take further steps, including the following:

1. *Sheriff's sale.* You, as a judgment creditor, may obtain a writ of seizure and sale from the court that gave the judgment. You then file the writ with the sheriff in the county or region where the debtor's assets are located. The sheriff can then seize and sell the debtor's assets, except for necessities—for example, automobiles, tools of a trade, and clothing—which are protected under the *Execution Act*. The sheriff then divides the proceeds from the sale on a pro rata basis among all creditors who have filed a writ of seizure and sale against the judgment debtor.

    There are drawbacks to using a sheriff's sale as a means of getting the money that the judgment debtor owes you. For example, there may be several judgment creditors with large judgments who have filed writs. They will share pro rata in the sale proceeds and may get more of the proceeds than you. In addition, the debtor's used assets may not have a high resale value, and you must use any sale proceeds first to pay the costs of the sale.

2. *Garnishment.* If you, as a judgment creditor, can find someone who owes the judgment debtor money, you may be able to obtain a garnishment order. A **garnishment order** is an order of a court requiring a person who owes money to a judgment debtor—the garnishee—to pay that money to the court, rather than to the debtor; once it receives the money, the court pays it to the judgment creditor. A garnishment order allows a judgment creditor to intercept, for example, accounts receivable that are owing to a judgment debtor from its customers. If the judgment debtor is a wage earner, the court can order the employer to pay a percentage of the wages into court. A garnishment order may continue in force until the judgment debtor's debt to the creditor is paid. Thus, it can act as a long-term diverter of funds from the garnishee to the judgment creditor.

judgment debtor examination
process in which a judgment creditor can question a judgment debtor under oath about his assets, liabilities, and income to provide information that assists the judgment creditor in satisfying the judgment

garnishment order
court order directed to someone who owes money to a judgment debtor, requiring this person to pay some or all of the money owing into court for payment out to the judgment creditor

Debt Proceedings in Small Claims Court

In Ontario, if you are a creditor and the amount of the debt is under $10,000, you can sue the debtor in Small Claims Court. There are a number of advantages: the court fees are much lower; the process is simpler and faster; and the evidence rules are relaxed, which makes it easier to prove a case. In Small Claims Court, you can either represent yourself or hire an agent—rather than a lawyer—to represent you. These proceedings are discussed in more detail in chapter 2 under the heading "The Litigation Process in Small Claims Court."

There are also advantages for debtors. They can ask to pay the judgment amount over time, a request that is rarely refused by the court. A debtor who has several judgments against her may ask the court for a consolidation order. Such an order requires the debtor to make periodic payments in an affordable amount into court; the payment is then divided among several judgment creditors, who may end up waiting years to be paid in full.

Debt Collection for Secured Creditors

If you are a secured creditor, you have simpler recovery methods at your disposal than if you are an unsecured creditor. You have the right to seize and sell the assets in which you have a security interest to recover what the debtor owes you. Once the sale is over, however, you have exhausted your security rights. If the sale of the security does not yield enough to pay the debt, you can still sue the debtor for the balance owing. In this suit, however, you are in the same position as any other unsecured creditor. You have no better claim against the debtor's remaining assets than anyone else.

As a secured creditor, you enjoy a number of advantages over unsecured creditors. Often, you can take action to recover the debt sooner than other creditors because your security agreement will allow you to seize and sell property as soon as the debtor defaults. You do not need a judgment or a writ of seizure and sale.

The security agreement may also define default as including actions other than non-payment of the debt. For example, it may define default as including misuse of the collateral by the debtor or the debtor's failure to pay a debt to another creditor. You are not required to obtain a court order in order to decide that a default has occurred. In the event that you choose to exercise a quick, self-help remedy, you can hire a private bailiff to seize and sell the collateral. Take care, however: where a secured creditor acts unfairly or oppressively, a court can void the security agreement between the creditor and debtor, and the creditor can be liable for damages. Consider the case of *Burns v. Financial Bailiff Services Ltd.* in this regard.

CASE IN POINT Punitive Damages for Trespassing Bailiffs

Burns v. Financial Bailiff Services Ltd., [2000] SJ no. 794 (QB)

Facts
Acting under a warrant of seizure, two bailiffs went to a native reserve with the intention of seizing a van that was subject to a chattel mortgage. While one bailiff knocked at the door of the residence of the debtors, the other bailiff entered the van. The second bailiff also entered the van later to avoid physical confrontation with one of the debtors.

Result
The court found that seizure of the van would have been unlawful under the federal *Indian Act*, which prohibits creditors from entering a reserve to seize the property of a native Indian or a band on a reserve. As professionals, the bailiffs knew or are deemed to have known this. The bailiffs therefore committed trespass, and the debtors were entitled to $3,000 in punitive damages awarded against the bailiffs and the company they worked for.

Business Lesson
Employ reliable bailiffs who know the law and are trained to act within their legal authority.

> ## Minimizing Your Risk
> ### Collect Your Debts Efficiently
>
> - Send a polite reminder, usually after 60 days from the due date.
>
> - Search for writs of seizure and sale, registration of personal property security interests, and bankruptcy to see if there are signs of financial collapse.
>
> - Approximately 90 days after the due date, send a demand letter.
>
> - If you have security, use the self-help remedies to seize collateral.
>
> - If you are an unsecured creditor, commence legal proceedings as soon as possible to stay ahead of any bankruptcy proceedings.
>
> - If you obtain a judgment, file writs of seizure and sale immediately, and carry out a judgment debtor examination to find out what assets may be available for seizure and whether a garnishment order may be effective.
>
> - Be ready to negotiate a settlement for less than what is owing, based on the likelihood of recovery of the debt and the costs of litigation. There is practical wisdom in the saying that a bird in the hand is worth two in the bush.
>
> - If you fail to recover the debt, remember that a bad debt is a business expense that is deductible from business income for tax purposes.

BANKRUPTCY AND INSOLVENCY

Suppose Woodhouse is unable to pay its debts, has been sued by creditors, and has a number of outstanding judgments against it that it is unable to pay. It may be time to consider bankruptcy. In law, Woodhouse is in a position to go into bankruptcy if its debts exceed $1,000 and it has committed one or more acts of bankruptcy, as defined in the *Bankruptcy and Insolvency Act*. An **act of bankruptcy** includes either being unable to pay debts as they come due (and not having assets that can be sold to pay them) or committing fraudulent or evasive acts to avoid creditors.

act of bankruptcy
being unable to pay debts as they come due or committing fraudulent or evasive acts to avoid creditors

If Woodhouse decides to declare bankruptcy, what happens? The general purpose of the *Bankruptcy and Insolvency Act* is to distribute a bankrupt's assets fairly among its creditors, then to discharge the bankrupt from further responsibility and allow it to start afresh. The Act operates by requiring bankrupt individuals and companies to turn over their assets to a trustee, who sells them and distributes the money from the sale to the bankrupt's creditors. A bankrupt who has not committed a fraud or other bankruptcy offence will be released from bankruptcy, with many of its assets gone, but with most of its debts discharged and cancelled. The bankrupt is then free to begin again, relieved of its load of debt.

You might ask why bankrupts should be able to escape their debts in this way. A short answer is that a discharged bankrupt, if freed of old debt, will be able to resume the commercial activity that ultimately benefits the economy and the consuming public as a whole. Creditors will recover at least some portion of what is owed to them, and they too will be able to continue engaging in useful economic activities and contribute to economic growth.

Web Link

Check www.bankruptcycanada.com for more information about bankruptcy and obtaining a trustee, and www.strategis.ic.gc.ca to conduct a bankruptcy search.

Bankruptcy Proceedings

If Woodhouse is in a financial position that is sufficiently insolvent for it to consider bankruptcy, it has a number of options. It may make a proposal to its creditors, make a voluntary assignment in bankruptcy, or wait for a creditor to petition it into bankruptcy. We examine each of these options in the following sections.

Proposal to Creditors

proposal to creditors
debt-restructuring proposal made under the *Bankrukptcy and Insolvency Act* or the *Companies' Creditors Arrangement Act*, which allows the business to continue operating and—if accepted—delays or avoids bankruptcy

trustee in bankruptcy
individual, usually an accountant, who is licensed under the *Bankruptcy and Insolvency Act* to administer a bankrupt's assets for the benefit of the bankrupt's creditors

official receiver
government official in the Office of the Superintendent of Bankruptcy who receives proposals, examines bankrupts under oath, and chairs meetings of creditors

A **proposal to creditors** is an arrangement put forward on behalf of a debtor to creditors under the provisions of the *Bankruptcy and Insolvency Act*. If, for example, Woodhouse finds itself unable to pay its debts as they become due, it may decide to make a proposal in order to avoid bankruptcy and continue to carry on business. To do this, it will retain the services of a **trustee in bankruptcy** or a proposal administrator, who is licensed by the Office of the Superintendent of Bankruptcy. The trustee or administrator will review Woodhouse's financial affairs with Woodhouse's management and prepare a proposal. The proposal will then be sent to the **official receiver**, a government official in the Office of the Superintendent of Bankruptcy. Once the proposal has been reviewed and approved by the official receiver, it is sent to Woodhouse's creditors. The creditors then vote as a group to accept or reject Woodhouse's proposal.

If the creditors accept Woodhouse's proposal, the proposal is then binding on Woodhouse and on all of its unsecured creditors. Secured creditors are still at liberty to seize Woodhouse's collateral, provided that Woodhouse has committed an act that amounts to a default under the security agreement between Woodhouse and the creditor. An accepted proposal means that Woodhouse will not go bankrupt and is not subject to other bankruptcy proceedings, so long as it abides by the terms of the proposal.

If the creditors reject Woodhouse's proposal, Woodhouse may make an assignment in bankruptcy and voluntarily go bankrupt, or any creditor may petition Woodhouse into bankruptcy. If, after a proposal is accepted, Woodhouse does not abide by its terms, it may also be forced into bankruptcy.

The proposal procedure we have just described should not be confused with the more complex and formal proposal procedure that is available to debtors under the *Companies' Creditors Arrangement Act*. It is a court procedure and is described later in this chapter.

Voluntary Assignment in Bankruptcy

If Woodhouse determines that its financial position is so precarious that bankruptcy proceedings are its only sensible option, it can voluntarily declare bankruptcy. By doing so, it assigns its assets (which are called its "estate," as though it has died) for the benefit of its creditors. It then files its assignment in bankruptcy with the official receiver, at which time it officially becomes a bankrupt. The trustee in bankruptcy then takes control of Woodhouse's estate.

The trustee's first action is to call a first meeting of Woodhouse's creditors. At this meeting, the creditors (and sometimes also the official receiver) are entitled to question the trustee and the bankrupt about the bankruptcy, the bankrupt's affairs, and the assets available to satisfy the debts owing to the creditors. A creditor, for example, may ask Woodhouse about salary increases for managers in the past year. The creditors may also elect inspectors from among their own ranks to oversee the liquidation of the estate. The trustee then sells the bankrupt's assets and distributes the proceeds to the creditors.

If Woodhouse is declaring bankruptcy for the first time, it can usually expect to be discharged from bankruptcy by the court within a year, without conditions. However, if a creditor objects to automatic discharge, a hearing must be held before a judge. At the hearing, the judge may decide to grant Woodhouse an absolute discharge from bankruptcy. This means that Woodhouse is relieved of the obligation of paying most debts that it incurred before bankruptcy. The *Bankruptcy and Insolvency Act* provides a few exceptions to this rule, most of which are inapplicable to companies; the debts that bankruptcy cannot extinguish are set out in figure 9.5.

If the judge makes Woodhouse's discharge conditional, Woodhouse might need to make additional funds available to creditors before it can enjoy the financial freedom afforded by discharge. The judge may also grant a suspended discharge, delaying a discharge until certain events have occurred. For example, a discharge may be suspended until a criminal investigation is completed or until objections by the trustee, the official receiver, or the superintendent of bankruptcy have been heard.

Involuntary Bankruptcy Petition

If Woodhouse remains optimistic about its financial future despite evidence that it is sinking further and further into debt, its creditors can take action. Any creditor to whom Woodhouse owes more than $1,000 (after deducting the value of any security that Woodhouse has given it), and who can identify an act of bankruptcy by Woodhouse that occurred within the last six months, may petition Woodhouse into bankruptcy. The most common act of bankruptcy that Woodhouse is likely to have committed is failing to pay its debts as they become due. The other act of bankruptcy, fraud, is difficult to prove and alleged relatively rarely.

Therefore, if Woodhouse owes Little Axe $10,000 and the account has been past due for three months, Little Axe is in a position to file a "petition for a receiving order" with the registrar of the Bankruptcy Court (a branch of the Superior Court in the province where Woodhouse carries on business). If the petition succeeds, which it will if Little Axe proves the debt, the court will make a receiving order. The **receiving order** appoints a trustee, who is usually nominated by a creditor. The trustee takes

receiving order
order that appoints a trustee in bankruptcy to take control of the bankrupt's property following a creditor's successful bankruptcy petition

Figure 9.5 Debts Not Extinguished by a Discharge from Bankruptcy

- an order or contract for family support

- an order for payment of damages for an assault

- an order for payment of restitution by a criminal court

- a fine

- a debt arising from a fraudulent act

- a debt in respect of a student loan if the debtor is still a student or has defaulted on the student loan within two years of having been a student control of Woodhouse's property and takes steps to sell the property on behalf of Woodhouse's creditors.

A petition for a receiving order can be risky and expensive for a creditor. If Little Axe's petition fails, Little Axe will probably be responsible for court costs. However, Little Axe may have sound reasons for taking a risk. If Woodhouse is insolvent and refuses to go bankrupt voluntarily, it will continue to deplete whatever business assets it has left. The sooner it is declared bankrupt, the sooner the trustee gets control of its assets. Assets of an insolvent company may disappear rapidly, leaving even less for creditors later on.

Little Axe may also be concerned about Woodhouse giving preference to another creditor over it. For example, Woodhouse's management may have an especially close relationship with the management of Rusty Saw, and Woodhouse may therefore prefer to pay Rusty Saw's invoices before it pays Little Axe's. Such an activity is known as a fraudulent preference and is illegal under the *Bankruptcy and Insolvency Act* and provincial statutes, such as Ontario's *Assignments and Preferences Act*. Rather than trying to recover funds diverted to Rusty Saw in a fraudulent preference scheme, Little Axe may be wise to take proactive steps to gain control of Woodhouse's remaining assets by means of the supervisory powers of the trustee in bankruptcy and the official receiver.

Viva Developments Inc. v. Icarus Properties Ltd. is a case that involves a fraudulent preference and a fraudulent conveyance under British Columbia legislation. The principles demonstrated in this case that prohibit fraudulent activity are analogous to those embodied in the *Bankruptcy and Insolvency Act*.

Companies' Creditors Arrangement Act

The *Companies' Creditors Arrangement Act* is a federal statute that provides an alternative to bankruptcy, particularly for large businesses with many creditors. The Act allows a company to make a proposal for paying its debts—through the courts—to its creditors, both secured and unsecured. Companies use the Act's protection in an effort to hold off creditors and bankruptcy proceedings by obtaining a court order.

Should Woodhouse obtain such an order, it will not go into bankruptcy; it will not be broken up and sold. Instead, while under the court's protection, Woodhouse will attempt to restructure its debt by proposing revised repayment terms to creditors. If Woodhouse's creditors accept Woodhouse's debt restructuring, they will usually receive less than they are legally entitled to or they will agree to postpone their right to payment for a longer time than they are legally required to wait. Woodhouse's creditors will make these concessions if they feel that they will fare better under a *Companies' Creditors Arrangement Act* proposal than under a bankruptcy, or if they believe that Woodhouse can be returned to financial health with a promise of eventual repayment of their debt. If the creditors refuse to accept the proposal, bankruptcy usually follows.

When Air Canada fell into financial difficulties after absorbing Canadian Airlines International, it took refuge under the *Companies' Creditors Arrangement Act*, which prevented bankruptcy proceedings from being initiated while it negotiated a proposal with its creditors. Negotiations were complex and prolonged. Creditors, such as airline employees, had to consider whether accepting pay reductions to keep

CASE IN POINT   Mortgage for Shareholders Equals Fraudulent Conveyance

Viva Developments Inc. v. Icarus Properties Ltd., [2004] BCJ no. 1858 (SC)

Facts

Between the time that the plaintiff corporation was awarded judgment against the defendant corporation and the time that the court quantified damages, the defendant granted a mortgage over land to its shareholders. The mortgage purported to secure shareholders' loans and management fees payable. The payment of management fees was approved by a resolution of the board of directors after judgment was granted. The amount of the shareholders' loans was inflated.

The defendant corporation also transferred property to its majority shareholder. The defendant claimed that the dominant intention of the transfer was to keep the company in business and to avoid foreclosure proceedings.

Result

The court found that the granting of the mortgage was void because it was a fraudulent conveyance, intended to "delay, hinder, or defraud creditors and others of their just and lawful remedies." The dominant intent of the mortgage was to secure the shareholders' loans and management fees, not to keep the company in business. The mortgage was therefore void as a fraudulent preference.

Business Lesson

Be aware that schemes to divert funds from creditors and others who are entitled to receive them may be fraudulent and illegal.

---

the company in business was preferable to the company's bankruptcy and their resulting job losses. After consideration by employee groups and lenders—and considerable bargaining—the parties eventually achieved a deal that permitted the airline to continue in operation and pay its creditors over time.

Minimizing Your Risk

Use Bankruptcy Proceedings When Necessary

- If you are a debtor, consider going voluntarily into bankruptcy only when it is clear that your company's debts cannot be paid when they are due and there is no realistic hope that the business's prospects will improve.

- If there is some hope of saving your business, use the relatively inexpensive proceedings available under the *Bankruptcy and Insolvency Act* to make a proposal to your creditors to restructure your debt.

- If you are an unsecured creditor, consider petitioning a debtor into bankruptcy only if the debt is large, there is ample evidence that the company is insolvent, and there is some prospect that something will be left after secured creditors have seized collateral.

- Remember that there may be less reason for a secured creditor to push a debtor into bankruptcy because seizing collateral may satisfy much of the debt.

Chapter Summary

This chapter has examined the related topics of banking, financing, and the debtor–creditor relationship from a business perspective—often that of Woodhouse Ltd., a financially challenged builder. We began our discussion with the general role of financial institutions and the methods they use to provide loans and transfer funds, particularly through negotiable instruments. We reviewed account agreements and the loan negotiation process. We then turned to the options available to business people when financing a business, considering both debt and equity financing. In addition, we examined the implications of borrowing money on both a short- and a long-term basis. We then turned to an examination of the debtor–creditor relationship, starting with the steps a creditor may take to investigate the creditworthiness of a business. We then reviewed the rights of both secured and unsecured creditors in the event of a default on a loan. Finally, we considered what happens when a business is unable to meet its financial obligations, including making a proposal to creditors, making a voluntary assignment in bankruptcy, being petitioned into bankruptcy, and seeking protection under the *Companies' Creditors Arrangement Act.*

KEY TERMS

act of bankruptcy
bill of exchange
caisse populaire
cheque
collateral
common shares
corporate bond
debt financing
default judgment
demand letter
drawee
drawer
equity financing

execution creditors
floating charge
garnishment order
general security
   agreement
holder
initial public offering
   (IPO)
judgment debtor
   examination
negotiable instrument
notice
official receiver

payee
payer
preferred shares
priority
promissory note
proposal to creditors
receiving order
secured creditor
secured loan
trustee in bankruptcy
unsecured loan
writ of seizure and sale

REFERENCES

Bank Act, SC 1991, c. 46.
Bankruptcy and Insolvency Act, RSC 1985, c. B-3.
Bills of Exchange Act, RSC 1985, c. B-4.
Burns v. Financial Bailiff Services Ltd., [2000] SJ no. 794 (QB).
Companies' Creditors Arrangement Act, RSC 1985, c. C-36.
Execution Act, RSO 1990, c. E.24.
Personal Property Security Act, RSO 1990, c. P.10.
Viva Developments Inc. v. Icarus Properties Ltd., [2004] BCJ no. 1858 (SC).

REVIEW AND DISCUSSION

True or False?

_F_ **1.** Bills of exchange are no longer used in Canada.

_F_ **2.** Banks have always been able to issue mortgages.

_T_ **3.** A company's capital structure reflects its balance of debt and equity financing.

_T_ **4.** A bankrupt emerges from bankruptcy free of most, but not necessarily all, debts and stripped of most, but not necessarily all, assets.

Multiple Choice

1. A cheque endorsed in blank is cashable
   a. by the payee named on the front of the cheque only
   b. by the payer only
   c. within 30 days
   d. by anyone

2. A consumer note
   a. bears no interest prior to the payment date
   b. is not transferable
   c. sometimes offers the maker a defence against payment
   d. is not a negotiable instrument

3. A floating charge
   a. crystallizes when a debtor defaults
   b. is used by unsecured creditors
   c. is a form of equity financing
   d. is a form of security held jointly by multiple creditors

4. Before it is eligible for a loan, a new business may need to
   a. pledge security
   b. prepare a written business plan
   c. provide a cash flow analysis
   d. do all of the above

5. A general security agreement covers
   a. the ranking of a debtor's various creditors
   b. the details of a company's capital structure
   c. a description of the security pledged, and a description of the actions that constitute a default
   d. all of the above

6. Creditors can obtain information about potential debtors
   a. by conducting a search for security interests through a public registry
   b. by conducting an execution search
   c. by conducting a bankruptcy search
   d. by all of the above

7. A proposal to creditors is
    a. a business plan presented to a bank to obtain a loan
    b. part of the petition of a debtor into bankruptcy
    c. an arrangement by the debtor to pay creditors without going bankrupt
    d. a voluntary assignment in bankruptcy
    e. c and d

Short Answer

1. How does secured credit differ from unsecured credit?

2. What is an initial public offering?

3. What is the difference between common and preferred shares?

4. What are the advantages and disadvantages of debt and equity financing?

5. What methods are available to unsecured creditors to enforce their rights?

Discussion and Debate

1. Following the bankruptcy of Woodhouse Ltd., the trustees scheduled a first meeting of creditors, in which the creditors had the opportunity to question the bankrupt and the trustee in bankruptcy about the events leading to bankruptcy, the assets, and the administration of the bankrupt's estate. The creditors learned the following:
    a. Just before bankruptcy, Brian X. Woodhouse, Woodhouse's general manager, sole shareholder, and president, transferred two company vehicles into his own name after paying $3,000 to the company for the vehicles. Was this permissible?
    b. Brian personally guaranteed a number of loans for Woodhouse. Before making the loan guarantees, Brian transferred his interest in the family home, his car, and a vacation property to his spouse. After the loans were guaranteed, and when the business was in trouble, he also transferred a share portfolio to his spouse. Are either of these transfers permissible?
    c. Brian's Aunt Emma had given a loan to the company. When the business was in trouble, Brian paid the loan back while not making payments on other loans. Was this permissible?

2. Woodhouse has several bills due at the end of the week. It does not have enough cash in its current account to cover the cheques that it needs to send out to these creditors. However, it knows that by the week's end, it should receive a cheque from a customer that will cover these debts. Woodhouse therefore writes the cheques to its creditors, even though at the time the cheques are written there is not enough in the account to cover them. Woodhouse's account agreement with the bank provides that the bank has the right to hold a cheque for a reasonable period until it clears the payer's account before crediting the amount to the payee's account. The bank has not previously exercised this right against Woodhouse. If the bank holds the customer's cheque until after Woodhouse's cheques to creditors are dishonoured, does Woodhouse have any recourse against the bank?

Glossary

acceleration clause
contractual term providing that payment of the entire debt becomes due on default

accommodation
human rights concept that refers to making changes that allow a person or group protected by the *Human Rights Code* to participate in the workplace

act of bankruptcy
being unable to pay debts as they come due or committing fraudulent or evasive acts to avoid creditors

administrative law
body of rules created by government agencies and applied to government agencies to monitor their decision-making powers

administrative tribunal
government body that functions like a court and makes decisions regarding administrative matters

adverse impact discrimination
workplace policy that unintentionally affects certain groups in a detrimental way

agency agreement
contract between principal and agent that describes the agent's rights and authority

agent
person who has the authority to act on another's behalf

aggravated damages
a subcategory of non-pecuniary damages awarded for intangible harm, such as harm to reputation or humiliation

alternative dispute resolution (ADR)
settlement of conflict through a process other than the court system

amortization period
length of time required to pay entire mortgage debt

articles of incorporation
document that creates a corporation

assault
tort in which the defendant threatens the plaintiff with physical harm

bailee
party in a bailment that is in temporary possession of the bailor's personal property

bailment
legal relationship that arises when personal property is borrowed, rented, stored, or found by a person other than its owner

bailor
party in a bailment that owns the personal property

balance of probabilities
standard of proof in civil (as opposed to criminal) law indicating that one version of events is more probable than another

bargaining unit
a group of the employer's employees whom the trade union is entitled to represent

battery
tort in which the defendant engages in unwanted physical contact with the plaintiff

bid-rigging
illegal trade practice in which bidders conspire to influence a contract price by having certain bidders place artificially high bids to favour another party to the scheme

bill of exchange
document signed by a drawer ordering a drawee to pay a specified sum to a payee immediately or on a later fixed date

bona fide occupational qualification (BFOQ)
reasonably necessary job qualification or requirement imposed because it is necessary for job performance

breach of contract
failure to fulfill contractual obligations

burden of proof
requirement that a certain party prove a particular fact at trial

business structure
method of carrying on business that dictates all aspects of a business's creation and operation

caisse populaire
credit union based primarily in Quebec but also operating for francophone clientele in other parts of Canada

caveat emptor
Latin maxim that translates roughly to "buyer beware"

certification
approval by a labour relations board that gives a union the right to negotiate on behalf of a bargaining unit

chattels
movable, tangible property

cheque
negotiable instrument under which the drawee banking institution pays the payee from the bank account of the payer

choses in action
intangible personal property, such as negotiable instruments and intellectual property

collateral
property that a borrower makes available to a lender to sell, in order to repay the amount due on a loan if the borrower defaults

collective agreement
contract between a union and an employer that governs the terms and conditions of employment for union members

common law
rules contained in decisions made over time by judges

common shares
shares whose dividends are paid at the discretion of a corporation's management on the basis of the company's profits after dividend payments have been made on preferred shares

condition
important term of a contract whose breach frees the non-breaching party from all further obligations under the contract

condition precedent
a clause in a contract specifying that something must happen before a party is required to perform his obligations under the contract

condition subsequent
occurrence of an event or circumstance that results in the termination of contractual obligations

conditional offer
offer subject to the fulfillment of one or more conditions

condonation
implied acceptance by an employer of the conduct of an employee by permitting the conduct to continue without warning, discipline, or corrective action

consideration
something of value given up by each party to a contract

conspiracy
act of planning or working together or both, on the part of two or more parties, to jointly commit an illegal activity

constitution
document that establishes the basic framework under which all other laws are created and the basic principles to which all laws must conform

constructive dismissal
fundamental breach by an employer of an employment contract that entitles an employee to consider herself dismissed and to sue the employer for wrongful dismissal

consumer
purchaser who buys or otherwise obtains goods for her own use, not for business purposes

contract
an agreement between two or more parties that is enforceable by law

contract law
rules that govern the enforcement of private agreements

contributory negligence
role that a plaintiff may play in negligently contributing to the cause of, or aggravation of, her own injury

cooling-off period
period set by statute during which a consumer who has made a contract can change his mind and repudiate it

copyright law
branch of law that protects the exclusive right to copy creative work

corporate bond
company's written promise to repay the buyer of the bond both principal and interest at specified intervals

corporate seal
imprint made on corporate contracts and other documents that communicates the intention to bind the corporation

corporation
method of carrying on business by means of a legal entity that is distinct from its creators and enjoys almost all the rights and obligations of an individual

counteroffer
proposal that accepts an offer on terms differing from those in the offer

criminal law
rules that govern the standard of acceptable behaviour in society, the breach of which results in fines and imprisonment

damages
losses suffered as a result of the commission of a tort or the breach of a contract, or compensation awarded for these losses

debt financing
borrowing money from a lender

deductible
out-of-pocket payment that an insured must make that is deducted from the insurance payment

deeds
records of title

defamation
tort based on harm to a person's or business's reputation through false statements made by the defendant

default
mortgagor's failure to fulfill her obligations under a mortgage

default judgment
a judgment based on the plaintiff's claim if the defendant has failed to file a statement of defence

defendant
party who is sued in a lawsuit

deliverable state
condition in which goods are finished, packaged, labelled, and ready to ship

demand letter
letter, usually written by a creditor's lawyer, stating that the debtor to whom the letter is addressed has defaulted, and that the debtor must pay the full amount, including interest on the principal sum owing, by a given date, or face legal action

director
person who makes major decisions regarding the business of the corporation; the director is elected by, and accountable to, the shareholders

disclaimer clause
clause in a contract that limits the amount or type of damages that the parties might otherwise be required to pay; also known as a "limitation of liability clause"

discovery
procedure after exchange of pleadings where both parties disclose all information, including producing documents, relevant to the case

discrimination
negative or singular treatment of a person or group on the basis of a prohibited ground of discrimination under the *Human Rights Code*

distress
remedy allowing landlord to seize and sell tenant's personal property when rent is unpaid

drawee
the person or institution to whom a negotiable instrument is sent for payment

drawer
person who drafts and sends the bill of exchange to the drawee for acceptance

due diligence
defence that claims a person did everything reasonable to prevent an offence from occurring

due diligence defence
defence to strict liability offence requiring accused to demonstrate that he took all reasonable steps to avoid committing a prohibited act

duress
pressure to enter into a contract by way of threat of physical or economic harm

duty of care
legal duty owed by one person to another based on a relationship or on the doctrine of foreseeability

duty to mitigate
obligation to take all reasonable steps to lessen losses suffered

employment equity
range of measures promoting a representative workforce; federal employment equity legislation and programs focus on four designated groups: women, visible minorities, people with disabilities, and aboriginal people

endorsement
additional terms added on to a standard form or existing contract

environmental law
rules that govern protection of the environment, restrictions on the exploitation of natural resources, and development in cities and rural areas

equal pay for equal work / equal pay for work of equal value (pay equity)
concept obliging employers to pay female and male employees who perform substantially the same jobs in the same workplace at the same rate, unless a legislated exception applies

equity financing
raising money by issuing and selling shares in a corporation or using retained earnings to meet short- or long-term financial needs

exclusion clause
clause in a contract that excuses parties from their contractual obligations in specified circumstances

exclusive dealing
practice whereby a commercial party requires another commercial party to deal exclusively with it in order to secure a business advantage

exclusive possession
possession of real property to the exclusion of others

execution creditor
creditor who has obtained a judgment and seeks to enforce (execute) it

express term
term specified in writing

fair information principles
10 principles, set out in the *Personal Information Protection and Electronic Documents Act* (PIPEDA), that guide the collection, use, protection, and disclosure of personal information

false imprisonment
tort in which the defendant unlawfully restricts the freedom of the plaintiff

federal system of government
system whereby law-making powers are divided between the federal and provincial governments according to subject matter

fiduciary duty
duty to act in good faith, with reasonable care and confidence, and in the corporation's best interests; enhanced duty of care that flows from a relationship of special trust, such as a relationship between a doctor and a patient

fiduciary employee
employee who holds a position of trust, could significantly affect an employer's interests, and has special obligations to the employer

fixed tenancy
right to rent real property for a specified period of time

fixtures
property, such as shelving or sinks, that is attached to buildings

floating charge
class of collateral, such as inventory, where a creditor allows a debtor to dispose of items in the class

force majeure
significant and unanticipated event—such as a natural disaster—that is beyond the control of the parties and makes fulfillment of contractual obligations impossible

forfeiture
remedy allowing landlord to regain possession of leased premises when rent is unpaid

forseeability
expectation of whether a reasonable person could predict that a certain result might follow from his actions

franchise
right to operate a business using the name, products, business methods, and advertising of another business

frustration
a legal doctrine that allocates the risk of loss in the event that a contract becomes impossible to perform and the contract is silent regarding the issue

fundamental fairness
principle encompassing the right to be heard, the right to hear the case against you, and the right to reply to the case

future goods
goods that have not yet come into being at the time a contract is made, such as an agricultural crop, or goods that have not yet been manufactured

garnishment order
court order directed to someone who owes money to a judgment debtor, requiring this person to pay some or all of the money owing into court for payment out to the judgment creditor

gender-neutral job evaluation system
system that evaluates the relative value of jobs in a manner that does not favour factors found in jobs traditionally performed by men

general partnership
partnership that is not registered with the government as a limited or limited liability partnership

general security agreement
pledge, often used by a debtor's bank, of most of a debtor's assets to cover short-term loans made over an extended period

goodwill
business's good reputation

grievance
dispute arising in a unionized workplace with respect to matters covered in the collective agreement

grievance arbitration
an external process for resolving disputes that arise under the collective agreement

guarantee
contract whereby a party assumes responsibility for another party's financial obligations if that other party defaults on payment

harassment
course of vexatious comment or conduct that is known or ought reasonably to be known to be unwelcome

holder
person who is assigned the right to be paid on a promissory note by the creditor originally entitled to be paid

implied term
term that will be inserted by law into a contract when necessary to give effect to the parties' intentions

incorporator
individual or other corporation that causes a corporation to come into existence by filing the required documentation

indemnity clause
clause in a contract that requires one of the parties to pay for any losses or expenses that the other party may incur as a result of claims related to the contract

independent contractor
self-employed worker who accepts specific projects, usually from several businesses

independent legal advice
legal advice regarding a contract obtained from a different lawyer than the lawyer who drafted the contract

industrial design law
branch of law that protects the visual appearance of a product, including its shape, patterns, and ornaments

initial public offering (IPO)
first offering of shares by a corporation to the public through a brokerage firm to raise capital for use by the company

injunction
order of a court requiring a party to discontinue an action or prohibiting a party from taking a proposed action

insurable interest
interest that causes insured to benefit from the existence of property and to suffer from its loss

intangible property
things whose value does not arise from their physical attributes

intellectual property
things created by the mind or intellect, such as logos and inventions

intentional tort
injury deliberately caused to a plaintiff by a defendant

interest-based or principled negotiation
form of negotiation where each party listens with an open mind to the concerns of the other

interference with economic relations
tort based on intentional harm, through illegal acts, to a party's means of earning money

interim injunction
temporary injunction, pending a final hearing; see "injunction"

joint and several liability
financial responsibility requiring all parties to contribute equally but also making each party responsible for the entire amount owed

joint health and safety committee
committee composed of equal numbers of management and worker representatives generally required by the *Occupational Health and Safety Act* in workplaces with 20 or more workers

joint venture
temporary relationship created for the purpose of completing one or a series of business projects

judgment debtor examination
process in which a judgment creditor can question a judgment debtor under oath about his assets, liabilities, and income to provide information that assists the judgment creditor in satisfying the judgment

judicial review
process whereby a court reviews the decision of an administrative tribunal

jurisdiction
law-making authority

just cause
justification for dismissal without notice based on an employee's conduct

lapse
expiration of an offer

law
body of norms, or rules, by which society chooses to govern itself

lease
contract that sets out terms of property rental

legal risk management plan
plan that allows businesses to take action to prevent or reduce loss

liability
legal responsibility for injuries or losses suffered by another

limitation period
time period in which a lawsuit must be commenced, after which the right to sue is lost

limited liability partnership (LLP)
partnership composed of partners in certain professions, such as lawyers and accountants, who have the same liabilities as those in a general partnership except that partners are not liable for the professional negligence of other partners or employees supervised by other partners

limited partnership
partnership composed of a minimum of one general partner and one limited partner who provides money or property to the firm and shares in the profits but who does not participate in the business affairs of the firm and whose liability is limited to exclude any personal assets

liquidated damages clause
clause in a contract that provides for the payment of money if a certain event—usually a specified breach of contract—occurs; also known as an "acceleration clause"

litigation
process of resolving disputes through a formal court process

lockout
refusal by an employer to let unionized employees into a workplace; usually occurs while an employer and a union attempt to negotiate a new collective agreement

market restriction
a practice whereby a seller forces a buyer to restrict eligible resale customers for the seller's goods

merchantable quality
quality sufficiently high to allow goods to be placed for sale as they are, without the need for repairs or other intervention

minor
person under the age of majority

minute book
book that holds corporate records, such as minutes of meetings

misrepresentation
false statement of fact

mortgage
loan secured by real property

mortgage term
period, usually between one and five years, during which a stipulated interest rate applies

mortgagee
party who loans funds to a mortgagor; usually a financial institution

mortgagor
owner of real property who borrows funds from a mortgagee

municipal bylaws
rules passed by municipal governments

negligence
failure of a person to act reasonably, with the result being harm to someone else

negotiable instrument
financial document, such as a cheque, that promises to pay the bearer a specified amount, and that can be transferred to a third party

nepotism policy
employment policy that allows an employer to discriminate in favour of, or against, her close relatives or the close relatives of employees

non-pecuniary damages
damages that cannot be readily quantified in financial terms

non-unionized employee
employee whose terms and conditions of employment are based on an individual employment contract rather than a collective agreement negotiated between an employer and a union

notice
verification, under a registration system, that a creditor has an interest in the property of a debtor

nuisance
tort in which the defendant interferes with the use and enjoyment of the plaintiff's property

occupier
person or company that has control over land or buildings, including owners and tenants

occupiers' liability
subcategory of negligence that imposes liability on occupiers of land or buildings for any harm caused to visitors, invitees, or trespassers

officer
person responsible for the day-to-day operation of a corporation; the officer reports to the director

official receiver
government official in the Office of the Superintendent of Bankruptcy who receives proposals, examines bankrupts under oath, and chairs meetings of creditors

omission
failure to act

Ontario Labour Relations Board
tribunal that mediates and adjudicates labour relations (and other) matters arising in Ontario

option agreement
contract in which a party gives something of value to keep an offer open for a specified period of time

paramountcy
highest in power or jurisdiction

parol evidence rule
common-law rule stating that if the language of a written contract is clear and complete, courts will not look at evidence beyond the contract to interpret it

partnership agreement
contract signed by all partners that sets out how the partnership will operate and how it will end

partnership or firm
method of carrying on business whereby two or more persons operate a business, with no legal separation between the owners and the business

passing off
tort based on one party's attempt to distribute its own knock-off product or service on the pretense that it is the product or service of another party

patent law
branch of law that protects the unauthorized manufacture, use, and sale of inventions

pay in lieu of notice
payment as a substitute for receiving adequate notice where an employee is dismissed without just cause

payee
person who receives payment on a negotiable instrument

payer
person who pays, or honours, a negotiable instrument

pecuniary damages
damages that can be readily quantified in financial terms

periodic tenancy
right to rent real property for an indefinite period of time, where both landlord and tenant have the right to terminate the tenancy after providing notice

personal information
under the *Personal Information Protection and Electronic Documents Act* (PIPEDA), any information about "an identifiable individual," whether recorded or not

personal property
movable, tangible things, including physical objects that are not attached to land or buildings, and intangible property

plaintiff
party who commences a lawsuit (the suing party)

poisoned work environment
workplace plagued with insulting or degrading commentary or actions related to a prohibited ground of discrimination under the *Human Rights Code*

policy
insurance contract describing the rights and obligations of an insurer and an insured

positional negotiation
form of negotiation where a party takes a position with the intention of deviating as little as possible from that position

precedent
legal rule set out by the court in a decided case that can be applied to a new case

predatory pricing
practice whereby a seller sets her prices unreasonably low (usually eliminating any profit margin or selling at a loss) to drive competitors out of the market

preferred shares
shares for which dividends are paid before any dividends are paid on common shares

pre-incorporation contract
contract entered into between a third party and the incorporators of a soon-to-be-incorporated business

presumption
a legal assumption that is made, subject to a party proving otherwise

price discrimination
practice whereby a supplier systematically offers different pricing terms and conditions to competing customers on sales of equal volume

price maintenance
practice whereby a seller attempts to control the resale price of goods by preventing a retailer from discounting the price

principal
person who has given another the authority to act on her behalf

priority
position in a ranking system that creates the order in which competing creditors can satisfy their claims against a debtor's property

private corporation
corporation whose shares are held by one person or a small group of people and are not offered to the public

private law
rules that govern the relationship between individuals (or corporations) where there is no government involvement

private property
things owned by individuals, businesses, or other organizations

privity of contract
doctrine that restricts the operation of a contract to those who are parties to it

product liability
subcategory of negligence based on a defendant's liability for harm caused to others because of his defective or dangerous products

professional negligence
tort based on a professional's failure to provide services that meet that profession's standards

progressive discipline
discipline imposed by an employer in steps that increase in severity

promissory estoppel
a remedy available to a party that relies on a gratuitous promise to her detriment

promissory note
document in which the maker, or promisor, promises to pay the promisee a sum indicated in the note, either on demand or on a fixed date in the future

property law
collection of rules that confer rights of ownership, possession, and transferability over things

proposal to creditors
debt-restructuring proposal made under the *Bankrukptcy and Insolvency Act* or the *Companies' Creditors Arrangement Act*, which allows the business to continue operating and—if accepted—delays or avoids bankruptcy

prospectus
document containing detailed financial information about a corporation that is required before sale of shares to the public

public corporation
corporation whose shares are offered for sale to the public

public law
rules that govern the relationship among governmental agencies and between government and individuals (or corporations)

public property
things owned by the government for the benefit of society

punitive damages
sum generally added to a damage award that is intended to compensate the plaintiff for a defendant's outrageous conduct

quantum
amount

quiet enjoyment
tenant's right to use leased property for intended purpose without interference from landlord or others under his control

ratification
approval by union members of a collective agreement

ratify
acknowledge corporate liability for a contract entered into on behalf of a business before incorporation

real property
immovable things, including land, buildings, and fixtures

reasonable notice
period of time an employee should be given between notification of dismissal and end of employment

reasonable person
fictional person who, in negligence law, applies the appropriate standard of care in a given situation

rebuttable
capable of being refuted

receiving order
order that appoints a trustee in bankruptcy to take control of the bankrupt's property following a creditor's successful bankruptcy petition

refusal to deal
inappropriate refusal, by a commercial party for its own advantage, to enter into commerce with another party,

despite the second party's willingness to meet the commercial party's business terms

regulations
rules created by staff of the Cabinet providing practical details of how a statute is to be implemented

release
document that absolves the breaching party of liability for any contract-related claims that the non-breaching party might make in the future

rescind
treat as if the contract were never made

restrictive covenant
clause in an employment contract that restricts an employee's activities, especially after employment ends; for example, a restrictive covenant might prohibit an ex-employee from disclosing confidential information about the employer

restrictive trade practices
practices, some of which are defined by the *Competition Act*, that tend to limit freedom of trade and competition in the marketplace

reviewable practices
commercial practices that seem to offend the *Competition Act* and that therefore may be subject to review by the tribunal

revocation
taking back of an offer

right to reinstatement
employee's right, provided by statute in some circumstances, to return to the job; for example, an employee who is terminated for going on pregnancy leave may be reinstated by an order of the Ministry of Labour

rule of law
concept that every person has equal rights before the law and that the law is supreme—nobody is above the law

rules of construction
common-law rules used in interpreting disputed contracts

seal
symbol, stamp, etc., on a contract that indicates an intention to be legally bound; takes the place of consideration

secured creditor
lender who has the right to sell an asset owned by the borrower to pay the loan if the borrower defaults

secured loan
loan for which a borrower provides collateral that the lender may sell to pay the loan if the borrower defaults

seller's lien
security interest under the *Sale of Goods Act* that allows a seller to keep and resell goods to discharge an insolvent buyer's debt

severance pay
one-time lump-sum payment made to a terminated employee in circumstances set out in the Ontario *Employment Standards Act, 2000*

sexual harassment
course of vexatious comment or conduct based on sex or gender that is known or ought reasonably to be known to be unwelcome

share certificate
document that represents the ownership of shares of a corporation

shareholder
owner of a corporation who shares in the profits of the business

shareholders' agreement
contract that governs the relationship between shareholders or between shareholders and a corporation, or governs how the corporation conducts its business

sole proprietorship
method of carrying on business whereby one person owns and operates the business, with no legal separation between the owner and the business

solicitor–client privilege
protection that prevents a solicitor from revealing in court communications between a lawyer and the client

specific goods
goods that exist at the time a contract is made and are specifically chosen or pointed out by the buyer

specific performance
requirement by a court that a party complete her obligations under a contract

standard form contract
contract that is drafted by one of the parties and imposed on the other with little or no opportunity for negotiation

standard of care
degree of care that a person must take to prevent harm to others

standard of proof
degree to which a party must convince a judge or jury that the allegations are true

stare decisis
principle that requires judges to follow decisions of higher courts in similar cases

statement of claim
court document notifying a defendant of a lawsuit against him and the reasons for the proceedings

statement of defence
court document notifying the plaintiff in a lawsuit that the defendant is denying the claim, and identifying the defendant's arguments

statute law
rules created by both the federal Parliament and provincial and territorial legislatures

strict liability offence
offence in which proof that an accused performed the prohibited act is sufficient to sustain a conviction, regardless of intention, unless the accused demonstrates that he took all reasonable care to avoid committing the prohibited act

strict liability tort
unintentional tort that requires no proof of negligence

strike
collective refusal to work by a group of unionized employees that usually occurs while an employer and a union attempt to negotiate a new collective agreement

tangible property
physical things

tax law
rules that govern the keeping of records and payment of taxes imposed by federal, provincial, and municipal governments

third party
outsider to a dispute or proceedings

tied selling
practice whereby a seller requires a buyer to buy one product or service in order to gain commercial access to, or a better price on, another product or service

title
ownership

tort
civil wrong other than breach of contract, for which damages may be sought to compensate for any harm or injury sustained

tort action
lawsuit based on tort

tort law
rules that assign responsibility and provide compensation for wrongs resulting in injuries or damages sustained by people or property

trademark law
branch of law that protects words, symbols, and pictures associated with a business's name, brand, or product

trespass to land
tort in which the defendant, without the permission of the plaintiff, comes onto land occupied by the plaintiff

trustee in bankruptcy
individual, usually an accountant, who is licensed under the *Bankruptcy and Insolvency Act* to administer a bankrupt's assets for the benefit of the bankrupt's creditors

unascertained goods

goods that are not yet separated from the stock of the seller and set aside for a particular buyer

unconscionable agreement

agreement so inequitably one-sided that it is unenforceable

undue hardship

difficulty beyond that which an employer is required to endure when accommodating the needs of an individual or a group protected under the *Human Rights Code*

undue influence

pressure exerted on a weaker party that deprives that party of his ability to exercise his judgment or free will

unfair labour practices

actions by employers that interfere with the formation and activities of a union, including intimidation

unintentional tort

injury inadvertently caused to a plaintiff by a defendant

union

organization of workers that negotiates wages and working conditions as a group with an employer

unionized employee

employee whose terms and conditions of employment are based on a collective agreement negotiated between an employer and a union rather than on an individual contract of employment

unlimited liability

full responsibility for any debt incurred or loss caused by a business

unsecured loan

loan given without collateral in exchange for a simple promise to repay

venue

place where a contractual dispute will be litigated

vicarious liability

liability imposed on one party (often an employer) for the harmful actions or omissions of another (often an employee)

vicarious performance

carrying out of contractual obligations by employees of a business

void

unenforceable

voluntary assumption of risk

defence based on proof that a plaintiff knowingly entered into a risky situation and thereby assumed responsibility for any injuries

waiver of liability

acknowledgement of risks in an activity and an agreement to assume them

warranty

minor term of a contract whose breach requires the non-breaching party to continue to fulfill her remaining obligations under the contract

WHMIS

(workplace hazardous materials information system) national information system designed to provide essential information about hazardous materials in the workplace

workplace diversity

employment of people from diverse backgrounds in a workplace where all feel welcome and respected

writ of seizure and sale

court order directing a sheriff to seize and sell assets belonging to a judgment debtor and pay the money from the sale to a judgment creditor; also called a "writ of execution"

wrongful dismissal

dismissal without just cause in which an employer breaches her common-law duty to provide reasonable notice to an employee

Index